EDEXCEL
A LEVEL
HISTORY
ActiveBook included

Paper 3:

Germany, 1871–1990: united, divided and reunited

David Brown
Series editor: Rosemary Rees

ALWAYS LEARNING

PEARSON

Published by Pearson Education Limited, 80 Strand, London, WC2R 0RL

www.pearsonschoolsandfecolleges.co.uk

Copies of official specifications for all Edexcel qualifications may be found on the website:
www.edexcel.com

Text © Pearson Education Limited 2016

Designed by Elizabeth Arnoux for Pearson

Typeset and illustrated by Phoenix Photosetting, Chatham, Kent

Produced by Out of House Publishing

Original illustrations © Pearson Education Limited 2016

Cover design by Malena Wilson-Max for Pearson

Cover photo/illustration © Bridgeman Art Library/German Photographer (20th Century)/SZ Photo

The rights of David Brown to be identified as author of this work have been asserted by him in
accordance with the Copyright, Designs and Patents Act 1988

First published 2016

19 18 17 16

10 9 8 7 6 5 4 3 2

British Library Cataloguing in Publication Data

A catalogue record for this book is available from the British Library

ISBN 978 1 447 985365

Printed in the UK by CPI

Websites

Pearson Education Limited is not responsible for the content of any external internet sites. It is essential
for tutors to preview each website before using it in class so as to ensure that the URL is still accurate,
relevant and appropriate. We suggest that tutors bookmark useful websites and consider enabling
students to access them through the school/college intranet.

A note from the publisher

In order to ensure that this resource offers high-quality support for the associated Pearson
qualification, it has been through a review process by the awarding body. This process confirms
that this resource fully covers the teaching and learning content of the specification or part of
a specification at which it is aimed. It also confirms that it demonstrates an appropriate balance
between the development of subject skills, knowledge and understanding, in addition to preparation
for assessment.

Endorsement does not cover any guidance on assessment activities or processes (e.g. practice
questions or advice on how to answer assessment questions) included in the resource, nor does it
prescribe any particular approach to the teaching or delivery of a related course.

While the publishers have made every attempt to ensure that advice on the qualification and its
assessment is accurate, the official specification and associated assessment guidance materials are the
only authoritative source of information and should always be referred to for definitive guidance.

Pearson examiners have not contributed to any sections in this resource relevant to examination
papers for which they have responsibility.

Examiners will not use endorsed resources as a source of material for any assessment set by Pearson.

Endorsement of a resource does not mean that the resource is required to achieve this Pearson
qualification, nor does it mean that it is the only suitable material available to support the qualification,
and any resource lists produced by the awarding body shall include this and other appropriate
resources.

Contents

Aspects in breadth: prosperity and social change, 1871–1990

Aspects in depth: different approaches to the problem of difference

How to use this book

STRUCTURE

This book covers Paper 3, Option 37.2: Germany, 1871–1990: reunited, divided and united of the Edexcel A Level qualification. You will also need to study a Paper 1 and a Paper 2 option and produce coursework in order to complete your qualification. All Paper 1/2 options are covered by other textbooks in this series.

EXAM SUPPORT

The examined assessment for Paper 3 requires you to answer questions from three sections. Throughout this book there are exam-style questions in all three section styles for you to practise your examination skills.

Section A contains a compulsory question that will assess your source analysis and evaluation skills.

A Level Exam-Style Question Section A

Study Source 9 before you answer this question.

Assess the value of Source 9 for revealing the attitudes of East Germans to the fall of the Berlin Wall in 1989.

Explain your answer, using the source, the information given about its origin and your own knowledge about the historical context. (20 marks)

Tip
This question requires you to use this individual letter to assess the attitudes of East Germans on a whole to the fall of the Berlin Wall in 1989. Therefore, you will need to use your own knowledge of the historical context to judge to what extent this source is representative of the overall attitude of East Germans, and how it can help us to understand how the fall of the Berlin Wall affected the lives of the GDR's citizens.

Section B contains a choice of essay questions that will look at your understanding of the studied period in depth.

A Level Exam-Style Question Section B

How accurate is it to say that Germany achieved national unity between 1871 and 1879? (20 marks)

Tip
This is a difficult question that asks you first to consider how you could judge national unity. Think about the divisions in Germany at the start of 1871 and how the government tried to overcome them. In what ways could you say that Germany was a more united people in 1879 than when the country first formed in 1871? What were the remaining divisions and issues? How extensive were both unity and disunity within Germany?

Section C will again give you a choice of essay questions, but these will assess your understanding of the period in breadth.

A Level Exam-Style Question Section C

'Between 1871 and 1990, Government economic policies were the main factor in the success of the German economy.' How far do you agree with this statement? (20 marks)

Tip
This question requires you to assess why successful development in the German economy occurred between 1871 and 1990, and to weigh up how far government policy has been the main factor in these developments. How did government policies help the German economy? Were there successful areas of German economic development that occurred without government assistance, and in what ways did government policies hamper the successful development of the German economy?

The Preparing for your exam section at the end of this book contains sample answers of different standards, with comments on how they could be improved.

FEATURES
Extend your knowledge

These features contain additional information that will help you gain a deeper understanding of the topic. This could be a short biography of an important person, extra background information about an event, an alternative interpretation, or even a research idea that you could follow up. Information in these boxes is not essential to your exam success, but still provides insights of value.

EXTEND YOUR KNOWLEDGE

The 'stab in the back' myth
The idea of being 'stabbed in the back' referred to the belief that the German military had not been defeated on the battlefield, but instead that Germany had lost the war due to traitors in Germany who had betrayed the country. These were frequently depicted as socialists, Communists and Jews who had actively worked to ensure that Germany lost the war. Erzberger, for instance, was one of the key politicians blamed for Germany's defeat given his political actions in the July crisis of 1917. The exact origins of the term allegedly came about during a meeting between Ludendorff and the Head of the British Military Mission in Berlin in 1919, when Ludendorff explained that Germany lost the war due to being stabbed in the back by home front failures. The idea that Germany never really lost the war but was betrayed was a powerful myth that was used by right-wing political opponents to attack the new Weimar Republic as illegitimate and traitorous to Germany. Unsurprisingly, the 'stab in the back' myth was a key aspect of Nazi ideology. The idea that Jewish Communist traitors lost Germany the war was a powerful part of Hitler's anti-Jewish agitation.

Knowledge check activities

These activities are designed to check that you have understood the material that you have just studied. They might also ask you questions about the sources and extracts in the section to check that you have studied and analysed them thoroughly.

ACTIVITY
KNOWLEDGE CHECK

1 Read Source 7. What evidence does Ludwig Erhard use to argue that West Germany's economic growth since the Second World War has been impressive?

2 Using primary sources in history can be problematic. The fact that Erhard was responsible for the West German economy does make Source 7 subjective in its analysis. Despite this, in what ways is this source still useful for a historian studying West Germany's economic growth after 1945?

Summary activities

At the end of each chapter, you will find summary activities. These are tasks designed to help you think about the key topic you have just studied as a whole. They may involve selecting and organising key information or analysing how things changed over time. You might want to keep your answers to these questions safe – they are handy for revision.

ACTIVITY
SUMMARY

1 To what extent had Adenauer's government built a successful and stable democracy in West Germany by 1960?

2 5-3-1 activity:

a) Summarise the history of the FRG from 1949 to 1960 in five sentences.

b) Choose three key words that you think best define this period.

c) Choose one key word - be prepared to explain your answer.

Thinking Historically activities

These activities are found throughout the book, and are designed to develop your understanding of history, especially around the key concepts of evidence, interpretations, causation and change. Each activity is designed to challenge a conceptual barrier that might be holding you back. This is linked to a map of conceptual barriers developed by experts. You can look up the map and find out which barrier each activity challenges by downloading the progression map from this website: www.pearsonschools.co.uk/historyprogressionsapproach.

progression map reference

 THINKING HISTORICALLY Change (8a, b & c) (I)

Imposing realities

The shape of history is imposed by people looking back. People who lived through the 'history' did not always perceive the patterns that later historians identify. For example, some people living through the German industrial revolution may have understood that great change was taking place, but they would not have been able to understand the massive economic, social and political consequences of industrialisation.

Consider the beginning of the German industrial revolution:

1 What factors were crucial in starting the second industrial revolution that began in 1891?

2 Could anybody have challenged this decision?

3 Explain why someone living in Germany in the late 20th century would have been unable to make a judgement about the beginning of a new era.

4 Who living now might regard the beginning of the German industrial revolution as an important event?

5 What do your answers to these questions tell us about the structure of history as we understand it?

Getting the most from your online ActiveBook

This book comes with three years' access to ActiveBook* – an online, digital version of your textbook. Follow the instructions printed on the inside front cover to start using your ActiveBook.

Your ActiveBook is the perfect way to personalise your learning as you progress through your A Level History course. You can:

- access your content online, anytime, anywhere

- use the inbuilt highlighting and annotation tools to personalise the content and make it really relevant to you.

Highlight tool – use this to pick out key terms or topics so you are ready and prepared for revision.

Annotations tool – use this to add your own notes, for example links to your wider reading, such as websites or other files. Or, make a note to remind yourself about work that you need to do.

*For new purchases only. If the access code has already been revealed, it may no longer be valid. If you have bought this textbook secondhand, the code may already have been used by the first owner of the book.

Introduction
A Level History

WHY HISTORY MATTERS

History is about people and people are complex, fascinating, frustrating and a whole lot of other things besides. This is why history is probably the most comprehensive and certainly one of the most intriguing subjects there is. History can also be inspiring and alarming, heartening and disturbing, a story of progress and civilisation and of catastrophe and inhumanity.

History's importance goes beyond the subject's intrinsic interest and appeal. Our beliefs and actions, our cultures, institutions and ways of living, our languages and means of making sense of ourselves are all shaped by the past. If we want to fully understand ourselves now, and to understand our possible futures, we have no alternative but to think about history.

History is a discipline as well as a subject matter. Making sense of the past develops qualities of mind that are valuable to anyone who wants to seek the truth and think clearly and intelligently about the most interesting and challenging intellectual problem of all: other people. Learning history is learning a powerful way of knowing.

WHAT IS HISTORY?

History is a way of constructing knowledge about the world through research, interpretation, argument and debate.

Building historical knowledge involves identifying the traces of the past that exist in the present – in people's memories, in old documents, photographs and other remains, and in objects and artefacts ranging from bullets and lipsticks to field systems and cities. Historians interrogate these traces and *ask questions* that transform traces into *sources of evidence* for knowledge claims about the past.

Historians aim to understand what happened in the past by *explaining why* things happened as they did. Explaining why involves trying to understand past people and their beliefs, intentions and actions. It also involves explaining the causes and evaluating the effects of large-scale changes in the past and exploring relationships between what people aimed to do, the contexts that shaped what was possible and the outcomes and consequences of actions.

Historians also aim to *understand change* in the past. People, states of affairs, ideas, movements and civilisations come into being in time, grow, develop, and ultimately decline and disappear. Historians aim to identify and compare change and continuity in the past, to measure the rate at which things change and to identify the types of change that take place. Change can be slow or sudden. It can also be understood as progressive or regressive – leading to the improvement or worsening of a situation or state of affairs. How things change and whether changes are changes for the better are two key issues that historians frequently debate.

Figure 1 Fragment of a black granite statue possibly portraying the Roman politician Mark Antony.

Debate is the essence of history. Historians write arguments to support their knowledge claims and historians argue with each other to test and evaluate interpretations of the past. Historical knowledge itself changes and develops. On the one hand, new sources of knowledge and new methods of research cause *historical interpretations* to change. On the other hand, the questions that historians ask change with time and new questions produce new answers. Although the past is dead and gone, the interpretation of the past has a past, present and future.

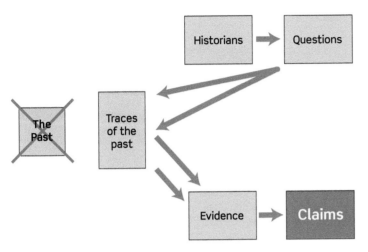

Figure 2 Constructing knowledge about the past.

THE CHALLENGES OF LEARNING HISTORY

Like all other Advanced Level subjects, A Level history is difficult – that is why it is called 'advanced'. Your Advanced Level studies will build on knowledge and understanding of history that you developed at GCSE and at Key Stage 3 – ideas like 'historical sources', 'historical evidence' and 'cause', for example. You will need to do a lot of reading and writing to progress in history. Most importantly, you will need to do a lot of thinking, and thinking about your thinking. This book aims to support you in developing both your knowledge and your understanding.

History is challenging in many ways. On the one hand, it is challenging to build up the range and depth of knowledge that you need to understand the past at an advanced level. Learning about the past involves mastering new and unfamiliar concepts arising from the past itself (such as the Inquisition, Laudianism, *Volksgemeinschaft*) and building up levels of knowledge that are both detailed and well organised. This book covers the key content of the topics that you are studying for your examination and provides a number of features to help you build and organise what you know – for example, diagrams, timelines and definitions of key terms. You will need to help yourself too, of course, adding to your knowledge through further reading, building on the foundations provided by this book.

Another challenge is to develop understandings of the discipline of history. You will have to learn to think historically about evidence, cause, change and interpretations, and also to write historically, in a way that develops clear and supported argument.

Historians think with evidence in ways that differ from how we often think in everyday life. In history, as Figure 2 shows, we cannot go and 'see for ourselves' because the past no longer exists. Neither can we normally rely on 'credible witnesses' to tell us 'the truth' about 'what happened'. People in the past did not write down 'the truth' for our benefit. They often had clear agendas when creating the traces that remain and, as often as not, did not themselves know 'the truth' about complex historical events.

A root of the word 'history' is the Latin word *historia*, one of whose meanings is 'enquiry' or 'finding out'. Learning history means learning to ask questions and interrogate traces, and then to reason about what the new knowledge you have gained means. This book draws on historical scholarship for its narrative and contents. It also draws on research on the nature of historical thinking and on the challenges that learning history can present for students. Throughout the book you will find 'Thinking Historically' activities designed to support the development of your thinking.

You will also find – as you would expect given the nature of history – that the book is full of questions. This book aims to help you build your understandings of the content, contexts and concepts that you will need to advance both your historical knowledge and your historical understanding, and to lay strong foundations for the future development of both.

Dr Arthur Chapman
Institute of Education
University College London

Germany, 1871–1990: united, divided and reunited

In the years 1871 to 1990, Germany would undergo profound developments that would not only shape the German nation, but also impact upon Europe and the world at large. Germany's unification in 1871 is one of the key moments in world history. Until 1866, Germany was divided into 38 states, but from 1866 to 1871, the largest German state, Prussia, under the leadership of Otto von Bismarck, pursued a policy of expansion, absorbing the other German states into a fully united nation, the German Reich, or Empire, which was officially proclaimed on 18 January 1871. Importantly, Germany had not been united through the mutual coming together of the 38 German states; instead, it had been formed under the dominant power of Prussia and through victories over its great rivals, Austria and France, which had created a huge surge of nationalist enthusiasm among the German people. The Prussian King was now the Kaiser of the German Empire, and the Prussian First Minister was his Chancellor. German unity had come about through nationalism fuelled by war and led by a Prussian elite who viewed notions of democracy unfavourably.

SOURCE 1

Official painting showing the declaration of the united German Empire in the Hall of Mirrors, Versailles, 18 January 1871.

1871 – 18 January: Southern German states unite with North German Confederation to form the German Reich

1871

1880 – Bismarck begins policy of 'state socialism' with the introduction of accident insurance

1880

1890 – March: Otto von Bismarck resigns as Chancellor of Germany

1890

1914 – August: Germany declares war on Russia and France

1914

1918 – October–November: Revolution begins in Germany; Kaiser Wilhelm II abdicates

1918

1929 – October: Collapse of US stock market sets off major economic crisis in Germany

1929

1933 – January: Adolf Hitler appointed Chancellor of Germany

March: Enabling Act passed, essentially dissolving the Weimar system and establishing Hitler as dictator

1933

1939 – September: Germany invades Poland; Britain and France declare war on Germany

1939

1949 – May: West German state of the Federal Republic of Germany (FDR) created under new constitution

1949

1989 – August: Thousands of East German refugees attempt to enter West Germany

October: Mass anti-government demonstrations in East Germany

November: East German government opens the Berlin Wall

1989

1875 — Social Democratic Party of Germany (SPD) formed

1888 — 9 March: Kaiser Wilhelm I dies

15 June: Kaiser Frederick III dies; his son Wilhelm II becomes Kaiser

1912 — Reichstag elections see SPD become largest party in Germany for the first time

1916 — Germany unofficially becomes a military dictatorship under Supreme Military Commanders Paul von Hindenburg and Erich Ludendorff

1919 — August: Constitution of the new republic (Weimar Republic) signed into law

1932 — July: Nazi Party becomes largest party in Germany after Reichstag elections

1934 — Hitler combines role of president and chancellor into title of 'Führer' after the death of President Hindenburg

1945 — April: Hitler commits suicide

May: Germany surrenders; end of war in Europe

1957 — March: European Economic Community (EEC) established with West Germany as founding member

1990 — March: First free elections held in East Germany

October: Germany re-established as one country

December: Helmut Kohl wins first all-Germany election

These aspects of Germany's origins would play a crucial role in the onset of the First World War and the Second World War, as well as undermining Germany's first major experiment with democracy between 1919 and 1933, a key factor in the rise of the Nazis and the dictatorship of Adolf Hitler.

Within Germany itself, the industrial developments from 1871 to 1914 changed society, and the rise of the urbanised working class led to new political movements that challenged the entrenched power of the Prussian elite. Socialist and Communist ideologies grew in influence, and the battle between the Prussian aristocracy to hold back rising agitation for greater democracy formed the basis of a tumultuous period of democratic and social change between 1871 and 1918. Following the far-reaching consequences of Germany's defeat in the First World War, Germany attempted to introduce one of the most democratic constitutions in history in the form of the Weimar Republic. However, the continuing power of the anti-democratic nationalist elite, the failure of the political parties to unite the German people behind the Weimar's democratic ideals, and economic turmoil in 1924 and, most importantly, in the early 1930s, all combined to advance the rise of an ultra-extremist, racist, nationalist movement led by Adolf Hitler that would come to power in 1933. Hitler's dictatorship led to the most horrific war in history; the mechanised genocide of six million Jews, as well as hundreds of thousands of homosexuals, intellectually impaired, Roma and Slavic peoples and trade unionists; and the eventual defeat of the German nation.

From this tumultuous event, the newly created nation of West Germany would embark on a remarkable path, successfully introducing a long-lasting democracy and rebuilding its economy, with the assistance of the United States, so that by 1960 it was the world's third largest economy, behind only the United States and the USSR. This dramatic transformation took place under the shadow of East Germany, ruled by a Communist dictatorship under the protection of the USSR, where, in Berlin, the Berlin Wall embodied the most literal image of this division. From 1945 to 1989, the divided Germany was at the heart of the Cold War between the United States and the democracies of Western Europe on the one hand, and the USSR and the Communist-ruled nations of Eastern Europe on the other. It was the battleground of ideologies, and it was the fall of the Berlin Wall in 1989 that signified the end of the Cold War, as democratic revolutions swept through Eastern Europe, changing the face of Europe once again. German reunification under a democratic parliamentary system in 1990 signified this new era in European affairs, as a re-emerging German nation would once again play a highly significant and powerful role as Europe's dominant industrial power, but this time as a responsible, democratic member.

Germany's history from 1871 to 1990 is one of the most frenetic and influential of all time. The nation was created, divided and then recreated; it underwent significant cultural and economic development, was the battleground of new political ideals, and was at the heart of the two largest wars in history. These developments fundamentally impacted not only the German people, but the entire population of Europe and the world at large, and they continue to do so in myriad ways even today.

3.1

Social change in Germany and West Germany

KEY QUESTIONS

- To what extent did German class structures change between 1871 and 1990?
- To what extent did the role of women in German society change between 1871 and 1990?

INTRODUCTION

Between 1871 and 1990, German society underwent incredible change. While in 1871 Germany had primarily been a rural-based society, where most workers engaged in agricultural industry, through the late 19th and early 20th centuries the country underwent rapid industrialisation. By 1914, the majority of German society lived in cities and were employed in the industrial sectors. Berlin had tripled in size and was Europe's third largest city after London and Paris. These changes had a dramatic effect on the country, leading to the growth of new working-class political activism that challenged the older order of German power. Mass industrialisation also prompted a rise in a new urban middle class, and a consequent decline in the traditional lower middle class engaged in German artisanship. Both of these developments would fundamentally alter German politics, as Germany's traditional leadership, consisting of the Prussian land owning elite, grappled with how to deal with the new socio-economic make-up of German society.

In society itself, the role of women and the family was also affected, as more and more women entered into the industrialised workforce and challenged the traditional German ideal of a woman's place being in the home. The First World War would only accentuate these critical developments, and the Weimar Republic that emerged found itself torn between those Germans who celebrated the new, modern political, social and economic culture of 1920s Germany, and those who longed for a return to the more conservative Germany of the pre-1914 period. In 1933, Adolf Hitler's Nazis proclaimed a new Germany that would embark on a radical course, the politics of which would have profound consequences for both men and women. From the ashes of the Second World War and a divided nation, West Germany would undergo profound industrial development, leading to greater social mobility and the supposed 'flattening' of Germany into a predominately middle-class society. New opportunities for employment would be opened up to young Germans in a way not possible before 1950.

However, despite the massive change from 1871 to 1990, in many ways the inequalities of German society, particularly in terms of the role of women, remained. Overall, the social change in Germany and West Germany between 1871 and 1990 was fundamental, not only in shaping the lives of the German people, but in the way it opened up new political developments that would have a profound effect on Europe and the world in the 20th century.

1875 – Social Democratic Party of Germany (SPD) formed

1883 – Free medical treatment for three million German workers introduced

1889 – German workers provided with a pension at the age of 70

1897 – Government introduces Protectionist Craft Laws to support German artisans

1912 – SPD becomes largest party in Reichstag after national elections

1870	1880	1890	1900	1910

1878 – Chancellor Bismarck introduces anti-socialist legislation, outlawing the trade union movement and the SPD

1885 – Society for the Protection of Women Workers' Interests formed by Emma Ihrer

1891 – Trade Union membership in Germany reaches 278,000

Six-week maternity leave introduced for German women

1911 – Separate insurance scheme established for white-collar workers

TO WHAT EXTENT DID GERMAN CLASS STRUCTURES CHANGE BETWEEN 1871 AND 1990?

The growth of the urban working class

The growth of Germany's working class that occurred after unification in 1871 had a profound effect on the social, cultural and political aspects of this new nation. Prior to 1871, the population of the divided German states had been mainly rural, with the economy centred on farming. Two-thirds of the German population lived in rural villages, whereas in Britain well over half the population lived in urbanised centres. However, following on from unification, Germany's population underwent rapid urbanisation due to the country's increasing industrial growth. By 1914, 66 percent of the German population lived in urbanised towns.

The swift **urbanisation** of the population created a range of new problems for Germany. These concerned conditions of housing and sanitation in the cities for this growing working class. This in turn changed German politics, as urbanised workers sought greater political representation in order to achieve better living and working conditions. The trade union movements flourished, and crucially, in 1875, the Social Democratic Party of Germany (SPD) was formed, focusing on representing the political views of the German working class. Trade union membership increased from around 50,000 in 1877 to 278,000 in 1891. Despite attempted persecution and anti-socialist legislation from Chancellor Bismarck, the SPD continued to grow in support, doubling its vote to 1.5 million between 1875 and 1890, and increasing its membership in the **Reichstag** from 12 to 35 members. Thus, the dramatic transformation of Germany from a predominately rural economy to an urban-based industrialised nation from 1871 onwards was to have a profound political effect that would challenge the traditional conservative powers within the country.

KEY TERMS

Urbanisation
The process by which more of the population leaves rural areas and moves to urban areas (built-up areas, such as a city or larger town). Urbanisation is generally associated with the process of industrialisation.

Reichstag
Technically refers to the German parliament building opened in 1894, but often used to refer to the German parliament itself from 1871 onwards. The German parliament is also known as the Bundestag.

Proletarian
A member of the working classes.

SOURCE 1 Karl Scheffler describes the gradual urbanisation of a village near Lubeck after 1870, in his autobiographical account of growing up in northern Germany.

Soon after the Franco-German War and the political unification of the German states, a change set in. At first, the change was barely noticeable, because the substance of what had grown slowly over centuries was robust. In the first decade after the war, things did not look much different in the city and the village. But then the new tendencies caught on all the more rapidly and thoroughly. Each year brought further changes, and soon nobody could escape the new circumstances of life. Even in the village one felt the desire to build, something that was characteristic of those years. At first several large factories were built a little further upstream. Initially, they just sat there rather curiously with their tall brick smokestacks in the middle of cow pastures. It was not long though, before houses in the style of the factory were built right next to them [the smokestacks], and the green of the meadows disappeared underneath huge piles of coal, rubble and garbage. Together with the factories came people to the village who had never been seen there before, except in their Sunday best as day-trippers. They were droves of workers – the kind who differ from rural and skilled tradesmen at first sight, because they had no training except for a few mechanical tasks, because they felt no occupational spirit, because they belonged to that class which was subsequently called **Proletarians**. Since the journey to the city was a long one, the need soon arose to create dwelling for these workers in the village itself. And because there was nothing suitable there, the first meagre apartment houses were put up. Tall, bare, multi-floor buildings stood isolated in the middle of fields. Poor families lived there side by side in squalor, without any comfort; an unkempt, quickly dilapidating backyard adjoined directly. The space between the houses was teeming with children. But they were the children of a new population. The poverty of these people was different from the poverty of the village farm worker. The industrial workers seemed to be degenerate; if they were really poor, it seemed as though foul smelling poverty was their natural element. The men were not brought up in the tradition of any particular occupation, the women were not housewives and mothers, and the children were little vagabonds who stole fruit from the gardens and trampled on the grain in the fields.

1918 – January: 400,000 Berlin workers go on strike
28 October: Political reforms introduced that remove special status of Prussian Junkers in the constitution

1935 – Lebensborn Programme established

1957 – West German women given the legal equality of their husbands

1966 – Number of 'guest workers' in West Germany grows to 1.2 million

1988 – Rita Süssmuth becomes first female President of the Bundestag

1920 1930 1940 1950 1960 1970 1980 1990

1919 – New Weimar Constitution grants German women the vote and guarantees female equality in education and pay

1932 – Unemployment in Germany reaches 31 percent

1933 – Nazi women's organisation Deutsches Frauenwerk formed
Laws restricting female employment introduced by new Nazi government

1949 – West German Basic Law guarantees legal equality of women

1956 – New legislation passed making it easier for West Germans to buy their own home

Despite attempts by Bismarck to undermine working-class support for the SPD (see below), the party continued to grow. In 1890, Bismarck proposed limiting the franchise (right to vote) and destroying the SPD completely; however, Kaiser Wilhelm II, who feared it could lead to revolution, rejected this and Bismarck was dismissed as chancellor. Subsequent chancellors extended Bismarck's social policies as a means of placating the working class and encouraging them not to support the SPD. Accident insurance was extended, child labour further restricted and sickness insurance lengthened. However, the German elite could not counter the political changes caused by the growth of the urban working class, and by 1912 the SPD had become the largest party in the Reichstag.

In the first two years of the First World War, the vast majority of the German working class, along with the SPD and the trade unions, supported the war effort. However, by the summer of 1916 this support was beginning to deteriorate. Industrial workers had begun to question the new restrictions on workers' freedom introduced by the Auxiliary Service Act in August 1916. This was followed by the extremely cold winter of 1916/17 that led to considerable food shortages. By 1918, the combination of food shortages, mass casualties and the Russian Revolution had led to large-scale political opposition among the working class. In January 1918, 400,000 Berlin workers went on strike and this soon spread to the rest of Germany, with over a million workers on strike within a month. The end of the war in November resulted in further unrest, leading to the eventual fall of the **Kaiserreich** and the creation of the Weimar Republic.

KEY TERM

Kaiserreich
The German empire formed from the unification of the North German Confederation and the southern German states.

The new Weimar Constitution guaranteed that employees would have equal rights with employers in determining working conditions and that workers would be guaranteed an eight-hour day. Urbanisation continued through this period, although at a slower rate. From 1870 to 1890, the population of Germany's large cities had doubled, and then doubled again from 1890 to 1910. However, from 1910 to 1940, the population of large urban areas only grew at a rate of 36 percent. By 1925, Berlin's population was over four million, a considerable growth considering that it was less than two million in 1919. Generally, conditions were quite good for the working class during the Weimar period, particularly from 1924 to 1929. Real wages increased by 9 percent in 1927 and by 12 percent in 1928. Two million new houses were built, alleviating overcrowding in the large German cities, and unemployment insurance for those out of work was established. The SPD continued to be the largest party in the Reichstag until 1932. However, the progress of the German working class was profoundly affected by the economic downturn after 1929. By January 1933, the number of German unemployed reached nine million. By 1932, unemployment had reached 31 percent, compared to ten percent in 1929. The economic crisis in the Weimar Republic fuelled the rise of the Nazi Party (officially known as the National Socialist German Workers'

Party, or NSDAP), although it should be noted that much of the German working class did not support Adolf Hitler's party, instead continuing to vote for the SPD or supporting the more radical Communist Party of Germany (KPD).

EXTEND YOUR KNOWLEDGE

The Social Democratic Party of Germany (SPD)
The economic development of Germany in the 1860s, and the difficult conditions faced by the new urban working class, led to the creation of numerous German socialist movements inspired by the work of the German philosopher Karl Marx. Marx argued that industrialisation and the growth of the urban working class would inevitably lead to the overthrow of the exploitative capitalist system.

In 1869, the Social Democratic Workers' Party had been formed in Prussia. With German unification in 1871, the differing socialist movements across Germany had sought greater unity, and in 1875 the Social Democratic Workers' Party joined with other workers' associations to form the Social Democratic Party of Germany (Sozialdemokratische Partei Deutschlands) or SPD.

However, despite being inspired by Marx, the SPD was not a revolutionary party. Instead, the party declared that only legal, democratic processes would eventually lead to greater political and social rights for Germany's workers. A key aim of the SPD was the push for constitutional reform, particularly in terms of the Prussian elite's unfair position, and the greater representation of Germany's workers in the political system. Despite Bismarck's attempts to persecute the new party, the SPD's influence on German politics developed quickly. By 1890, they were attracting well over a million votes in the Reichstag elections. By the start of the 20th century, it was the largest, most influential and best organised socialist party in the world. By 1914, the SPD was the biggest party in Germany, with over one million members. It was also the largest party in the German Reichstag, having won the 1912 election with around four million Germans voting for the SPD.

The impressive growth of the party, fuelled by the parallel development of Germany's urbanised working class, was seen as a considerable threat by both the old established Prussian Junker class (see the Extend your knowledge box on page 18) and the newly emerging class of industrial big business owners. Chancellors Bulow and Bethmann-Hollweg attempted to deal with this issue by pursuing a policy of weakening the SPD's popularity by introducing social reforms for the workers. At the same time, they encouraged conservative parties to work together to try to keep the SPD from gaining power in the Reichstag. However, these policies proved inadequate in stopping the growing popularity of the socialist party. The rise of the SPD from 1875 onwards, and the consequential response by conservative Germany, was a key factor shaping the German political scene, not only in the Kaiserreich, but also in the Weimar Republic, where the SPD continued to be the most popular political party up to 1932.

The SPD had taken power following the German revolution of 1919 and had played a major role in defining the political constitution of the new republic. The first three Weimar chancellors were from the SPD, and the party continued to be the most popular in German elections until the rise of the Nazis in the early 1930s. In 1933, the Nazis banned the SPD, and its members were either arrested or fled into exile. In 1945, it was re-established in West Germany, and was subsequently one of the two major parties in West German politics (the other being the Christian Democratic Union of Germany). From 1969 to 1982, the Chancellor of West Germany was from the SPD, and the party continues to play an important role in unified Germany today, making it the oldest party in German politics.

Under the Nazis, from 1933 to 1945, urbanised workers experienced increased employment, due to public work schemes and rearmament programmes, at the expense of their rights, with the Nazis banning trade unions and the ability to strike. The working class grew by around ten percent from 1929 to 1938, as the Nazis expanded German industry in preparation for war. Despite some working-class opposition to the Nazis, and the fact that they tended to be considerably under-represented among Nazi membership, worker discipline, even during the Second World War, continued to be high.

During the West German period, from 1945 to 1990, urbanisation increased even further, with the percentage of the working population remaining in rural communities falling from 23.1 percent in 1950 to 8.3 percent in 1970. West Germany's considerable economic growth fuelled greater movement to the large, industrialised centres. From 1950 to 1980, West Germany's population grew by 50 percent to 61.7 million. Of this population, 74 percent of the West German population lived in communities of over 10,000 by 1980; in the Communist East, it was only 57 percent. While living standards in the cities were relatively high in West Germany, the introduction of the 'guest worker' would change the demographics of the country's working class. These were workers, predominately from Turkey and Greece, who were brought into the country on fixed contracts and without permanent residency in order to fill labour shortages in industries such as electrical engineering and shipbuilding. From 1959 to 1966, this grew from 150,000 to 1.2 million guest workers. This was to have the effect of creating an 'underclass' of ethnic workers in German cities, who tended to be employed in the lowest-paid jobs and lacking the same employment rights as Germans. In total, the West German government recruited some 14 million guest workers. After 1973, the government ended the programme, but allowed many guest workers to remain in West Germany and settle with their families. Millions of Turkish workers settled in cities like Berlin, where they would have a profound effect on the cultural and economic life of Germany's urbanised centres.

EXTEND YOUR KNOWLEDGE

Gastarbeiter (guest workers)
Starting in 1955, West Germany made a series of agreements with Greece, Italy, Spain, Turkey, Portugal and Yugoslavia to allow workers from these countries into West Germany to work in areas of the economy that were underemployed. These workers were known as Gastarbeiter (guest workers), and from 1962 to 1973, 9.66 million Gastarbeiter entered West Germany. These foreign workers played an important role in West Germany's economic boom in the 1950s and 1960s. It was also hoped, by all the nations involved, that the Gastarbeiter would gain new skills which they could then take back to their country of origin and, in turn, help their economic development. The programme ended in 1973, as unemployment in Germany had grown to the extent that it was felt that the Gastarbeiter were blocking positions that the German unemployed could take. Although the majority of the Gastarbeiter returned home, they had a lasting impact on the social and cultural make-up of West German society. In 1989, research showed that of the 4.8 million foreign workers in Germany, around three million were either originally Gastarbeiter or were descended from Gastarbeiter.

SOURCE 2

Overview of German urbanisation, 1871–1980, adapted from T.W. Guinnane, 'Population and the economy' in S. Ogilvie and R. Overy (eds) *Germany: A New Social and Economic History since 1800, Vol. III* (2003).

Year	Percentage of German population living in rural areas	Percentage of German population living in urban areas of more than 100,000
1871	63.9	8
1890	53	26
1910	40	48
1939	30.1	59
1961	20.7	53
1980	6	67

ACTIVITY
KNOWLEDGE CHECK

1 Read Source 1. What changes does Karl Scheffler describe taking place in Lubeck after 1870 and how does he appear to feel about these changes? (Use quotes from the source to back up your argument.)

2 Using Source 1, Source 2 and your own studies, list the key changes taking place in Germany's urban population from 1871 to 1980.

3 Summarise the key political and social changes caused by these developments.

Bismarck's introduction of pensions and health insurance in the 1880s

The structure of government established by Chancellor Bismarck after 1871 was aimed at maintaining the Prussian elite's dominance over the German state. This was significantly challenged by urbanisation and the subsequent political demands of this growing working class. Bismarck and the Prussian elite viewed the political developments this unleashed, particularly the rise of the SPD, as a significant threat to the political order. In 1878, Bismarck introduced anti-socialist legislation, outlawing the trade union movement and the SPD, suppressing their newspapers and putting hundreds of leading members into jail. Parallel to this repression, however, Bismarck hoped to gain the support of Germany's working classes by introducing an extensive scheme of social security. In 1883, free medical treatment for three million workers and their families was introduced, funded jointly by both workers and employers. In 1884, accident insurance providing benefits to incapacitated workers was set up, completely financed by employers. In 1886, both accident and sickness insurance were extended to an extra seven million workers, and in 1889, workers were given a pension at 70, or earlier if they were disabled, a measure financed by employers, workers and the state. Bismarck's reforms set up Europe's first-ever widespread welfare system. Despite this, the legislation failed to achieve its political goals. The working class still continued to support the banned SPD.

The welfare system did not aim to actually improve working conditions, and Bismarck refused to consider legislation that would set working hours, restrict child labour or allow Sunday as a rest day. Much of the working class considered that, without the threat of the SPD, the welfare system would never have been introduced in the first place, consequently adding to the Socialist Party's support. Thus, Bismarck's pension and health insurance policies of the 1880s failed to stem the increasing politicisation of Germany's expanding working class.

EXTEND YOUR KNOWLEDGE

Otto Eduard von Bismarck (1815–98)
Otto von Bismarck was one of the most outstanding and influential European statesmen of the second half of the 19th century. It was his leadership that not only led to the unification of Germany, but shaped the type of nation it would become from 1871 onwards. In 1862, Bismarck had become President of the Prussian Ministry, and from this period onwards had embarked on a policy of unifying Germany under Prussia's leadership. He subsequently took Prussia into three wars: against Denmark in 1864, Austria in 1866 and France in 1870. Prussia was victorious in each of these conflicts, and every victory pushed Germany towards greater geographical unity and increased the power and dominance of Prussia. After the victory over Austria in 1866, Northern Germany was unified under the North German Confederation. In 1871, Bismarck used the victory over France to complete the unification of Germany. The still independent southern states had joined with the North German Confederation against France and now, with the sudden surge of nationalism brought on by victory, sought full unification. On 18 January 1871, the unification of Germany was completed. Bismarck's influence, however, did not end there. Bismarck ensured Prussian dominance of the new German state through the German constitution that he drew up. The key power of the new state was still in the hands of the Junker class.

Bismarck dominated the German political scene for the next 20 years as Chancellor of the German Reich, personally defining the key aspects of Germany's foreign and domestic policies. With respect to domestic concerns, he enacted a series of policies aimed at minimising the political consequences of Germany's industrial developments, namely the rise of the SPD. In March 1890, Kaiser Wilhelm II dismissed him, due primarily to the Kaiser's concern at the growing extremism of Bismarck's anti-SPD policies. Bismarck's influence on Germany, however, continued far beyond his removal as Chancellor in 1890 and his death eight years later. The nature of the constitution he had constructed and the power of the Junker minority it enshrined would be the key issues in Germany up to 1914, as new forces challenged the old privileged order.

EXTRACT

G. Barraclough, *The Origins of Modern Germany* (1947). Here Barraclough gives some explanation of the reasons Bismarck introduced social reforms.

Bismarck sought to take the sting out of labour agitation by introducing extensive schemes of social security; between 1883 and 1889 compulsory insurance for workers against sickness, accident and old age etc., was introduced in the hope of bringing the working class into **quiescence**. Neither repression nor **cajolery** was a success. Organised labour realised that it owed the benefits of Bismarck's social legislation ultimately to the Social Democrat party and its political pressure; and the party continued to grow.

SOURCE

3

William Harbutt Dawson, *Bismarck and State Socialism: An Exposition of the Social and Economic Legislation since 1870* (1891). Dawson was a British writer who wrote on various aspects of German politics and society. Here he assesses the reasons for Bismarck's introduction of social legislation in the 1880s.

While passing repressive legislation [against the SPD], Prince Bismarck let it be understood that he intended it go hand in hand with important social reforms. With one hand he would use the rod, and with the other apply **assuasive** means. He refused to believe that the working classes of Germany had committed themselves past recall to the theories of Socialism. He maintained rather that those who followed the lead of men like Bebel and Liebknecht [leading SPD politicians] were people of the '**baser** sort' and that the honourable and industrious sections of the army of labour still respected the law and had no wish to disturb the existing social system. His aim in promoting industrial reforms was to cut the ground beneath the Socialistic agitators by gradually removing those grievances of which they could with only too much justice complain. He told the Reichstag on October 9th, 1878: 'I will further every endeavour which positively aims at improving conditions of the working classes... As soon as a positive proposal came from the Socialists for fashioning the future in a sensible way, in order that the lot of the working man might be improved, I would not at any rate refuse to examine it favourably, and I would not even shrink from the idea of State help for the people who would help themselves.' The outcome of this and other declarations to the same effect was the promise, the imperial speech with which the Reichstag was opened in February 1879, of social reforms for the **amelioration** of the condition of the working classes. This promise was repeated several times during the next two years; and finally it was on February 15th, 1881, definitely announced, in an imperial message, that laws for the insurance of workpeople would without delay be laid before the Reichstag. Here in brief are the causes which led to Prince Bismarck's policy of State Socialism. They were on one hand economic, and on the other hand social. At a time when trade, industry and agriculture were alike bordering on ruin, and when society was being undermined by the misery and discontent of the working classes, all eyes turned to the State for **succour**. Self-help stood paralysed, unable to grapple with the terrible difficulties of the situation.

KEY TERMS

Quiescence
A state of quiet or inactivity.

Cajolery
Persuasion through flattery.

Assuasive
Calming.

Baser
Lowest or bottom part.

Amelioration
Improvement.

Succour
Help or assistance.

SOURCE 4

British cartoon published by *Punch* in 1878 showing Chancellor Bismarck struggling to get the jack of Socialism back in its box. The poem says that every effort of further repression simply encourages greater human desire for freedom. *Punch* was a very popular British magazine that focused on humour and political satire.

SEPTEMBER 28, 1878.]   PUNCH, OR THE LONDON CHARIVARI.   143

KEEPING IT DOWN!

WHAT, Bogey-scared, O Man of Blood and Iron?
  You'd try Repression's bad old recipe?
The Spectres which your strong-reared State environ
  You'd bind and box? An endless task, you'll see!
Down with the lid! the ugly inmate throttle!
  It will not do—your system will not work :
You'll find that, like the Geni in the bottle,
  'Twill out at last, in spite of tightest cork.

Jack-in-the-Box is sure to play you tricks, Sir,
  Unless you have the force to *break the spring.*
Repression ever acts as an elixir
  To human yearnings for a freer wing.

To lay the Social Spectre is your duty,
  You doubtless think ; but tyrant will in terror,
Because its Bogey does not *look* a Beauty,
  O'erlooks its heart of truth—a fatal error !

The incubus of iron Militarism,
  Cramped freedom, stifled thought, and crippled trade,—
These *will* breed discontent and Social schism,
  Dread forces 'gainst Autocracy arrayed.
The plan of Mrs. PARTINGTON won't pay, Sir.
  Your Measure, like her mop, you'll fruitless find.
Box up the Bogey for to-day you may, Sir;
  'Twill out to-morrow. Will can't bag the Wind !

THE PROPER PEOPLE TO DEAL WITH ORANGEMEN.—Peelers. | A MUSICAL RUN.—HANDEL and BACH for half-a-crown.

ACTIVITY
KNOWLEDGE CHECK

1 What comment is the cartoon (Source 4) making in respect to the rise of Socialism in 1870s Germany and Bismarck's attempts to stop it?

2 How does this help to explain why Bismarck introduced social reforms in the early 1880s?

THINKING HISTORICALLY | Evidence (6b)

The strength of argument

Look at the three sources on Bismarck's social reforms (Extract 1, Source 3 and Source 4) and answer the following.

1 Look at Source 4.

  a) What is weak about this source?

  b) What could be added to it to make it stronger?

2 Read Extract 1.

  a) What argument does this extract make?

  b) How might this argument be strengthened?

  c) If you compare Extract 1 to Source 3, what makes Source 3 a more useful source in understanding Bismarck's motivations for his social reforms?

3 Read Source 3.

  a) How has the explanation been expanded to make the claim stronger?

  b) Can you explain why this is the strongest argument of the three sources?

4 What elements make a historian's claims strong?

The artisan tradition and its impact

The industrialisation of Germany not only provided a political challenge to the Prussian elite, but also undermined the German artisan tradition. These were small, often family-owned businesses, some of which were hundreds of years old, which prided themselves on their skilled labour and hand-crafted goods. Differing trades were organised into guilds, which regulated such aspects as price, competition and the work of apprentices, thus ensuring the ongoing survival of the artisan shops and that skilled craftsmanship remained high. For many Germans, in an era of rapid change, the artisans were a powerful symbol of historical continuity, a living link to a key tradition of highly skilled workers crafting their goods by hand and passing down these skills from one generation to the next. Under rapid industrialisation after 1871, however, the artisan tradition came under severe threat. Mechanised factories could produce cheaper goods at a rate far beyond that which the artisan could produce by hand. Groups of artisan industry declined or completely disappeared, particularly in those small businesses working in dyes or weaving. From 1882 to 1895, one-man artisan businesses declined by 13.5 percent and suffered even further decline from 1897 to 1907. Economists feared at the time that the German artisan tradition was doomed to fade out entirely.

However, by 1900, it was clear that the artisan tradition, although being reduced, could survive in industrialised Germany. New methods and better tools allowed many artisans to adapt to increasing competition. Despite this, along with shopkeepers and small traders, Germany's artisans formed a particularly angry sector of society. The rapid change Germany experienced after 1871 significantly affected their traditional way of life. They felt challenged both by the political elite and the growing power of the Socialists and trade unionism. Unlike the working class and the upper and middle classes, they lacked specific political parties that represented their views. Although the government had attempted to gain their support by introducing protectionist craft laws in 1897, the fear of modernisation and accelerating industrialisation encouraged many artisans to embrace radical political parties who rejected Germany's social direction.

It is thus, perhaps, not surprising that skilled craftsmen, shopkeepers and small business owners provided the first solid basis of support for the fledgling Nazi Party in the early 1920s. Not only were the Nazis fervently anti-Communist, but also their original programme (known as the Twenty-Five Points) contained several policies meant to assist small traders. Wholesale businesses were to be shut down and their premises given to small traders at a cheaper lease rate, and small artisans were to be given greater consideration by the state. Skilled workers made up 33 percent of the Nazi membership in the 1920s, despite making up only 27 percent of German society as a whole. Many artisans felt that their positions were threatened by growing consumerism and the construction of large shopping complexes in Weimar Germany, and so were attracted to the Nazi Party, which promised to protect the artisan tradition.

When Hitler came to power in 1933, the Nazis introduced several measures that helped Germany's artisans. Trade unions were crushed and department stores were restricted, with all chain stores barred from growing any larger and unable to offer services such as shoe repairing, baking, barbering or food catering. Highly skilled artisans were protected from competition as the Nazis cracked down on the employment of low-paid, unskilled workers, and all new artisan shops had to gain official permission before being set up. From 1935 onwards, all new artisans had to pass the Master's Examination in their craft to ensure that a high level of skill was maintained. Nazi Party formations had to order their uniforms and boots from artisan traders. From 1931 to 1936, the number of artisan businesses rose by one-fifth. Despite this, the Nazis ensured that the artisan tradition remained lower in importance than the interests of big industry. Artisan suggestions that industry should be de-mechanised were completely rejected. As the Nazis launched mass rearmament through industrial production from 1934 onwards, it was clear that the German economy would prioritise big industry, not the artisan tradition.

In the last years before the outbreak of war, from 1936 to 1939, the number of artisan businesses began to decline, decreasing by 11 percent. From 1936 onwards, department stores began to grow again, increasing their turnover by ten percent up to 1939. This was due to the fact that they were major employers, able to keep around 90,000 Germans in work, as opposed to the small artisan craft shops. Nazi concern at unemployment thus encouraged them to help the larger chain stores survive and grow. As the war approached, the Nazis tried to restrict artisan businesses, declaring that the artisan trades of bakers, butchers, shoemakers and tailors were too numerous in Germany, and they began to close shops that they considered were not economically justified. Those artisans who survived these closures tended to persist during the war by forming co-operatives with other small businesses and thereby pooling their resources and sharing costs. Some artisan businesses also prospered by using slave labour, particularly Jewish prisoners, who they were able to put to work for extremely long hours and no pay.

Following the Second World War, West Germany, with assistance from the USA, underwent considerable economic growth. Despite the fact that this growth was driven by big industry, the artisan tradition was also to play an important role. Artisans were given special status within the West German economic model. The most important aspect of this special status was that artisan organisations were given the role of organising and overseeing the training of skilled workers. This ensured that artisan organisations had a key role to play in the highly industrialised West Germany. By 1955, over 3.5 million Germans were employed in artisan trades, a growth of one million since 1939. They were centred on those crafts linked to big industry, such as skilled metalworking, with fewer working in areas such as clothing or textiles. The co-operative element of German artisans that developed during the Second World War expanded even further in West Germany, enabling small businesses to prosper financially in a competitive economy. The role of the artisan tradition in West Germany was a unique aspect of its economy. The co-operation between big industry and the smaller skilled trades, combining mass production with skilled craftsmanship, helped build a particular reputation for West German exports, thereby ensuring that the artisan tradition would maintain a very important place in the new economy from 1945 to 1990.

EXTRACT

2 In 'Social structure in the twentieth century', from S. Ogilvie and R. Overy (eds) *Germany: A New Social and Economic History since 1800, Vol. III* (2003), Christina Benninghaus, Heinz-Gerhard Haupt and Jorg Requate assess the decline of the German artisan class during the 20th century.

During the twentieth century, the traditional-style middle groups of German society became even smaller and more differentiated. One clear indicator is the decline in the proportion of self-employed persons among German earners, a decline that accelerated rapidly after the Second World War. The number of craft workshops fell from 849,000 at the foundation of the Federal Republic to 500,000 in 1977... But at the same time as crafts and commerce were undergoing these profound transformations, the sphere of white-collar employees was expanding. The non-manual labour force, which largely meant white-collar employees, made up only 10 per cent of all earners in the German Empire in 1910, but 21 per cent in the Federal Republic by 1950, and 46 per cent by 1980... With the improved employment situation and the expanding consumer goods industry after 1960, one man shops and craft workshops lost the important social function that they had fulfilled in the nineteenth and the first half of the twentieth century, that of providing supplementary income for workers' families in periods of unemployment, sickness and old age... Nowadays German politics is dominated no longer by the **Mittelstand**, but rather by a vaguely defined 'middle'.

KEY TERM

Mittelstand
German word for lower middle class, mainly consisting of family-owned businesses and skilled artisans.

'The position of German artisans improved in the years 1871–1990.'

To what extent do you agree with this statement? (20 marks)

Tip

This question is asking you to make a judgement on how far policies and industrial developments improved the position of German artisans. This will require some consideration of their position from 1871, the changes under the Weimar period and the Nazis, and then in the period after 1945. In many ways, for example, the Nazis introduced policies that aimed at improving the position of German artisans, but you might also consider how their policies were not consistent and changed from the late 1930s and into the Second World War. You could also examine how far the West German policies on big industry helped German artisans to achieve their economic goals.

ACTIVITY
KNOWLEDGE CHECK

1 Read Extract 2. What does it argue has happened to the German artisan class since 1950 and what has been the political effect of this change?

2 5-3-1 exercise:

    a) Summarise the key developments of the German artisan class from 1871 to 1990 in five sentences.

    b) Then choose three key words that you believe best summarise these developments.

    c) Now choose one key word that best defines the development of the German artisan class from 1871 to 1990.

The slow decline of the landowning elite and the peasantry

Developments for the land owning elite, 1871–1918

The Prussian land owning elite, known as Junkers, were the pre-eminent political power in Germany. The Junkers, a hereditary aristocracy, had been the leaders of the Prussian government and army that had united Germany, and they enjoyed dominant positions in the social, political and administrative elements of this new nation. It was ruled by the Prussian dynasty, and was shaped by the traditions of the Prussian elite. The constitution ensured that the Prussian elite could veto any attempts at constitutional change; and crucially, the chancellor, who was appointed from the Prussian elite, did not have to consult with parliament when making decisions. The Junkers exercised power over Germany through the Prussian parliament, which had an unequal voting system, ensuring that the Junkers would always maintain a majority, as well as their control of the military and bureaucracy.

EXTEND YOUR KNOWLEDGE

Junkers

The Junkers were the Prussian nobility that emerged in the late 1700s. Through government protection, this nobility had carved out massive agricultural estates on which the Prussian peasantry worked under repressive conditions. In this extremely two-tiered class system, the wealthy, noble Prussian Junkers ruled the peasantry that made up the majority of the population. The word 'Junker' translates to 'young nobleman' and this class could usually be identified by the preposition 'von' or 'zu' in their surnames. The Junkers took up the most privileged positions in Prussian politics and the military, and dominated the Prussian state under the ruling royal family, the House of Hohenzollern. It was the leading Prussian minister Otto von Bismarck who would unite Germany, and the subsequent constitution ensured that the Junkers would now not only dominate Prussia, but would also define the most powerful class in the newly unified German nation. The Prussian king became Kaiser of Germany and the Prussian elite took up the most privileged roles in Germany. Despite gradual changes, the Junkers would continue to play a critical role in German politics up to the end of the Second World War.

Prussian wealth, however, was based on massive land holdings and thus relied on agricultural production, something that the economic and political changes driven by industrialisation and urbanisation undermined. Junker control over the Prussian population had been easier in an agrarian-based economy, as much of the peasantry worked on Junker-owned land, thus ensuring the allegiance of the peasants to the elite, who they relied on for their survival. However, two key aspects undermined Junker power after 1871. Firstly, as the peasantry declined rapidly, so too did support for the political parties that represented the Junkers in the Reichstag. If the economic basis of the Junkers declined, this in turn could lead to a decline of their strength as the German elite and the collapse of their political power in Germany. The peasantry was changing in its traditional political habits. Rapid urbanisation had disrupted their way of life, and in a similar manner to the German artisan workers, they began to pursue their own political organisation in an array of forms. Thus, in order to maintain their parliamentary majority, the Conservative Junker-based party formed an alliance with the National Liberals, who represented the upper middle classes and industrial elite. These two powerful groups essentially represented the old wealthy of German society (the Junkers) and the new wealthy (the industrial owners). Both feared the rise of the SPD and the growing demands of the working class, and were thus prepared to work together to ensure their political and economic positions.

By allowing the wealthy industrialists into the upper sections of German political power, the Junkers hoped to maintain their dominance, as well as ensuring that the upper middle classes would have a powerful incentive to work with them, thus lessening the possibility of political change. Despite this, the coalition (political alliance) between the traditional Conservatives and the National Liberals contributed to the slow decline of the land owning elite. While maintaining their social status and control of the military, however, the Junkers had to compromise with big business, and German political policy moved further and further in a direction that favoured the industrialists. This growing political power of the newly wealthy industrial classes slowly undermined the previous complete dominance of the Junkers. The Junkers also faced another challenge in the shape of a **federalised** Germany. Previously, the Junkers had dominated the independent state of Prussia. Now the situation was made more difficult by the fact that the Junkers asserted political dominance over all of Germany, a situation challenged by those in other states, particularly Baden and Bavaria.

SOURCE
5 Georg von Siemens (cousin of the founder of Germany's electrical industry) writing in 1901, concerning the power of the Prussian agrarian elite.

> That government would go so far to accommodate the agrarians was not expected on our side. But for twenty-five years now these people have occupied all official positions and, by means of the bureaucracy, have secured the domination of the parliamentary bodies. If a government has a choice, it always goes along with the powerful ones, and right now the powerful ones are the excellently organised conservative agrarians, while the liberals feud with each other, like the Jews at the time of the siege of Jerusalem by Titus.

Thus, by the start of the 20th century the key political issue in Germany focused on the power of the Junkers. There was growing anger from the increasingly large working class, who opposed the Junker/industrialist alliance that aimed at restricting both their political and social rights. There were riots in Prussia after the 1908 state election in which the SPD achieved only seven seats with 23 percent of the vote, as opposed to the Junker Conservatives, who achieved 212 seats with only 16 percent of the vote. The Junkers blocked attempts to change the political system. In 1912, the political power of the working class, which had been growing since 1871, was most clearly demonstrated when the SPD became the largest party in the Reichstag, winning over four million votes and 110 seats. This was seen by the Junkers as a disastrous challenge to their entrenched power; in reality, however, very little changed. The SPD was wary of appearing revolutionary and was determined to prove both its responsibility and its loyalty to the German system. It pursued gradual political change within the existing political framework, and by 1914 there had been no change to the existing order.

By the time of the First World War, Germany had reached a point of political standstill. The socialist-dominated Reichstag was increasingly in disagreement with the Junker Chancellor Bethmann Hollweg, and the southern German states were pushing for a greater say in German politics. However, members of the Prussian landowning elite still held their dominant positions within the military and government and opposed any attempts at change. They also continued to have the support of the middle classes and industrialists, who also feared the SPD. The power of

KEY TERM

Federalised
The system of federalism refers to a type of government where power is shared between a central government and the political units that make up the country, usually known as states or provinces. The powers of government are thus divided between central government authority and state authority. In Germany, for instance, the central government controlled foreign policy, while the states controlled education. This constitutional arrangement is known as a federation. Today, the best-known example of a federal government is the United States of America, although Germany, despite some differences from the Kaiserreich, is still a federal system made up of 13 states (as opposed to 25 states in 1871). The significant difference between the German federal system of today and the German federal system of 1871 is that Prussia no longer exists in modern Germany.

the Junkers, although undergoing slow erosion since 1871, appeared to be in no particular danger of revolutionary change at the onset of the First World War in August 1914. It was only through the events of the war that the Junkers' power over Germany was completely destabilised.

EXTEND YOUR KNOWLEDGE

Class structures in the Kaiserreich

The society that emerged in Germany during its rapid industrialisation from 1871 onwards was quite rigid in its defined class structures and lack of social mobility. Landowners, industrialists, artisan shopkeepers and urban workers tended to pursue their own separate issues, with the idea of a united German nationality playing a secondary role to these defined class concerns.

The Prussian land owning elite, the Junkers, was the most powerful group, with privileged positions in the Kaiser's court, the army and bureaucracy. They also benefited from special tax privileges. However, a new powerful class was also emerging at this time, in the shape of the wealthy industrial-owning elite. This group, consisting of industrialists such as the Krupps, Thyssens and Hugenbergs, was considerably wealthy and believed they should benefit from political influence equal to their importance to the German economy. They shared with the Junkers a fear of the SPD and the rise of socialist politics.

In this sense, it is important to understand that the new powerful industrialists were not a direct political challenge to the Junkers. Instead, the Junkers were prepared to work with the industrialists to stop the SPD. In turn, the industrialists did not challenge the Junkers, but instead sought both a lifestyle and influence in German politics that reflected that of the Junkers. Rich industrialists, for instance, often purchased landed estates and military commissions for their children, thus allowing them to take their place in German high society alongside the Prussian elite. The emerging conservative combination of the traditional Prussian elite with the new industrialists would shape the anti-socialist politics of the Kaiserreich and Weimar Germany, and would eventually play a considerable role in the ascendancy of Adolf Hitler to the German chancellorship in January 1933.

EXTRACT

William Carr, in *A History of Germany, 1815–1985* (1987), here assesses the power of the Junkers in the early 20th century, and growing opposition in Germany to this privileged class.

At the beginning of the twentieth century the burning political issue in Germany was not the future of the Reichstag but the need for reform of the **archaic** Prussian constitution. In the Reichstag Conservatives were only a small party, politically isolated after 1909 and unable to prevent the passage of progressive legislation. Yet in Prussia the conservative position was virtually **unassailable**. They had a stranglehold over the civil service, they controlled the upper chamber and had close on a majority in the lower house, which was still elected by the outmoded three-class system. Their entrenched position in the army and at court enabled Prussian landowners to exert a great deal of influence on imperial policy as well. The offensive against Prussian conservatism was started by a Radical, Theodore Barth, with a motion in 1900 calling for reform of the Prussian constitution. It was promptly defeated but Barth reintroduced it annually in the **Landtag** and focused public attention on the problem. It was becoming more acute in the early years of the century for other reasons. In the first place the democratisation of the South German states was proceeding apace; in 1905–1906 Wurttemberg decided to elect all members of its lower house on the basis of **universal suffrage**. Secondly, in 1900 the Socialists decided to take part in Prussian elections for the first time; the fact they could only obtain seven seats with twenty-three per cent of the poll at the local elections of 1908, whereas the Conservatives with sixteen per cent had 212 seats, illustrated the glaring injustice of the prevailing system. There were working class demonstrations in Prussian cities, ending in clashes with the police, and the emperor hastily agreed constitutional changes. Nothing came of it.

ACTIVITY
KNOWLEDGE CHECK

Using Source 5, Extract 3 and your own studies, list all the ways in which members of the Prussian Junker elite were given a favoured position in Kaiserreich Germany.

Developments for the land owning elite during the Weimar Republic

By August 1918, it was clear that Germany was losing the war. Political and social opposition was growing against the conflict, and there were mass demonstrations and strikes in the streets of Germany. In September, the Prussian military leadership of Lieutenant General Erich Ludendorff and Chief of General Staff, Paul von Hindenburg, recommended to Kaiser Wilhelm II that Germany should approach the President of the United States, Wilson, and ask for an immediate truce. However, President Wilson believed that lasting peace could only be achieved by democratic nations, so General Ludendorff recommended to the Kaiser that Germany be reformed into a parliamentary democracy. On 28 October, political reforms, pushed through by the new government under the reformist Chancellor Prince Max of Baden, confirmed that the Prussian elite would no longer dominate the military or the government, and the unfair voting structure for Prussian state elections was abolished. This was not enough for the majority of the German population, and revolution subsequently swept through the country. On 9 November, the Kaiser was forced to abdicate and the first civilian government in Germany was established under the SPD. The Junker-led establishment that had existed since 1871 had been overthrown.

This, however, was not the end of their political influence in Germany. The SPD's fear of Communist revolution, fuelled by uprisings taking place within Germany, encouraged the SPD leader Ebert to make a deal with the German army. Ludendorff's successor, General Groener, promised to protect the new civilian government if Ebert, in turn, promised not to reform the leadership of the military. This was known as the Ebert–Groener Pact. This undoubtedly helped the fledgling government in maintaining the loyalty of the German army and ensuring the crushing of the numerous Communist uprisings that took place between 1918 and 1922. However, it would have serious implications for the Weimar Republic by upholding the power of the Junkers through the military. Although they had technically been stripped of their power due to the end of the Kaiserreich constitution and the creation of the new Weimar Republic, the Junkers still held significantly powerful positions within the new system. The key heads of the military, men such as Hans von Seeckt, commander-in-chief of the military from 1920 to 1926, Franz von Papen, Chancellor of the Weimar in 1932, and critically, Paul von Hindenburg, who became President of the Weimar Republic in 1925, were all Junkers. These powerful Junkers viewed the democratic ideals of the Weimar Republic with distaste, and believed in the return to an authoritarian system supported by the military, and possibly led by the Kaiser. Using their powerful positions, they undermined the Weimar Republic in a variety of ways. In 1920, for example, Seeckt refused to follow orders to fire on a right-wing coup driven by angry army officers and Free Corps. Known as the Kapp Putsch, it was only defeated by the resistance of workers and civil servants. More importantly, it was the political scheming of Papen, along with Hindenburg, with the support of military leaders and the land-owning elite, that led to the appointment of Adolf Hitler as Chancellor in 1933. Papen hoped he could use the popular support of the Nazis to establish a dictatorship in Germany and then remove Hitler from power, returning to a Junker-dominated authoritarian state.

Developments for the land owning elite during the Nazi dictatorship and post-1945

Due to Hitler's clever political manoeuvring, however, this never occurred. Hitler's relationship with the Junkers was complex. On 30 June 1934, Hitler crushed the Nazi SA (see Chapter 5, page 116), a move that won him the support of the military leadership. However, after the death of Hindenburg in 1934, Hitler assumed the role of Chancellor-President (or Führer) and the political power of the Junker class considerably declined. Powerful Junkers in the German government, such as Papen, were removed from their position, and, importantly, in 1938, Hitler assumed control of the army, enabling him to remove leading Junker generals who were becoming wary of his aggressive foreign policy. Despite this, the majority of the military leadership, still dominated by the Junker class, maintained their loyalty to the Nazis through the Second World War. In July 1944, however, a small group of military leaders became concerned about the progress of the war and attempted to assassinate Hitler. The Junker Count von Stauffenberg carried out the attempted bombing, but its failure led to the discovery of the plot and the execution of around 5,000 people. The consequence of this was the final destruction of Junker power in Germany, as Hitler wiped out the old imperial military leadership that he believed had become disloyal.

After the Second World War, the end of the land owning aristocracy in Germany was compounded by the fact that the main Junker lands in East Germany were made part of Poland, and members of the Junker class were forced to give up their properties. In Communist East Germany, large Junker land holdings that were still in Germany were split up into smaller farms and run by the state, and large aristocratic manor houses that had existed for centuries were destroyed. By 1952, the power of the Prussian land owning elite, which the 1871 constitution was meant to ensure lasted forever, had finally come to an end.

Developments for the peasantry, 1871–1918

Linked to these developments in respect of the Junkers was the position of the German peasantry. Over the course of the 20th century, one of the key changes in German society was the decline of the agricultural sector as a factor in the overall economy. In 1900, agriculture made up 30 percent of the German national product, but by 1989 this had reduced to barely two percent. This was mirrored by a reduction in those German workers engaged in the agricultural sector, from 49 percent in 1871 to only two percent in 1989.

During the Kaiserreich, there was considerable political discussion concerning the ongoing role of agriculture within a rapidly industrialising society. The powerful Junker class relied on its massive farm holdings for its wealth and therefore had a vested interest in protecting the rural economy. It was Junker pressure that led Bismarck to introduce protective tariffs in 1879, to stop the import of cheaper grain from Russia and the United States. In 1893, the largely Junker-backed Agrarian League pressure group was formed to fight against any moves by the government to weaken tariffs against agricultural imports.

Developments for the peasantry during the Weimar Republic and Nazi dictatorship

The loss of workers during the First World War affected Germany's agricultural production, as did the fact that fertiliser and fuel had to be prioritised for the war effort. Consequently, Germany suffered from fairly acute food shortages during the war. In the 1920s, better farming practices from Denmark and the Netherlands, combined with growing competition from world markets, also challenged German agriculture. Even before the Great Depression, the German agricultural sector suffered from a price slump that led to widespread bankruptcy and the closure of a large number of farms. This crisis was further exacerbated by the worldwide economic depression that began in 1929.

The Nazis promoted rural Germany as the real heart of German tradition and culture, as opposed to the 'degenerate' cities. The Nazi Party romanticised the unchanging nature of Germany's rural villages. German farming life, with its link to the land, its traditional cultural practices, as well as its defined roles for both men and women, supposedly represented the backbone of 'pure German stock'. In 1933, the Nazis introduced laws that protected farms from forced sales or from being broken up, and guaranteed high agricultural prices for German produce. However, the Nazis were helpless to stop the continuing decline of the peasantry, as the recovery and growth of the German industrial economy encouraged further migration from rural areas into the cities. The requirements of the Second World War and the need for Germany to be self-sufficient increased the pressure on German farms to raise production, despite a continuous decline in the agricultural workforce.

Developments for the peasantry, post-1945

Following the end of the Second World War, West German farms benefited from better farming practices and mechanisation. This led to greater efficiency in the West German agricultural sector, as land was consolidated into larger farms, thereby improving the productivity of the country's rural economy. Farming machinery and agricultural prices were subsidised by the West German government, and the demand for German produce remained high among German consumers. The restructuring of German agriculture, however, did lead to a considerable decline in the workforce. Between 1950 and 1960, the rural sector lost 50 percent of its workers and the agricultural population continued to decline due to the economic opportunities of West Germany's industrial growth. The development of the West German economy in the 1970s led to further reduction in both the rural population and in agriculture's importance in the German national product as a whole. Overall, from 1871 to 1990, the German peasantry and the rural economy they were employed in underwent a considerable decline.

THINKING HISTORICALLY Change (7a)

Convergence and divergence

Political change in Germany, 1871–1945

1871	1912	1919	1933	1945
Germany established under political dominance of Junkers	SPD becomes largest party in the German Reichstag	Weimar Republic established which places full power in civilian government	Adolf Hitler becomes Chancellor of Germany	Adolf Hitler destroys power of the Junker class

Social change in Germany, 1871–1945

1871	1883–84	1918	1931	1943
Germany undergoes mass urbanisation leading to growth in working class	Chancellor Bismarck introduces social reforms for workers	Anger at the war leads to over one million German workers going on strike	Economic devastation leads to mass unemployment across German society	Growing concern in German society at progress of the Second World War

1 Draw a timeline across the middle of a landscape piece of A3 paper. Cut out ten small rectangular cards and write the above changes on them. Then place them on the timeline, with political events above the line and social below. Make sure there is a lot of space between the changes and the line.

2 Draw a line and write a link between each change within each strand, so that you have four links that join up the changes in the *political* part of the timeline, and four that join the social changes. You will then have two strands of change: *political and social*.

3 Now make as many links as possible across the timeline between political change and social change. Think about how they are affected by one another and think about how things can link across long periods of time.

You should end up with something like this:

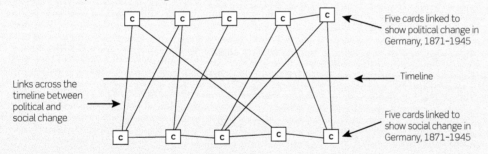

Now answer the following questions.

4 How far do different strands of history interact with one another? Illustrate your answer with two well-explained examples.

5 At what point do the two strands of development converge (i.e. when do the changes have the biggest impact on one another)?

6 How useful are the strands in understanding the change in political power in Germany from 1871 to 1945?

ACTIVITY
KNOWLEDGE CHECK

1 Summarise the key changes to the Prussian land owning elite from 1871 to 1945.

2 What were the most important elements shaping the gradual decline in power of the Prussian landowning elite? List them in order of importance.

3 The Junker class had completely lost its influence in German politics by the Second World War. How far do you agree with this statement? Provide evidence both for and against the statement, and then a write a final conclusion answering this question.

The rise of the white-collar workers

Taking place parallel to the growth of the German working class, as industrialisation accelerated after 1871, was the rise of a new German middle class of white-collar workers, both in state and private industry. This too was to have a crucial impact on German politics, the growth of the economy and the greater need for jobs in administration, teaching, scientific research and the legal profession, as Germany's cities expanded. In Prussia, for example, the civil service grew from only 40,000 in 1850 to 250,000 by 1907. The number of schoolteachers expanded by 43 percent between 1891 and 1913, and the number of doctors more than doubled between 1876 and 1913.

The expansion of industry and its growing sophistication meant more jobs were required in research and development, skilled mechanical expertise, marketing, sales and finance. This led to greater opportunities for social mobility in the Kaiserreich, as many Germans from the traditional lower middle classes were instead able to take up higher-skilled, better-paid positions as white-collar workers. This new white-collar middle class tended to be the children of artisans, the lower middle class, who now found greater prospects through education into the professions offered by Germany's industrial development. From 1882 to 1907, the number of self-employed artisans as a percentage of the German workforce decreased from 25.4 percent to 18.8 percent, while the number of white-collar workers increased from 4.7 percent to ten percent.

The rise of this new middle class was to have important political and social consequences for Germany. The white-collar workers tended to have better pay, housing and health than the working class. The new middle class viewed themselves as separate from the working class, and from the 1890s began to organise themselves into political pressure groups that argued for greater recognition of their particular importance to German society. In 1901, for example, various white-collar political groups organised themselves into a Co-ordinating Committee that argued for a separate state insurance scheme for white-collar workers, asserting that it should be different to that offered to the working class. In 1911, they were successful, and a different insurance scheme for white-collar workers was introduced. This government decision had the important effect of reinforcing the growing class divisions within the Kaiserreich, marking out clear differences between the working class and the new middle class. The new middle class also affected the traditional politics of Germany. Just like the working class, they tended to be critical of both the government and the traditional system that favoured the Junkers. Some of the white-collar workers voted for the SPD, while others took a more radical path. The German Middle Class Association, for example, was extremely racist, anti-Semitic and nationalist, and rejected all forms of parliamentary democracy. Consequently, the government introduced nationalist, policies that they hoped would unite the new middle class, the lower middle class, industrialists and the aristocracy in support of the Kaiser and against the SPD, although this was not always successful.

By 1912, the class of white-collar workers was more powerful than ever before. Although they feared the growing power of the SPD, they also shared with the working class a belief that the German system required political change, and at times the middle-class parties were prepared to work with the SPD in the Reichstag in order to challenge the entrenched governmental system dominated by the Prussian elite. This occurred particularly in the southern German states, where there was, understandably, a greater feeling against Prussian power. Just as most Germans did, the white-collar class supported Germany's entry into the war in 1914. As the war progressed, however, many white-collar workers found their standard of living dropping considerably, to the same level as that of the working class, and by August 1916 there was a growing movement against the war within this section of German society. In fact, it was the middle-class political leader, Matthias Erzberger, of the Centre Party, who made the strongest call for peace in July 1917, and Erzberger aligned himself with the SPD in voting for an end to the war. The vote was carried by 212 votes to 126, representing what was also taking place in German society, as the white-collar middle class was increasingly siding with the working class in their demands for an end to the war.

This unity, however, did not last much beyond the foundation of the Weimar Republic in 1919. The white-collar middle class was particularly fearful of the Communist uprisings taking place in the early period of the Weimar, which they believed threatened their position in society. More importantly, however, unlike during the previous Kaiserreich, although members of the white-collar middle class still viewed themselves as superior to the working class, their economic situation was relatively no better and in some cases worse. The economic crisis of hyperinflation that the Weimar experienced in the early 1920s, followed by depression from 1929, affected white-collar workers severely. There was a growing sense of economic insecurity and unease about the political direction of the Weimar Republic. During the war, the shortage of white-collar workers was made up for by a dramatic increase in the number of working women, as well as the entry of newly trained workers and previously retired ones who took up their old roles. This caused growing issues with unemployment as white-collar workers returned from the war. This was further accentuated following on from hyperinflation in 1923. The economic devastation caused by this financial crisis primarily affected the middle classes, resulting in the emergence of a white-collar working class. This forced more people to look for work, thus saturating the market. While the number of white-collar workers doubled in Germany from 1907 to 1925 (blue-collar workers only increased by 20 percent during the same time), unemployment remained higher than for the working class. The white-collar working class did not enjoy the same increase in real wages as the working class between 1924 and 1929, and unemployment remained high. A government report in 1928 asserted that 183,371 white-collar workers were unemployed. Problematically, white-collar workers did not receive the same state benefits as blue-collar workers, and some 90,000 white-collar workers were forced to live without any unemployment support.

SOURCE

 Hans Georg was a sociologist who was interested in the emergence of the white-collar working class, and its role and impact on German society. In this article, 'Our Stand at the Abyss', of 26 January 1921, Georg notes the distinctions between white-collar workers and blue-collar workers and the importance of social mobility in German society.

White-collar employers used to belong to the Mittelstand. That the income of a white-collar employee was usually not much higher than a worker's, indeed often lagged behind it, does not refute this but only proves that the social position of an occupation does not absolutely and without exception depend upon its economic ranking. Who would seriously deny that the life style of white-collar employees was not superior to that of the workers! White-collar employees dressed better, lived in nicer homes, possessed higher quality household goods, pursued educational opportunities, attended lectures, concerts or theatrical performances and read good books. Their standard of living approximated that of the propertied class, not perhaps in range and freedom but in type. The reasons for their proud appearance are neither beyond explanation nor solely a response to the demands of their occupation. It was a thoroughly justified expression of a deeper need, of a more refined intellectual and spiritual education. There is no denigration of the manual worker in this statement, though there is perhaps a reproach directed at the independent unionists and party socialists, who, mistaking the facts, have subjected 'white-collar proletarians' to ridicule. These slanders of the middle class were also wrong when they claimed that white-collar employees had merely invented the prized relationship between themselves and their superiors as that of being co-workers. Their appraisal of this relationship undoubtedly waned over time but never entirely disappeared. While workers could be turned out of the factory from one day or one week to the next, white-collar employees could be dismissed only four times a year, and, moreover, had to be given six weeks' notice. But even this limited right of dismissal was generally not invoked, even when a decline in business would clearly have made it tempting. The resulting existential security of white-collar employees once again contributed to their adoption of the ways of thinking and life-styles of the higher social classes... It is impossible to overestimate the value of these classes. The leading strata of the population and economy are replenished and renewed from their ranks. They are in turn renewed by the most capable recruits from the proletariat, which is consequently the particular significance of the latter. It is a permanent – note the word well – mediate between the bottom and the top.

ACTIVITY
KNOWLEDGE CHECK

What does Source 6 reveal about the attitudes and importance of the emerging white-collar working class in 1921?

The loss in earnings and the high unemployment rate nurtured a feeling of antagonism within the middle classes towards the Weimar Republic, a factor only further accentuated by the depression. In Berlin alone, 60 percent of university graduates were out of work by 1933. Nazi policies calling for an end to women in the workforce definitely appealed to many male white-collar workers, who believed this to be a factor in their unemployment. However, the voting patterns of white-collar workers were not uniform; those in the state sectors, primarily the civil service, voted in large numbers for the Nazis, while those white-collar workers in more manual positions, and who lived in more working-class districts of big cities, tended to vote for the SPD. Where the Nazis had strong support was among young white-collar workers, who saw little prospect for work in the economic climate of the Weimar after 1929, with youth from the white-collar working class making up 20 percent of new Nazi Party members between 1929 and 1932. Under the Nazis, white-collar workers enjoyed particular rights not shared by industrial workers. While blue-collar workers could be fired with only a week's notice, white-collar professions required six weeks' notice. Many white-collar workers found that their employment opportunities could be helped immensely through Nazi membership, and by the end of the first year of Hitler's time in power, they were 65 percent over-represented within the Nazi Party (while blue-collar workers remained 30 percent under-represented). The economic development and modernisation of the Nazi economy saw a 25 percent increase in the white-collar population between 1933 and 1939, compared to only a ten percent increase among blue-collar workers during the same period. The proportion of white-collar workers to other workers in Germany now reached one in every four, a massive increase since 1895, when only one in every 13 workers had been from the white-collar class. Critically, white-collar workers experienced a ten percent pay rise in comparison to 1928, while the 1928 blue-collar income stagnated. Under the Nazis, white-collar workers enjoyed better status in terms of pension schemes and insurance benefits compared to blue-collar workers, and even had a form of address, 'Sie', which gave them greater status than industrial workers, who were addressed by the less formal 'du'. Unsurprisingly, the white-collar class of workers in Germany were consistently loyal to the Nazis, even during the Second World War.

ACTIVITY
KNOWLEDGE CHECK

1 What does Source 7 demonstrate about the Nazi relationship with the German civil service?

2 What would be some possible concerns about using this photo as a source of evidence?

3 Using what you have already read, how far does this photo show an accurate portrayal of the Nazis' relationship with German white-collar workers?

SOURCE

Adolf Hitler speaking to German civil servants at a rally in Nuremberg in 1933.

As previously discussed, the newly constituted nation of West Germany that followed the fall of the Nazis and the division of Germany underwent rapid industrial growth in the 1950s. This, in turn, drove a massive expansion of white-collar work in Germany. As the economy shifted in the 1970s and 1980s, from one dominated by industry to one more focused on service, new generations of German workers were drawn into the white-collar class. In 1890, white-collar workers made up around ten percent of the workforce; by 1940, this had increased to 20 percent, and by 1980, this had reached 35 percent of West Germany's workers. The largest group in the West German workforce was educated, white-collar workers employed in either the service or manufacturing areas. This transformation of Germany from 1871 to 1990, into a society dominated by the middle-class, white-collar professions, has had an important political and social effect on the country.

Social mobility after the Second World War

Following the devastation of the Second World War, the new nation of West Germany rebuilt itself as one of the world's most successful capitalist economies. One of the key successes of this economy was that it provided for a more equal society. This has been referred to as the *nivellierte Mittelstandsgesellschaft*, the levelled middle-class society. This idea asserts that West Germany developed an economy that had less of a social and financial gap between the differing classes, with most Germans existing in the 'middle', instead of in a stratified society where there is a larger gap between the very rich and the very poor. Some of the key reasons for this were the destruction of the Junkers and the wealthy landed classes during the Second World War, the massive expansion of the white-collar class and the improved position of the working class. Higher wages, greater social security and full employment, combined with social mobility, ensured a high standard of living within the new Federal Republic of Germany.

The demand for skilled labour, firstly as a key aspect of West Germany's industrially based economy in the 1950s and 1960s, and then, from the 1970s onwards, towards higher education and the service industry, ensured that West German society had a high level of generational mobility. From 1950 to 1964, real wages in West Germany doubled. This in turn fuelled greater consumerism within German society. During the 1950s, government policy drove house building, and a law was passed in 1956 making it easier for Germans to buy their own house. New tax allowances allowed workers to deduct commuting expenses from vehicle purchases, thus making it easier to purchase a car. Those who had suffered most in the war were assisted by the Equalisation of Burdens Law of 1952, which, over two decades, transferred 90,000 million deutschmarks from those who suffered the least during the war to those who had been most devastated by it. This, in turn, helped to provide economic opportunities to millions of Germans who may otherwise have found it difficult to rebuild their lives following the Second World War. Subsequently, more Germans found themselves able to enjoy a standard of living that had previously been open only to the wealthiest in German society. German wage earners had only constituted nine percent of car owners in 1950, but by 1960 made up over 50 percent. General living standards across West Germany rose by 58 percent between 1953 and 1960, in comparison to Britain, where they increased by 25 percent. There was a considerable increase in the building of modern apartments, consumer culture and access to greater leisure time for many Germans.

The move from an economy based on heavy industry to one focused on the service industry in the 1970s allowed more young Germans to enter the middle class. The transformation of German society continued into the 1980s; by 1989, 66 percent of the German workforce was employed in the service industries, with the largest working group centred in the educated middle class. Despite these positive developments, social mobility was not possible for all West Germans. Major differences in wealth and status still existed, particularly in terms of the 'guest workers', who formed a new underclass and worked in the least protected, lowest-paid and most difficult jobs in the German economy. Blue-collar families had less access to generational mobility, with those from more professional backgrounds at a distinct advantage in terms of education and employment opportunities. Most significantly, much of this social mobility was primarily judged through male occupations. West German women were discouraged from entering the workforce, and those who did predominately laboured in jobs of low status and low pay. While social mobility in West Germany undoubtedly led to continued changes in the class structure, with more and more Germans entering the middle class as the blue-collar and agricultural sectors declined, the argument that this, in turn, meant West Germany was developing into a classless society was somewhat exaggerated.

EXTRACT

4

In *Interpretations of the Two Germanies, 1945–1900* (2000), Mary Fulbrook here challenges the concept that social mobility after the Second World War meant that West Germany was developing into a 'classless society'.

Although some analysts have claimed that West Germany was developing a relatively classless society, with universal affluence allegedly obscuring social differences and regional accents denoting only area of birth, not position in a social hierarchy, nevertheless major differences in wealth and status remained. Most notably a new, ethnically distinct 'underclass' of 'guest workers' (Gastarbeiter) developed, predominately employed in the most disagreeable and least well-remunerated jobs, under the worst conditions as far as such matters as employment rights, health and safety measures or level of union protection were concerned. And at the top of the hierarchy the predominance of members of the old aristocracy (whether or not they dropped the 'von' from their surnames) was still to be observed. Social mobility continued to be largely structurally induced – that is, related to changes in the class structure as a whole, with the shrinking of the agricultural and blue-collar sectors inevitably implying a degree of inter-generational mobility – with the acquisition of educational credentials to a considerable degree serving to legitimate the inheritance of social status. But with a plurality of elites – in politics, finance, business, academia, the law, the churches and other professions – there was no single route to the top in a society that might be unequal but was still relatively open. A professional and well-to-do background remained, of course, a distinct advantage – as did being male. Women in the West continued to have 'their' social class measured primarily in terms of their father's or husband's occupation. Insofar as they took up paid employment outside the home, women tended to remain in lower-status, less well-paid, often part-time or temporary employment, with minimal help by way of state nurseries or provisions for after school childcare.

ACTIVITY
KNOWLEDGE CHECK

1 What were the main factors affecting the growth of the white-collar working class between the years 1871 and 1990? Break your answer down into the differing periods: Kaiserreich, Weimar, Nazi and West Germany.

2 How accurate is it to describe West Germany as a 'classless' society? Provide evidence to support your argument.

TO WHAT EXTENT DID THE ROLE OF WOMEN IN GERMAN SOCIETY CHANGE BETWEEN 1871 AND 1990?

Roles in the family and the workplace in the 19th century

The role of women in German society during the 19th century tended to be quite traditional. Given the significance of Prussian culture in the newly unified country, the role that women played in the militarised society of Prussia tended to dominate German values after 1871. Men were viewed as, primarily, soldiers and defenders of the home and fatherland, who were prepared to lay down their lives for their nation. A woman's role, on the other hand, was to fulfil her patriotic duty through maternal care, providing emotional support to the family and tending to the sick and needy of society. The roles of men and women were thus quite differentiated. Germany's national civil code legalised the lower status of women, asserting that the man had authority in all matters relating to his family's children, administrative power over his wife's property and wealth, and power of attorney (ultimate control) over his wife's legal contracts. Women were denied the vote, and were restricted in the areas of education, work and politics. Women, it was believed in 19th-century Germany, should focus on their traditional maternal duty, caring for their family, and were too fragile to play a larger part in society. Kaiserreich Germany was thus a quite strictly hierarchical society, which enforced, through law, the dominant position of men over women.

Growing industrialisation after 1871, and the subsequent development of the working class, did see more women enter the workforce. However, the German industrial economy was quite segregated between men's and women's work. The female sectors of work were considered to be textiles, garment making and food processing. These were the lowest-paid, least skilled areas of the economy and tended to lack union protection. Men were considered to be the main breadwinners, so women's work was solely subsidiary, and thus worthy only of low pay and restricted from positions in heavy industry or in management, which were seen as areas of employment fit only for men. Even where men and women worked together, women's work was deemed 'unskilled' as compared to men's, which was officially designated 'semi-skilled', thus allowing for lower pay and worse conditions, as well as confirming the lower place of women within the workforce.

Women who worked were still expected to take the full burden of family-raising and domestic tasks, thus adding to the difficulties many women within the working class were forced to endure. However, the welfare provisions introduced by Bismarck contained specific benefits for women. By 1891, women were guaranteed six weeks of maternity leave and an 11-hour working day. Women were also not allowed to be employed in the mining industry. Importantly, working women were allowed more time off at lunch and on Saturdays, so that they could perform their domestic duties. Although this offered protection for women, it was focused on the idea that the proper place for women was in the home. Women were still subordinate to men, and the extra time women were provided with during work hours confirmed their primary duty as raising children and tending to the domestic needs of their families. Within the Kaiserreich there was a growing concern that industrialisation was leading to more and more women entering the workforce. This was considered undesirable, as it was believed that work was the cause of poor health among women, leading to infant mortality and miscarriages, thereby threatening not only the health of Germany's families, but also the nation itself. In an attempt to counteract this protective legalisation was introduced which aimed to reinforce the key divisions between men's place in the workforce and women's place at home, caring for the family.

Not all Germans accepted this position of women, however. In 1885, a group of women, led by Emma Ihrer, established the Society for the Protection of Women Workers' Interests, which helped support working women, mainly through providing the services of doctors and lawyers without charge. The society campaigned for women's rights, and had some success in pressuring the Reichstag to conduct an official survey of wages in the clothing industry. The group had over a thousand members by 1886, when the government banned it. Ihrer continued her campaigns, and in 1890 became the first and only woman elected to the General Commission of German Trade Unions, using this key position to campaign for greater rights for working-class women. The discrimination against women in Germany was also challenged by the SPD, the only political party that called for an end to Germany's discriminatory legal system and campaigned for women's right to vote. It had its own women's section, led by feminist Clara Zetkin, which published the SPD's women's newspaper *Die Gleichheit* ('Equality'.) It was Zetkin who helped to found the first ever International Women's Day on 19 March 1911, to try to bring greater attention to the plight of women, not only in Germany, but also in the world at large. One of the SPD's most prominent and active members was the female socialist, Rosa Luxemburg.

However, women such as Zetkin and Luxemburg were certainly an exception to the position of the average German woman in society. Other feminist groups formed, such as the middle-class Bund Deutscher Frauenvereine (Union of German Feminist Organisations, BDF), which campaigned for the rights of middle-class women to have equality in education and politics, and to be allowed to organise their own financial affairs. The BDF was founded in 1894 and grew significantly following its creation, although it only focused on the rights of middle-class women. The Federation of German Women's Associations was also created during this time and focused its campaign on reforming German's discriminatory civil code. Despite the agitation of the SPD and the numerous feminist organisations, the government refused to change Germany's civil code, and the restricted role of women remained relatively unchallenged until after the First World War.

The impacts of the First World War

During the First World War, women played a significant political role in opposing the conflict. In 1914, Zetkin, Luxemburg and Luise Kahler had been among the few SPD members who rejected their party's policy of supporting the war. This was a particularly brave stance, given that the majority of the population and all the Reichstag's political parties, including the SPD, supported the war in its early stages. Zetkin went as far as to organise the international socialist women's anti-war conference in Berlin in 1915. Both Luxemburg and Zetkin were arrested several times during the First World War due to their opposition to the war.

Economically, the war also changed the position of women in Germany. While the actual number of German women working did not change, the type of work they engaged in clearly did.

The shortage of male workers saw women enter into previously barred industrial positions; working in industries such as chemical, iron, steel and engineering. Women took up key positions in the German postal and transport sectors, work that had previously been seen as outside their capabilities. Many German women experienced a new sense of freedom, as they became the primary breadwinners in the family for the first time, a development that helped to establish an enhanced position for women in German society. Women's work was now promoted by the government as essential for Germany's survival, a considerable change from the degrading attitude given to women's work before 1914.

SOURCE

8 Young German women working on cartridges in a munitions factory during the First World War, c1916.

This growing role of women in politics and the economy was enhanced further following the First World War, as the new Weimar Constitution granted all women the vote, a move that had a key effect in changing the traditional role of women in German society. The Weimar political parties encouraged the participation of women in politics, believing that this would help them attract the female vote. Women members made up 9.6 percent of the new Weimar parliament in 1919, and although this would represent a high point for female membership, the percentage of female Reichstag members remained at around six to seven percent throughout the Weimar period. Although this may appear small, it was a considerable development from before 1914, and it is worth considering that women made up only two percent of the British parliament and one percent of the United States' House of Representatives at the same time. Women also made up 6.1 percent of the members in Germany's state parliaments. The Weimar Constitution moved away from the Kaiserreich's civil code, instead guaranteeing female equality in education and equal opportunity employment in the civil service, as well as equal pay. The BDF grew from 300,000 members in 1914 to 900,000 during the 1920s.

The impact of the First World War had led to the emergence of the so-called 'double earners'; married women who also worked, a development that in turn enhanced the economic independence of many German women. Women's new-found independence during the war, their enhanced status and greater employment opportunities, combined with the terrible loss of around two million men during the First World War, meant the traditional idea of marriage for many young women now became less possible, and this led to the emergence of a new type of German woman. This 'new Weimar Woman' challenged German traditional culture; she was typically defined as urbanised, financially independent, single and sexually active, a follower of United States' fashion, who spent her evenings at nightclubs. For many conservative Germans, the emergence of the 'new Weimar Woman' represented the breakdown of German society taking place under the Weimar Republic, as this new femininity challenged the traditional family structure.

SOURCE

9 Elsa Herrmann, in *This is the New Woman* (1929), defines how the 'New Woman' is different from the older generations of German women.

To all appearances, the distinction between women in our day and those of previous times is to be sought only in formal terms because the modern woman refuses to lead the life of a lady and a housewife, preferring to depart from the ordained path and go her own way. In fact, however, the attitude of the new woman toward traditional customs is the expression of a world view that decisively influences the direction of her entire life. The difference between the way women conceived of their lives today as distinguished from yesterday is most clearly visible in the objectives of this life. The woman of yesterday lived exclusively for and geared her actions towards the future. Already as a half grown child, she toiled and stoked her hope chest for her future **dowry**. In the first years of marriage she did as much of the household work as possible herself to save on expenses, thereby laying the foundation for future prosperity, or at least a worry free old age. In pursuit of these goals she helped her husband in his business or professional activities. She frequently accomplished incredible things by combining her work in the household with this professional work of her own, the success of which she could constantly observe and measure by the progress of their mutual prosperity... Her primary task, however, she naturally saw to be caring for the well being of her children, the ultimate carriers of her thoughts on the future... In stark contrast the woman of today is orientated exclusively toward the present. That which is decisive for her, not that which should be or should have been according to tradition. She refuses to be regarded as physically weak being in need of assistance – the role the woman of yesterday continued to adopt artificially – and therefore no longer lives by means supplied to her from elsewhere, whether income from her parents or her husband. For the sake of her economic independence, the necessary precondition for the development of a self reliant personality, she seeks to support herself through gainful employment. It is only too obvious that, in contrast to earlier times, this conception of life necessarily involves a fundamental change in the orientation of women toward men which acquires its basic tone from concerns of equality and comradeship.

KEY TERM

Dowry
Money or property given by the bride to her husband at marriage.

SOURCE 10 1920s Weimar fashion for the 'new Weimar Woman'.

However, despite these changes, many aspects still remained the same for German women. For the most part, the traditional attitude to women persisted, with the role of wife and mother viewed as the preferable outcome for all young German women. If German women were to work, it was expected that they would do this before they were married, after which they would settle down to fulfil their domestic duties, raising their children and looking after their homes while the men worked. Despite the lofty ideals of the Weimar Constitution, working women were still predominately found in the jobs of the lowest status and least pay. Overall, while the impact of the First World War and the political ideals of the Weimar Republic did contribute to more opportunities for German women than found in the Kaiserreich, to a larger extent this was still not the experience for the majority of German women, and the traditional attitude to women and their role in society remained largely unchanged from the 1890s.

Nazi policies

SOURCE

 11

From a speech by Hitler to the National Socialist Women's Section, 8 September 1934. Here, Hitler argues against the Weimar's ideas of political and social emancipation of women.

> The slogan 'Emancipation of Women' was invented by Jewish intellectuals and its content was formed by the same spirit. In the really good times of German life the German woman has no need to emancipate herself. She possessed exactly what nature had necessarily given her to administer and preserve... If the man's world is said to be the State, his struggle, his readiness to devote his powers to the service of his community, then it may perhaps be said that the woman's is a smaller world. For her world is her husband, her family, her children and her home. But what would become of the greater world if there were no one to tend and care for the smaller one?... the sacrifices which the man makes in the struggle of his nation, the woman makes in the preservation of that nation in individual cases. What the man gives in courage on the battlefield, the woman gives in eternal self-sacrifice, in eternal pain and suffering. Every child that a woman brings into the world is a battle, a battle waged for the existence of her people... So our women's movement is for us not something which inscribes on its banner as its programme the fight against men, but something which has as its programme the common fight together with men.

The Nazi attitude to women primarily reflected the traditional German view, which drew a clear demarcation between the roles of men and women in society. In many ways it differed little from the Prussian perspective of the 19th century. The Nazis' glorification of the violent, militarised, masculine culture of the First World War informed their ideal of the German man as one who saw military duty, patriotism and sacrifice for his country as the highest honour. Women's duty was therefore to serve their country by ensuring they gave birth to a plentiful race of healthy Germans, who would contribute to the country's cause and were raised with the correct ideals, focused on nationalism and duty to the nation. The independent 'new Weimar Woman' was thus seen as a threat to this ideal, and Nazi propaganda persistently depicted her as a danger to the social fabric of German society: the decadent, immoral woman who was a product of the Weimar Republic and the liberal, modern Germany it represented.

The Nazis reflected older German thinking, whereby the traditional family was the core of the nation: it ensured the ongoing health of Germany; if the traditional roles of men and women were challenged and the family structure itself was to break down, it would threaten the nation's strength and vigour. The Nazis were not alone in this perspective, and shared the same beliefs of many conservative women, who argued that the proper place for German women was in the home, nurturing their children, thus ensuring the continued well-being of the nation. The Nazis' electoral breakthroughs in the early 1930s were well supported by women voters, although this had little to do with the party's anti-feminist ideology. Instead, it appears that along with the hardship brought about for many women by the depression, as for their male counterparts, women now had the added burden of looking for work and caring for the family while husbands struggled for work, and it was this that led them to vote for the Nazi Party.

Once in power, the Nazis quickly implemented a range of policies aimed at forcing women out of employment and back into the home. All feminist and female working groups were banned, and women were barred from government employment and practising medicine or the law. Female assistant teachers were dismissed and women were barred from jury service. Subsequently, the number of female secondary school teachers declined by 15 percent between 1933 and 1935. A ten percent limit was placed on female enrolment at German universities (at that stage, women made up 20 percent of university students) and an interest-free family loan was provided to young German couples if the wife refrained from working. The syllabus for girls at primary and secondary school now focused primarily on domestic science. The wearing of make-up was discouraged, as it was seen as 'unGerman', and the police were ordered to reprimand women they saw smoking in public. Being thin was believed to restrict a woman's ability to give birth, so Nazi propaganda encouraged women not to concern themselves with their weight. German women were encouraged to dress in 'feminine' fashion, and the wearing of skirts instead of slacks was promoted. Healthy German women were encouraged to contribute to the new race of Germans by having as many children as possible, with financial incentives provided for large families, and the Mutterkreuz (Mother's Cross) awarded to those who either had eight (gold cross), six (silver cross) or four children (bronze cross).

The Nazi women's organisation Deutsches Frauenwerk (DFW) was established in September 1933, aimed at providing education about domestic work and child-rearing to German women. The Nazi slogan for women was 'Kinder, Kirche, Kuche' (children, church and kitchen).

However, although reflecting traditional elements, Nazi policy towards women was a divergence not only from the Weimar, but also from the previous Kaiserreich. While in the Kaiserreich the traditional attitude to women was one of middle-class domesticity, the Nazis saw women's duty as more actively breeding Germany's new 'master race'. This required the physical and racial fitness of women in a manner not conceived of previously. Abortions were banned, and genetic 'counselling centres' were set up to ensure that young couples planning on having a family were of the 'right' genetic stock and would thus have strong, healthy, 'German' children. Most radically, in 1935, the Nazis established the Lebensborn Programme, which provided an adoption system for 'racially pure' unmarried mothers to give up their babies to SS officer families, so that the children could be raised by 'racially pure and healthy' Nazi parents. The removal of the social stigma associated with extramarital pregnancies and adoption was also meant to stimulate a rising birth rate of Aryan children, by encouraging unmarried women to have children as long as they were 'racially pure' by the Nazi definition. Conversely, those deemed 'racially unfit', such as Jews, prostitutes, disabled or mentally ill people and other so-called 'undesirables', were discouraged from having children; and between 1933 and 1945, the Nazis engaged in forced sterilisation, euthanasia and mass murder to ensure that only 'racially fit' children were born.

SOURCE

12 Jutta Rudiger, head of the Nazi League of German Girls, 1937 to 1945, speaks about her experiences, in an interview conducted in the early 1990s. Here she questions some of the claims surrounding the Lebensborn Programme.

I still hear today that the Third Reich encouraged out of wedlock pregnancies. In fact, the slogan 'Give the Führer a child' was the work of a few fanatics during the war. I got letters from the front asking me where I got the idea of encouraging girls to get pregnant. The whole thing was new to me. I made some inquiries in party circles, and was told my correspondents had been listening to enemy propaganda! It's true that Himmler once spoke to the leaders of the League of German girls and said that when so many soldiers were dying in the war, if a man got a girl pregnant and then went back to the front, we should be generous and assume that they plan to get married, especially if the man was killed. An unmarried mother should not be driven to suicide, as earlier was so often the case. We agreed and said 'Good. If a woman is expecting a baby, the League of German Girls will help her.' But even Himmler never went so far to say 'you must give the Führer a child,' or 'every woman should get pregnant.' He didn't dare. All of us were glaring at him, and he probably noticed it. At the end of his speech he even said that any SS man who seduced a minor would be severely punished. The SS Lebensborn homes, the 'Wells of Life' were not breeding farms, but places where unmarried mothers could go to have their children in peace, away from the reproaches of their relatives. We in the League felt even more strongly about using women in combat. Even in 1945 Arthur Axmann, Schirach's successor as Reich Youth Leader, told me that Martin Bormann wanted me to make BDM girls available for military service. Bormann planned to create a women's battalion. I said spontaneously, 'That is definitely out of the question! There's no way I will allow it! First, if we're so desperate only the women can save us, then it makes no sense anyway. Second, I am of the opinion that for purely biological reasons, women can't be used as fighting soldiers. It contradicts their nature. Women bring life into the world; they don't destroy it.'

Despite their policies, overall the Nazis failed in their attempts to restrict the female labour force. As industrialisation driven by the preparation for war increased, a greater female presence in the workforce was required, primarily as they provided a cheap workforce essential to the Nazi economy. By 1939, women still made up 33 percent of the workforce, only a very slight decrease from 37 percent in 1933. In the clothing industry they constituted 66 percent, and even in the metalworking industry, an area that was definitely not seen as a healthy profession for women, they still made up 12 percent of the workforce. The drive for rearmament required more female employment in the critical sectors of semi- and unskilled work. Recognising these developments, the Nazis even rescinded the marriage loan qualifications in 1937 so that they applied to all German women, not just those who did not work in the labour market. In 1938, concerned at the increase of women seeking work in better-paid commercial sectors of the economy, the Nazis also introduced a new compulsory 'duty year' for all unmarried women under 25 who wanted to seek employment, which directed them into the clothing, textiles and tobacco industries. Women's pay even increased at a faster rate compared to German men between 1935 and 1938.

During the Second World War, the Nazis, unsurprisingly, sought greater participation of women in industry to help the war effort. In 1943, three million German women between the ages of 17 and 45 were conscripted into work, with only those who were deemed in poor health or who had one child under six or two under 14 years old exempted. The policy was a failure overall, however, with only 900,000 extra women actually entering the workforce. Despite this, by the end of the Second World War, women made up 60 percent of Germany's wartime labour force. Hitler and Joseph Goebbels both became concerned that continued pressure on women not to wear make-up, not to smoke and to dress in skirts (which was virtually impossible given the industrial work women were engaged in) might turn women against the Nazis, given the already overwhelming pressures of the Second World War.

However, overall, the Nazis were unable to overcome the difficulties of their contradictory policies. While on the one hand they wanted women to return to the home and take up their traditional roles as mothers and domestic carers, on the other hand their military and industrial plans required a modernisation of the economy and the mass mobilisation of the entire workforce, one in which women had to play a crucial role. By 1938, it was clear that the Nazi prioritisation of rearmament clearly outweighed their attempts to limit women's employment in the German economy.

ACTIVITY

KNOWLEDGE CHECK

1 Examine Source 11. How would you describe Hitler's attitude to the role of women in German society as shown from this speech?

2 With reference to Source 12 and your own studies, how far do you agree that the Nazis overwhelmingly failed to achieve their goals in regard to German women? Use evidence to support your argument.

The Second World War and post-war opportunities

The development of West Germany after the Second World War had a particular focus on reconstructing the traditional German nuclear family following the devastation of German life caused by the war. The benefits programme introduced in the 1950s, known as the Kindergeld, was based on a situation whereby the male would be the main worker and the female and children would be at home. The benefits would only go to families with three or more children, thus excluding many working women, either single or widowed by the war, who mostly did not have such large families. The pension scheme introduced in 1957 also discriminated against women, as it was based on total earnings and wage structure throughout one's working life; women who had been engaged in part-time work or had taken time out for maternity would not receive the full amount. Female membership of political parties was considerably low, sitting at only 4.4 percent. The West German Basic Law of 1949 did guarantee the legal equality of women, but in many ways the traditional ideal of a woman's place in society was not fundamentally different in 1950s West Germany to the attitudes persisting since the 19th century. It was not until 1957 that West German wives were given legal equality with their husbands, and it was a further two years until a father's complete authority over all matters relating to the family's children was removed.

By 1980, despite the massive expansion of the German economy, women made up only 39 percent of the labour force, a bare six percent increase from the Nazi economy of 1938, and only two percent more than in Weimar Germany. The demands of the massively expanding labour market had been filled primarily by the increase in immigrant guest labour, not an increase in the employment of German women. However, in terms of female employment, just as they had since 1871, women still worked mainly in the jobs of lowest status and pay in the economy: 93 percent of all part-time workers were women, and on average women's pay was 30 percent lower than that of West German men. There were, however, increased opportunities for women in education. Women made up 30 percent of higher education students in 1960, in comparison to 20 percent in the Weimar period, and this rose to 37.9 percent in 1980. In the 1970s, a growing feminist movement, inspired by similar groups in the United States and elsewhere in Europe, began to push for greater opportunities for women in West Germany. This pressure led to several legislative changes: women were finally granted complete equality in marriage; a woman could seek employment without her husband's permission; and divorce was made easier for women to obtain.

SOURCE 13 A Nazi propaganda poster of 1934 promoting the League of German Girls. The slogan translates as 'Association of German girls in the Hitler Youth'.

By the early 1980s, female admissions to university equalled the number for men, and female students made up 41 percent of university students in 1989. The government created a national officer for women's affairs in 1980, responsible for working towards female equality in West Germany. There was also some progress for women in the political sphere, with Rita Sussmuth becoming the first President of the Bundestag in 1988 (similar to the role of speaker in the British parliament).

Despite this, up to 1989, West Germany remained a country where men dominated the higher positions of employment. While women made up 75 percent of total staff at hospitals and 50 percent of school staff, only four percent of German physicians and 20 percent of school principals were women, and only five percent of all West German university professors were female. The social status of West German women was still primarily judged in terms of either their father's or their husband's employment. Looking at the entire period from 1871 through to 1989, it is thus clear that, despite a lot of developments, many aspects pertaining to women's roles in German society still remained the same.

A Level Exam-Style Question Section C

'The position of women in German society has shown little change throughout the years 1871–1990.' How far do you agree with this statement? (20 marks)

Tip

This question is asking you to make a judgement on the extent of change in German women's lives over this long period. You may want to consider the ways in which the position of women in the Kaiserreich was in many ways similar to those in West Germany after 1945. However, in the Weimar period, as well as West Germany after 1970, there was a considerable increase in women's participation in politics and society. However, to what extent this led to an overall change to women's position in German society is questionable.

ACTIVITY
KNOWLEDGE CHECK

Compare the Nazi propaganda poster for the League of German Girls (Source 13) with the picture of the 'new Weimar Woman' (Source 10).

1 What differences can you see between the two images?

2 How far did the Nazi depiction of the ideal German woman differ from the image of the 'new Weimar Woman'?

3 What were the key differences between the Nazi belief in the role of women in society and the position in society of the 'new Weimar Woman'?

ACTIVITY
SUMMARY

1 Looking back over the period 1870 to 1990, what do you consider to have been the most important social change taking place in Germany, and why? You could consider the rise of the urban working class, the decline of the artisan tradition, or the end of Junker influence, among other important developments. Provide evidence to back up your argument.

2 How far do you agree that Germany became a fairer society between 1871 and 1990? Provide evidence to support your argument.

3 'The majority of changes to the role of women in German society were short-term and had no lasting impact between 1871 and 1990.' How far do you agree with this statement? Come up with evidence to back up your answer from across the time period covered in this chapter.

4 To what extent do you agree that, despite Hitler's claims, the Nazi state imposed little change on German society? Summarise the evidence both for and against this statement and then give a good conclusion.

WIDER READING

Berghahn, V. R. *Imperial Germany 1871–1918: Economy, Society, Culture and Politics*, Berghahn Books, revised and expanded edition (2005)

Fulbrook, M. *A History of Germany 1918–2008: The Divided Nation*, Wiley-Blackwell, third edition (2009)

Jefferies, M. *Contesting the German Empire 1871–1918*, Blackwell Publishing (2008)

Retallack, J. *Imperial Germany 1871–1918*, Short Oxford History of Germany series, Oxford University Press (2008)

3.2 Economic change in Germany and West Germany

KEY QUESTIONS

- How far did the German economy change from 1871 to 1990?
- To what extent did the role of government policies influence German economic developments from 1871 to 1990?

INTRODUCTION

Between 1871 and 1990, the German economy underwent a period of considerable change and development. From the industrial revolution, which began in the second half of the 1800s, to the policies of Adolf Hitler, through to the creation of West Germany and its key role in the integration of Western Europe's economic system, there is no doubt that Germany's economy has shaped European history. From the mid-1800s up to 1914, Germany's industrial might boomed and an industrial revolution transformed the country into Europe's premier economic power. This incredible growth would shape the policies of the Kaiserreich and play a key role in the nation's drive towards the First World War. Due to defeat, and the impact of the reparations the victorious Allies demanded from Germany, the economy was required to rebuild, and in the 1920s experienced a somewhat superficial economic boom fuelled by loans from the USA.

The economy's reliance on the United States subsequently led to Germany suffering from the worst effects of the global depression in the early 1930s, with unemployment at levels previously unseen. This economic crisis influenced the rise of the Nazis, who revitalised the German economy and brought back high rates of employment via a system overwhelmingly focused on rearmament and the preparations for war. Their policies culminated in Germany's devastating defeat in the Second World War, and by 1945 it appeared that Germany might never regain the economic power it once held. However, through the support of the United States and the policies of its government, West Germany experienced an economic development almost unparalleled in European history, and within a decade had risen from the ashes of the Second World War to become the third biggest economy in the world. Under the leadership of Konrad Adenauer, West Germany was central to the creation of an integrated Western Europe, being a founding member of the European Economic Community, an organisation that would begin the path to European Economic Co-operation and the establishment of the European Union.

1873 – German economy falls into depression

1890 – German economy begins period of considerable economic growth, known as 'second industrial revolution'

1916 – Auxiliary Service Act to mobilise more workers for German war industry established

1929 – October: Wall Street Crash wipes out millions of dollars from American stock markets

1930 – September: National elections held; Nazis achieve 18.2 percent of the vote

1880 1890 1915 1920 1925 1930

1879 – Germany introduces protective tariffs on agriculture and industrial exports

1898 – First naval bill passed to create 17 new German naval ships

1923 – French occupation of the Ruhr

Government response leads to hyperinflation crisis

1928 – German agriculture suffers severe crisis due to worldwide slump in food prices

1931 – June: Three major banks in Germany collapse, setting off a severe financial crisis

Overall, what is therefore apparent through these 130 years is that understanding Germany's economic development is critical to both European and world history. Germany's economic dominance has influenced the course of some of the most important events of the 20th century, both in a positive and a negative sense. Certainly the development of modern Europe can be much better understood through the study of economic change in Germany and West Germany between 1871 and 1990.

HOW FAR DID THE GERMAN ECONOMY CHANGE FROM 1871 TO 1990?

Germany's considerable economic growth during the 19th century began in the period before the country was politically unified. Germany experienced industrial revolution in the 1850s, mainly due to worldwide economic growth. The first major area of industrial development related to the railways and heavy industry, such as steam engines and machine tools. The growth of Germany's railways was considerable. From 1845 to 1870, the railway network grew by six times, from 3,280 kilometres of track to 19,575 kilometres. Large banks fuelled this industrial revolution through investments, while labour from the declining artisan economy flooded into the growing urban centres, such as Berlin, providing the cheap workforce needed for these new industries. Trade between Prussia and France, Belgium, Britain and Italy expanded. New technologies, such as steam engines and railways, helped to expand Germany's mining industries considerably, and the extension of the railways allowed German states to transport more of their raw materials at a greater pace throughout the country and into Europe. German exports, mainly of coal and iron to Austria-Hungary, the Netherlands, Belgium, France, Russia, Switzerland and Italy, increased at a rapid rate in the 1850s and 1860s (from 1845 to 1860, exports grew by over 70 percent), as did worker productivity.

This remarkable development, however, did not immediately continue with Germany's unification. Instead, from 1873, Germany experienced a considerable economic crisis. Overinvestment and corrupt practices combined with an economy that was naturally slowing, as the railways reached a point at which they could no longer expand, thereby slowing Germany's industrial growth. This depression lasted from 1873 to 1890. However, from the 1890s up to the First World War, Germany underwent another industrial boom. This has been called 'the second industrial revolution' and was driven by the development of a considerable number of new technologies combined with increased levels of industrial investment. German scientists invented the world's first electrical generators and synthetic dyes. German companies invested heavily in research and development and then benefited from the new technologies developed by their scientists. The country also possessed a skilled workforce and management, who were able to adapt new technology and inventions from outside of Germany quickly, and use them to improve German industry, thus ensuring that Germany was not restricted by out-of-date practices. New industries such as advanced machine tools, chemicals and electricity were the main parts of this second industrial revolution. Electrical output, for example, increased by 18 percent every year from 1890 to 1913. The urbanised population grew at a substantial rate, thus increasing the need for further electrification of German cities, as well as providing jobs in construction, as the need for more housing expanded. In 1883, Deutsche Edison Gesellschaft was formed, later known as AEG, one of the first major industrial companies focused on electricity. Their leading rival was Siemens and Halske, another expanding electrical firm.

The reasons for 19th-century industrial growth

SOURCE 1

German economic growth 1870–1913, from F.B. Tipton 'Government and economy' in S. Ogilvie and R. Overy (eds) *Germany: A New Social and Economic History since 1800, Vol. III* (2003).

	1870	1913
Gross Domestic Product (millions of 1990 dollars)	44,101	145,068
Share of world product (%)	2.4	5.7
Gross Domestic Product per capita (1990 dollars)	1,913	3,833

1932 – January: Unemployment peaks at six million
July: National elections held; Nazis become largest party in Germany with 37.3 percent of the vote

1934 – Dr Hjalmar Schacht appointed Reich Minister of Economics and introduces 'New Plan'

1936 – German economy comes under the direction of Goering as Plenipotentiary for the Four-Year Plan

1942 – Albert Speer appointed Minister of Armaments and Munitions and begins reorganisation of German war economy

1947 – British and Americans merge their occupational zones in West Germany into one area known as 'Bizonia'

1948 – American government provides 17 billion US dollars worth of aid to Western European economies in policy known as the Marshall Plan

1951 – Co-determination established as basis for worker representation in West German industry

1955 – Agricultural Act (also known as Green Law) introduced to protect German agriculture from foreign competition

1957 – Treaty of Rome creates the European Economic Community

1962 – Common Agricultural Policy established

1935   1940   1945   1950   1955   1960

Those workers employed in the construction industry increased by nearly one million from 1895 to 1911. Germany's industrial growth outstripped the other industrialised economies of mainland Europe, such as France, but was never able to reach the economic output of Great Britain or the United States. However, in terms of new technologies such as electricity and chemicals, Germany was the undoubted world leader and had developed a reputation for technological excellence. German growth was also fuelled by **cartelisation**. The economic crisis in the 20 years after 1874 had encouraged companies to merge, therefore reducing competition and allowing for more stable employment, as it was less likely for these large **conglomerates** to go out of business. This led to the concentration of German heavy industry in the hands of several massive cartels by the 1890s, such as the Rhenish-Westfalian Coal Syndicate and the Steelworks Association, and the two most famous German family-owned businesses: the massive steel producer Thyssen AG, founded by August Thyssen in 1891, and the largest company in Europe, Friedrich Krupp AG. The lack of competition in German industry, combined with the massive profits and economic stability of these giant cartels, encouraged further investment from German banks, thus expanding the growth of these companies and aiding German industrial production and trade.

A considerable increase in Germany's population, from 50 million in 1890 to 60 million in 1910, also aided Germany's industrial boom, by providing not only an expanding workforce, but also a huge domestic market that sustained the growth of Germany's industries. In simple terms, Germany had the largest population in Europe and thus the largest domestic market, a key factor in the industrial boom leading up to the First World War. The German population was also relatively young, which aided the expansion of its workforce. Germany also had massive reserves of raw materials, such as iron ore in Alsace-Lorraine and huge coalfields in the Ruhr area, as well as considerable reserves of potassium salts and coal tar necessary for the chemical industry. Ship building developed as considerable attention was given to improving Germany's river and canal systems. Consequently, this growth drove forward Germany's ability to export through its increasing naval fleet.

Germany's fast pace of growth was enhanced by Chancellor Caprivi's commercial treaties, which were signed with numerous countries between 1890 and 1894, including Italy, Austria-Hungary, Russia, Belgium, Switzerland and Romania. These treaties lowered **tariffs** on imports from these European countries on cattle, timber, rye and wheat. In return, these countries guaranteed Germany a market for their exports for at least 12 years. These commercial agreements significantly enhanced the German export market, making Germany the biggest industrial nation in Europe by 1900. Between 1872 and 1914, the value of German exports increased by around £365 million, its share of world trade trailing only slightly behind Britain's.

SOURCE

Robert Franz, in an article in 1910 titled 'The statistical history of the German banking system', describes how the German banking system contributed to the success of German industry.

Technical and economic reasons were the cause which in the first instance led to the amalgamation of coal and iron works, particularly during the last years, and these same factors tend more and more to bring about the establishment of great consolidated works combining the production of the raw material with that of the half finished and manufactured articles. This development would not be possible at all, or would meet with great difficulties, without a corresponding organisation of the money and credit markets i.e. without strong banks which are in a position to carry through the necessary financial transactions. Developments of industry and banking showed the same tendency and mutually influenced each other to a large extent. It can be said that the banks created the industries, since the funds which are gathered by the banks in increasing volumes are mainly the result of the increasing productivity of capital invested in industrial undertakings. It is true however that the creative power which in a comparatively short time placed German industry in its present commanding position took its origin with the men who put to practical use and in the interest of economic progress of the nation the achievements and inventions of the domain of science and technique. It is the undisputed merit of the persons at the heads of the banks that they appreciated those endeavours and supported them by advancing the requisite **capital**, oftentimes incurring great risks for the banks. The entire development was, moreover, vigorously furthered by a commercial and tariff policy favourable to industry, though it must be said that this policy was abandoned to a certain extent with the new customs tariff of 1902, the revision of the tariff and the renewal of our commercial treaties have been undertaken and carried out under the motto 'greater tariff protection for agriculture.'... The progressive industrialisation of Germany and the large increase of its population caused on the one hand increasing imports of industrial and **auxiliary** materials as well as of foodstuffs, and on the other steadily growing exports of industrial products. As a result Germany's share in the world's commerce shows a rapid growth.

The government also heavily subsidised Germany's economic growth. As Germany approached 1914, military expansion drove industrial production further, advanced by the fact that a German scientist had invented synthetic ammonia, a key ingredient in the production of nitrates for explosives.

By 1914, German industry had reached an impressive level. It now produced two-thirds of Europe's steel, mined more than half of Europe's coal, led the continent in chemicals, electrics and cotton, and produced 20 percent more electrical energy than Britain, France and Italy combined. Its currency was nearly as strong as the British pound (the pound was the world's key currency), and it was Britain's most serious economic rival.

ACTIVITY
KNOWLEDGE CHECK

1 Read Source 2. What factors does Robert Franz believe were key to Germany's economic growth in the early 20th century?

2 What specific examples from your previous reading support his arguments?

Change (8a, b & c) (I)

Imposing realities

The shape of history is imposed by people looking back. People who lived through the 'history' did not always perceive the patterns that later historians identify. For example, some people living through the German industrial revolution may have understood that great change was taking place, but they would not have been able to understand the massive economic, social and political consequences of industrialisation.

Consider the beginning of the German industrial revolution.

1 What factors were crucial in starting the second industrial revolution that began in 1891?

2 Could anybody have challenged this decision?

3 Explain why someone living in Germany in the late 19th century would have been unable to make a judgement about the beginning of a new era.

4 Who living now might regard the beginning of the German industrial revolution as an important event?

5 What do your answers to these questions tell us about the structure of history as we understand it?

Change in German industry during the 20th century

German industry underwent substantial change and development throughout the 20th century, twice having to rebuild after military defeat, in the First World War and then the Second World War.

The First World War had required the mobilisation of the entire German industry. Despite having the largest and most modern industry in Europe at the start of 1914, Germany lacked key aspects required for modern warfare, such as cotton, rubber and petroleum, as well as special metals such as copper and tin. The director of AEG, Walther Rathenau, helped to establish the War Raw Materials Department in 1914, which, under the control of Rathenau, reorganised the German war industry to ensure that Germany had sufficient raw materials to wage war. By August 1915, Rathenau had been reasonably successful. German scientists had also made major breakthroughs in producing synthetic materials to replace those elements they were unable to import. Most importantly, German scientists discovered how to manufacture nitrates from air using a new process, a considerable technological advancement that allowed Germany to produce sufficient nitrates for explosives, despite being cut off from Chile, which had been its main supplier before the war.

The government established numerous agencies to control industry centrally. The Central Purchasing Company, set up in 1916, organised German imports from neutral countries and attempted to maintain some elements of German trade despite the war, while the Imperial Grain Office controlled food rationing and supplies. Under Hindenburg and Ludendorff, the Auxiliary Service Act was established; this directed the labour of all men aged between 17 and 60, although it excluded the industrial mobilisation of women and children. The Supreme War Office was given substantial control over German industry and labour; one of its key roles was deciding which workers in which industries would be exempt from military conscription. The Supreme War Office had some successes in iron and steel, as well as munitions production, although Germany still continued to suffer from serious problems in coal and transport supplies.

At the war's end, the newly established Weimar Republic faced considerable challenges in terms of the German economy. The war debt was more than 140,000 million marks; the currency had lost considerable value; German trade had been destroyed; foreign investment had dried up; and inflation was pushing up the cost of living for German citizens. This situation was compounded by the loss of the economically important areas of the Saarland and Upper Silesia, in the Versailles settlement of 1919, and the imposition of reparations in 1921 that demanded a payment of two billion marks a year. In comparison to the considerable growth and developments of German industry that had categorised 19th-century Germany, the Weimar's growth rates and technological advancements were quite minimal. German exports, however, did recover after the war at a considerable rate. There was an expansion of manufacturing and investment in industry, and the fact that German products were relatively inexpensive overseas helped the economic transition from war to peacetime. The French occupation of the Ruhr, and the subsequent hyperinflation crisis of 1923 to 1924, slowed Germany's industrial production, but with the end of hyperinflation, resumed production in the Ruhr and the assistance of the Dawes Plan helped to rebuild German industry.

EXTEND YOUR KNOWLEDGE

Hyperinflation (1923–24)

The hyperinflation crisis that affected the Weimar Republic in the early 1920s was one of the most damaging inflationary crises of the 20th century. It was caused by several factors. Government financing during the war had been based on the understandable belief that Germany would win the war and force the defeated Allies to pay off the German war debt. Instead, the value of the German mark fell after the war. This high inflation turned into hyperinflation in 1923 when the French and Belgian armies occupied the German Ruhr, due to their belief that Germany was not paying war reparations properly. The German government advised workers in the region to go on strike and the Ruhr industry came to a stop. However, to pay the workers on strike, the government printed more money, a policy that progressively made the German currency worthless. By the end of 1923, one US dollar was equal to 4.2 trillion German marks. This caused financial chaos, as many Germans' life savings became effectively worthless. A whole wheelbarrow full of German marks was needed simply to buy a loaf of bread. At the end of 1923, the Reichsbank was printing 100 trillion mark notes. The crisis ended when the government called off the Ruhr strike and introduced a new German currency, the Rentenmark. However, the social problems caused by hyperinflation, the destruction of middle-class savings and the lack of trust in the German government and the banks would have a lasting effect that would play some part in the even greater economic issues faced in the early 1930s.

SOURCE

3   This political cartoon is from 1923, the period of hyperinflation in Germany. A starving mother covered in bank notes holds up her starving child and cries out for food.

ACTIVITY
KNOWLEDGE CHECK

1 The power of this political cartoon (Source 3) lies in the contrast between the bank notes and the starving mother and child. Explain the political message the cartoon is making.

2 How far is Source 3 an accurate comment on the effects of hyperinflation?

The renewal of the German economy under the new currency, the Rentenmark, and massive investment from US financial institutions, drove a resurgence of German industrial production. By 1927 it had reached pre-war levels, and **gross national product (GNP)** grew significantly from 1925 to 1929. German industrial bosses travelled to the United States, where they observed new organisations of production, particularly the use of assembly lines. The introduction of these new techniques in German industry allowed them to boost production without expanding their workforce. In the Ruhr, for instance, the workforce declined by 33 percent, yet production increased by 18 percent per working hour.

SOURCE

4 The report of the Commissioner of the Reichsbank on the state of the Weimar economy at the end of 1928. Here he evaluates the positive and negative aspects of the economy.

With the present Report a period of four years closes. If we compare the present position with that of four years ago, we note a very great advance alike in regard to the economic development of the country as a whole and in regard to the position of the Reichsbank in particular. There has been a far reaching reorganisation and **rationalisation** of the industrial system of Germany; the standard of living of the masses of the people has appreciably risen, and in the case of a great part of the working class has again reached or surpassed the pre-war level. The marked fluctuations of the first few years have made way for a more steady line of development, and an increasing power of resistance is clearly revealed. Those who foretold that the symptoms of decline from the highly favourable conditions of a year ago were about to take on the form of a rapid and serious depression, underestimated the country's economic power of resistance. At the same time there are still considerable branches of the national economy which have had an inadequate share in the general recovery. If the general position were to change fundamentally for the worse – there are at the present no signs of such a change – this would presumably be more apparent. The position of agriculture, though here and there improvement is apparent, remains on the whole less favourable that that of the rest of the national economy. The possibilities in this case of compensating out of the business the high rate of interest which has to be paid, or alternatively of passing it on to the consumer, are considerably less than they are in other economic branches... It was to be foreseen that after the war and the inflation, which followed the war a marked demand for new capital would make itself apparent for the purpose of improving the machinery of production as well as for public purposes... The largely modernised machinery of production at the present time provides work for four million more workers than it did before the war within the same territorial limits, and a great number of public requirements which for a long time had remained unsatisfied have since been able to be met. The price, however, which has been paid for these results is a new annual burden of interest in relation to foreign countries, which at present is undoubtedly over half a million reichsmarks.

ACTIVITY
KNOWLEDGE CHECK

1 According to Source 4, what were the positive and negative aspects of the Weimar economy in 1928?

2 Are there any other negative aspects of the economy that you would add to Source 4?

3 'Source 4 is overly positive of the Weimar's economic condition by the end of 1928.' Provide evidence for and against this assertion.

The financial crisis set off by the 1929 stock market crash in the United States led to a massive crisis in German industry. The high rates of industrialisation in the German economy meant it was hit worse than its neighbours, such as Italy and France. The Nazi Party, which had come to power during the depression, focused German industry on public work schemes, self-sufficiency and rearmament. By 1934, unemployment had been halved, and by 1939 there was a labour shortage in German industry. The building and metal industries increased substantially.

KEY TERMS

Gross national product (GNP)
An economic statistic that is calculated by looking at the market value (i.e. selling price) of all products and services produced in one year by citizens of a particular country. It is used to compare economic performance and growth between countries.

Rationalisation
Making a company more efficient.

Road construction and growth of the German car industry were a key aspect of Germany's industrial rejuvenation in the mid-1930s. The government invested heavily in work creation schemes and German industry to get the economy back on its feet. From 1936, the Four-Year Plan was launched, focusing German industry on armaments production, and by 1938, 44 percent of government expenditure focused on rearmament alone. The preparation for war meant there was an increased investment in ensuring Germany was self-sufficient, and industry made greater efforts to produce synthetic forms of rubber, petrol and oils. Nazi control over industry was increased, and the economic direction of the German economy was towards war. This saw the German economy massively distorted towards large-scale industries, such as steel and coal production, and the subsequent decline of consumer-based manufacturing.

The economy during the Second World War made significant use of the lands Germany invaded and occupied, putting millions of slave labourers to work in munitions production and farming. Inefficiency and infighting within the Nazi economic sector hampered the production of armaments, and production only began to rise after it was reorganised under the Central Planning Board, established by Albert Speer, Minister of Munitions and Armaments from 1942. Better techniques of mass production and reorganisation of industry were introduced, and the allocation of raw materials to the differing sectors of the economy improved. Industrial production in wartime Germany actually reached its peak in 1944, despite the mass bombings Germany was enduring.

With the end of the Second World War and the division of Germany, the new nation of West Germany began to rebuild the economy that war had destroyed. Through the economic programme of Ludwig Erhard, and enhanced by US investments through Marshall Aid, German industry began to redevelop. This was boosted in the early 1950s by the Korean War (1950–53), which required the type of industrial goods that Germany had always excelled at. GNP trebled throughout the 1950s. The West German economy, however, had changed: from a focus on heavy industry and mining in the earlier period of the 20th century, to one driven by the advanced machinery industry, electronics, automobiles and service industries, such as banking and education. Economic revival, in turn, drove the house-building industry. This change continued as the economy modernised further into the 1980s, as consulting, advertising and research began to play an important part in the West German economy.

Mass unemployment from 1930 to 1932

The Great Depression that played such a large part in the eventual end of the Weimar Republic began in the United States in October 1929. A catastrophic collapse in the stock market led to American investors losing around 40,000 million US dollars in only a month. This had the effect of wiping out US loans in Europe; a particular problem for Germany, as it was the country most reliant on American investment for its economic growth. By 1930, many short-term US loans had been withdrawn. This situation was made worse after the September 1930 election, in which the Nazi Party made significant gains: the growing fear of American investors at the rise of political extremism in Germany prompted the further withdrawal of US loans. In June 1931, 1,000 million marks in loans were withdrawn from Germany and three major banks in Germany collapsed. This set off mass panic among German savers, who desperately attempted to withdraw their funds, thus heightening the now catastrophic banking crisis.

Parallel to the economic collapse in Germany, the worldwide economic downturn resulted in a mass decline in global imports. For a country such as Germany, whose economy was reliant on exports, this was a further blow. Factories closed down and unemployment rose by 2.1 million between the end of 1929 and December 1930, and then steadily climbed by another three million to its peak of six million in January 1932. Unemployment and the banking collapse caused economic despair unparalleled in modern German history. It is estimated that around 40 percent of the workforce was unemployed, although in industries such as machine building it was 48.9 percent, and in shipbuilding an incredible 63.5 percent. The government under Chancellor Bruning believed the solution was to raise taxes and slash unemployment benefits, a policy that increased the suffering of Germany's unemployed. Growing despair, mass poverty, starvation and a general deterioration in town life, with factories left dormant and town parks overgrown, became common.

SOURCE
5

SOURCE
5 Germans in Berlin line up outside Postscheckamt, Berlin, to withdraw their savings during the banking crisis of 1931.

The growth of extremist parties

The massive numbers of unemployed young men led to the growth of extremist private armies, such as the Nazi SA and the SPD's Reichsbanner. This was due to the fact that these groups' military organisation and street battles against their opponents gave disenchanted, unemployed young men a purpose. By 1932, the SA had grown from 100,000 to 400,000 strong. There were mass clashes in the streets and at political rallies. German politics now largely centred on the streets and the growing violence between political parties.

EXTEND YOUR KNOWLEDGE

The Nazi SA

The Sturmabteilung, known by the abbreviation SA, was the violent paramilitary wing of the Nazi Party, formed in the early 1920s. They provided protection for Nazi rallies and attacked the political meetings of their opponents, such as the Communists. They were recognised by their brown shirts. During the Great Depression their numbers increased dramatically, as young unemployed men found in the SA an outlet for their anger and disillusionment with German society, as well as a purpose for their lives, which had been affected by mass unemployment.

The impact of the Great Depression

The Great Depression had been partly caused by the US stock market crash, but the over-reliance on American loans, the lack of domestic investment, the decline of the agricultural sector and the focus on a small range of export sectors as the basis of economic growth, all combined to make Germany the most vulnerable country to any downturn in the US economy. Bruning's attempts to alleviate the crisis only deepened it further. Industrial production plummeted and unemployment rose. This economic downturn was felt across German society, with industrial workers, teachers, white collar workers and civil servants all suffering a decline in their standard of living. Bruning continued to pursue a policy of cuts in wages and public expenditure while increasing taxes. He hoped that Germany's economic situation would convince the Allies to lift the First World War reparations, and in June 1932 he was successful, with the Bank of International Settlement agreeing to end Germany's payment requirements.

However, the financial means by which he had achieved this aim had brought about greater economic depression and further anger among the German population.

The Nazi Party exploited the suffering caused by the Great Depression by establishing their own soup kitchens and charity fundraisers, and by 1931 they were feeding around 200 people a day in some areas. When Bruning called an election in 1930 to gain a mandate for his economic policy, the consequence, instead was a considerable rise in the extremist parties, with the Nazi Party increasing its vote from 800,000 to 6.4 million and gaining 18.2 percent of the vote (compared to only 2.6 percent in 1928), while the German Communist Party increased its vote to 4.4 million, up from 3.3 million in 1928, and took 13.1 percent of the vote. Bruning was removed on 30 May 1932 and replaced by a new Chancellor, Franz von Papen, who simply continued Bruning's economic direction. In July 1932, Papen also called an election to try to gain support for his economic programme. This time the Nazis became the largest party in the Reichstag, with 37.3 percent of the vote. Voting with the Communists (who, while hating the Nazis, also hoped for the eventual destruction of the Weimar Republic), the Nazis could now hamper the effective running of the Reichstag, forcing through a no-confidence motion in Chancellor von Papen, so another election was held at the end of 1932. This time, however, the Nazi vote declined, although it was still the largest party in Germany.

The economic strife Germany was still suffering, the inability to find a popular leader, the deadlock in the Reichstag and the growing violence on the street all helped to influence the German political elite and President Hindenburg to appoint Adolf Hitler as Germany's Chancellor on 30 January 1933. Without the Great Depression, it is difficult to see how the rise of the Nazis from their position in 1928 to power in 1932 could have taken place. The consequences of mass unemployment, the inability of the ruling politicians to deal with the situation and the ability of the Nazis to exploit the hardships, all contributed to the subsequent fall of the Weimar government and the destruction of the democratic experiment founded in 1919.

SOURCE

In Betty Scholem's letter to her son, written in 1931, she describes the effects of the economic depression on Germany.

My Dear Child, your letter of the twenty second arrived on the thirtieth. Meanwhile, you should already have received two letters from me describing the terrible situation. Technically, I'm in no position to give you a complete picture of the collapse, which you'd need in order to really understand what's happening. The year 1930 was still a good one. We were a bit in the red; but given more or less normal business, we still hoped to make it up eventually. We never would have taken such a long trip if we'd had an inkling that such a crisis lay ahead!! It hit us like a catastrophe. An enormous fall in the demand for price tags caused our debts to swell. Just as all business came to a halt, the bank failed; so there was no one to speak to. The banks went into a government holding company, which showed no interest in the debts of customers. All of this happened at once. It looks as if we'll lose everything. It's cold comfort to know that the entire commercial sector is in the same position and that more shops are going under than staying afloat. Since everywhere you look there's desert, you see no chance to plant anything new. The situation is desperate. I cannot continue to maintain my own house and household – this much seems certain. A pity isn't it. My mama, hardly a wealthy woman, at least died in her own apartment. Of all the possible alternatives left to me, moving in with Erich seems the best. Hermine is leaving on the first of September, and Martha will move into her room. As long as we can still keep the house, I want to stay in my own apartment. For now, the rent of 170 marks is still easy to come up with. Martha helps with the cleaning, and for lunch I go upstairs. I make my own breakfast, and evenings I'm mostly out. As an innocent victim of Germany's crisis, I will have to place my existence upon the famous 'other basis' and enjoy the last good thirty years of my life like a fine tasting stew.

ACTIVITY
KNOWLEDGE CHECK

1 What impression does Source 5 give of Berlin during the banking crisis of 1931?

2 In what ways does Source 6 confirm this impression?

3 In what ways are Sources 5 and 6 valuable to a historian studying the problems Germany faced in the early 1930s, and why?

4 What are the potential issues with both sources?

The post-war 'economic miracle'

The West German economic boom that took place in the 1950s is often described as the 'post-war economic miracle'. To what extent it was a 'miracle' – that is, it has no rational explanation – is heavily debated by historians, but there is little argument that West Germany underwent impressive economic growth from the 1950s into the 1960s. By 1963, West Germany was the strongest economic power in Europe and the third biggest economy in the world. This economic growth was driven by several factors. Firstly, Germany had been the second biggest economy in the world prior to the Second World War and, despite the destruction caused by the war, there remained a considerable number of workable factories still standing in West Germany in 1945. Secondly, West Germany had a large population of skilled labour that provided the basis of its economic recovery. Thirdly, the West German economy benefited from American assistance in the form of Marshall Aid (see page 59 for more detail). West Germany received around 99 million US dollars, which it used to expand the coal-mining, railway, electrical, steel and iron industries.

As stated earlier (see page 44), the West German economy benefited from the Korean War, which further boosted industrial production. A global economic boom from 1951 enhanced the demand for products which the West German economy was in a strong position to provide. The German car industry grew substantially and the desire for high-quality West German products worldwide could barely be met. The growth in the prosperity of the West German economy, along with the need to rebuild after the Second World War, led to a massive house-building programme, which enhanced domestic industries that were not linked to the export market. **Gross domestic product (GDP)** grew by 12 percent in only five years. The industrial growth was helped by a co-operative union sector that restricted wage increases, and a massive influx of 3.6 million refugees from East Germany, who, being predominately young and highly skilled, enhanced the West German economy. Given the context of the Second World War, West Germany did not bear the costs of the massive rearmament that some of its competitors were going through in the early 1950s as a consequence of the Cold War.

Industrial relations were also different from the rest of Europe. The West German economy was unique in its introduction of co-determination in 1951. This policy meant that any business with over 1,000 employees in the iron and steel industry had to allow representatives of the workforce to have a say in the running of the business. In 1952, the establishment of Works Councils, which facilitated joint discussions between employers and employees, further enhanced this. These policies were successful in establishing a relative harmonisation of industrial relations in West Germany, and they minimised the number of days lost to strikes, for example in comparison to France and Britain.

By 1958, West Germany had near full employment, and the demand for labour meant it was more difficult to restrict wage rises. However, a slowdown of the West German economy took place in the early 1960s as it transitioned from **heavy industry** to one more based on the **service industries**. These two factors combined saw growth slow in comparison to Italy and France, which now recorded higher growth rates. Although still a healthy economy, the so-called 'economic miracle' had essentially ended by 1963. It has been subsequently argued by historians that the 1950s was less an 'economic miracle', and instead the re-establishment of one of the world's most powerful economies, which had been disrupted by both World Wars. Despite this, there is no doubt that the period between 1950 and 1963 was impressive in terms of West Germany's economic development.

> **KEY TERM**
>
> **Gross domestic product (GDP)**
> The monetary value of all goods and services produced in a country over a certain period. It is used to measure a country's economic health.

> **KEY TERMS**
>
> **Heavy industry**
> Industries working in large-scale manufacturing of equipment or the extraction of raw materials. The production of railways or ships, coal mining or steel production would be regarded as heavy industry.
>
> **Service industry**
> Industry that produces services for consumers as opposed to tangible goods. This could include accounting, education, computer services and trades.
>
> **Monopoly**
> A situation in which one company dominates the market for a particular product.

SOURCE

Ludwig Erhard speaking on the West German 'economic miracle' in 1957. Erhard was the West German Minister of Economics, and is considered the 'father' of the 'economic miracle'. He believed in a free market economy and the freedom of competition, that together would serve the social target of 'prosperity for all'.

Impairment of competition is a near constant threat, and one that comes from all sides. This is why the preservation of free competition is one of the most important tasks belonging to a state based on a liberal social order. I do not exaggerate when I say that a law against **monopolies** should be considered an indispensable economic basic law. If the state were to fail in this area, it would mean the end of the 'social market economy'.

... 'Prosperity for all' and 'Prosperity through competition' are inextricably linked: the first postulate identifies the goal; the second, the path that leads to it.

These few remarks already reveal the fundamental difference between the social market economy and the old-style liberal economy. Entrepreneurs who believe that they can demand cartels as a result of

KEY TERM

OEEC

The Organisation for European Economic Co-operation was an economic organisation to aid the recovery of Western Europe after the Second World War, made up of 18 countries, including France and the UK.

A Level Exam-Style Question Section C

How accurate is it to say that the post-war 'economic miracle' was the most impressive period of German industrial growth in the period 1871–1990? (20 marks)

Tip

This question is asking you to weigh up the successful stages of German economic growth over a long period of history. In what way was the post-war 'economic miracle' impressive? Once you are confident with this understanding, weigh it up against other successful periods, such as the second industrial revolution before the First World War, the Weimar Republic in the 1920s, and the Nazi economy of the 1930s. In what way would these periods of economic growth be more or less impressive than the post-war economic boom in West Germany?

KEY TERM

Depreciated currency
This refers to when a country's currency loses its value in relation to other international currencies.

modern economic developments place themselves on the intellectual level of those Social Democrats who conclude that automation leads to a state-run, planned economy.

This reflection surely illustrates my idea that it is infinitely more useful to increase prosperity through expansion than to try to reach prosperity through a pointless quarrel about a different distribution of the national income.

Success has proved me right. As a result of German economic policy, the profit that everyone derives from the economy has continued to grow year upon year. Between 1950 and 1962, for example, private consumption – as expressed in 1954 prices – rose from DM [Deutsche Mark] 69 billion to 175 billion. This is one of the most remarkable increases on the international stage. According to calculations by the OEEC, the index of private consumption in West Germany rose – price adjusted – (1950 = 100) to 236 in 1961; during the same period, the index figure rose to 127 in Great Britain, to 137 in Sweden, to 162 in France and to 139 in the USA.

Even if the pre-war period is used as a basis for comparison, West German development easily exceeds the average of all OEEC countries. Even the most revolutionary reform of our social order would never have succeeded in increasing the private consumption of this group or that, even by a fraction of what was actually achieved; any such attempt would have led to the paralysis and stagnation of the national economy.

ACTIVITY
KNOWLEDGE CHECK

1 Read Source 7. What evidence does Ludwig Erhard use to argue that West Germany's economic growth since the Second World War has been impressive?

2 Using primary sources in history can be problematic. The fact that Erhard was responsible for the West German economy does make Source 7 subjective in its analysis. Despite that, in what ways is this source still useful for a historian studying West Germany's economic growth after 1945?

Change in German agriculture during the 20th century

German agriculture, 1914–20

In terms of agricultural production, the First World War caused severe shortages. The depletion of both young men and horses for the front line damaged the farming sector, and much of the agricultural work had to be taken up by women and children. Combined with the damaging winter of 1916 and 1917, this meant that food supplies were substantially curtailed, particularly from 1917 onwards. However, after the war, the agricultural sector actually benefited from hyperinflation, as the **depreciated currency** enabled farmers to pay off their mortgages much more easily. However, this improvement in the German agricultural industry was extremely short-lived.

The slump in agricultural prices in the 1920s

Even before the Great Depression of the 1930s, German agriculture suffered a significant economic downturn during the 1920s. During the First World War, many countries significantly expanded their agricultural production. The subsequent oversupply of food led to a worldwide drop in agricultural prices that hit German farmers particularly hard. It can be argued that German agriculture was suffering from depression as early as the 1920s. It is clearly the case that the rural sector did not feel the benefits of the economic growth the Weimar Republic experienced between 1924 and 1925. By 1931, wheat prices had fallen to a third of prices prior to 1920. Weimar agriculture was in a particularly vulnerable state. Unlike its foreign competitors, there was low investment in better farming techniques and technology, and little attempt to restructure and rationalise the sector. The decline in available labour, as discussed previously, exaggerated the problems, as did Weimar taxes on agriculture, which were nearly four times higher than those during the Kaiserreich.

In terms of the agricultural sector, despite the decline in the number of German workers involved in farming, some 30 percent of the working population was still engaged in either agrarian or forestry-based work in 1925. The large Prussian landholdings from before the Weimar Republic still existed, but there was an increase in smaller, peasant-owned farms. Market and price controls established by the war still existed in some form. However, the collapse of agricultural prices in the 1920s, combined with a diminishing labour force, led to a decline in agricultural productivity and growth, and the farming sector never enjoyed the short-term boom of the mid-1920s, as experienced by industry.

Despite attempting to protect farmers by subsidising agriculture and introducing protectionist policies, in 1925, the level of rural indebtedness and bankruptcy continued to rise, increasing by around 20 to 30 percent in the late 1920s. In 1928, the agricultural sector was hit by a further crisis as agricultural prices crashed again due to further worldwide overproduction. The price of wheat and rye dropped by around 35 percent and the price of cattle also declined significantly. Between 1928 and 1932, agricultural income dropped by 40 percent, and the average income in the agricultural sector was 44 percent below the national average. German agricultural production fell and the migration of workers from the country to the city accelerated. There was considerable anger and growing resentment among farmers and rural workers, who felt that the Weimar Republic was not doing enough to help rural communities during this crisis.

In some rural areas, such as Schleswig and Holstein, there were tax strikes, mass protests and the bombing of government offices. Unsurprisingly, it was in these depressed rural areas that the Nazi Party first started to gain support. Although the Nazis gained only 2.6 percent of the national vote in the 1928 election, they did particularly well in the depressed rural areas of Schleswig and Holstein, Lower Saxony, Thuringia and Upper Bavaria. The focus on depressed rural areas appeared to be the best means of expanding the Nazi vote, and the Party paid much greater attention to agricultural-based regions following the election.

The Great Depression drove the agricultural crisis further. After 1929, prices declined again and rye exports were practically non-existent (rye exports had been two tonnes in 1922). Bankruptcy and rural decline grew, and despite some attempts by the state to assist agriculture through the Osthilfe Programme, the anger of rural communities at what they perceived as a decade of neglect and hardship meant there was little support for the Weimar government. The Nazis were fast becoming the party of agricultural protest, and in their breakthrough election of 1930 they made their biggest gains in areas dependent on small family-owned farms.

EXTEND YOUR KNOWLEDGE

Osthilfe Programme

Osthilfe translates as 'Eastern Aid' in English. The Weimar government introduced it between 1929 and 1930, to try to help agricultural areas in Eastern Germany that were going bankrupt. It was politically questionable from its very beginnings, given that it targeted one particular group in only one area of Germany during an economic depression that was hurting all Germans. The key reason why the Eastern agricultural area was chosen for aid was that it was still dominated by the politically influential Junker class. The programme ended in scandal after it was revealed that wealthy Junkers had wasted much of the funds of the Osthilfe on expensive cars and holidays.

EXTRACT

1

Eric Weitz, in *Weimar: Promise and Tragedy* (2007), assesses the issues facing agricultural areas during the Weimar period.

The collapse of world commodity prices sent agriculture reeling into depression as early as the mid-1920s. The 'golden years' certainly did not apply to Weimar's agrarian sector. And farmers were quick to blame socialists and Jews for all of their woes. Indebtedness was the **scourge** of agriculture. Farmers climbed out of debt during the inflation and managed almost immediately to sink back in. Always eager to buy more land, they invested too heavily when the terms of trade were in their favour, and suffered when prices collapsed and they could no longer carry their mortgages. Moreover, they bemoaned the shortage of labour they endured, especially the **paucity** of girls and young women willing to put up with the strain of agricultural labour. On the farms girls and women endured sixteen to seventeen hour working days, dirty conditions and heavy lifting, all under the ever watchful eye of the owner of the farm and his wife...To the utter dismay of farmers and officials, thousands upon thousands of young women fled the rural areas for factories and the city. The work may have been no easier, but at least they did not suffer under the constant gaze of their employers. They felt freer, while farmers and officials **foisted** upon them the blame for the crisis of agriculture.

KEY TERMS

Scourge
A thing causing great suffering.

Paucity
Smallness of quantity.

Foisted
Imposed an unnecessary or unwelcome thing on someone.

ACTIVITY
KNOWLEDGE CHECK

Read Extract 1. Apart from the agricultural price slump, what are the other reasons that Weitz gives for the rural depression in Germany in the early 1920s?

The agricultural industry during the Nazi period

Despite Nazi propaganda that mythologised the German peasantry, the decline in farming continued through the 1930s. This was partly due to the increase in German industry that required an ever increasing labour force. The focus on self-sufficiency did help German farms, as food imports into Germany were restricted. However, investments in the modernisation of farming techniques and mechanisation lagged behind Nazi investment in industry. This, combined with the ever decreasing agricultural labour force, saw a decline in both the standard of living of German farmers and agricultural production. The Nazis attempted to combat this in 1938, by giving greater subsidies to the agricultural sector, but the decline in farming continued, mainly as a consequence of Nazi policies that favoured the preparation for war. Between 1933 and 1938, it is estimated that almost one million people left the rural part of Germany to look for work in the cities, the highest rate of internal migration in Germany during the 20th century.

German agriculture in the post-Second World War period

The trend of a declining labour force in the agricultural sector continued in West Germany, reaching record levels by the end of the 1960s. The nature of Germany's division had left West Germany with relatively few farms, apart from areas of meat production, forcing it to become a major importer of food. However, farmers maintained a strong political influence, and in 1955 the West German government introduced the Agricultural Act (also known as the Green Law), which would support agricultural prices through protective tariffs on some agricultural imports. Rising domestic consumption combined with these tariffs to contribute to a ten percent increase in agricultural production. However, the Green Law was unable to stop the overall long-term decline of the agricultural sector. While non-agricultural employment increased by around nine million from 1950 to 1970, the agricultural labour force declined by 1.6 million. Government policies that enabled farmers to consolidate their farms, combined with greater mechanisation and improved farming techniques, meant that West German farms grew in size, but required less of a labour force to work them. The growth of the service economy and job opportunities available also prompted further urbanisation and the decline of Germany's rural population. The importance of the agricultural sector of the economy declined consistently through the history of West Germany, and by 1989 it only contributed around 1.6 percent of its GDP, a decline from 11 percent in 1956, with the number of farms dropping from 1.6 million in 1950 to 630,000 in 1990.

EXTEND YOUR KNOWLEDGE

Agricultural Act 1955

With the end of the Second World War and Germany split into two sections, West Germany faced an acute shortage of food. Despite the considerable imports needed, the West German government wanted to make sure that German farmers were able to sell their products at a price that would enable them to invest and develop German agriculture. Price controls were brought in and German food prices remained high, despite the fact that worldwide food prices actually declined in the early 1950s. This West German policy culminated in the Agricultural Act of 1955, which also came to be known as the Green Law. German agriculture was protected with guaranteed high prices, regardless of the efficiency of the farms. The policy aimed to support German agriculture and maintain a decent standard of living for German farmers while stabilising agricultural prices. The policy was undoubtedly beneficial for German farmers; however, it meant German food prices remained high and it provided no incentive for German farmers to improve the efficiency of their farming practices.

TO WHAT EXTENT DID THE ROLE OF GOVERNMENT POLICIES INFLUENCE GERMAN ECONOMIC DEVELOPMENTS FROM 1871 TO 1990?

The introduction of protection, 1879

The campaign for protective tariffs that reached its peak in 1879 was a response to a slowdown in the German economy that had begun several years before. The German economy had expanded too quickly, with too many businesses being set up that were not sustainable in the long term. In 1873, the German economy crashed and over 150 companies went bankrupt. German industry contracted and the rate of economic growth slowed considerably. At the same time as these events were occurring, German agriculture was also facing difficulties. Russia and the United States were developing as major exporters of wheat, and this, combined with several poor harvests in Germany, meant the country was soon reliant on imports, particularly wheat from Russia. As German wheat prices dropped and exports declined, smaller farms faced bankruptcy. The solution put forward by both industrialists and landowners was for greater protectionism in the German economy.

A new pressure group, the Central Association of German Industrialists, was formed in 1876 and exerted pressure on Chancellor Bismarck and the German government to introduce reform. They pointed to the fact that the worldwide economic downturn had seen the majority of industrialised nations introduce tariffs (except for Great Britain). However, there was still significant opposition to tariffs within the German parliament, and a broad section of Germany's political parties supported free trade. In 1876, a bill to set tariffs on pig iron imports was defeated in the Reichstag. Bismarck, however, was determined to pursue the policy of tariffs. In terms of Germany's agriculture, a long-term price slump in German farming could threaten the wealth of the Junkers, undermining their powerful role in Germany. Tariffs on agriculture could both protect Junker power, by ensuring they maintained the wealth gained from their large farms, and raise revenue for the struggling German economy.

The political implications of tariffs

There was also another political incentive for Bismarck to introduce protection policies. From 1871 to 1878, the most powerful political party in Germany had been the National Liberals. This party rested on the support of the new middle class of educated professionals and pushed for greater political reform in the German system, a point that Bismarck viewed with concern. Due to their size in the Reichstag, Bismarck was forced to work with the National Liberals, but tariff reform offered an opportunity to break this dependency. The National Liberals were committed to free trade. In the 1878 election, Bismarck used this to campaign against the National Liberals by openly supporting protectionist policies. He proclaimed that tariff policy was patriotic, as it aimed to support Germany against foreign competition, and that those who backed free trade were therefore actively working against their own country's well-being. It was a powerful message. Many previously National Liberal voters, such as the smaller farmers and peasantry, who had been consistently supportive of liberal policies, now switched to the pro-tariff Conservatives backed by Bismarck. The National Liberals consequently lost 29 seats, mostly to the pro-tariff Conservatives. In 1879, the Reichstag passed the protective tariff law, with two conservative parties, most of the Centre Party and some right-wing National Liberals backing the bill.

Bismarck had achieved two political aims: he had significantly weakened the National Liberals by splitting the party over the issue of tariffs, and he had enhanced the power of the Conservatives in the Reichstag. Although those in heavy industry were disappointed that tariffs on iron were lower than those on agriculture, they were grateful to Bismarck for supporting the movement to protectionism. The industrialists grew closer to the Junkers, united over their support for both Bismarck and tariffs, in an association known as the 'alliance of steel and rye'. This was significant in creating a new conservative elite in Germany that incorporated the older, established class of the Junkers with the newly emerging, economically powerful industrialists. This conservative political bloc would attempt to restrict any attempt at democratic change in Germany over the next 40 years.

The National Liberals, who had been the key political party of the 1870s, now split into two parties: the Progressives, which believed in free trade, and the National Liberal Party, which backed Bismarck. The split undermined the liberal political movement and it never regained the influence on German politics it had once enjoyed.

Economically, the protectionist policies of 1879 did advance Germany's agricultural and industrial sectors in the short term. They boosted the price of German agriculture and helped revitalise industry by strengthening the domestic market. However, the lack of cheaper imports of wheat from Russia meant the overall cost of bread went up, a fact German workers resented. This deepened the already problematic class divide, as policies appeared to benefit the wealthy Junker class at the cost of the working class and poorer in society, although the reality of this perception has been an area of debate among historians.

David Blackbourn, in *History of Germany 1780–1918: The Long Nineteenth Century* (2003), assesses the overall effects of the 1879 tariffs.

> Consumers certainly paid more than they would have done given a **free market** in agricultural produce, for protectionism kept German food prices above world levels. It is less clear that the Junkers were, as so often claimed, the predominant beneficiaries. True, the East Elbian staple, rye, received favourable treatment; protection raised the price of fodder for peasants practising **animal husbandry**; and the higher cost of rye bread left consumers with less to spend on peasant dairy produce and the like. But tariff duties were also levied on peasant produced grains (wheat, oats, barley, as well as rye) and research suggests that middle and large peasants benefitted substantially. Protection was similarly extended to almost everything in which peasants had an interest, including horses, cattle, fruit, vegetables, wine, and wood. Other measures were also introduced to help the peasants. … All in all, agricultural protectionism was neither a Junker ramp, nor did it completely distort the pattern of German primary production by preventing diversification away from grain growing, even if it is true that the Empire produced more rye than it would have done in the absence of tariffs.

KEY TERMS

Free market
An economic system where prices are set without government control or tariffs.

Animal husbandry
The cultivation and breeding of animals.

ACTIVITY
KNOWLEDGE CHECK

1 Why were protectionist tariffs introduced by the government in 1879?

2 Which factors were purely economic and which were political? Which factor (economic or political) do you think was the main reason for the introduction of tariffs?

3 According to Blackbourn (Extract 2), why is it inaccurate to argue that tariffs were introduced simply to benefit the Junkers?

The building of a large navy from 1898 to 1914

The construction of a German navy that could rival Britain's – at that time the world's dominant naval power – was in large part driven by the personal desires of Kaiser Wilhelm II. On coming to power in 1888, Wilhelm had quickly ordered the restructuring of the navy's administration to increase its efficiency. In terms of construction, however, the navy stagnated and was in decline by 1895. Yet the inspiration for an expanded navy came to play a larger part in the Kaiser's thinking at the end of the century, in response to the political problems then plaguing the country. At the same time, nationalist ideas concerning the need for Germany to assert its power internationally in a way that was equal to its military and economic strength were becoming much more prominent. Kaiser Wilhelm II was one of the key promoters of this ideal, being obsessed with the idea of transforming Germany into the world's dominant power. To achieve this, he believed that Germany had to invest in the construction of a powerful navy; the fact that the German navy was only seventh in the world by 1897 did not equate with his dream of a Germany rivalling France and Britain and expanding its colonies across the globe. The building of the navy was also a potential solution to Germany's growing political divide.

There was considerable enthusiasm among Germany's academic and middle classes for the construction of a powerful navy that would secure the country's place as one of the world's great powers. Thus, the building of a large navy would help to secure popular support for the Kaiser, uniting the middle classes in their support for this ambitious mission. The navy was also new and therefore could represent the nationalist hopes of all Germans. The army, which was largely unchanged in its structure since 1871, was dominated by the Prussian elite and therefore did not hold the focus of German-wide nationalism in the way that a powerful navy could. The industrialists, for whom such a project would drive on industrial production, would also support the building of the navy. Trying to find a so-called 'middle ground' in German politics, which would unite previously diverse class and political movements in their common desire for the construction of a powerful German fleet, was thus a powerful motivation for Kaiser Wilhelm II's actions. There were international factors as well. Germany's relationship with Britain had been tested over questions concerning territory in East Africa and Germany's support of the Boers during the conflict over Transvaal in 1896.

While Germany was wary of committing to an actual conflict against the power of Britain, the Kaiser was growing increasingly concerned about the restrictions placed on Germany due to its inadequate naval fleet. From 1896 onwards, the Kaiser became increasingly focused on the German navy, believing that this was the key factor in defining power in international affairs.

Thus international desires, combined with domestic political motivations, inspired the focus on the navy as a solution to the issues Germany faced. The Kaiser's original plan floundered, however, due to its inability to inspire the Reichstag to provide the necessary funds required to expand the navy. In 1897, the Kaiser appointed Admiral Alfred von Tirpitz as secretary of state for the navy. Tirpitz subsequently established the Navy League, a pressure group with the support of several key industrialists, which carried out a press campaign supporting naval expansion. The navy was promoted as a nationalist project that was essential if Germany were to achieve great power status. In 1898, Tirpitz introduced a bill into the Reichstag that would create 17 ships in only seven years. This time the bill narrowly passed by 212 votes to 139. The Kaiser, however, was not content with only 17 ships, and in 1900 a second bill was presented to the Reichstag to increase Germany's shipbuilding. Once again the bill was accompanied by a strong propaganda campaign to build up popular support for the construction of a great navy. This bill also passed, and Germany's navy increased to 36 ships. Further naval bills were passed in 1906, 1908 and 1912, each one not only adding more ships, but also ensuring that the German navy kept up with the most modern naval technology.

By 1914, Germany had doubled the size of its navy and was the second biggest maritime power in the world after Great Britain. This massive expansion had significant consequences for Germany's foreign relations. The British believed that Germany's naval expansion was primarily aimed at challenging British naval power, so the German naval expansion sparked an arms race between the two countries centred on the building of a superior navy. Britain developed its relationships with France and Russia, as all three were united by their fear of Germany's increasingly militaristic foreign policy. Britain began to see Germany as its main enemy, and Germany's increasing diplomatic isolation would prove problematic for European relations leading up to 1914. Secondly, the construction of the navy did not achieve its domestic goals. Despite the hopes of the Kaiser, the navy never really united the middle classes in their support of Germany's ruling class, and the SPD continued to increase in support, eventually becoming the largest party in the Reichstag in 1912.

SOURCE

In Kaiser's Wilhelm II's 'A place in the sun' speech, which he gave to the North German Regatta Association in 1901, he argued for Germany's right to greater international power, and the importance of building a new navy to achieve this.

In spite of the fact that we have no such fleet as we should have, we have conquered for ourselves a place in the sun. It will now be my task to see to it that this place in the sun shall remain our undisputed possession, in order that the sun's rays may fall fruitfully upon our activity and trade in foreign parts, that our industry and agriculture may develop within the state and our sailing sports upon the water, for our future lies upon the water. The more Germans go out upon the waters, whether it be in races or regattas, whether it be in journeys across the oceans, or in the service of the battle flag, so much the better it will be for us. For when the German has once learned to direct his glance upon what is distant and great, the pettiness which surround him in daily life on all sides will disappear. Whoever wishes to have this larger and freer outlook can find no better place than one of the **Hanseatic cities**... we are now making efforts to do what, in the old time, the Hanseatic cities could not accomplish, because they lacked the **vivifying** and protecting power of the empire. May it be the function of my Hansa during my year of peace to protect and advance commerce and trade! As head of the Empire I therefore rejoice over every citizen, whether from Hamburg, Bremen or Lubeck who goes forth with this large outlook and seeks new points where we can drive in the nail on which to hang our armour. Therefore, I believe that I express the feeling of all your hearts when I recognise gratefully that the director of this company who has placed at our disposal the wonderful ship which bears my daughter's name has gone forth as a courageous servant of the Hansa, in order to make for us friendly conquests whose fruits will be gathered by our descendants!

KEY TERMS

Hanseatic cities
Commercial confederation of German guilds and their market towns that dominated Baltic maritime trade in the 15th century.

Vivifying
Making more interesting or intense.

ACTIVITY
KNOWLEDGE CHECK

1 From Source 8 and your previous reading in this chapter, what were the main reasons why Kaiser Wilhelm II and members of his government wanted to construct a large German navy?

2 What are the key aims the Kaiser sets out in Source 8?

3 Why would this speech from 1901 have alarmed Britain and France?

The impact of Nazi policies

During the Nazi Party's rise to power, Hitler had been purposely vague on economic policy, promising to overcome the considerable unemployment levels without offering any real detail on how this would be accomplished. His first major economic decision was to appoint Dr Hjalmar Schacht to President of the Reichsbank on 16 March 1933. From August 1934 to November 1937, Schacht was also Reich Minister of Economics, a position from which he played a key role in Nazi economic policy. Schacht was a Nazi sympathiser at the time, but he was not a member of the party or a dedicated follower. He had a strong background as a financial expert and had held the role of President of the Reichsbank in the 1920s. One of his first main policies was a major overhaul of Germany's banking system to avoid another banking collapse in the future. A new Supervisory Office for Banking was established that oversaw and regulated the German banking system. Schacht believed that, instead of making cuts to try to bring Germany out of the Great Depression, they should spend considerable amounts on public investment, thereby going into debt, in order to revitalise the Germany economy. Between 1933 and 1935, 5,000 million marks were invested in public works programmes, and unemployment subsequently fell from 2.7 million in 1934 to 1.7 million in 1935.

SOURCE 9

A Nazi rally in 1935 of the Work Soldiers Organisation. All unemployed men between 16 and 25 were conscripted into the Work Soldiers for massive public building projects, such as the building of the Autobahns.

1 Look at Source 9. What impression do you think this official Nazi photo intends to make about the Nazi Party with regard to the German economy?

2 The Work Soldiers Organisation was a popular aspect of Nazi economic policies. Why do you think this would have been the case in German society during the mid-1930s?

Mefo bills

The key problem for Schacht, however, was how to restart the Germany economy, particularly in terms of rearmament, without investing in a manner that would cause inflation. His main solution to this problem was the introduction of the 'mefo bills' in 1933. These were government contracts to large industrial companies that were not paid in cash, but instead as government agreed credit that would be paid in four years' time. In this way, the government was able to use deficit financing for big industry, but did not have to pay the money immediately, only after the economy began to rebuild, thereby avoiding inflationary spending. It also hid the government debt from the German people, as technically the government was not actually spending cash to aid Germany's economic recovery. The Reichsbank issued 12,000 million marks worth of mefo bills to German industry, primarily for financing rearmament. Mefo bills also financed 50 percent of arms expenditure from 1934 to 1936. As the economy recovered and unemployment dropped, the government was able to move away from this type of deficit financing and use taxation and government loans to drive industrial production.

EXTEND YOUR KNOWLEDGE

Mefo bills

Mefo comes from 'Metallurgische Forschungsgesellschaft', a fake company established by Hjalmar Schacht to hide the large amounts of money Germany was spending on rearmament. The fake company issued 'mefo bills', convertible into Reichsmarks, to pay for rearmament production. As the 'Mefo' company did not actually exist, the payments could be hidden, and thus the Nazis were able to disguise both their rearmament policies and the considerable debt they were creating through their economic policies.

Rearmament under the Nazis and the 'New Plan'

Although consumer goods were part of the recovery, the main basis of German industry was rearmament. From 1933 onwards, the armed forces placed orders for military equipment with around 2,800 German firms. These were disguised from the world by both the military and German industry; for example, Krupp's took contracts for a German agricultural tractor programme that was actually a massive investment in the construction of military tanks. Aeroplanes that were designated for commercial use were instead part of the reconstruction of the German air force. Employment in the armaments industry boomed: explosive manufacturers, for example, more than doubled their workforce. The raw materials industry could barely keep up with demand. This created a **balance of payments** problem, as Germany began to import the raw materials required for rearmament in huge amounts without increasing exports. This was driven further by the greater spending power of the German people as the economy improved, which increased the demand for imports.

To solve this problem, Schacht introduced the 'New Plan' in September 1934. The 'New Plan' regulated German imports by signing a series of agreements with south-eastern European countries and Latin America. The imports were paid for with German marks, but the deal specified that the marks could only be used to either buy German goods or invest in industries that the German economy required. Through the 'New Plan', Germany was essentially able to import the raw materials required for rearmament and use this to subsidise its export industry. The south-eastern European countries were willing to enter into these deals with Germany, as their own export industries lacked markets and Germany could help their economies through its massive requirements for raw materials. The 'New Plan' also had the political purpose of increasing German political influence in south-eastern Europe, by making the economic well-being of these smaller nations dependent on Germany. From 1933 to 1936, therefore, the primary aim of the German economy was focused on overcoming the Great Depression and increasing German employment.

KEY TERM

Balance of payments
A country's record of all economic transactions in a particular year. Ensuring that the difference between payments coming in and going out of the country is not too great is crucial to maintaining a healthy economic system.

The Four-Year Plan, 1936

From 1936 onwards, the focus shifted to massive rearmament and the drive to war. Schacht was sidelined and he eventually resigned in 1937. Instead, the economy came under the direction of Herman Goering as **Plenipotentiary** for the Four-Year Plan.

Schacht had become concerned that the German economy was focusing too much on rearmament and not enough on consumer products. The economy was being distorted by the fact that the majority of German employment was in the armaments industry. However, the money earned by the German people could not be spent on German consumer products, as industry overwhelmingly produced products for the military. Thus imports were still increasing at an unsustainable rate. Schacht argued that there should be a slowdown of rearmament and a greater investment in German industry producing consumer products. This was unacceptable to Hitler, who instead sidelined Schacht and prioritised the Four-Year Plan under Goering. Nazi control over industry was increased, and the economy was directed towards preparation for war. Schacht's concerns over deficit spending were disregarded, as the government increased armaments expenditure on a massive scale. Public debt increased, but restricting wage increases and consumer spending controlled inflation. The financing of housing and private industry was blocked, and a ban on the issuing of mortgages was put in place. The Four-Year Plan invested in synthetic materials in order to make Germany self-sufficient and less reliant on overseas imports, a policy known as autarchy. The production of synthetic rubber, petrol and oil was prioritised. The Four-Year Plan had mixed success. It massively increased Germany's military capability, but not at the rate Hitler demanded. It improved Germany's production of synthetic fuels by 130 percent, but this made up only 18 percent of overall demand.

EXTEND YOUR KNOWLEDGE

The Four-Year Plan and the 'guns or butter' speech
The Four-Year Plan introduced in 1936 under Herman Goering signalled a change in direction for the Nazi economy, away from the more cautious policies of Hjalmar Schacht and towards a more direct focus on rearmament in preparation for war, regardless of any concerns over the economic consequences. At a mass rally in Hamburg on 17 January 1936, Goering articulated this idea in a speech where he argued, 'We have no butter, comrades, but I ask you: would you rather have butter or guns? Shall we bring in lard, or iron ores? I tell you, being prepared makes us powerful. Butter only makes us fat!' This became known as the 'guns or butter' concept, whereby Germany would forgo the benefits of consumer products so that they could focus on developing weapons to make the country more powerful. In reality, the speech was simply brilliant propaganda. Hitler did not want to move away from consumer production entirely, and the Nazi economy, while focused on rearmament, was also aimed at ensuring that its citizens were content. Overall, it could be argued that the Nazi economy always aimed mostly at 'guns', but with a little bit of 'butter'.

From 1936, German industry was focused in a greater way on armament production, but the economy was never placed on a 'total war' footing, as Hitler still wanted to protect the German standard of living and the rising demand for consumer products. Thus it was really only a partial mobilisation of industry for war, and Hitler predicted that the economy would not be completely ready for war until around 1942. The Nazi economy had been successful in both rearmament and managing consumer levels without a rise in inflation.

However, by 1939, the economic policy of the Nazis was becoming arguably unsustainable, as the government continued with massive rearmament while trying to restrict consumer spending by keeping down wages and increasing taxation. Problematically, the German population was growing, but the Nazis were still trying to restrict the consumer goods industry, particularly in the area of housing construction. How long they could have persisted in this direction if the war had not begun at the end of 1939 is still open to considerable debate. With the onset of the Second World War, the Nazi economy faced several significant problems, as outlined further by Source 10.

SOURCE 10

An SPD analyst sets out the issues with the Nazi economy in 1938. The SPD had been banned in 1933 and its members either left Germany or faced arrest and imprisonment. However, some members remained in Germany and secretly made reports on the situation there. These reports were sent to the exiled SPD organisation in Prague and Paris, known as Sopade, and were subsequently published under the title, *Germany Report of the Sopade*.

Can one keep down consumption permanently at its present level without building up an explosive charge? One must not only consider the consumption of foodstuffs but also the consumption of consumer durables and the expansion of the consumer goods industries in proportion to the growth of the population. The most important consumer durable is the dwelling. One can neglect housing construction for a few years, as occurred during the war. But, in the process, such a demand for housing develops that afterwards extraordinary efforts are necessary to get on top of the worst housing shortage. Similarly, the expansion of the consumer goods industries can cease for a time, but, in the process, one creates for the future a dangerous 'contraction in the capacity for foodstuffs', particularly if one encourages the procreation of children as much as the Nazis do. Since the same steel and the same cement, the same copper and the same wood are used for rearmament and for the installation of the autarchy programme as for the construction of dwellings and for the expansion of the consumer goods industries, and since human labour power, which is required for the production of all these goods, is only available in a limited amount, the resource limitations to the expansion of rearmament have finally been reached. (Through the annexation of Austria these limits have once more been somewhat extended because in Austria there are reserves of labour and industrial capacity which have not yet been used. But these reserves will soon have been used up as well.) In a money economy all resource constraints express themselves as financial constraints… As far as the individual is concerned, the most important constraint on consumption continues to be the size of his purse. The quality and amount of the foodstuffs, clothing, shoes, radios which someone can buy is still determined in the first instance by the size of his net income – after the deduction of all taxes, social security contributions, contributions to the Labour Front, 'donations' etc… It follows from this that the most important method of 'diverting' production from the consumer goods sector to the rearmament industries consists in pinching the consumer's purse as hard as possible. That can be achieved by keeping down wages or by raising taxes and contributions. And both of these are indeed happening.

ACTIVITY
KNOWLEDGE CHECK

1 How useful to historians is Source 10 for revealing the problems in the German economy at the end of the 1930s?

2 To what extent would you agree with the assessment made in Source 10?

The German economy during wartime

As discussed previously, the economy was only partially mobilised for war. Despite this, the speed of the Nazis' early victories meant the burden on the German economy was bearable in the first years of the Second World War. There were few restrictions on the German economy and consumer expenditure fell only slightly. However, with the invasion of the USSR in 1941, the economy slowed and the demands on the military increased; thus the problems with the economy became more apparent. One of the major issues was the nature of Hitler's governing style. There was little cohesion or attempt to rationalise the economy. Instead, three competing agencies – the Ministry of Munitions, the Ministry of Economics and the Ministry for War – all had overlapping control over the war economy, a situation that caused both confusion and a lack of direction for war production. Hitler opposed the forced employment of women on ideological grounds, and feared that a significant reduction of consumer goods would lead to the opposition of the German people towards the regime. Thus, despite the grandiose plans for German military expansion that Hitler proposed, production of army weapons actually declined in 1941.

At the beginning of 1940, Hitler ordered a massive increase in military production and appointed Fritz Todt as Minister of Armaments and Munitions, to try to streamline the economic confusion. Todt rationalised arms production by freeing it from interference from both the military and Goering's organisation for the Four-Year Plan. Industry was given greater control over managing its own efficiency; subsequently, prioritisation focused on the army, rather than the air force and navy, as it was apparent that fighting in Eastern Europe would not end quickly. When Todt died in a plane crash on 7 February 1942, Albert Speer replaced him. As discussed previously, Speer reorganised the German war economy.

Central planning of raw materials was placed under Speer, allowing him to better organise the exploitation of German raw materials for arms production, thus reducing the wastage that was prevalent in the war economy. By 1943, armaments production per head was 32 percent higher than in 1939. Speer reduced the number of tank and vehicle models, which allowed for greater productivity. He made better use of factory floor space and assembly line production, cutting the time it took to produce tanks and increasing engine production for planes by 200 percent. The manufacture of munitions per worker rose by 60 percent between 1939 and 1944, and the production of weapons increased overall by 130 percent, despite the actual number of workers available increasing by only 11 percent.

SOURCE

11 Albert Speer, in *Inside the Third Reich* (1970), describes the problem with the Nazi war economy and its unfavourable comparison with the war economy of the United Kingdom.

It remains one of the oddities of this war that Hitler demanded far less from his people than Churchill and Roosevelt did from their respective nations. The discrepancy between the total mobilisation of labour forces in democratic England and the casual treatment of this question in authoritarian Germany is proof of the regime's anxiety not to risk any shift in the popular mood. The German leaders were not disposed to make sacrifices themselves or to ask sacrifices of the people. They tried to keep the morale of the people in the best possible state by concessions. Hitler and the majority of his political followers belonged to the generation who as soldiers had witnessed the Revolution of November 1918 and had never forgotten it. In private conversations Hitler indicated that after the experience of 1918 one could not be cautious enough. In order to anticipate any discontent, more effort and money was expended on supplies of consumer goods, on military pensions or compensation to women for the loss of earnings by their men in the services, than in the countries with democratic governments. Whereas Churchill promised his people only blood, sweat and tears, all we heard was Hitler's slogan: 'The final victory is certain.' This was a confession of political weakness. It betrayed great concern over a loss of popularity which might develop into an insurrectionary mood. Alarmed by the setbacks on the Russian front, in the spring of 1942 I considered total mobilisation of all auxiliary forces... 'Our feelings tell us that this year we are facing the decisive turning point in our history,' I also declared publicly in April 1942, without suspecting that the point was impending: with the encirclement of the Sixth Army in Stalingrad, the annihilation of the Africa Corps, the successful Allied land operations in North Africa, and the first massive air raids on German cities. We had also reached a turning point in our wartime economy; for until the autumn of 1941 the economic leadership had been basing its politics on short wars with long stretches of rest in between. Now the permanent war was beginning.

ACTIVITY
KNOWLEDGE CHECK

1 Read Source 11. According to Albert Speer, why was the German economy performing so poorly during the Second World War?

2 What other factors not mentioned in the source could be added to support Speer's argument that Germany's economic organisation was not sufficient for the demands of the Second World War?

A final development in the Nazi economy took place in 1944, with the appointment of Joseph Goebbels as Total War Plenipotentiary. His task was to produce a new, more extreme focus on the war effort. Industries producing non-essential items such as toys were shut down, work leave was banned and employment of domestic servants was restricted so that these women could be employed in war industries. However, his policies failed to have much of an impact. The number of women employed for war production, for example, increased by only 271,000 from the start of Goebbel's initiatives until the end of the war. As the losses in the war increased, skilled workers were conscripted into the army and were replaced by older workers who were not qualified for the work required, thus increasing inefficiency in the war production. By the end of 1944, the German war economy was able to continue at a barely efficient rate, due to the fact that foreign workers made up 20 percent of the workforce.

Overall, Nazi economic policies went through three stages: the recovery from the Great Depression between 1933 and 1936, the preparation for war through the Four-Year Plan between 1936 and 1939, and the waging of the war itself from 1939 to 1945. While successful in its earlier goals of fighting unemployment, this was based overwhelmingly on rearmament and war production. Germany was never able to overcome its shortages and inefficiencies of organisation and production in a manner that was required for the considerable demands of the Second World War.

The impact of Marshall Aid

The Second World War had devastated the German economy. Its cities had been destroyed by the massive Allied bombing campaigns and its industries lay in ruins. The revival of the German economy to the levels it had been previous to 1939 seemed almost impossible. There were other troubling political questions to solve. Following the war, the issue of the future of both Germany and Europe became an acute area of disagreement between the Western powers of Britain and the United States on the one hand and the Soviet Union on the other. Germany was divided into four occupational zones under the respective control of the Soviet Union, Britain, France and the United States. The Soviet Union insisted on heavy reparations for German industry and refused to consider Germany as an economically unified country. In early 1946, the US government announced that as a response, American troops would remain in Germany as long as Soviet troops remained in their occupational zone, and that the United States would not continue to respect Soviet restrictions on German industrial production.

In January 1947, the British and Americans united their occupational zones into one body known as 'Bizonia', thus signifying the division of Germany into two economic zones, one under Western capitalist influence and the other under Soviet control. The growing American determination to resist the spread of Communism in Europe was confirmed on 12 June, when US President Harold Truman announced that the USA would offer economic and military assistance to all 'free peoples' struggling against Communism. This had been preceded by a speech at Harvard University by the US Secretary of State, General George C. Marshall, on 5 June, when he promised massive economic aid to Europe. In February and March 1948, a six-power conference, called the London Conference, met in London and backed the Marshall Plan, and once final confirmation passed through US Congress in April 1948, 17 billion dollars of aid, known as Marshall Aid, was made available to Western European nations, including West Germany.

The United States sought the industrial recovery of Europe, as this would not only help to stop the growth of Communism, but would also boost the US economy, as a healthy European economy would provide markets for American goods. This had to include their zone of West Germany, as the United States understood that Europe's economic revival after the Second World War would be accelerated by the re-emergence of the powerful German economy. Germany received around 2.7 billion dollars of the Marshall Plan.

The impact of Marshall Aid is vigorously debated between historians. According to a US government report in the 1950s, Marshall Aid was crucial because it 'fired the engine of the German economy'. The Marshall Plan, it was argued, helped the revival of investment in German industry from domestic financial institutions by rebuilding confidence in the emerging West German economy. It was thus crucial in restarting the flow of capital within the West German economy. There is no doubt that the Marshall Aid was well administered by the West German government, which used it to invest in industry, and then reinvested the accumulated interest and repayments made by industries back into government finances. Through this, the Marshall Plan funds for investment in the West German economy grew between 1952 and 1969, providing a strong financial basis for West Germany's expanding industrial system. It is estimated that Marshall Aid paid for 37 percent of West German imports, and much of the money received through the Marshall Plan was invested in improving the railway, electrical and steel industries.

However, many historians have questioned the impact of Marshall Aid. The West German economy was beginning to emerge from the war as early as the summer of 1945, and had achieved 40 percent of pre-war output by 1946. Capital for investment, as well as labour for industry, was in ample supply before Marshall Aid arrived in 1948. It thus assisted West Germany, but did not kick-start the economy in the manner argued by the government. Marshall Aid instead helped to accelerate the considerable growth of the West German economy that was already taking place.

SOURCE
12

A West German government poster from 1949, promoting the Marshall Plan and the economic policies of the ruling Christian Democratic Party. The sign says 'Warning! Construction Work'. The writing in white says 'It goes ahead through the Marshall Plan'.

What is less open to debate is the political impact of the Marshall Plan. The plan encouraged greater co-operation between Western European nations. The aid was administered by the OEEC, and participation in this common organisation brought about the closer co-operation of the occupying powers of West Germany, as well as laying the foundation for the greater integration of Western European economies. This, in turn, led to France integrating its zone with 'Bizonia', thereby creating 'Trizonia' in June 1948, unifying the Western-occupied areas into one entity.

In this way, the Marshall Plan played a critical role in the division of both Germany and Europe. The Eastern Communist bloc refused Marshall Aid, marking a clear separation between those in Western Europe, under the economic protection of the United States, and those in Eastern Europe, under the economic protection of the USSR. This also confirmed the separation of West Germany and its development as a liberal capitalist nation. The integration of West Germany in a manner compatible with the Western economic system defined its economy and set it decisively apart from the socialist economic system concurrently developing in East Germany. Finally, as a West German report in 1949 made clear, the Marshall Plan was critical in leading to the acceptance of the newly created nation of West Germany on the international scene, a factor that could be argued to be of greater importance than any economic impact the Marshall Aid money may have provided.

EXTRACT

3 D.G. Williamson assesses the significance of the Marshall Plan, in *Germany from Defeat to Partition 1945–1963* (2001).

To many West Germans in the 1950s it was axiomatic [self-evident] that the Marshall Plan triggered the West German boom. Yet in strictly economic terms, it played a relatively small role in the economic recovery. In February 1948 Erhard had optimistically predicted that the Plan would provide the investments and imports necessary for rebuilding the industrial infrastructure of the Bizone. The reality was very different. By December 1948, out of $99 million worth of aid, only $22 million was in the form of industrial goods, the majority of which was cotton. At its peak in the last quarter of 1949, Marshall Aid accounted for 37 per cent of West Germany's imports, but by 1952 this had declined to 3 per cent. As part of the Marshall Plan, America also loaned the FRG [Federal Republic of Germany] dollars to pay for imports, which German consumers then purchased with Deutschmarks. These marks were called 'counter-part' funds and were paid into a special account. Erhard had hoped that they would be made available to invest in the consumer goods industries, but the Marshall Plan administrators in Germany insisted they could only be used to buy vital equipment to break bottlenecks in key sectors of the economy. Although the funds only amounted to about 6.7 per cent of the total investment in West German industry, they were used with considerable effect to expand the capacity of the railways, the electrical, iron and steel industries and above all coal mining, for which they provided in 1949 47 per cent of the total investment. The real significance of the Marshall Plan lay in creating a stable environment in which the West German economy could expand.

ACTIVITY
KNOWLEDGE CHECK

1 Look at Source 12. What message is the political poster trying to make concerning the Marshall Plan?

2 Read Extract 3. In what ways does D.G. Williamson disagree with Source 12, and why?

3 In Extract 3, what does Williamson argue is the main success of the Marshall Plan?

The impact of membership of the European Community and the Common Agricultural Policy post-1956

The first Chancellor of West Germany, Konrad Adenauer, believed that West Germany's economic future was intrinsically linked both to the United States and to greater integration with Western Europe. The results of the extreme nationalism of the Nazis also gave a boost, particularly with younger West Germans, to the idea of a movement towards a wider pan-Europeanism. Some even backed the idea of a complete movement away from nation states towards a united Europe. Beyond Germany, countries such as France feared the potential power of a unified Germany. Thus, if West Germany could be integrated into a united Western European economic organisation, this would make unification with East Germany – tied to the USSR and under a different economic system – much more difficult. As discussed previously in this chapter, the co-operation required within the OEEC also helped to encourage further integration of the Western European economies.

The first key development in this movement towards greater economic co-operation came in April 1951, with the formation of the European Coal and Steel Community (ECSC), which combined the heavy industrial sectors of France, West Germany, Italy, Belgium, the Netherlands and Luxembourg into one common market. The West German government agreed to the ECSC for two reasons: politically, they hoped that their involvement in the ECSC would contribute to Western Europe's acceptance of West Germany as a new, co-operative member of the post-war Europe; economically, the ECSC would expand the market for German goods. The ECSC was successful and led to the six nations deciding in June 1955 to expand their economic union.

The Treaty of Rome and the creation of the European Economic Community

After two years of negotiation, on 25 March 1957, the Treaty of Rome established the European Economic Community (EEC). The Common Market established by the EEC, which abolished tariffs between member states, greatly benefited West German exports. West Germany's industrial products were in high demand among the other EEC members, and by 1981, 45 percent of German exports went to EEC member states, while 47 percent of Germany's imports came from within the EEC. By 1987, West Germany had clearly established itself as the main economic power within the EEC. The EEC was heavily dependent on West Germany's membership, and without its contribution to the EEC's budget, many of its policies would have been unsustainable. This economic dominance also had political benefits, as West Germany was able to utilise its trade links to build considerable influence within European affairs. Parallel to West Germany's industrial integration with Western Europe was the effect of the EEC's Common Agricultural Policy (CAP), established in 1962.

The Common Agricultural Policy (CAP)

At the time of the Treaty of Rome, agriculture was a major industry of the original six members. Each government heavily intervened in its agricultural industry, making the shared goal of creating a common market for agriculture particularly difficult. It was felt, however, that creating the CAP was critical. If each nation subsidised its agricultural industry differently, thereby creating different food prices, this could have an effect on industrial competition between the nations, thereby contradicting the very concept underpinning the creation of the EEC. It therefore took four years of complex negotiations to create the CAP, which came into force at the beginning of 1962.

The CAP was based on three principles: free circulation of goods between countries, implementation of common prices on agricultural goods and the maintenance of stable exchange rates. Over the next eight years, common prices were established on a range of products, including wheat, rice, oils, milk, fruit, vegetables, sugar and wine. The immediate effect in West Germany was a drop in food prices, as the agreed common prices were less than the prices in West Germany prior to the CAP. West German agricultural exports increased, especially in milk, sugar and butter. Between 1971 and 1977, for instance, West Germany's share of sugar exports within the EEC rose by 19 percent.

However, the overall impact of the CAP was to somewhat distort West Germany's agricultural sector. The CAP included a fund to subsidise the modernisation of agriculture of the member states. To pay for this and keep prices at a set level the CAP was considerably expensive, at times reaching 70 percent of the EEC's budget. Given that West Germany was a highly industrialised nation, with a small agricultural sector, and a net importer of food, subsidising the agricultural sector was not economically productive. At times, West Germany was spending about 30 percent of its total expenditures on the CAP. This was mainly due to the political lobbying of the influential agricultural sector in West Germany. The guarantee of high prices saw farmers overproduce and create large surpluses that the EEC had promised to buy. Excess production was stored in so-called 'olive oil lakes' or 'mountains of grain', or was simply destroyed. Farmers could avoid making improvements to inefficient systems of agriculture due to the lack of competition, and the restriction on food imports, particularly from the United States, saw food prices gradually rise, with EEC food prices being around two to five times higher than world market prices by the 1970s. By 1989, two-thirds of the net value of West Germany's agricultural sector came from state subsidies, and the CAP consumed 50 percent of the entire EEC budget. West German farmers undoubtedly saw their standard of living increase, despite the reduction of the agricultural sector as a percentage of the overall West German GNP. However, it is somewhat debatable whether the CAP was beneficial in its overall impact on West Germany.

A Level Exam-Style Question Section C

'Between 1871 and 1990, government economic policies were the main factor in the success of the German economy.' How far do you agree with this statement? (20 marks)

Tip

This question requires you to assess why successful development in the German economy occurred between 1871 and 1990, and weigh up how far government policy has been the main factor in these developments. How did government policies help the German economy? Were there successful areas of German economic development that occurred without government assistance, and in what ways did government policies hamper the successful development of the German economy?

ACTIVITY
SUMMARY

1 'The post-war "economic miracle" was little more than a continuation of Germany's economic development that had simply been interrupted by war.' Looking at the period from 1871 to 1990, find evidence both for and against this statement.

2 How accurate is it to argue that Germany's decision to enter into the Common Agricultural Policy had mostly negative effects? Provide evidence to support your argument.

3 What would you consider the most successful government economic policies in Germany in the period 1871 to 1990, and why?

4 What would you consider the most negative policies? Again, provide evidence to support your view.

WIDER READING

Berghahn, V.R. *Imperial Germany 1871-1918: Economy, Society, Culture and Politics*, Berghahn Books, revised and expanded edition (2005)

Ferguson, N. 'The German inter-war economy: political choice versus economic determinism', in Fulbrook, M. (ed.) *Twentieth-Century Germany: Politics, Culture and Society 1918-1990*, Bloomsbury (2001)

Hitchcock, W.I. 'The Marshall Plan and the creation of the West', in Leffler, M.P. and Westad, O.A. (eds) *The Cambridge History of the Cold War Volume I: Origins*, Cambridge University Press (2010), pp. 154-74

Mombauer, A. and Deist, W. (eds) *The Kaiser: New Research on Wilhelm II's Role in Imperial Germany*, Cambridge University Press (2003)

Noakes, J. and Pridham, G. (eds) *Nazism 1919-1945 Volume 2: State, Economy and Society 1933-1939*, University of Exeter Press (1984)

O'Dochartaigh, P. *Germany since 1945* (Studies in Contemporary History), Palgrave Macmillan (2004)

Ogilvie, S. and Overy, R. (eds) *Germany: A New Social and Economic History since 1800, Volume III*, Hodder Arnold (2003)

Tooze, A. 'The economic history of the Nazi regime', in Caplan, J. (ed.) *Nazi Germany*, Short Oxford History of Germany series, Oxford University Press (2008), pp. 168-95

3.3 Ruling the Second Reich, 1871–79

KEY QUESTIONS

- How far did the political system successfully overcome the key divisions facing Germany in 1871?

- To what extent did the Reichstag impact on German regional and social divisions between 1871 and 1879?

- How far was Bismarck successful in achieving his key foreign and domestic political goals between 1871 and 1879?

INTRODUCTION

In 1871, the North German Confederation united with the southern German states to form the new, united German Empire known as the Kaiserreich. At its head was the Prussian king, now known by his title Kaiser Wilhelm I; and the Prussian Chancellor, Otto von Bismarck, had been the main figure behind unification. Although this may be seen as the end of a process that finally brought the German states together, in many ways it was just the beginning of an even more difficult task: that of creating a united German people who shared belief in the Kaiser and his empire. The German states had developed separate identities over hundreds of years, and divisions based on religion, geography, ethnicity and culture were still prominent within the new German state of 1871. Through his leadership, Bismarck helped to craft a new German constitution that attempted to create an integrated and unified Germany under the supreme guidance of the Prussian state. The federal states were able to retain a considerable amount of power, but were still subservient to Prussian leadership. Through the Reichstag, German men were able to vote in the democratic process. Bismarck hoped this would help to integrate Germans within the new political system and nullify the calls for greater democratic liberalisation.

To help achieve this unity, Bismarck co-operated with the most popular political party, the National Liberals, who hoped to achieve a Germany both economically and politically unified through liberal values. Together, Bismarck and the National Liberals launched the *Kulturkampf*, a policy of discrimination aimed at the Catholic Church in Germany, which they believed was the main force impeding German unity. In schools and universities, a new German nationalism was taught as a subject, celebrating unification as the destiny of the German people, and encouraging unity through patriotism and faith in the Kaiser. Bismarck encouraged this strong sense of nationalism by attempting to unite the German people against enemies of the Reich, whether against the Catholics in Germany or the old enemy of France. From 1871 to 1879, then, Germany grappled with the consequences of unification and the type of nation this new empire should be. While great progress

1815 – Congress of Vienna consolidates 360 German states into 38 separate states loosely affiliated under the German Confederation

1870 – Formation of the Catholic Centre Party

1874 – January: Second Reichstag elections – National Liberals the most popular party, with 29.7 percent of the vote

1875 – Socialist Workers Party of Germany founded

April: *Berliner Post* publishes 'Is War in Sight?'

1815 // 1865 // 1870 1871 1872 1873 1874 1875

1867 – North German Confederation founded after Prussia's victorious war over Austria in 1866

June: Creation of the National Liberals Party

1871 – Independent southern German states combine with North German Confederation after victorious war over France in 1870 to form the united German Empire under Kaiser Wilhelm I

Bismarck launches the *Kulturkampf* against the Catholic Church in Germany

March: First Reichstag elections – National Liberals the most popular party, with 30.1 percent of the vote

was made in forging a new German people, Bismarck's policies against the Catholics and socialists, and his final break with the National Liberals, meant that the nation still retained many of its class and religious divisions as it entered the second decade of its existence.

HOW FAR DID THE POLITICAL SYSTEM SUCCESSFULLY OVERCOME THE KEY DIVISIONS FACING GERMANY IN 1871?

Trying to reconcile unity and division

The movement towards German unification had a long and complex history. For much of the 19th century, politicians, historians, philosophers and writers grappled with the key question of what it meant to be German. At the Congress of Vienna in 1815, the previous 360 German states had been consolidated into 38 **sovereign states** that were loosely connected through the German Confederation. The states were independent, but through the German Confederation they co-operated in some limited aspects, for example through a common defence policy. Ideas of German nationalism were growing. However, a long history of separate states meant the connection to regional identity and the ruling families of the differing areas remained very strong. Germany was also divided along religious lines, with the Catholic area of Bavaria, for example, quite separate in its political outlook and values from the predominately Protestant state of Prussia.

> **KEY TERM**
>
> Sovereign state
> A state that administers its own government and is not dependent upon or subject to another power.

The idea of 'Germany' was largely geographical; the main concept of German, as put forward by nationalist writers in the early 19th century, focused on language as the key definer of national identity. However, the idea that all those who spoke German were unified in their national identity was rather vague in comparison to France and Britain, which were cohesive sovereign states where the population was united by its shared citizenship. Linguistic unity was only one aspect of identity and was not strong enough on its own to overcome historical cultural and religious divisions, which had developed over hundreds of years. Additionally, the two biggest and most powerful states in the German Confederation, Prussia and Austria, incorporated large populations that did not speak German or consider themselves ethnically German. Austria, in particular, viewed calls for German unification as a threat to both its royal family and its powerful position in the German Confederation.

The role of Prussia

The eventual unification of Germany into one united sovereign state was not an equal process shared by all members of the German Confederation. Instead, it was a process driven by Prussia and under its military and political dominance; driven by a combination of the massive industrial growth experienced by the German states in the 1850s, the inspiration of Italy's wars for unification taking place at the same time, and the coming to power of the more liberal Prince Wilhelm in Prussia in 1858, the national question took on greater prominence. The Prussians were determined to control the process, in order to ensure that the emerging nation would be under their control. After the wars against Austria and France, Germany became a united nation in 1871. However, the key questions that nationalists wrestled with at the start of the 19th century remained. What it meant to be German was still rather vague, and the many divisions between differing areas of Germany did not simply evaporate with unification.

Problematically, German unification was not a shared process. Instead, it was driven by Prussia, which now essentially ruled the newly created nation. Most significantly, the Prussian prince, Willhelm, was crowned Kaiser of Germany, symbolising Prussia's power over the newly created state and the ruling dynasties of the other German regions. Thus, while 1871 had been the culmination of a long process aimed at creating a united German nation, it was actually the beginning of the process to create a united German people.

1878 – July: Fourth Reichstag elections – National Liberals and Centre Party tied, winning 23.1 percent of the vote each

October: Anti-socialist legislation introduced, which prohibits socialist meetings in Germany

1879 – Bismarck brings the *Kulturkampf* to an end
Reichstag votes to introduce protective tariffs on some imported goods

1890 – March: Otto von Bismarck resigns as Chancellor of Germany

1894 – The Bavarian Chlodwig zu Hohenlohe-Schillingsfürst becomes the first non-Prussian Chancellor of Germany

1880	1885	1890	1895

1877 – January: Third Reichstag elections – National Liberals the most popular party, with 27.2 percent of the vote

1880 – Split in the National Liberals and the creation of the Liberal Union party

1892 – German flag adopted

One-third of the new German state was Catholic, and many viewed themselves as a discriminated minority within the Protestant-dominated Germany. Beyond the Catholic population, however, many Germans, including Junkers, southern Germans, non-Prussians, particularly in Hanover, and many within the German peasantry, viewed the newly created nation with distrust. Thus, the constitution of Germany constructed by Bismarck aimed to achieve two main functions: to enshrine Prussian power, while at the same time overcoming some of the key divisions within Germany.

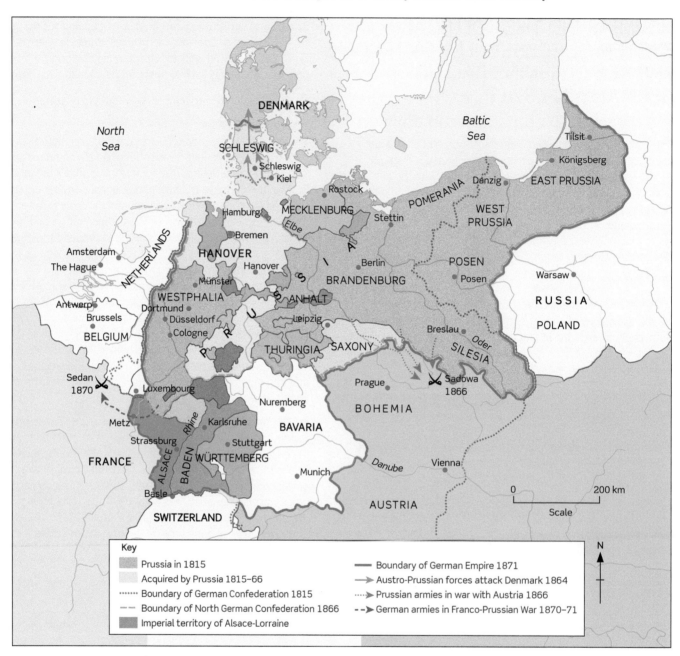

Figure 3.1 The division of Germany, 1815–71.

The potential for dynastic rivalry between Germany's many royal families was overcome by allowing the 22 different royal rulers to maintain substantial power under the Prussian King, who was also German Emperor. The constitution proclaimed that all the German sovereigns were equal, although it was clear that as the Emperor controlled the civil service and the military this was not really true. Under the constitution, the Emperor took precedence over the separate states through his ability to proclaim imperial law, which superseded state powers. Despite this, the constitution dealt successfully with the difficult question of how to integrate the royal families, who had ruled over the separate German states before 1871, into one unified nation dominated by a single emperor. The constitution also established an elected parliamentary body, the Reichstag. Although its role in German politics is questionable, it served as a key aspect of unification. Universal **suffrage** for all German men over 25 meant the Reichstag elections were the only aspect of the political process that Germans from across the country could engage in equally. This democratic engagement provided a powerful sense of German unity. The creation of a single currency, sole measurements and weights, a national legal system, a national civil service, a German military, and the linking up of Germany's railway system, all helped to establish a greater sense of a unified nation, as did the creation of national symbols such as the German flag in 1892. Kaiser Wilhelm I played a key role through his dignified but restrained leadership, which helped to bring him the emotional respect of all Germans, thereby helping to create a unifying figure in the Kaiser and the German Empire he represented.

KEY TERM

Suffrage
The right to vote. The Kaiserreich had universal male suffrage, meaning that all men could vote. In comparison, at the same time in Britain, only two out of every five men had the vote.

EXTEND YOUR KNOWLEDGE

The Congress of Vienna (1815)
The Congress of Vienna of 1815 was a major conference between the great powers of Europe that sought to settle the critical issues of Europe following the Napoleonic Wars. Many issues in respect of European security and national territory were discussed. In terms of German unification, the Congress of Vienna was a major step along the path to eventual unification in 1871. Prussia was significantly expanded, gaining territory in both the western and eastern parts of Germany. Its power and strength would grow further over the following decades, to the point where it could challenge the other great German-speaking power, Austria. In terms of unification, however, the Congress was critical, as it reduced the previous 360 separate states of Germany into only 38, and bound them into a loose unity under the German Confederation, governed mainly by Austria. Although the German Confederation was a rather weak administrative body, the fact that Germany had now consolidated into only 38 states and that these states were, at the very least, discussing issues of defence and the economy with each other, was a key step in the eventual creation of a unified German nation.

The military is also a good example of the way in which the German constitution attempted to reconcile unity and division. The German army was made up of four separate armies: those of Prussia, Bavaria, Saxony and Wurttemberg. Each separate army owed allegiance to the king of that particular state. However, in a time of war, the emperor would be in charge of the entire military, and the Prussian command would thus take the lead over the army. So constitutionally, the sovereign powers of Bavaria, Saxony and Wurttemberg still played an important role in the German military and did not simply have their powers taken away, but in practice, the Prussian military elite, led by the emperor and the Junkers, essentially controlled the German military.

This hybrid form of unification shows the complexities in creating a unified Germany that reconciled the two rather contradictory aims of maintaining the dominance of the Prussian elite while integrating all German citizens into a common identity within the nation. Prussian influence in politics and the military was clearly disproportionate, and many diverse religious and regional groups within the newly created nation were uneasy about its predominant power. At times, Bismarck sought to overcome this by generating a defensive German nationalism focused on alleged threats to the Empire, predominately from France. Although successful, it was only able to create a short-lived and somewhat superficial sense of shared German identity. However, while there were clearly limits to German unification, given the historical separation of the German states and the vast array of differing cultural, regional and religious identities this had created, the first ten years after 1871 were quite successful in forging a sense of shared German citizenship within the newly created Reich.

SOURCE

A painting from 1871 celebrating German unification, by Anton von Werner. The northern and southern states of Germany are depicted as two ancient German warriors, shaking hands after their victory over France. Above them is an angel who holds the German crown in her hands.

Ludwig Pfau was a poet, journalist and politician. In this article, 'Centralisation und Federation' written in 1864, he sets out the key aspects of disunity between the German people, and argues that true unity and freedom for Germany cannot come about through centralisation under Prussian power, but a federal state, where all German states, including Prussia, are merged equally within the German nation.

The fragmentation faced by Germany is not limited to the country itself, but extends to the people. The discord of minds is the moral impediment that prevents the unity of territories. Absolutist, constitutional, and socialist endeavours are splintered by Catholic, Protestant, and philosophical viewpoints to such an extent that each party has at its heart the most opposing elements. If material fragmentation is to come to an end, this spiritual fragmentation must first be overcome. However, concealment and deferral does not lead to the internal unity of the people; instead, differences must be revealed and reconciled; this is the only way to exert a beneficial effect on the political development of the nation.

The root principle of the political question, in Germany and every other country, is this: the divine right of monarchs or sovereignty of the people; authority or state rule; dogma or reason; force or law; **subjugation** or freedom. No matter how one looks at it, the same contradiction arises again and again, and when applied to the structure of the national state, it comes down to centralisation or federation.

The nature of the question of German unification does not boil down to monarchy or republic, Austria or Prussia, greater Germany or lesser Germany, but to centralisation or federation. Those who support the divine right of kings, authority, dogma, force, and serfdom must logically vote for centralisation; in contrast, those who champion sovereignty of the people, self-rule, reason, the rule of law, and freedom must logically strive for federation... Centralisation and the divine right of kings prevail in Berlin just as much as they do in Vienna. Moreover, His Majesty non possumus, the King and Lord who finds his crown on the altar and behaves infallibly towards parliament and the people, just as his ministry behaves irresponsibly, is fundamentally nothing but a pseudo-Protestant pope and a tsar from the Uckermark [a northerly region of Prussia]... Reactionary Prussian rule must also step aside, allowing the great civilising power of the nation can take its place. For in relation to the internal development of the German Empire, Prussian **hegemony** is no better than the Roman Empire.

KEY TERMS

Subjugation
Bringing under control.

Hegemony
Predominance of one state or social group over all others.

ACTIVITY
KNOWLEDGE CHECK

1 What impression is the painting by Anton von Werner (Source 1) trying to give of German unification?

2 What key problems relating to German unification does Source 2 set out?

3 What solution to the problems of German unification does Source 2 propose?

4 How far does Pfau's argument (Source 2) differ from the painting celebrating German unification by Anton von Werner (Source 1)?

The federal government and the *Länder*

As previously discussed, before unification Germany had consisted of 38 separate states. The northern states had been consolidated into the Northern German Confederation after Prussia's successful war against Austria and the German states of Saxony, Hanover and Hesse-Cassel in 1866. During the successful war against France in 1870, the southern German states of Bavaria, Baden, Wurttemberg and Hesse-Darmstadt, driven by the mass wave of nationalism generated by the war, requested to join with the Northern German Confederation into a united Germany. However, the integration of the states within the newly created nation was a complex arrangement. While wanting to be part of a unified Germany, states such as Bavaria were also wary of giving up complete power to Prussia.

The constitution of 1871 established Germany as a federal state, with the separate states retaining certain powers, albeit under the dominance of Prussia. Each of the 25 states, or *Länder*, was allowed to retain its own constitution. This meant that many of the states were quite different in the way they were governed. Bavaria, for instance, was relatively liberal, while the Grand Duchy of Mecklenburg-Schwerin had a constitution that pre-dated the French revolution and had no elected parliament until 1918. The states also retained control over education, transport, direct taxation, policing and health. Additionally, the southern states enjoyed certain privileges not given to the northern states, due to deals Bismarck made with the southern states to encourage them to join with the Northern Confederation in 1871. As discussed on page 67, one of the compromises agreed to through negotiation of the southern states with Bismarck was the formation of a unified military through four separate armies that were still controlled by the sovereigns of Bavaria, Saxony and Wurttemberg, as well as the Prussian ruler who was now also Emperor of Germany. The southern states were also allowed to retain their own railway and postal systems, and were exempted from the taxes on beer and spirits that the northern states had to pay. On the other hand, the federal government was able to set national tariffs, control the banking system and set the direction of German foreign and economic policy.

EXTEND YOUR KNOWLEDGE

Federal government
The system of federalism refers to a type of government where power is shared between a central government and the political units that make up the country, usually known as states or provinces. The powers of government are thus divided between central government authority and state authority. In Germany, for instance, the central government controlled foreign policy, while the states controlled education. This constitutional arrangement is known as a federation. Today, the best-known example is the United States of America, although Germany, despite some differences from the Kaiserreich, is still a federal system made up of 13 states (as opposed to 25 states in 1871). The key difference between the German federal system of today and the German federal system of 1871 is that Prussia no longer exists in modern Germany.

The *Länder* and the Bundesrat

The power of the *Länder* was centred on the Upper House of Parliament, known as the Bundesrat. The Bundesrat was made up of the delegates of the state governments, who were selected according to the constitutions of the separate *Länder*. The number of representatives for each state in the Bundesrat depended on the size of the state; Prussia, for instance, took up 17 of the 58 Bundesrat seats, while Bavaria only had six and the smaller states only one. The Bundesrat represented the will of the German states, having the power to veto legislation passed by the Reichstag, and with some advisory powers over German foreign policy. Fourteen votes were needed to veto legislation, so in theory states could work together to undermine Prussian dominance. However, in practice this never happened, as the smaller states were afraid of challenging Prussian power.

While the Bundesrat proclaimed to uphold the federalist state in Germany and allow all of the *Länder* a say in national policy, in reality the constitution was set up in a manner that ensured Prussia's position. Firstly, the fact it had 17 members in the Bundesrat while only 14 votes ensured a veto, meant that it always had the ability to veto legislation it found unfavourable. Secondly, the Prussian parliament (Landtag) was elected through a restricted franchise that was based on a three-class system. The voters were separated into three classes based on how much tax they paid: the highest taxpayers, the middle taxpayers and the lowest taxpayers. Although the lowest taxpayers represented 85 percent of the population and the top only five percent, each section of taxpayers elected exactly one-third of the parliament. In some areas, this meant that one considerably wealthy person made up a third of the votes on their own. To ensure even further that the right type of Prussians made up the parliament, the voters did not even vote directly for their members, but for an electoral college, which then chose whom the members of the Prussian Landtag would be. This meant that 14 delegates to the Bundesrat from Prussia always represented the interests of the wealthiest in Prussian society, mainly the Junkers. This ensured their political dominance over the German political system, as they could block any legislation emanating from the Reichstag that they found unfavourable to their privileged position.

The constitution itself, despite its federal structure, enshrined Prussian dominance within the structures of power. The Kaiser would always be the Prussian King, and, along with the Prussian elite, he had supreme control over the German military and government appointments, thus ensuring that policy would remain favourable to the interests of the Prussian elite. Essentially, in terms of the German federal system, the constitution could be defined as one where the states were given enough power by Bismarck to keep their leaders content, while at the same time guaranteeing that Prussia remained, overwhelmingly, the dominant power within this political structure. Having said this, even Prussia was not immune from the changes brought about by its integration within a unified Germany. Prussia could not be governed without consideration of the desires of the other states, and the Prussians could not dominate all aspects of government. By the 1890s, the Kaiser had appointed several non-Prussians to key positions within the Reich government, and most critically, the Chancellor of Germany from 1894 to 1900 was a Bavarian, Chlodwig zu Hohenlohe-Schillingsfürst.

SOURCE

3 In this speech, made in November 1871, Socialist leader August Bebel denounces the lack of constitutional and political rights for the German federal states and the dominance of Prussia over the German system.

Gentlemen! Today I find myself in a position, together with gentlemen from both the Right and the Centre, to vote against the motion, although we do so for different reasons. This, of course, will not prevent the Reich Chancellor's press organ, the **Norddeutsche Allgemeine Zeitung**, from stating in tomorrow's political overview that today's vote is yet more proof of the cooperation of the 'blacks' [Centre Party] and the 'reds' [Socialist Party]. [laughter] Gentlemen, that side has voiced serious misgivings on the grounds that, if this motion were to pass, the jurisdiction of the Reich's authority would have to be extended, and this has prompted these gentlemen to speak against the motion. We once took a strong stance against the extension of powers in the North German Confederation, but not because we were particularly in favour of the existence of small states – God forbid, Gentlemen! – but simply because we told ourselves that, in the face of Prussia's absolutist-military appetite in the small states - and despite the Reich Chancellor's remark that their liberalism still lagged far behind Prussia's – constitutional life in the small states was more rounded, and generally allowed an opposition party at least slightly more independent movement. However, Gentlemen, recent years have seen a considerable decline in these conditions, especially over the last year. The establishment of the North German Confederation meant that the small states were denied any independent action or work, and the establishment of the German Reich, built on 'fear of God and pious conduct', drew the southern German states into this state of impotence, putting an end to their independent activities. Today Gentlemen, the small states – we, as Social Democrats, have had sufficient experience of this in recent years – do little more than play policy bailiff for Prussia. [laughter] The persecution our party has suffered in Saxony – where laws that were already reactionary were used against us in the most arbitrary, reactionary way with regard to freedom of assembly, freedom of association and freedom of the press – has shown us that the small states have lost any liberal spirit they once had, along with the ability to put up any resistance against the pressure they face from Berlin.

KEY TERM

Norddeutsche Allgemeine Zeitung
Conservative newspaper in the Kaiserreich, which was a strong supporter of Bismarck.

ACTIVITY
KNOWLEDGE CHECK

1 What reason does Bebel provide in Source 3 for why the Socialists voted against the extension of power by the North German Confederation?

2 According to Bebel, what did the founding of the North German Confederation do to the small states of northern Germany?

3 In a similar way, what did the founding of a united Germany do to the southern German states?

4 According to Bebel, what has happened in Saxony, and what does this show about Prussian power in Germany?

TO WHAT EXTENT DID THE REICHSTAG IMPACT ON GERMAN REGIONAL AND SOCIAL DIVISIONS BETWEEN 1871 AND 1879?

The impact of regional and social divisions

The nature of democracy in Germany in 1871

The constitution of 1871 had established the German parliament, known as the Reichstag, as the lower house of Germany, consisting of political parties elected through a popular vote of all German men aged 25 or above. Although being generally sceptical of democracy, Bismarck believed that allowing Germans a democratic vote would help to minimise more liberal influences and encourage continued support for the monarchy. His view was that denying any form of democracy would simply encourage further political opposition. In some ways, the Reichstag was a superficial form of democracy. Bismarck legislated that Reichstag members would receive no payment, thus making it extremely difficult for those of the less privileged classes to run for election. While the Reichstag had to pass all legislation, it had restricted powers to initiate legislation, instead responding to legislation presented to it by the Reich government or the Bundesrat. The Bundesrat could veto all legislation it did pass, and neither the Chancellor, nor the military chiefs, nor the Kaiser had any responsibility to the Reichstag. If the Reichstag rejected legislation that the government wanted passed, the Kaiser could dissolve the Reichstag and call new elections. Overall, then, it could be argued that the Reichstag was a somewhat restricted and insincere form of democracy.

Tensions arising from regional divisions and a multinational Reich

Regional divisions also largely impacted the political parties within the Reichstag. The National Liberal Party, for instance, which supported the German Empire, was mainly based in the north, while the German People's Party, who opposed the creation of a unified Germany, was based in the south. The previously mentioned Centre Party represented Catholic interests, and thus its support was strongest in the German areas of the south, such as Bavaria and Baden, as well as the Rhineland, Silesia and the Polish population of the eastern side of Prussia. The German Conservative Party, on the other hand, mainly represented the interests of the land owning Junker class of Prussia. However, in many ways, the Reichstag served a crucial role in creating a unified German nation. The elections constituted a unifying national political process whereby Germans from across the country could exercise their voice on how the country should be run. Within the Reichstag itself, the right to debate allowed objections and dissent to at least be voiced in an open forum. This was important in trying to overcome the serious regional and social divisions that affected the new nation.

Along with the regional divisions already discussed, Germany was also a multinational Reich, incorporating regions populated by Poles, Danes and French peoples. These groups faced discrimination and were treated with suspicion due to their questionable loyalties to Germany, given their different ethnic backgrounds. Consequently, each of these ethnic groups formed its own separatist or nationalist parties and ran in Reichstag elections, doing well in the elections between 1874 and 1881. Social divisions also impacted on the Reichstag and could at times take on regional aspects as well. The popular National Liberals represented the educated and wealthy middle class of Germany and were thus best represented in Saxony, Hanover, Baden and industrial areas of the Rhineland. The key impact of the growing social divisions within Germany, however, was the rise of the Socialist Workers' Party of Germany (the SAPD only became known as the SPD in 1890). As discussed in Chapter 1, the rapid urbanisation of German society, combined with the depression of the 1870s, encouraged the appeal of socialism as a political ideology during this decade. The specific needs of the new German working class led to the formation of the SAPD in 1875, and it made gains in 1877 and 1878, although it only attracted around seven percent of the vote at this stage.

Overall, then, it could be argued that the regional and social divisions represented by the political elections through the 1870s clearly demonstrated the problems apparent in the new German Empire. It is debatable how far the political elections worsened the divisions within the recently unified nation or simply represented them, but it is clear that the Reichstag showed that the pre-existing divisions previous to 1871 remained a powerful force in shaping the political attitudes of the German people. Thus, the political scene in Germany from 1871 to 1879 can appear to be quite negative, wracked as it was by regional, social and religious tensions, and with parties hostile to the new German nation doing well in Reichstag elections, particularly in 1874.

However, it should also be noted that the Reichstag was very important in giving a political voice to these minorities who, over time, came to be more and more integrated within the German system. For instance, nationalist and separatist parties won around ten percent of the vote in 1874. Over time, however, the Polish, Danish and French minorities became more assimilated within Germany, as new generations attended German schools, were conscripted into the army and increasingly saw themselves as part of the German nation. This can be seen clearly in Reichstag voting, where the Polish and French moved from voting for nationalist and separatist parties to predominately voting for the Catholic German political party, the Centre Party. Critically, despite the political tension and division within Germany between 1871 and 1879, the Reichstag elections and parliamentary debate ensured that these issues never developed into violence against the state. Although democracy in Germany was somewhat restrained, it still came to be viewed as the best means for outsider groups opposed to aspects of the Reich to show their dissent at the overall government system, as opposed to turning to anti-government violence.

Year	National Liberals	Liberal Left	Conservatives	Centre Party	SPD	Others
1871	30.1%	9.3%	23.0%	18.6%	3.3%	15.7%
1874	29.7%	9.0%	14.2%	27.9%	6.8%	12.4%
1877	27.2%	8.6%	17.7%	24.8%	9.1%	12.6%
1878	23.1%	7.8%	26.6%	23.1%	7.6%	11.8%

Figure 3.2 Reichstag results, 1871–78. Adapted from G. von Hohorst, J. Kocka and G.A. Ritter (eds) *Sozialgeschichtliches Arbeitsbuch, Vol. 2, 1870-1914* (1978).

EXTEND YOUR KNOWLEDGE

The constitution of the Kaiserreich

The constitution of 1871, constructed by Bismarck, can often be quite confusing for students. This is because it was a complex attempt to give German people a democratic say in the system through the Reichstag elections, while ensuring that the Kaiser and the Prussian elite retained real power. This created a political system that was neither a democracy nor an absolute monarchy, but was something of a combination of the two. The Kaiser had considerable powers to appoint and dismiss the chancellor and government ministers. He also had absolute control over foreign policy and the military, and could dissolve the Reichstag and call new elections. The chancellor, appointed by the Kaiser, was not accountable to the Reichstag. The Bundesrat was constructed in a way that ensured that the Junkers, who could use it to ensure that their political interests were always favoured, always dominated it. While this appears to indicate that Germany was a considerably authoritarian state, it is important to note that Germany allowed more men to vote in the Reichstag elections than qualified in Britain at the same time. The Reichstag did have some important powers, particularly its power to pass or reject the military budget. It is also important to note that the German constitution granted freedom of the press and freedom of assembly (right to protest), and these rights were more progressive than in many European countries at that time in history. Overall, then, it is very hard to assess how democratic or authoritarian the constitution was because it shared attributes of each.

SOURCE

In *The Founding Program of the National Liberals*, published in June 1867, the National Liberals set out their goals for the unification of Germany. They consider the role of liberal ideology and the Reichstag in creating a unified, democratic German nation.

We see the unification of all of Germany under one single constitution as the most important task we face today. Bringing a monarchic federal state in line with the requirements of the constitutional law is a difficult undertaking, and one that has never been accomplished to this day in the history of mankind. The constitution of the North German Confederation has neither fully accomplished this task, nor concluded it in a satisfactory manner. We believe that the new constitution represents the first essential step on the road to a German state rooted in liberty and power. As a matter of urgency, all available forces must be employed to encourage the accession of southern Germany, as allowed for by the constitution, but under no circumstances should it weaken or cast doubt upon the unified central government... Just as our party endeavoured to make improvements at its earliest stages, so, from the next session of the Reichstag, will it work without pause to continue to develop the constitution. We saw in Parliament the nation's living forces united. With our assistance, universal and equal suffrage, direct elections, and the secret ballot have become the foundation of public life. We are not oblivious to the associated risks, so long as the police powers continue to curb freedom of the press and the rights of assembly and association, as long as primary schools are crippled by regulations and elections are subject to the effects of bureaucracy; especially since the withholding of daily allowances limits a person's eligibility to stand for election. However, although these guarantees could not be achieved, the risks have failed to deter us. It is now up to the people to speak out in favour of clean elections. As a result of their hard-fought struggles, the people will be able to express themselves faithfully, and once this happens, general suffrage will become the sturdiest **bulwark** of freedom. It will clear away the shadows of the estates system that persist today and, finally, we will achieve equality before the law, as we were promised.

KEY TERM

Bulwark
An object serving as a defence or protection of something.

ACTIVITY
KNOWLEDGE CHECK

1 After reading Source 4, what five key words would you use to define the political goals and ideology of the National Liberals?

2 To what extent did the Reichstag have effective political influence in Germany from 1871 to 1879?

3 What key problems with German unification were demonstrated by the nature of the Reichstag parties?

THINKING HISTORICALLY — Cause and consequence (7a & b)

Questions and answers

The questions that historians ask vary depending on what they think is important. It is the questions that interest us that define the history that is written. These questions change with time and place. Different historians will also come up with different answers to the same questions, depending on their perspectives and methods of interpretation, as well as the evidence they use.

Below are three historians who had different areas of interest.

Thomas Carlyle	Karl Marx	Sir Charles Oman
• A political historian who lived in the 19th century • He was interested in the idea that great men shape history	• An economic and political historian who lived in the 19th century • He was interested in the role of the lower classes and how they contributed to historical change	• A military historian who lived in the late 19th and early 20th century • He was very interested in the minute detail of warfare, including how armies were organised and what tactics they used

These are some key aspects relating to German unification.

The creation and role of the Reichstag, 1871	The entrenchment of Prussian authority in the German constitution of 1871, written by Bismarck	Prince Wilhelm of Prussia being crowned Kaiser of Germany in 1871
The Prussian three-tier voting system	The creation of the German Workers' Party in 1875	The success of nationalist and separatist parties in the 1874 Reichstag elections
The German army organised under the leadership of Prussia, Bavaria, Saxony and Wurttemberg	The politics and actions of Bismarck in forging a unified Germany	The creation and role of the Bundesrat in 1871

Work in groups of between three and six to answer the following questions.

1 Which of these events would have been of most interest to each historian? Explain your answer.

2 Each take the role of one historian and devise a question that would interest them about each of the events.

3 Discuss each event in turn. Present the questions that have been devised for each historian and offer some ideas about how they would have answered them.

4 For each event, decide as a group which question is the most interesting and worthwhile of the three.

Answer the following questions in pairs.

5 Identify the different ways that each historian would approach writing on the politics and actions of Bismarck in creating a unified German empire.

6 In what ways would Carlyle and Marx differ in their explanations of the significance and role of the Reichstag? What would be the focus of their arguments?

Answer the following questions individually.

7 All three historians may produce very different accounts and explanations of the same piece of history. Of the three historians, whose account would you prefer to read first? Explain your answer.

8 Do the differences in these accounts mean that one is more valid than the others?

9 Explain why different historical explanations are written by different historians.

10 Explain why different explanations of the same event can be equally valid.

HOW FAR WAS BISMARCK SUCCESSFUL IN ACHIEVING HIS KEY FOREIGN AND DOMESTIC POLITICAL GOALS BETWEEN 1871 AND 1879?

Bismarck's co-operation, and eventual break, with the National Liberals

The National Liberal Party was the most popular Reichstag party in the first decade after German unification. Politicians who supported Bismarck's creation of a unified German nation had formed the party in 1867. The party was led by Rudolf von Benningsen and mainly represented the interests of the industrial and professional middle classes. The party held a strong patriotic belief in German unification, and its ideology focused on two key areas: national unity and the promotion of civil liberties. The Liberals were strong advocates of free trade, believing that a truly united Germany with a single economic system and no protectionist policies was the best means of expanding middle class and industrial wealth, as well as building a truly unified nation. In the first German election held in 1871, the National Liberals achieved 30.1 percent of the vote, the most of all the political parties, and considerably higher than the nearest challengers, the Centre Party, which achieved 18.6 percent. In the elections of 1874, the Liberals' vote dropped slightly to 29.7 percent, but they still remained the biggest party in the Reichstag.

Bismarck was prepared to work with the National Liberals at this time, and a considerable amount of liberal legislation relating to free trade was passed in the early stages of German unification. Freedom of movement restrictions were removed, so that Germans could travel freely within Germany to look for work. Laws restricting the charging of interest on loans were removed, and weights and measurements were standardised across Germany. The Reichsmark became the sole legal currency of Germany, and import duties on certain metal products were removed. Through these policies, Germany moved towards an economic integration that broke down the barriers between the previously independent German states and helped to unify their economic system, thus providing the basis for the economic growth that Germany would experience from the 1890s onwards.

Bismarck was prepared to work with the National Liberals for two reasons. Firstly, beyond free trade and economic unity, the National Liberal ideology also supported constitutional change towards greater democracy and civil liberties for Germans. Given that they were the largest party, their policies could not simply be ignored. Bismarck therefore hoped, through co-operating with the National Liberals in economic policy, that the educated middle classes who voted for the National Liberals would remain happy with the German system and the economic benefits it was providing, and thus be less concerned about the fact that Bismarck was resisting the liberal push for greater democracy. In essence, he hoped to trade off economic concessions in place of political concessions. Secondly, both Bismarck and the National Liberals feared the Catholic support for the Centre Party, which they believed was a threat to national unity. The National Liberals therefore supported Bismarck's attempts to restrict the actions of the Catholic Church in Germany (see the later section on the *Kulturkampf*). Thus, up to 1879, Bismarck was prepared to co-operate with the National Liberals, although it should be noted that, importantly, this did not mean he supported their ideology. Instead, while Bismarck saw positives in the fact that the most popular party in Germany supported German unity, and he always expected to have to govern with the support of the middle classes represented by the Liberals, he also opposed the key ideology of the National Liberals, which pushed for greater democratic change.

By the mid-1870s, the tension over Bismarck's refusal to extend parliamentary power was growing between the Chancellor and the National Liberals, particularly those within the National Liberal Party who were further to the left in their ideology. For Bismarck, the solution to this problem was to try to find a means of splitting the National Liberals, and then work with the more right-wing conservative elements of the party. As discussed in the previous chapter, the economic downturn of the 1870s provided this opportunity. For Bismarck the strong push for tariff reform was driven by political considerations as much as it was by economic concerns. Tariff reform was strongly supported by the Conservative Party, which represented Junker interests, as well as small farmers and peasants, many of whom had previously voted for the National Liberals. In the 1878 campaign, the strong message put forward by Bismarck on tariff reform, and the portrayal of those who supported free trade as traitors against German interests, undermined the National Liberals, whose vote declined to 23.1 percent.

The defining split in the National Liberals came in 1879 over the vote concerning the introduction of protective tariffs, where the more conservative elements of the National Liberals supported protectionist policies. By August 1880, the party had officially split between those on the more conservative right, who remained with the National Liberal Party, and those on the left who formed the Liberal Union.

The consequences of Bismarck's split with the National Liberals

Bismarck had achieved his goal of splitting the party and pushing the National Liberals in a more conservative direction, and over the next decades the National Liberal Party became more conservative in its ideology. However, Bismarck soon found that his political manoeuvres actually made his task of governing Germany more difficult. The decline of the National Liberals meant that the Centre Party, which represented Catholic interests, became the largest party in the Reichstag. Given Bismarck's opposition to Catholic policy in Germany, this made the Reichstag much more difficult for the Chancellor to manage. The division of the National Liberals into two parties also split the vote, and it was no longer possible for a coalition between the National Liberals and the Conservative party to hold a majority in the Reichstag, weakening the Reichstag's overall support for Bismarck's policies. Lastly, the left liberals gained support, with the Progressive Party and the new Liberal Union Party winning 21.1 percent of the vote between them in the 1881 election. The two parties soon merged to become the German Free Minded Party, and in 1884 became the second most popular party in Germany after the Centre Party. The two biggest parties in Germany by 1884 were thus ones that were in many ways opposed to the political goals of Bismarck. Between 1881 and 1886, Bismarck's ability to manage the Reichstag was therefore severely weakened, and he found himself politically isolated. He had achieved his aim of dividing the National Liberals, but the political consequences were not the positive gains he had expected.

SOURCE

5 This American magazine cartoon from 1879 shows Bismarck as the total master of parliament, expertly subduing the political parties of the Reichstag.

THE GREAT GERMAN RINGMASTER

SOURCE

A letter from Max von Forckenbeck to Franz von Stauffenberg, dated 19 January 1879. Both men were prominent National Liberals. Here, Forckenbeck sets out his concerns at Bismarck's policies and calls for the National Liberals to keep campaigning against protectionist tariffs.

The Bismarck System is developing at a frightening pace, just as I have always feared. Universal conscription, unreasonable and exorbitant indirect taxes, a disciplined and slighted Reichstag, and public opinion that has been tainted by the conflict of all material interests and thereby rendered powerless – this is indeed politics based on the powerlessness of the peoples, the demise of any constitutional liberal development, and at the same time a terrible threat to the entire Reich and the young Kaiserdom. As things stand, does the National Liberal Party and its current politics, its current program, and its current structure present a suitable instrument to counter such dangers? Are we not being led deeper into the quagmire with every step? Isn't pure opposition becoming a duty? These questions have continued to torment me amidst the pressure of difficult business. On the morning of the second Christmas holiday [26 December], I was visited by Lasker. As soon as he started talking, it was clear that he was plagued by the very same questions. We arranged a gathering for New Year's Eve. The meeting consisted of Benda, Rickert, Bamberger, Lasker, and myself. Braun had been invited but did not attend. The draft legislation regarding the Reichstag discipline was not yet known in detail. We agreed that Lasker should draft a short programme: a.) Resistance to the arbitrary domestic Bismarck policies that rush everything and throw everything into a state of confusion. b.) Only the needs of the Reich can determine the extent to which indirect taxes are raised, i.e. only to replace state contributions. c.) No import duties may be imposed on essential commodities, grain or livestock. For this reason and others, [there is] opposition to the letter dated 15 December.

SOURCE

The Liberal Secessionists Declaration of 30 August 1880, in which the Liberals, who were leaving the National Liberals to form the Liberal Union Party, set out the reasons for their division.

Over the past two years, we have become ever more certain that, in the face of fundamentally altered circumstances, the National Liberal Party is no longer driven by the unity of political attitudes that was once the sole basis of its power and influence. Based on this conviction, the undersigned hereby tender their resignation from the National Liberal Party. The effectiveness of a truly constitutional system, which the German liberal party has relentlessly pursued since its inception, is the only way to ensure a stable path for the smooth and ongoing development of our national unity, which is rooted in the Kaiser and the imperial constitution. We believe that the essential conditions to achieve our goal are these: that the liberal party unite over central issues and that the confusing and gruelling struggles between different liberal factions come to an end. It is the shared responsibility of the entire liberal party to firmly resist the retrogressive movement and adhere to our hard-won political liberties. Economic freedom is closely linked to political liberty, and the long-term material welfare of the nation is guaranteed by the solid foundation that economic freedom provides. Imperial tax reform can only move forward by safeguarding constitutional rights while relinquishing the people from all unnecessary burdens and removing such indirect taxes and duties, which primarily disadvantage the poorer classes by shifting the tax burden towards them. For Germany, more so than any other country, **ecclesiastical** and religious freedom is the fundamental condition for internal peace. That freedom, however, must be guaranteed and regulated through independent constitutional legislation, the implementation of which should remain independent of ulterior political motives. **Inalienable** constitutional rights must be preserved and schools must not be placed under the authority of the church. We are prepared to come to an agreement on this basis. However, speaking as members of the liberal party, these will remain the leading views for us under any circumstances.

KEY TERMS

Ecclesiastical
Relating to the Church.

Inalienable
Something that cannot be altered or taken away.

ACTIVITY
KNOWLEDGE CHECK

1 In Source 6, what are Forckenbeck's major concerns with Bismarck's political activities?

2 What does Source 6 demonstrate about the confusion in the National Liberal Party about how to deal with Bismarck's policies?

3 What was Forckenbeck's suggestion on how the National Liberals should deal with Bismarck's political policies?

4 Using Source 7 and your reading of this chapter so far, determine to what extent Forckenbeck was successful in convincing the National Liberal Party to follow his three suggestions.

5 After reading Source 7, summarise the reasons why the Liberal Union Party split with the National Liberals.

The *Kulturkampf*

The *Kulturkampf* ('struggle for civilisation') was the name given to the anti-Catholic legislation pursued by Bismarck and the National Liberals in the early part of the 1870s.

The Catholic Church and the new German constitution

In 1864, the Catholic Church in Rome had denounced the values of liberalism and secularism in the Syllabus of Errors. In 1870, the Church made the Declaration of Papal Infallibility, which declared that the pope's spiritual powers had authority over secular power in respect to the political allegiance of Catholics. The National Liberals opposed both these declarations; firstly because the Catholic Church opposed the very ideology the party was built upon, and secondly because the pope's declaration in 1870 would undermine the hoped-for unity of the German nation, ultimately formed in 1871. If one-third of Germany's population was more loyal to the pope and the Catholic Church in Rome than to the German nation, this was clearly a threat to the national unity that the National Liberals and Bismarck were dedicated to creating. Furthermore, the Centre Party, which represented the interests of German Catholics, opposed the constitution of the German state when it was founded in 1871. The Centre Party had been formed in 1870 and aimed to protect the rights of the Catholic minority in Germany, who they believed could be under threat given the considerable Protestant majority in the new Germany. The rights of Catholics had been protected in Prussia by the constitution of 1850, and the Centre Party fought to ensure that those rights were not undermined by the new German constitution of 1871. In the old German Confederation formed in 1815, which included Austria, just over half of the population had been Catholic. However, with the exclusion of Austria after its defeat by Prussia in 1866, the Catholic population was now the minority. The Centre Party thus focused on protecting Catholic rights despite this change. The Centre Party called for the continuing independence of Church institutions and opposed any form of secularisation in areas such as education and marriage. While not opposed to German unification, they argued for a less centralised Germany that gave greater autonomy to the German states, an idea directly opposed to the type of unified Germany envisioned by the National Liberals.

EXTEND YOUR KNOWLEDGE

The Syllabus of Errors (1864) and the Declaration of Papal Infallibility (1870)
These were key statements published by the Vatican in 1864 and 1870. The Syllabus of Errors set out the Catholic Church's stance on various philosophical and political questions. It was seen at the time as a reaction against modernism and the general European movement away from Catholic monarchies to secular democracy. The Declaration of Papal Infallibility, published in 1870, asserted that the pope's moral teachings were to be the guiding principle for all Catholics, and took precedence over the values and education put forward by the state where Catholics were residing. This was a critical doctrine that was resented by many progressive, liberal leaders throughout Europe, who believed in a democratic state governed by secular, liberal values. This also called Catholic loyalty into question: if there were a difference between the state's values and Catholic values, whom would Catholics have true loyalty to? For both the National Liberals and Bismarck, the pope's declaration was a challenge to German unity, as it meant that Catholics could never have full allegiance to Germany, as their first allegiance was to the pope.

Bismarck's concerns about the Centre Party

For Bismarck, however, the major concern with the Centre Party was its support not only for German-speaking Catholics, but also for those Catholic non-German ethnic groups within Germany, such as the Catholic Polish and the French of Alsace and Lorraine. Bismarck was already suspicious of the Catholic population, given that most Catholics had sided with Austria against Prussia in the war of 1866. Now the Church supported Polish language teaching and the autonomous desires of Alsace and Lorraine, as well as calling for a war against Germany's ally Italy, in order to help the pope regain the lands lost when Italy unified as a nation in c1870. This only reinforced Bismarck's belief that Catholics were an outside group, antagonistic to Prussia and the formation of the new German Reich. The Church's encouragement of Polish students to continue speaking Polish was particularly galling to Bismarck.

The suppression of all other languages except German was a key aspect of Bismarck's policy to unify all the German people and weaken non-German identities within the Reich. The speaking of Polish meant that this ethnic group retained a separate identity and maintained a Polish nationalism that was disconnected from the German nationalism that the German government was promoting in schools. For Bismarck, it was crucial for Germany's stability that Polish youth were 'Germanised' and came to see their loyalty as belonging to Germany; the Church's promotion of the Polish language was therefore a serious obstacle to this policy. Additionally, the fact that the Centre Party was fast becoming the main party for those groups that opposed the German state was a serious concern for the Chancellor. Not only Poles and Alsace-Lorrainers, but also Danish and Hanoverian Germans were growing in their support for the Centre Party. These non-Catholic minorities had come to view the Centre Party as the main political voice for those who opposed the manner in which Germany had been unified under Prussian dominance. To Bismarck, all these factors, along with the pope's claims of sovereignty over German Catholics, made German Catholic politicians and priests a dangerous 'enemy to the empire' or *Reichsfeinde*. Bismarck and the National Liberals shared this point of view, both seeing the Centre Party and the Catholic Church as an impediment to the development of a unified, patriotic German nation. For the liberals, the quarrel was also intellectual, given the Church's opposition to the development of liberal values and education.

The *Kulturkampf*: the campaign against Catholic institutions and power

Bismarck initially attempted to persuade the Vatican to withdraw its support for the Centre Party, but this was rejected. Subsequently, Bismarck, with the support of the National Liberals, launched a campaign against Catholic institutions and power within Germany. Known as the *Kulturkampf*, it began with the establishment of laws allowing state authorities to inspect Catholic schools and banning the Jesuit priestly order from Germany. In 1873, these laws were followed by the Prussia May Laws, which set out a range of laws establishing state control over the Catholic Church in Germany. The state would have power over the education and appointment of priests. However, these policies failed to achieve their goals, so a further wave of even more repressive measures was carried out, with Church property seized, clergy not appointed by the German state expelled from Germany, and the introduction of the so-called 'Bread-Basket Law', which withdrew financial support from any priest who did not publically declare his support for the German state. By 1879, 1,800 priests had been either jailed or exiled from Germany, and the German state had seized Church property worth 16 million Reichsmarks. Violence had also erupted, as the army was called upon to break up Catholic protests against the *Kulturkampf* measures.

Despite the harsh measures, the *Kulturkampf* failed to achieve its goals. Instead, the persecution actually reinforced Catholic separation from the German state. The attack by the German state against the Catholic minority only strengthened Catholic support for the Centre Party, which they felt was the best means of defending Catholic rights. The Centre Party became one of the few parties to draw voters from across Germany's divided classes, gaining votes from bankers, peasants, landowners and workers, for example, drawn together by their Catholic faith and feelings of persecution. During the *Kulturkampf*, the Centre Party vote increased from 18.6 percent in 1871 to 27.9 percent in 1874, and by 1878 they were the equal biggest party in the Reichstag, with the same share of the vote as the National Liberals. The *Kulturkampf* also had the effect of ostracising the German Catholic population, who became more defensive and removed from wider German culture. Being Catholic became a considerable issue in terms of finding employment, particularly in the civil service, and there were very few Catholics among Germany's business and financial leaders. In terms of education, the Catholic population was further disadvantaged, with Protestant males 50 percent more likely to go to university.

By 1879, the *Kulturkampf* had essentially ended, as Bismarck no longer found it politically helpful. As discussed previously, Bismarck was moving against the National Liberals by the late 1870s and thus needed the support of the Centre Party to push through protectionist policies in the Reichstag. Furthermore, Pope Pius IX, who had strongly supported the Centre Party, died in 1878 and was replaced by Leo XIII. This new pope was much more willing to talk with the German government and find areas of compromise between the Church and the state. The Prussian Conservatives and the royal family also opposed the *Kulturkampf*. For the Kaiser, the Church's opposition to the secularisation of society and the weakening of religion's influence was something he supported. Although quite prejudiced against Catholicism, many Junkers also believed, along with the Kaiser, that religion was an important force against the values of liberalism they opposed; whether that religion was Catholic or Protestant did not particularly matter. Therefore, the push for protectionist policies, alongside the ending of the *Kulturkampf* by the end of the 1870s was, for Bismarck, also an attempt to regain the support of the Kaiser and the Junkers.

Over time, German Catholics became more assimilated within the German nation. However, the feelings of persecution enforced by the *Kulturkampf* were to leave a lasting impact on relations between the Catholic and Protestant denominations throughout the period of the Kaiserreich.

SOURCE 8

This cartoon, 'The Berlin Bullfighter', published in *Punch* on 17 April 1875, depicts Bismarck subduing the raging bull of Catholicism. Note the papal hat worn by the bull.

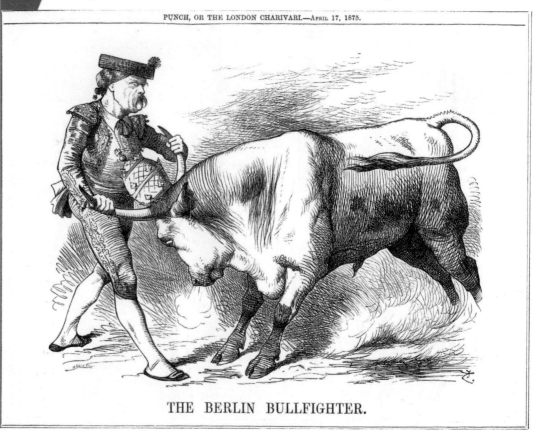

PUNCH, OR THE LONDON CHARIVARI.—April 17, 1875.

THE BERLIN BULLFIGHTER.

SOURCE 9

Eduard Husgen was a leading Catholic writer and campaigner. In 1871, he was dismissed from judicial service in Prussia due to his links with the Centre Party's newspaper. Here, writing in 1907, he describes some of the motivations and impacts of the *Kulturkampf*.

KEY TERM

Ultramontane
Where supreme papal authority is recommended in matters of discipline and faith.

That which we refer to as the *Kulturkampf* involved the mobilisation of sectarian opposition to Catholicism, the marshalling of state power at upper and lower levels, and the use of every resource that education and property had to offer against anything that was Catholic in name or even remotely associated with the Catholic Church. In those days, it hovered over our fatherland like a poisonous atmosphere, like a form of disease. Catholic and enemy of the Empire; Catholic and unpatriotic; **ultramontane** and anti-patriotic; supporter of the Centre Party and opponent of cultural aspiration of any kind – according to popular belief, these terms could be used interchangeably. It was good form, as it were, to make it clear to Catholics that they were politically and socially inferior and deny them equality in both the public and private sphere. As Reichstag representative Hanel announced in parliament on January 12, 1882, when people started to feel ashamed as a result of the situation, 'engaging in the *Kulturkampf* was necessary, correct, and patriotic, and even a requirement if one were to be accepted in high society. One simply had to follow with blind determination each and every demand raised by the government and the Conservatives regarding Church legislation, or run the risk of seeming somewhat indecent, at least from a political perspective.' It should be noted, however, that sometimes the Progressives and National Liberals were even worse than the Conservatives. Sectarian and political contrasts left a gaping rift running through society, dividing families and breeding discord. As a matter of fact, any Catholic with steadfast convictions was regarded as a second-class citizen. Indeed, even Catholic men who were not affiliated with the Centre Party and identified instead with its political opponents were not taken seriously and were met with a certain degree of mistrust, unless they distinguished themselves by showing particular enthusiasm in the battle against their co-religionists.

ACTIVITY
KNOWLEDGE CHECK

1 What image does the cartoon (Source 8) give of Bismarck in his fight with the Catholic Church?

2 What were the key reasons for the *Kulturkampf*?

3 How successful was Bismarck in achieving the political aims of the *Kulturkampf*?

4 To what extent does the cartoon (Source 8) represent the reality of the *Kulturkampf* and Bismarck's political battle with the Catholic Church?

A Level Exam-Style Question Section A

Study Source 9 before you answer this question.

Assess the value of Source 9 for revealing the reasons for the *Kulturkampf* and its effects on German Catholics.

Explain your answer, using the source, the information given about its origin and your own knowledge about the historical context. (20 marks)

Tip
For this question you will need to weigh up the origin of the source. The fact that the author was a victim of the Kulturkampf *is obviously important. However, that does not mean that the perspective of the author is subjective or an exaggeration. Think about what information the source provides about the* Kulturkampf *and then consider your own knowledge in order to evaluate the value of the source when studying the* Kulturkampf *and its effects.*

The appeal to nationalism to achieve unity

As you have already read, despite the creation of the German nation in 1871, regional, political and religious divisions, which undermined attempts to forge a patriotic allegiance that united all Germans in their allegiance to the state, persisted. As discussed previously, one of the key problems was the lack of symbols that could unite the German people: there was no national flag, no national anthem and the national holiday that celebrated Germany's defeat of France at the Battle of Sedan in 1870 was opposed by many within German society. Southern states did not play a large role in the Battle of Sedan and preferred to celebrate the victories over France that they contributed to. Additionally, many socialist politicians viewed the holiday as a celebration of Prussian militarism and refused to recognise the holiday. Thus, the aim to create a German nationalism became a key government aim. Parliament introduced policies that sought to create a national *reichsdeutsche* identity. Primary schools, high schools and universities were required to teach nationalism as a subject, and students were encouraged to see 1871 as the fulfilment of a historical destiny that led to the formation of the great, unified Germany. The school curriculum focused considerably on instilling the values of loyalty to the Kaiser and obedience to the Kaiserreich. Regular street processions celebrating great national victories were held, and student textbooks proclaimed the glory of the Kaiser. There was a strong, conscious effort in government policy to create a **homogeneous** nation which shared the same nationalist values. Running parallel to this educational policy, Bismarck believed in a strong policy of cultural nationalism towards minority groups such as the Polish in order to 'Germanise' them. Schools enforced the teaching of German over Polish or French, for instance, and Bismarck believed that only by enforcing this German cultural identity could the nation consolidate its empire and ensure that it was not under threat from external enemies. From the late 1870s, this policy was accelerated even further, with the expulsion of foreign Poles and Jews from Germany, and the use of the institutions of education and the military to enforce a German identity on ethnic minority areas, particularly in terms of German Poles.

KEY TERM

Homogeneous
Consisting of parts that are the same or uniform in their composition.

SOURCE 10

Children's board game from the Kaiserreich that allowed German children to role-play as Prussia in their defeat of Austria in 1866.

The promotion of a distinct German nationalism not only had the effect of integrating Germans into the new nation, it also served an important domestic political role for Bismarck. Even before 1871, he had argued that nationalism could be used to mobilise public opinion in favour of government policy, and after unification he frequently engaged the threat of *Reichsfeinde* (enemies of the Empire) to rally the support of the German people. These enemies could be outside of the German state, such as France, or within the German state itself, such as the Catholic Church, as seen previously in this chapter. The targeting of alleged enemies of Germany was intended to achieve two key goals: firstly, the greater national integration of the German people, united by their patriotic hatred and fear of this enemy and, secondly, to divert attention to this supposed threat and away from the call for greater democratic reform in the German political system. In 1878, for example, Bismarck used two assassination attempts on Wilhelm I to declare that socialism was a threat to the German nation. This was despite the fact that the attempted assassins had no connection with socialism or the SPD. Anti-socialist legislation was introduced that prohibited socialist meetings and gave the police the power to randomly search, arrest and exile socialist politicians. The law was called 'the Law for Combating the Criminal Aims of Social Democracy', and the fear of this internal enemy, determined to pursue revolution within Germany, was a key means of attempting to bind the middle classes together in their support for the conservative institutions of the German state. Through Bismarck's policies, Catholics (who were seen as loyal to the pope) and socialists (seen as more loyal to the international ideology of Communism) were thus deemed as threats to the unity of the German nation, as they did not share the nationalist goals and loyalty to the Kaiser and Germany believed in by the majority of Germans.

While Bismarck was successful in encouraging national unity through an appeal to nationalism, as well as utilising this for political gain, the more worrying aspect was that this national identity was considerably based around militaristic ideals, fear of external and internal enemies, and strongly promoted the superiority of German culture. Over the next 20 years, this form of nationalism was to take on a more aggressive character and was one of the key factors fuelling German military aggression in the 20th century.

SOURCE 11

Kaiser Wilhelm I welcomes Chancellor Bismarck during the German national day of Sedan, in Berlin in September 1873, to commemorate Germany's victory over France that led to German unification.

Kaiser Wilhelm I. begrüßt den Fürsten Bismarck bei Einweihung der Siegesfäule in Berlin am 2. September 1873. (Text S. 390.)
Nach einer Skizze von R. Warthmüller gezeichnet von C. Gerlach.

SOURCE
12
Florentine Gebhardt, in *Blätter aus dem Lebensbilderbuch* (Pages from Life's Picture Book) (1930), describes her days as a primary school student, celebrating Germany's national day of Sedan.

As a garrison town, Crossen was twice as patriotic and royalist as other towns. Even the **frugal** town authorities wanted to mark Sedan Day with the celebrations it deserved, probably digging a little deeper into the town's pockets than they did on other occasions. Each citizen contributed as much as he could. It goes without saying that every house was bedecked with black-white-red flags, which were left over from the arrival of the troops in 1871, and the streets where the afternoon parade would take place were decorated with leaf garlands, which were either hung across the streets or on individual houses. Naturally, we children were up much earlier than usual, even though the school celebration was not due to start until 9 or 10am. In the town's secondary schools, the celebration took place in the assembly hall, first for the upper classes of the boys' school and then for those of the girls' school. The elementary schools probably only had class celebrations; I cannot say for certain. Simply being allowed to set foot in the hallowed ground of the assembly hall, which usually remained locked, made it a grand occasion. I gazed at the large glass cabinets along the walls in shy admiration, taking in the stuffed animals (teaching aids for the boys' school) and the bust of the Kaiser behind them. With a feeling of festive anticipation, I took my place on the bench between my schoolmates – but not without first casting a furtive glance to see whether they, like me, were in their Sunday best. In the morning, I had to wear my woollen Sunday dress; the white dress was saved for the outing. Since I was not involved in the ceremony, there was no need to don my Sunday white. Then the event itself got underway. One of the teachers delivered the celebratory speech, which we did not pay much attention to; a few chosen pupils sang their well-rehearsed songs; and an even more select few recited their poems. The envious non-elect were harsh in their criticism – well, any of us could have done that! After the cheer for the Kaiser and the [Prussian] national anthem marked the end of the celebration, we were dismissed with the reminder to reassemble in the schoolyard at 1.30pm.

ACTIVITY
KNOWLEDGE CHECK

1 How is German nationalism promoted in the painting showing the national day of Sedan (Source 11)?

2 How is German nationalism encouraged through the board game shown in Source 10?

3 Looking at Source 12, in what way was education used to promote German nationalism? List all the ways in which German nationalism was promoted among German youth.

4 Using Sources 10 to 12, summarise the key aspects of German nationalism that were officially promoted between 1871 and 1879.

A Level Exam-Style Question Section B

How accurate is it to say that Germany achieved national unity between 1871 and 1879? (20 marks)

Tip
This is a difficult question that asks you first to consider how you could judge national unity. Think about the divisions in Germany at the start of 1871 and how the government tried to overcome them. In what ways could you say Germany was a more united people in 1879 than when the country first formed in 1871? What were the remaining divisions and issues? How extensive was both the unity and disunity within Germany?

The War in Sight crisis

The War in Sight crisis of 1875 had its roots in both the *Kulturkampf* and Bismarck's concern with the actions of Germany's old enemy, France. By 1875, France had recovered considerably from its defeat by Germany in 1871, It had also seen the overthrow of a more peaceful republican government and the implementation of a new royalist government, which aimed to increase its prestige amongst the French population through an aggressive foreign policy. Bismarck was concerned at this more assertive France and believed that, being a Catholic country, France might try to encourage Catholic opposition within Germany. The French government had done nothing to stop French Catholic bishops from attacking the *Kulturkampf* policy, and in 1874, Bismarck informed the French government that there would be a threat to peace in Europe if the French government sided with the Vatican against German domestic policy.

There was also growing concern in the German military at the French Army Organisation Law of 1873, which increased the number of French infantry battalions from three to four. The government estimated that by 1878, France would have around 800,000 trained men it could call on in case of military conflict, an increase of around 80,000. The German military leader, Helmuth von Moltke, even considered that the growth of the French military strength might force Germany to take steps towards a preventative war; that is, attacking France first, before it had the means to attack Germany. Bismarck was not a supporter of Moltke's belief in preventative war, but he was concerned about the actions of the French government. Bismarck believed that the best way to challenge France was to build pressure on its government. On 5 April 1875, the German newspaper *Kölnische Zeitung*, with Bismarck's encouragement, published an article that described a fearful picture of Catholic conspiracy, incorporating the French and Austrian governments, aimed against Germany. This was followed, on 9 April, by an article in the popular German newspaper *The Berliner Post*, which asked 'Is War in Sight?' The article made clear to the German public that many within the German government believed that it was. Bismarck had organised this press campaign to try to put pressure on France.

The *Berlin Post* and *Kölnische Zeitung* articles caused considerable alarm both in Germany and in the major European capitals. This was followed by German diplomatic action that encouraged the idea that Germany was seriously considering a preventative war against France. Moltke's report on French military expansion was sent to the British government, and a German diplomat in Russia told the French ambassador in Berlin that many Reichstag politicians were seriously considering a preventative war. The Russian, French and British governments were considerably alarmed by the possibility of war. The Tsar of Russia visited Germany, with the support of the British government and Queen Victoria, for private talks with the German Kaiser. On leaving the talks, the Russian Chancellor Alexander Gorchakov informed the press that he believed peace had now been assured. The pressure from Russia and Britain forced Bismarck to back down in his attacks on France. Bismarck, however, was furious with Gorchakov, believing that Russian influence had undermined his policy against France. Bismarck was also angry at Britain's interference in German affairs. Bismarck felt he had been humiliated and undermined by Russian actions, and by the fact that the direction of German policy had been set by private discussions between the Kaiser and Tsar, which he, as Chancellor, had been excluded from. The War in Sight crisis also demonstrated the influence of the German military on governmental policy, as well as the problems with Bismarck's use of the press to mount political campaigns.

The crisis did lead to Bismarck being more careful in his rhetoric towards France. Following the crisis, he stopped speaking about anti-German Catholic conspiracies and instead concentrated on diplomatic concerns. Critically for Germany, though, in 1873, Germany had made an alliance with Russia and Austro-Hungary, known as the Three Emperors League. The War in Sight crisis weakened the league by damaging Russian/German relations, and subsequently encouraging a growing unease in Europe towards the diplomatic goals of the new German nation.

EXTEND YOUR KNOWLEDGE

Bismarck's foreign policy and the Three Emperors League

Bismarck's foreign policy between 1871 and 1879 focused on consolidating the German empire. In this regard he made it clear that, unlike other European powers, Germany had no interest in imperial expansion of overseas territories. Instead, his key focus was to engage in alliances and agreements with other European powers that would maintain stability in Europe (thus allowing Germany to continue to develop economically without interruption), ensure German strength as a power in Europe and maintain the diplomatic isolation of Germany's main enemy, France. One of the key aspects of this was the Three Emperors League, a diplomatic treaty between Germany, Russia and Austro-Hungary that guaranteed that they would help each other if they were attacked by a fourth power. This ensured that France could not form an alliance with Russia or Austro-Hungary, thereby highlighting its military and diplomatic isolation. In this way, the War in Sight crisis was a blow to Bismarck's foreign policy, as it weakened the relationship between Germany and Russia and made European powers more concerned with Germany's foreign policy aims: two key aspects that Bismarck's foreign policy aimed to avoid.

EXTRACT

1 A.J.P. Taylor, in *Bismarck: The Man and the Statesman* (1955), assesses the consequences of the War in Sight crisis for Bismarck.

Bismarck gave way [to Russian and British pressure] with the masterly grace which he knew how to use when necessary. The crisis turned out to be a false alarm, even helped to improve Franco-German relations. It left only a lasting estrangement between Bismarck and Gorchakov. Bismarck did not forgive the Russian interference and alleged that Gorchakov had announced to his ambassadors: 'Peace is now assured.' Gorchakov on his side was not sorry to humiliate the man who had once described himself as Gorchakov's admiring pupil; and he said in private: 'Bismarck is ill because he eats too much and drinks too much and works too much.' Though this was true, Gorchakov like others would have done well to remember that Bismarck, even when ill (or perhaps most when ill) was more formidable than most men when well. The 'war in sight' crisis was a casual episode in Bismarck's policy, and it seemed to leave no mark on domestic affairs.

EXTRACT

2 William Carr puts forward his assessment of the impact of the War in Sight crisis, in *A History of Germany 1815–1985* (1987).

So the 'War in Sight' crisis ended in a defeat for Germany and a diplomatic victory for France. True, Britain and Russia would not have moved a finger to aid France had she attacked Germany, as the new order in Europe suited them perfectly well. More to the point, the crisis made it plain that these powers would not allow Germany to destroy France and become absolute master of Europe. Bismarck was angered by the turn of events. He could not bear to be outmanoeuvred and never forgave Gorchakov for his part in the *démarche* [diplomatic interference], in fact his enmity towards the Russian chancellor probably had permanent effects on his attitude to Russia. The whole crisis brought home forcibly the real danger of a war on two fronts and undoubtedly impressed him with the need for the utmost caution in the future.

 THINKING HISTORICALLY   Evidence (6c)

Comparing and evaluating historians' arguments

Good history is not about being right (in the sense of gaining definitive access to the truth about the past). Good history is well-argued and grounds the claims that it makes about the past in credible ways. In other words, we can have as many acceptable accounts of the past as there are well-argued answers to historical questions.

Read Extracts 1 and 2, on the consequences of the War in Sight crisis, and then answer the following questions.

1 Compare the two accounts and identify factual statements or claims that they both agree upon. Make a list of these points.

2 Look carefully at how the historians use language. Do they both use equally cautious language in making their claims, or is one more confident and assertive than the other? What effect does this have on their portrayals of Bismarck?

3 Extract 1 is from a biography of Otto von Bismarck, while Extract 2 is about the overall history of Germany. How does this change your reading of each source on the War in Sight crisis?

4 How does the purpose of the text shape the historians' arguments? Are both of the historical accounts equally credible or are there reasons to prefer one account to another?

A Level Exam-Style Question Section B

To what extent did Bismarck successfully achieve his political goals in the years 1870–79? (20 marks)

Tip

This question is asking you to establish what Chancellor Bismarck's political goals were between 1870 and 1879, and to then consider how far he went towards achieving them. The question is not simply whether Bismarck achieved these goals or not, but the extent to which he achieved them. This is an important distinction you need to take into account.

ACTIVITY
SUMMARY

1 In the period between 1871 and 1879, what would you consider to be the biggest divisions within Germany following unification?

2 List the ways in which the government attempted to overcome these divisions, then rank these factors in terms of success, i.e. which were the most successful government policies in overcoming German division and which were the least successful?

3 How far would you agree that unified Germany was essentially a state ruled by Prussia between 1871 and 1879? Think about factors that both support and argue against this idea, and then come up with an overall answer.

4 Thinking about this entire chapter, how far do you agree with the statement that 'Despite unifying in 1871, Germany remained a substantially divided nation in the first decade of its existence'?

 WIDER READING

Berghahn, V.R. *Imperial Germany 1871–1918: Economy, Society, Culture and Politics*, Berghahn Books, revised and expanded edition (2005)

Jefferies, M. *Contesting the German Empire 1871–1918*, Blackwell Publishing (2008)

Pulzer, P. *Germany 1870–1945: Politics, State Formation and War*, Oxford University Press (1997)

Retallack, J. (ed.) *Imperial Germany 1871–1918*, Short Oxford History of Germany series, Oxford University Press (2008)

Taylor, A.J.P. *Bismarck: The Man and the Statesman*, Hamish Hamilton (1955)

Williamson, D.G. *Bismarck and Germany 1862–1890*, Longman (1986)

3.4 The birth of democratic Germany, 1917–19

KEY QUESTIONS

- To what extent did the First World War cause political and social division in Germany between 1914 and 1918?
- To what extent did the German Revolution alter the political system between 1918 and 1919?
- To what extent did the foundation of the Weimar Republic in 1919 achieve a new unity for the German nation based on democratic values?

INTRODUCTION

At the onset of the First World War, the German nation appeared to be both politically and socially united in a manner that had not been achieved since its foundation in 1871. The divisions that had been so prominent previously faded away in the patriotic outpouring that dominated the first two years of the war. However, as the war dragged on past 1916, the old fractures in the German system began to raise their heads once again. Worker strikes and class divisions, accentuated by arguments concerning Germany's war aims and heightened by starvation, became more prominent. Anger grew within the Reichstag as the war dragged on, pursued by a military dictatorship that had essentially taken over the running of the country. By August 1918, it was evident that Germany had lost the war. Desperate to offset possible revolution, the military leadership implemented political reforms and finally passed the running of the country onto the Reichstag parties for the first time.

However, the reforms came too late, and the anger and shock at Germany's defeat in November 1918 led to the German Revolution, the eventual abdication of the Kaiser and the end of the political system that had ruled the country since 1871. Its replacement, the Weimar Republic, promised to usher in a new constitution and unify the German people through the liberal values of democracy and freedom. From its beginnings, however, the extremist political forces of both the right and the left opposed it. The decisions made by the first Chancellor, Friedrich Ebert, to deal with the problems the Weimar faced would have serious repercussions that continued to haunt the new Republic throughout its short existence, and still provide exhaustive debate among historians today. The end of the First World War was thus a time of severe upheaval, political renewal, violence and revolution; a tumultuous and unique historical period that would shape the nature of this influential country in the years leading up to the Second World War.

1914 – 4 August: SPD shows support for the war

Kaiser acclaims German unity in speech to the Reichstag

1916 –August: 'Silent Dictatorship' of Hindenburg and Ludendorff established as supreme political power in Germany

1917 – April: 200,000 Berlin workers strike against worsening conditions in Germany

USPD founded by breakaway members of the SPD

United States declares war on Germany and its allies

July: Centre Party leader Erzberger calls for an end to German involvement in First World War

1918 – January: One million workers strike in Germany

March: Treaty of Brest-Litovsk ends war between Germany and Russia

| 1914 | // | 1916 | 1917 | 1918 |

1914 – December: Liebknecht becomes first SPD member to oppose German involvement in First World War

1916–17 – Winter: Turnip Winter – Germany undergoes severe famine

1917 – Bethmann-Hollweg forced to resign as Chancellor and replaced by George Michaelis

October: Radical Communist Bolshevik Party seizes power in Russia

1918 – August: War turns decidedly against Germany

29 September: Ludendorff informs Kaiser Wilhelm II that Germany has lost the war

TO WHAT EXTENT DID THE FIRST WORLD WAR CAUSE POLITICAL AND SOCIAL DIVISION IN GERMANY BETWEEN 1914 AND 1918?

Strains of war, tensions and military dictatorship, 1917

The onset of the First World War in August 1914 brought to an end a long period of peace and economic growth that stretched back to 1871. The start of the war was greeted by great patriotic feeling across German society. Undoubtedly, this was heavily mixed with a high level of anxiety at the economic consequences of the war, as demonstrated by the large numbers of Germans hoarding food or withdrawing savings from banks, but overall the war appeared to have erased many of the acute divisions that still plagued German society. In 1912, the SPD had become the largest party in the Reichstag, a development which the elite of German society viewed with considerable alarm. The Kaiser and his government had been concerned that the SPD might not support the war, so plans to arrest SPD members and close down socialist newspapers were being considered. Instead, the SPD accepted the German Chancellor's assertion that the war was necessary as a German defence against the repressive Tsarist regime of Russia. On 4 August 1914, the SPD voted for war credits (domestic loans to pay for Germany's war).

Across Germany, industrial-, upper-, middle- and working-class Germans were united in their support for the war. Even the Polish population of Germany, which had been seen up to this point as potential enemies of the German nation, were supportive of the Reich's declaration of war. This spiritual and political togetherness that the war created was known as the ***Burgfriede***, the spirit of 1914, by which Germany had supposedly swept away the old divisions emanating from 1871 and had instead forged a new unity founded on patriotic fervour. This was best summed up by the Kaiser's statement after the war credit vote in August: 'I know no parties anymore, only Germans'. Indeed, the *Burgfriede* did remain fairly strong in the first two years of the war, based on a clear belief among the public that the war was progressing

well for Germany. The German High Command, which ensured that only positive news about the war was available in Germany, perpetuated this feeling. This was despite the fact that by 1916 Germany had undergone some significant military failures, particularly on the Western Front.

KEY TERM

Burgfriede
This word was actually a German medieval term that referred to a truce made between warring parties or individuals if they were visiting or staying in a castle at the same time. The term was used during the First World War to signify that, in a similar way, political opponents had now put aside their differences for the defence of Germany against its enemies.

However, by winter 1916, the strains of the war were beginning to reopen the key divisions within German society that were present before 1914. Critically, the division between rural and urban areas of Germany became worse than in the previous period. This was driven by Germany's growing food shortage. Germany was a country reliant on food imports for a third of its overall supply. An Allied naval blockade, combined with the depletion of agricultural workers and the military requisitioning of food, led to rising food prices and growing shortages. Poor government policies accentuated the problem. In 1915, the government had killed 35 percent of the country's pigs in order to save grain, leading to an eventual meat shortage and the high price of meat. The winter of 1916–17 had been particularly cold, resulting in the failure of the potato crop and the so-called '**Turnip Winter**'.

KEY TERM

Turnip Winter
The European winter of 1916–17 was particularly cold, making worse the poor conditions both soldiers and civilians were suffering due to the First World War. In Germany there were even greater issues with food, as the potato crop, a main staple of the German diet, was destroyed by poor autumn weather in 1916. The failure of the potato crop, combined with the Allied blockade, meant that Germans were forced to rely on turnips for their main food source. The lack of food, combined with the freezing winter, contributed to starvation and mounting opposition to the war.

1918 – 3 October: Prince Max of Baden becomes Chancellor with a government appointed from Reichstag members for first time

29 October: Kiel Mutiny breaks out

7 November: Socialists seize power in Bavaria and declare it an independent Socialist Republic

1919 – January: Attempted Communist revolution crushed by Freikorps

Constituent assembly elections held with centre democratic parties successful

April: Freikorps crushes Communist Republic in Bavaria

1918

1919

1918 – 9 November: Prince Max announces abdication of Kaiser and hands power to SPD leader Friedrich Ebert

10 November: SPD/USPD coalition forms the new government of Germany

1919 – June: German government signs Versailles Treaty and is forced to accept Article 231, asserting German guilt for First World War

11 August: New Weimar Constitution passed by assembly

SOURCE
1   Cheering crowds in Berlin after war has been declared against Russia on 1 August 1914.

ACTIVITY
KNOWLEDGE CHECK

1 What does Source 1 possibly reveal about the feeling towards war in Germany in 1914?

2 In what way does Source 1 support the assertion that the *Burgfriede* was widely supported in 1914?

3 In what ways should we be careful about using Source 1 to make generalised arguments about the feeling in Germany after war was declared in 1914?

The food shortages brought about a growing anger that split rural and urban areas of Germany. Starving urban populations believed that rural areas were hoarding food and were able to live off their own animals and produce, and thus were immune to the problems facing the cities. Rural populations, on the other hand, were angered by the shortages of labour they faced and the growing prices associated with farming, as well as the criticism from Germans in the cities and the government's searches of farms for possible hidden food.

Morale was highly affected by the lack of food, as poor diet led to a considerable growth in malnourishment, disease and rising mortality rates among the very young and elderly of German society. During the First World War, 750,000 Germans died of diseases related to starvation. Protests and riots over the desperate situation started to take place, and resentment, not just between rural and urban areas, but also between the classes (as the working class and *Mittelstand* (see Chapter 1, page 17) believed the upper classes had greater access to the black market), threatened the *Burgfriede*. The demand for better wages that would enable working-class Germans to purchase food was a key factor in the mounting strikes that began in 1916. By April 1917, 200,000 workers were on strike in Berlin, with one of the key concerns relating to further bread rationing. Starvation, combined with the war itself, weakened the 'spirit of 1914'. German casualties had reached 2.5 million by 1917 and there appeared to be no end in sight. The continuation of the war promised little more than further starvation and increasing demands on the German workers. The fabric of German society, which had been considerably divided before 1914, was becoming even more fractured by 1917.

Workers in the city resented the growing controls and demands placed on them, as well as government inaction over the desperate shortage of food. Those living in rural areas were angered by price controls that, combined with the lack of agricultural workers, restricted their ability to make a living. The focus on mass industrial production and the incentives provided to big business threatened the small business artisans of the *Mittelstand*, while the middle class found their status in German society threatened by the war, as wages stagnated, servants became harder to find, and savings invested in rent or war bonds declined as the war progressed. Many within these differing classes, however, shared a strong feeling of resentment and anger towards the Prussian elite. The Prussian elite enjoyed taxation privileges up until 1916, and their ability to use their status to acquire food not available to average Germans contradicted the idea that the German people were linked by their shared suffering in the war effort.

By 1917, the belief that all of German society was making the same sacrifices for the war effort, a key concept sustaining the *Burgfriede*, had essentially collapsed. Many Germans were beginning to question whether the war was even worth continuing. This doubt was accentuated, in turn, by the political situation that had essentially turned the running of government over to the German military. The military had been granted wider powers over government administration at the start of the First World War and played a central role in both social and economic mobilisation. The Kaiser's lack of military understanding had effectively led to him being ignored by the military. Considerable pressure was placed on the chancellor Bethmann-Hollweg to allow the German military command to pursue the war in any way it saw fit. From August 1916, Germany was effectively run by a military dictatorship, and the anger and resentment from many Germans that the war was simply being continued to fulfil the wishes of the Prussian military elite grew to a crisis point by 1917.

SOURCE 2

Paul von Hindenburg, in a letter to Chancellor Bethmann-Hollweg on 27 September 1916, sets out his concerns regarding lack of food for workers in Germany.

Your Excellency knows what tremendous tasks face our munition industry if a successful result of the war is to be attained. The decisive factor is the solution of the labour problem, not only as regards the numbers of workpeople, but specially as regards the provision of ample food to enable each individual to put forth his maximum effort... it does not seem to me to be sufficiently recognised everywhere among the officials that the existence or non-existence of our people and Empire is at stake... It is impossible for our working people to maintain their full strength if they do not succeed in obtaining a sufficient supply of fat, allotted to them on a proper basis. I beg your Excellency most urgently to impress upon all Federal Governments, administrative and communal authorities, the seriousness of the situation, and to demand that they shall use every means to provide sufficient nourishment for our munition workers, and unite all leading men of all parties as leaders of the Army at home behind the plough and the lathe to work together and arouse the *furor Teutonicus* (German fury) among the tillers of the soil as well as among the townspeople and the munition workers.

SOURCE 3

The Portuguese Ambassador in Berlin discusses his observations of Germany in 1916 in a report to the Portuguese government.

The German people are feeling the pinch of the war. The lack of butter, bread and other necessary commodities is severely felt. But the people are far too disciplined to do more than grumble, for a long time to come. The result of the war is not in doubt, but the Allies must be prepared for a protracted and sullen resistance on the part of Germany, and ought not to underestimate the difficulty of wearing down the spirit of a people, which, after all is profoundly patriotic and schooled to accept with fatalistic resignation the decisions of its Government. The word 'fatalism' best expresses the mood of Germany today. Warlike enthusiasm has gone. Hope of a sweeping victory has departed, but nothing justifies the supposition that the German masses are likely to revolt against the authorities for many a long day. The allies must therefore redouble their efforts to render the blockade increasingly stringent and make up their minds to the fact that, though half beaten, Germany is far from recognising in practice the hopelessness of her plight.

ACTIVITY
KNOWLEDGE CHECK

1 What impression do Sources 2 and 3 give of Germany at the end of 1916?

2 How far do Sources 2 and 3 agree with each other? Are there any key differences or similarities?

3 Using your own studies on Germany in 1916, how far would you say that Sources 2 and 3 provide an accurate depiction of the situation facing the country at this time?

The roles of Hindenburg and Ludendorff

The roles of Paul von Hindenburg and Erich Ludendorff were critical during the First World War. From August 1916 up to the end of the war in 1918, they essentially ruled Germany in the so-called 'silent dictatorship'. After the failure of the German offensive at Verdun, where German losses had reached 200,000 by May 1916, Chancellor Bethmann-Hollweg made the decision to replace the German Chief of the General Staff Erich von Falkenhayn. Bethmann-Hollweg chose Paul von Hindenburg as his replacement.

Hindenburg had been the commander of the German troops during the Battle of Tannenberg in 1914, when the German army had completely destroyed the Russian Second Army. This victory had made him and his second-in-command, Erich Ludendorff, heroes with the German people, and Bethmann-Hollweg hoped he could use this acclaim, and the widespread respect for Hindenburg held by many of Germany's politicians, to help bring about a more united support for Germany's war effort. The decision instead turned out to be a fateful one for Bethmann-Hollweg: both he and the Kaiser were essentially sidelined, as Hindenburg and Ludendorff established complete supremacy over German policy during the war. The Kaiser was no longer consulted on military matters and Bethmann-Hollweg was forced to accept Hindenburg's and Ludendorff's decisions, due to the fact that Ludendorff simply threatened to resign if their policies were not followed. The popularity and support for Hindenburg and Ludendorff meant that the Chancellor could not risk the two military leaders stepping down. In this way, the German political system that had existed from 1871 was essentially ended, as the country came under an unofficial military dictatorship.

Hindenburg and Ludendorff set the economic, military and political direction of Germany: they established the Auxiliary Service Act (see Chapter 2) that defined the economic basis for Germany's war efforts; they defined the aims of the German war effort; and used their power to dismiss and appoint ministers and chancellors. In military terms, Hindenburg and Ludendorff were determined that the war should go on until Germany achieved a victory that would allow the country to make substantial territorial gains, a *Siegfrieden*. This was known as the **Kreuznach Programme**, and it called for annexation of the Baltic region, all of Poland, Luxembourg, French coal and iron fields, economic dominance and some territorial acquisition of Belgium, control of the Romanian oil fields, as well as territory in the Balkans that would be given to Germany's allies, Austria and Bulgaria. Bethmann-Hollweg believed the plans were unrealistic and unachievable, but he was forced to accept them by the military dictatorship in April 1917.

Ludendorff was also instrumental in forcing through the military strategy of unrestricted submarine warfare, a tactic in which any ship making its way to British port would be targeted. Bethmann-Hollweg was against the policy, believing that it was ineffective and would only help to bring the United States into the war. The German military, however, prevailed, and in spring 1917, unrestricted submarine warfare commenced. The strategy was, as Bethmann-Hollweg predicted, inadequate, and, along with the German attempts to encourage Mexico to attack the United States, uncovered by the British secret service in the **Zimmerman telegram**, was one of the key reasons for the USA's entry into the war against Germany on 6 April 1917. The USA's entry into the First World War in 1917 was also prompted by the sinking of American ships caused by Germany's unrestricted submarine warfare, most notably the *Lusitania* in 1915, which resulted in the death of 128 Americans (1,198 passengers of the *Lusitania* died in total).

Politically, Ludendorff, in particular, exercised considerable power. The Russian Revolution of February 1917 had inspired a renewed call for political reform in Germany, from both left-wing politicians and many within the German working class. Desperate to resist a revolution in Germany, Bethmann-Hollweg had encouraged the Kaiser to promise reforms in his Easter message. The Kaiser duly asserted that at the end of the war he would reform the Prussian electoral system. Bethmann-Hollweg had wanted the Kaiser to make a stronger statement, but Ludendorff had worked to ensure that the Kaiser's promises were vague and insubstantial. Even then, Ludendorff denounced the promises as weakness in the face of the Russian Revolution and continued to fight against any proposal for political reform. In July 1917, he helped force through Bethmann-Hollweg's resignation and forced the Kaiser to appoint George Michaelis, a weak figure who the 'silent dictatorship' could easily control. Reichstag members correctly saw him as simply a puppet chancellor, described by one SPD member as 'the fairy angel tied to the Christmas tree at Christmas for the children's benefit'. When Foreign Secretary Richard von Kuhlman pursued a policy towards Russia that the military

KEY TERMS

Siegfrieden
Essentially translates to 'peace with victory'. This was the concept that Germany could not end the war without making substantial territorial expansion.

Kreuznach Programme
A substantial plan for a massive expansion of German territorial and economic power if Germany had won First World War. The programme was opposed, not only by Bethmann-Hollweg, who believed the goals were unattainable, but also by a growing number of SPD members, who argued that it went far beyond the defensive motivations that supposedly drew Germany into the war in August 1914.

Zimmerman telegram
An offer by the German government, sent by telegram to the Mexican government in January 1917, encouraging the Mexican government to join with Germany if the United States joined the war against Germany. In return, the German military would provide military assistance, enabling Mexico to seize Texas, New Mexico and Arizona. The Foreign Secretary of the German Empire, Arthur Zimmerman, sent it. The message was intercepted and decoded by British intelligence and made public.

considered weak, Hindenburg and Ludendorff forced his resignation by spying on him and spreading malicious stories about his private life to the press.

Overall then, the 'silent dictatorship' exercised substantial power from 1914 to 1918, particularly Ludendorff, who was instrumental in setting the political and military direction of the country. In 1918, it would again be Ludendorff who was key in making the crucial decisions in shaping the new German political structure that would emerge from the end of the war.

Erzberger's Peace Resolution

The breakdown of the *Burgfrieden*, combined with the Russian Revolution of February 1917, the United States' entry into the First World War and the military's insistence on the Kreuznach Programme, culminated in the political crisis of July 1917. The Kaiser's vague promises in the Easter statement had failed to placate the growing anger of the working class, driven by starvation and anger at the progress of the war. Inspired as well by events in Russia, there were strikes involving around 1.5 million workers during 1917. Many within the SPD were also concerned about military conflict with the United States. The war had been justifiable as a defensive necessity against Tsarist aggression, but it was less easy to justify war against the United States, a country whose democratic system a substantial number of SPD members viewed as a political inspiration. Bethmann-Hollweg's acceptance of the Kreuznach Programme angered left-wing Reichstag members. The SPD leadership called on the Chancellor to distance himself from the military's demands for annexation and to introduce firm political reforms. The main call for an end to the war, however, was led by a prominent member of the Centre Party, Matthias Erzberger.

At the start of the war, Erzberger had been a strong supporter of German military action, calling for a massive war of annexation aimed at Belgium, Poland, the Baltic, Ukraine, parts of France, and French and Belgium territories in Africa, along with a huge bill of reparations paid to Germany by its defeated enemies. However, by 1917 he had completely altered his viewpoint. He had conducted his own research into Germany's military tactics and had concluded that unrestricted submarine warfare was a complete failure. He made his own visit to the Eastern front, where he witnessed the progress of the war and discussed the situation with the German military command. By June 1917, he was concerned about the growing strength of Germany's enemies and the continuation of the war with no end in sight. He visited Vienna, where he also learnt that the Austro-Hungarian Emperor believed that they needed to remove their country from the war by the end of 1917. July 1917 was also the period in which the Reichstag needed to discuss the extension of war credits that they had voted through in 1914. Erzberger used these deliberations to make his concerns known to the Reichstag. He made two speeches to the Main Commission of the Reichstag (a select group of politicians investigating whether to recommend the Reichstag vote through further war credits), where he set out detailed criticism of Germany's situation in the war and his doubts about any possible victory that would allow for annexation. He called for a 'Peace Resolution', a peace without victory that would bring the war to an end without the achievement of the Kreuznach Programme. An Inter-Party Committee was set up, with members of the Centre Party, National Liberals, SPD and Progressives agreeing to draft the Peace Resolution. On 19 July 1917, a Peace Resolution was approved in the Reichstag by a substantial majority of 86 votes. The resolution called for a lasting peace, based upon friendly understanding amongst peoples and the eschewing of use of force, territorial annexations and oppression in all its forms.

Erzberger's victory in the Reichstag, however, did not have the effect he had desired. Ludendorff and Hindenburg, while being vehemently opposed to the Peace Resolution, saw it as an excellent opportunity to push for the removal of Bethmann-Hollweg as Chancellor. Using the Chancellor's loss of support in the Reichstag, the military leaders offered their resignations, claiming they could no longer work with Bethmann-Hollweg. The Kaiser explained the situation to the Chancellor, who duly offered his resignation on 13 July. Erzberger had hoped the Chancellor would be replaced with a stronger figure who would be able to control the 'silent dictatorship', but this was naive political optimism. Instead, as discussed previously, Ludendorff and Hindenburg forced the Kaiser to appoint Michaelis, a weak Chancellor whom they could easily control. The military ignored the Reichstag's resolution and forced Michaelis to insist that any discussions on an end to the war with Britain and its Allies had to include annexation of territory for Germany, thus ensuring that any proposed peace talks were doomed to failure. Ludendorff helped to found the new Vaterlandspartei

(Fatherland Party), a mass party of conservative and middle-class nationalists, supported by the military, prominent industrialists and media tycoons, which called for rigid adherence to the Kreuznach Programme. By 1918 it had over a million members, and with the assistance of the army's own propaganda service, it disseminated a strong message against Erzberger's Peace Resolution. Erzberger's goals had essentially failed. Despite the prominence of his resolution, the removal of Bethmann-Hollweg, which he had supported, actually strengthened the military dictatorship and meant that the war simply continued beyond 1917 in order to achieve military goals that were increasingly unachievable.

EXTRACT

1   Gordon A. Craig, in *Germany 1866–1945* (1978), sets out the motivation for Erzberger's Peace Resolution and the involvement of Ludendorff.

Erzberger had been making an independent study of tonnage figures and had reached the conclusion, which the navy rejected while refusing to refute his calculations, that the submarine campaign was a total failure and that Germany must seek a negotiated peace. On 10 June he had a conference with Bauer (Ludendorff's chief political agent), who told him that Ludendorff shared his scepticism of naval claims, and was already planning a winter campaign. He painted a dark picture of Germany's military condition and the growing strength of the enemy and spoke of the necessity of preparing the people psychologically for the sacrifices that were to come... Shaken by Bauer's revelations, Erzberger was also worried by two other matters. He was aware that the new Austrian Emperor Charles and his Foreign Minister, Czernin, were convinced that the Habsburg Empire must have peace before the end of the year and he was also concerned over intimations from the leaders of the Majority Socialists that, when the issue of war credits was posed again in July, they might have to vote negatively in order to protect themselves against their schismatic left wing, which at Easter time had organised an Independent Socialist party dedicated to the speedy termination of the war. Goaded on by these cares, the Centrist leader decided to share them with his parliamentary colleagues and did so with devastating effect. At the beginning of July the Main Committee of the Reichstag began its deliberations on war credits. In two speeches before this body, Erzberger gave a detailed and frightening picture of Germany's military prospects and called upon the Reichstag to pass a resolution expressing readiness to negotiate for a peace without forced annexation.

ACTIVITY
KNOWLEDGE CHECK

1 According to Extract 1, what were the main reasons for Erzberger's call for an end to the war?

2 Why do you think Ludendorff encouraged his political agent Bauer to tell Erzberger the war was not going well for Germany? (Hint: Think about the outcome of Erzberger's actions.)

3 What does this tell us about Ludendorff as a political leader?

Emergence of the Independent Socialist Party

The events of 1917, however, had led not only to growing divisions between the Reichstag and the military, but also to a decisive split in the SPD itself. The first war credit vote in August 1914 had been supported unanimously by the SPD. However, by December 1915, there was growing disenchantment within the SPD at the party's continuing support for the war. In the war credit vote of that month, 20 members of the party rejected the party line and voted against a continuation of war credit. The leader of the SPD, Hugo Haase, had by now changed his views on the war and felt that he could no longer lead the SPD when the majority of members still backed the German war effort. Although they shared Haase's concerns over the military leadership, the majority of the SPD felt that opposition to the war was an act of treason that would hamper any attempts to push for greater political reform once the war was over. Haase subsequently resigned and was replaced by Friedrich Ebert.

In March 1916, the growing tension led to 18 SPD members breaking away from the party and establishing the Labour Fellowship. In April 1917, inspired by events in Russia, the mass strikes in Berlin, growing anger at the progress of the war and the SPD's weakness to stand against the military, the split within the SPD was formalised by the creation of a new party, the Independent Social Democratic Party of Germany (USPD), with Hugo Haase as its first leader. The USPD was also loosely affiliated with the Spartacus League and the Revolutionary Shop Stewards. The Spartacus

League had been founded by former members of the SPD who had been against the war from the very start in 1914, led by Wilhelm Liebknecht and Rosa Luxemburg. They had been imprisoned from 1916 to 1918 for agitating against Germany's involvement in the war. In December 1914, Liebknecht had been the first Reichstag member of the SPD to break ranks and vote against war credits. Luxemburg and Liebknecht were further to the left than Haase and were supporters of the Bolsheviks (the leading Russian Communist party) led by Lenin in Russia. The Revolutionary Shop Stewards was a working-class political group that helped to initiate and support the strikes taking place in Berlin.

The affiliation of the Spartacus League and the Revolutionary Shop Stewards with the USPD helped the new party to become a type of umbrella group for those Germans on the left who had lost faith in the SPD and wanted a stronger push, both for an end to the war and for substantial political reform and possible revolution in Germany. By January 1918, the USPD had around 120,000 members and was instrumental in strikes of that month of around one million workers calling for a better distribution of food and an end to the war. These strikes led to a decisive break with the SPD, who accused the USPD of unpatriotic action that damaged Germany's war efforts at a crucial time. The military leadership asserted that the USPD had stabbed Germany in the back. In reality, the strikes did little to actually affect Germany's military strength, which had deteriorated through the country's struggles since 1914. The USPD's creation and support, however, pointed to growing divisions and tensions within the country, and this concern over the war and the future of Germany was to reach its culmination in 1918.

TO WHAT EXTENT DID THE GERMAN REVOLUTION ALTER THE POLITICAL SYSTEM BETWEEN 1918 AND 1919?

Constitutional reforms from above, 1918

The strikes of January 1918 had clearly demonstrated the precarious nature of Germany's situation in the war. A decisive victory that showed the war had been worth fighting appeared to be the only way the old order could maintain its power and hold back the growing calls for political reform. Problematically, however, this meant fighting on to achieve a victory with annexation in the face of growing protests, as well as the increasing likelihood that these goals were unachievable. However, in October 1917, the German military appeared to have been given one final chance to achieve its military goals and bring the war to a successful conclusion. The radical Communist Bolshevik party, led by Vladimir Lenin, had seized power in Russia and sought to consolidate its power by fulfilling its key promise of bringing Russia's participation in the First World War to an end. The German military was in a strong position on the Eastern front and was able to take advantage of the Bolsheviks' desire to bring an end to the war by insisting on extremely strong terms. On 3 March 1918, the Bolsheviks concluded the **Treaty of Brest-Litovsk** with Germany, ceding Poland, Lithuania and parts of Latvia to Germany and accepting that Estonia and Ukraine would be German protectorates with puppet governments loyal to Germany. The treaty also imposed significant reparation payments on Russia. The treaty was approved by a majority in the Reichstag, with only the USPD voting against it.

Victory now seemed to be possible, and Ludendorff was able to move 52 divisions from the Eastern front to the Western front for one final offensive. Despite initial success, however, by July, the Allies had counter-attacked. Reinforced by over one million fresh American troops, the Allies now began to make major gains against the German army. On 8 August, Germany suffered what Ludendorff described as the 'black day of the German army', as the British army took 16,000 German soldiers prisoner and British troops overran German positions on the Western front. Despite the German army's sustained but orderly retreat over the next few months, Ludendorff and Hindenburg clung desperately to the hope that they could continue the war. However, on 29 September 1918, their key ally Bulgaria pulled out of the war, a move that forced Ludendorff to accept that the war was essentially over. It was at this point that the German military leader decided to make the political concessions that could help to excuse the military from taking responsibility for the problems its leadership had caused. At the Spa Conference on 29 September 1918, Ludendorff informed the Kaiser that the war was lost and that political changes had to be made if the old regime was to survive.

On 3 October, Prince Max of Baden, who, despite his royal position as Prince of Baden, had a liberal political outlook, was appointed Chancellor. During the war, he had worked to assist German prisoners of war and had strongly opposed the tactic of unrestricted submarine warfare. For the first time in the Kaiserreich, the government of the new Chancellor was made up of Reichstag members from the SPD, the Centre Party and the Progressives. Ludendorff, who up to this point had resisted any moves towards political reform, had insisted on this change.

There were three key reasons for Ludendorff's change in direction. Firstly, the military feared that the announcement that the war was lost and that Germany was now seeking an armistice could set off a revolution. Moderate political reforms might be enough to ensure that the majority of German people were satisfied and stave off the demand for greater changes. Secondly, US president Woodrow Wilson insisted that peace between nations had to be based on democratic values; thus Germany's transformation into a democratic state could help the leadership negotiate a more favourable armistice with the Allies. Wilson made it clear that he would only negotiate with the people's representatives, not military leadership. Thirdly, and probably most importantly, Ludendorff understood that forcing the political parties to negotiate what was going to be a difficult surrender to the Allies would allow the military leadership to pass the blame for Germany's defeat onto the Reichstag politicians. Ludendorff believed that the Reichstag parties' actions against the military leadership in July 1917, and the role of left-wing politicians in encouraging strike action, had been a key reason for the country's defeat. In Ludendorff's own words, these politicians 'must now eat the soup which they have served us'. He would later claim that the reason Germany lost the war was not due to military weakness, but because it had been 'stabbed in the back' by socialist traitors.

EXTEND YOUR KNOWLEDGE

The 'stab in the back' myth

The idea of being 'stabbed in the back' referred to the belief that the German military had not been defeated on the battlefield, but instead that Germany had lost the war due to traitors in Germany who had betrayed the country. These were frequently depicted as socialists, Communists and Jews, who had actively worked to ensure that Germany lost the war. Erzberger, for instance, was one of the key politicians blamed for Germany's defeat, given his political actions in the July crisis of 1917. The exact origins of the term allegedly came about during a meeting between Ludendorff and the Head of the British Military Mission in Berlin in 1919, when Ludendorff explained that Germany lost the war due to being stabbed in the back by home-front failures. The idea that Germany never really lost the war but was betrayed was a powerful myth, used by right-wing political opponents to attack the new Weimar Republic as illegitimate and traitorous to Germany. Unsurprisingly, the 'stab in the back' myth was a key aspect of Nazi ideology. The idea that Jewish Communist traitors lost Germany the war was a powerful part of Hitler's anti-Jewish agitation.

The role of Prince Max of Baden

On 3 October 1918, Prince Max wrote to the US president asking for an armistice. The government then set about making constitutional reforms. The Prussian three-class franchise was abolished and the constitution changed, so that the army and navy were responsible to the Reichstag, not the Kaiser. The Chancellor and his government were made accountable to the Reichstag, and further democratic reforms were introduced in several German states that, up to this point, had resisted political change. On 28 October, the reforms were passed. In only three weeks, Germany had become a constitutional monarchy. Two days prior to this, Ludendorff had resigned, after failing in his attempt to convince the military and the Kaiser that they should try to continue with the war instead of accepting Wilson's armistice terms, primarily that Germany had to immediately stop unrestricted submarine warfare. With the military leadership removed and Germany having established a constitutional monarchy, Prince Max replied to President Wilson, asserting again that Germany was ready for an armistice and reiterating the political reforms that had been made. This was a 'revolution from above', where those in power had instigated change in an orderly fashion. For the SPD leader Ebert, these reforms were substantial and there was no pressing need to go beyond them. Germany had become a constitutional system under the monarchy, a system that moderates within the SPD, along with the Centre Party, National Liberals and the Progressives, were content with. However, events from late October onwards were to ensure that the attempt by the military, Prince Max and the Reichstag leaders to hold off revolution in Germany by implementing reform had come too late to stop the German people's push for a more radical political direction.

SOURCE

A 1942 German right-wing political cartoon linking the 'stab in the back' myth to anti-Semitism. The cartoon depicts Jews in Germany as responsible for the defeat of the German army in the First World War. The source is the Berlin Franz Eher, the central publishing house of the Nazi Party, established in 1920.

ACTIVITY
KNOWLEDGE CHECK

This political cartoon (Source 4) was published in 1942. What does this tell us about the enduring legacy and power of the 'stab in the back' myth?

SOURCE

The diary entry of Colonel von Thaer, for 1 October 1918, upon hearing from Ludendorff that the war was lost. Colonel von Thaer was transferred from his previous post as Chief of German Staff of the 4th Reserve Army in France, to work with the Supreme Command of Ludendorff and Hindenburg in April 1918. His diary is a key source in understanding how Ludendorff created the myth that the war was lost, not because of the army's failure, but because of anti-German socialist betrayal.

Terrible and appalling! It is so! Indeed! As we were gathered together, Ludendorff stood up in our presence, his face was pale and filled with deep worry, but his head was still held high. A truly handsome Germanic hero figure. He said roughly the following: It was his duty to tell us that our military condition was terribly serious. Any day now, our Western Front could be breached. He had had to report this to His Majesty the Kaiser recently... Together with the General Field Marshal, he [Ludendorff] had answered that the Supreme Army Command and the German Army were at an end; the war could no longer be won, but rather an unavoidable and conclusive defeat awaited. Bulgaria had already been lost. Austria and Turkey, both at the end of their powers, would also soon fall. Our own Army had unfortunately also been heavily contaminated with the poison of Spartacus-socialist ideas, and the troops were, he said, no longer reliable. Since the 8th of August the situation had rapidly gotten worse. As a result, some troops had proven themselves so unreliable that they had had to be quickly pulled from the front. If they were replaced with other troops willing to fight, they would be received with the label 'Strike breakers' and challenged not to fight anymore. He said he could not operate with divisions that were no longer reliable. It was thus foreseeable, he went on to say, that the enemy in the near future, with the help of American troops anxious to fight, would succeed in a great victory, a breakthrough in grand fashion. As a result, the West Army would lose its last hold and retreat in full disbandment across the Rheine and carry the revolution back to Germany. This catastrophe, he said, must be avoided by all means. For the cited reasons we could no longer allow ourselves to be beaten. Therefore, the Supreme Army Command demanded of His Majesty the Kaiser and of the Chancellor that a proposal for the bringing about of peace be made to President Wilson of America without delay, for bringing about an armistice on the basis of his 14 Points.

SOURCE

In his memoirs, *Out of My Life*, written shortly after the war (1920), Paul von Hindenburg describes Germany's difficult situation in 1916, but claims that he did not believe the war would end in 1918 and thought that Germany could have fought on.

When the conduct of operations was entrusted to me I regarded the country's morale as serious, though it had not collapsed. There was no doubt that people at home had been bitterly disappointed by the military events of the last few months. Moreover, the privations of daily life had materially increased. The middle classes in particular were suffering very severely from the economic situation, which affected them exceptionally intensely. Food had become very scarce and the prospects of the harvest were only moderate... In the middle of August 1918 I did not consider that the time had come for us to despair of a successful conclusion of the war. In spite of certain distressing but isolated occurrences in the last battle, I certainly hoped that the Army would be in a position to continue to hold out. I also believed that our public at home would be strong enough to survive even the present crisis. I fully realised what the homeland had already borne in the way of sacrifices and privations and what they would possibly still have to bear. Had not France, on whose soil the war had now been raging for four years, had to suffer and endure far more? Had that country ever been cast down by failure during the whole of that time? Did she despair when our shells fell into her capital? I believed that our public would keep this in mind even in this serious crisis, and stand firm if only we at the front continued to stand firm too.

ACTIVITY
KNOWLEDGE CHECK

1 In what key ways does Thaer's diary entry (Source 5) disagree with Hindenburg's memoirs (Source 6)?

2 According to Source 5, why does Ludendorff believe the war has been lost and that he now has to try to end it?

3 Despite the difficult situation from 1916 onwards, why did Hindenburg (in Source 6) believe the war could have continued past 1918?

4 Using your own knowledge, what would you say are the key weaknesses in Hindenburg's assessment (Source 6)?

5 Who does Hindenburg appear to be blaming for Germany's defeat in 1918 and how does he use the comparison with France to do this?

Disintegration, defeat and revolution, 1918–19

By the end of October 1918, Germany had transformed its political system. The reforms, however, were not enough to resist the calls for further change. Part of the problem was the final realisation that the war was over. While the German people had a general sense that the final offensive had not been successful, the announcement that Germany was seeking an armistice came as a sudden shock. To many, the political system did not appear to have changed enough. The Kaiser was still on the throne, an unelected prince was still Chancellor, and the war continued to drag on. Woodrow Wilson's reply to the German government was made public in late October, and it was clear from his notes that he viewed the Kaiser as a major impediment to peace. There was a growing call for the abdication of the Kaiser by the German public, as well as by politicians and some within the military. Wilhelm II refused to accept that his abdication was a necessity for Germany to be able to conclude the war, and on 29 October he departed Berlin and made his way to the principal German military headquarters, in the Belgian town of Spa, in order to escape the growing calls for his abdication as Kaiser.

Events, however, were progressing rapidly. On 28 October 1918, the naval leadership had ordered the German fleet at Kiel to engage in one last suicidal attack against the British navy. The German navy had been inactive since 1916, and the leadership feared that their insignificance in the war could hamper the future of the navy. They therefore believed they needed one final battle to regain honour for the navy. It is also possible that the naval leadership hoped to sabotage the armistice negotiations; crucially, the assault had not been discussed with the government. The German sailors, however, who had suffered from poor conditions throughout the war, were unwilling to give their lives in a pointless battle when the war was already lost. On 29 October, they began demonstrations in Kiel, and soon their protest movement had spread from northern Germany to all major cities, as the sailors used the German rail system to publicise their message. The Kiel Mutiny sparked the German 'revolution from below'. Beginning in Kiel and soon spreading to all parts of Germany, revolutionary councils formed by workers, soldiers and sailors began to appear. This was a grass-roots form of democracy inspired by the **soviets** of the Russian Revolution. The councils were elected in chaotic mass meetings for example, of striking workers or mutinying sailors, who then promised to negotiate with government officials, the army or industrial bosses to bring about proper political change in Germany.

In Russia, the soviets had been a key part of the Communist revolution. For the German military, Prince Max and the moderate SPD, the councils were a dangerous development that signalled the possibility that Germany could follow a similar path. By early November, mass protests filled Berlin, and striking workers and soldiers were electing more revolutionary councils. The actual State of Germany was now also in danger. On 7 November 1918, the socialist Kurt Eisner seized power in Bavaria and declared an independent Bavarian Republic. Prince Max and the SPD leader Ebert now believed that the only way to stop a full-blown revolution and the disintegration of Germany was to give in to the demands of the protestors and force the abdication of the Kaiser. On 9 November, a mass strike took place in Berlin. Ebert informed Prince Max that only a democratic government could bring the revolution to an end. Ebert himself was not a supporter of the councils, but believed in a constitutional government. Prince Max decided he had to take decisive action. On 9 November, the German political system of 1871 came to an end. Without informing Wilhelm II, Prince Max announced that the Kaiser would abdicate his throne and that Prince Max would hand power over to the first civilian Chancellor of Germany, Friedrich Ebert. The Kaiser, who was still in Spa, tried to reject Prince Max's announcement, but was informed by the new head of the German military, Wilhelm Groener, that the army was no longer loyal to the Kaiser. When the Kaiser's most loyal military leader, Hindenburg, confirmed this, Wilhelm II was forced to accept Prince Max's announcement and he left for exile in Holland.

On 11 November 1918, the SPD, in coalition with the USPD, formed the government of Germany, and on the very same day, representatives of the new government travelled to the Western front in France to sign the armistice and bring the war to an end. Freedom of speech, religion and the press was established; political prisoners were released; and equal voting rights for men and women were proclaimed. Ebert announced that the revolution was now over. Despite this assertion, it took until at least April 1919 for the SPD leadership to finally quell the 'revolution from below' and ensure the political unity of Germany. Ebert's leadership was to critically define the manner in which this took place and the consequences it would subsequently have for the future of the new German political system.

KEY TERM

Soviet
The term comes from Russia and refers to a local council, representing workers' and soldiers' rights, which was formed during the Russian Revolution of 1917. These soviets were democratic grass-roots political organisations that were elected by workers and soldiers to represent their views. They had some administrative political power and would eventually play a key part in the Communist revolution. The German workers' and soldiers' councils were inspired by the soviets in Russia and hoped to develop greater representation of soldiers and workers in the German political system.

EXTRACT 2

From Richard Bessel, 'Germany from war to dictatorship,' in M. Fulbrook (ed.) *German History since 1800* (1997). Bessel discusses why the move towards parliamentary government could not avert the German revolution and the main issues the new government faced.

Parliamentary government – the great goal of the revolutionaries of 1848 – was inaugurated in Germany on 28 October 1918, when the Reichstag passed a law stipulating that henceforth the Reich government was dependent upon the confidence of the parliament. By the time the Kaiser abdicated and fled to Holland, Germany already had had effective parliamentary government for over a month – in the form of the government of Prince Max of Baden, which rested on the majority support in the Reichstag rather than the confidence of the Emperor. Yet the depth of the social and political divisions which had grown since 1914 was such that when Germany's military rulers Paul von Hindenburg and Erich Ludendorff – realising that the war was lost and that Germany needed a parliamentary government in order to negotiate with the Allies – opened the door to a genuine parliamentary system, the change was almost superfluous. Indeed, on the same day that Germany finally formally achieved parliamentary government, 28 October 1918, the naval mutiny began in Wilhelmshaven. Political reform very quickly gave way to political revolution. The divisions exacerbated by the war not only undermined the imperial political system; they also constituted an extraordinarily difficult and damaging legacy for the democratic system put into place following the defeat in 1918... From the outset the new governmental system lacked the support of a large proportion of the German population, many of whom had been shocked by defeat and revolution, still felt loyalty to the Kaiser, regretted the crumbling of the rigid social and political lines of authority embodied in the imperial system and refused to accept the legitimacy of the new regime. Thus, from the moment of its birth, the first successful attempt to establish a governmental system in Germany on the basis of popular sovereignty was burdened by the fact that a large proportion of the German people did not recognise its legitimacy.

ACTIVITY
KNOWLEDGE CHECK

1 According to Bessel (Extract 2), why could the changes introduced by Hindenburg and Ludendorff not stop political revolution in Germany from breaking out?

2 With reference to Extract 2, what was the main problem facing the new government after the abdication of the Kaiser?

The roles of Ebert, Scheidemann and Rosa Luxemburg

As the first civilian chancellor, Friedrich Ebert was critical to the type of political system that would emerge following Germany's surrender in November 1918. Thus it is crucial to understand that Ebert, despite being leader of the SPD, was determined to establish an ordered, democratic system that was not based on more radical left-wing ideas. Ebert had not even wanted Germany to become a republic after the abdication of the Kaiser. Instead, he hoped that one of the Kaiser's sons would take the throne, thus ensuring that Germany continued as a constitutional monarchy. This, however, had been made impossible by the actions of another prominent SPD member, Phillipp Scheidemann, who held the position of Secretary of State. Following his appointment

as Chancellor on 9 November 1917 by Prince Max, Ebert had hoped to quieten the crowds and stop any further disorder in Germany. He issued a proclamation asking the German crowds to simply return to their homes. Instead, a large crowd started to gather at the Reichstag, demanding that Ebert make a speech. Ebert refused, but Scheidemann was concerned by the fact that he had been informed that the leader of the Spartacists, Karl Liebknecht, was about to proclaim that Germany was a Soviet Republic. Hoping to seize the initiative, Scheidemann went out to the balcony of the Reichstag and spoke to the crowd, ending with the words, 'Long live the German republic!' With these fateful words, Scheidemann ensured that the German monarchy was no more. Ebert was furious, telling Scheidemann that he had no right to declare Germany a republic, but he also felt that he could not contradict Scheidemann's declaration now that the large crowd had heard it, fearing that if he tried to install a new Kaiser there would simply be more unrest.

On 10 November 1918, Ebert formed a new coalition government with the USPD. Ebert's key goal at this stage, beyond ending the war, was to stop any further revolution in Germany. To do this he needed to ensure that the army returned in an ordered fashion and was loyal to the new government, helping it to stop the ongoing issues in Bavaria and close down the soldiers' and workers' councils. Ebert believed that a parliamentary government was essential to Germany and that the councils posed a threat to this type of democratic system. To guarantee that he achieved his aims, Ebert was prepared to make a deal with the old order of German society. On 9 November, he telephoned the head of the German army Wilhelm Groener and the two agreed on a critically important deal. Groener would support Ebert and the new government if Ebert promised to leave the army unreformed. This was known as the Ebert–Groener Pact, a vital agreement in which Ebert promised, with the military's assistance, to restrict the power of the soldiers' councils and establish an ordered system based on a parliamentary government. This was followed by a deal between the main trade unions and the industrialists on 15 November. Known as the Stinnes-Legien Agreement, the trade unions promised to respect private ownership of industry if the industrialists recognised the trade unions as the only representatives of the German workers, and if an eight-hour day was introduced. These deals ensured that the government under Ebert had vital support from the military, the trade unions and the wealthy industrialists.

The Freikorps

Ebert's main concern was the radical left, who he believed wanted to provoke revolution and turn Germany into a Communist state like that in Russia. In his goal to stop this from happening, he was aided by the **Freikorps**. These were paramilitary organisations made up of returning soldiers and Germans too young to have served in the army. The Freikorps were violent and stringently anti-Communist. They also had strong connections with the army, who supplied them with weapons. Despite their vehement hatred of democracy, Ebert welcomed the Freikorps' assistance at this stage as a means of suppressing left-wing revolutionary organisations.

SOURCE 7

German military forces awaiting attack by Spartacus forces during the Berlin uprising, 1919.

KEY TERM

Freikorps

Translates to 'free regiment' in English and refers to German military mercenary forces that had a long history in Germany, dating back to the 18th century. After the First World War, the Freikorps were irregular paramilitary forces, not officially part of the military, but they enjoyed unofficial financial and ideological support from the German army. They were predominately made up of decommissioned veterans who still wanted the discipline of the army, and young Germans who had not been able to serve in the army as the war ended too soon. The Freikorps were violent and strongly anti-Communist, and were used by the Weimar government to put down attempted Communist uprisings between 1919 and 1920. When the government tried to disband the Freikorps in 1920, they mounted their own failed coup. These extreme right-wing groups were the training ground for many Nazis, who started in the Freikorps and were later attracted to the right-wing ideology of Adolf Hitler. In 1933, the Freikorps officially amalgamated with the Nazi Party.

SOURCE 8

Spartacus forces in defensive positions during the uprising in Berlin, 1919.

Straßenkämpfe in Berlin.
Zweifronten-Barrikade in der Schützenstraße.

ACTIVITY
KNOWLEDGE CHECK

Compare the two photos (Sources 7 and 8) above, showing both the military and the Spartacists during the 1919 attempted uprising by the Communists. How can these images help us to understand why the Spartacists were defeated?

The first major action of the Freikorps came in January 1919. In December 1918, Karl Liebknecht and Rosa Luxemburg had broken with the USPD and formed the KPD, the Communist Party of Germany. In early January 1919, during protests against the removal of the left-wing Berlin chief of police Emil Eichorn, the KPD declared a Communist revolution and occupied buildings in Berlin. Both Ebert and the military leadership looked to the Freikorps to restore order, believing they could be better relied on to crush the revolution than the regular army troops. Despite being a key leader of the KPD, Rosa Luxemburg had argued that the time was not right for a revolution, believing that the majority of the German working class did not support their actions. However, the majority of the party voted for revolution and Luxemburg felt that she had to go along with the party's choice. It was a fateful decision. Over three days between 10 and 13 January, the Freikorps crushed the revolution, murdering captured Communist prisoners. On 15 January, Liebknecht and Luxemburg were arrested, tortured and brutally murdered.

This brutal crackdown, however, did not put an end to attempted revolution. In early March, the Freikorps were used to subdue another Communist uprising, this time murdering around 1,000 people in Berlin. In April, Freikorps were used again, this time to crush the Bavarian Soviet Republic, executing the Communist leadership and thousands of its supporters. Further unrest took place sporadically across Germany, but the Freikorps were instrumental in ensuring that any left-wing threat to the new government was summarily crushed. At the same time, the Freikorps were critical in the crushing of the workers' and soldiers' councils.

By August 1919, the German revolution was essentially over. Ebert had succeeded in stopping left-wing revolution and ensuring that the councils played no further part in government. It is somewhat questionable how far the revolution brought about radical political change. The Kaiser had abdicated and Germany had a new, civilian government that held power through an elected Reichstag. The key reforms, however, went little beyond what Prince Max had established in October 1918. Critically, Ebert had chosen to leave the military leadership unreformed; thus it was still dominated by the Prussian elite who had no belief in democracy or the new SPD government. Even more worryingly, he had relied on the vicious, anti-democratic Freikorps to crush the workers who wished for greater political change. Whether Ebert did what was necessary to ensure order and stability for the new government, or was a traitor to the ideals of socialism that his party claimed to represent, is still a matter for debate. What is unarguable is that his decisions would shape the new republic; most critically, his decision to rely on an unreformed military and violent militia gave these institutions a particular position of strength in 1919. Once they had destroyed the radical left, they would subsequently come to focus their anger on the government Ebert had been so instrumental in establishing.

EXTRACT

3   Eric Weitz, in *Weimar Germany: Promise and Tragedy* (2007), sets out Ebert's political aims and his concerns about the future form German democracy should take.

From the very moment he took office, the Social Democrat Friedrich Ebert worked feverishly to channel political energies down disciplined, regulated paths. More than anything else, Ebert feared that the Russian Revolution would be replicated in Germany. Ebert and his colleagues believed deeply in democracy and the replacement, eventually, of capitalism by a social organisation of the economy. But what their Russian counterparts had accomplished, they also believed, was the creation of economic chaos and political terror, they very antitheses of democracy and a progressive social system. The massive project of restoring order and creating liberty in Germany required careful organisation. Germans were hungry and cold; food and coal had to be procured, men put back to work, democratic institutions constructed. Germany would not, could not, tolerate 'Bolshevik conditions' as he and his supporters repeated time and again. Ebert believed that government had to be legitimated through democratic procedures, namely the vote. German democracy had to be placed on a firm foundation and only a new constitution could do that. Moreover, a free election and a new constitution would rein in his more radical coalition partner, the USPD, and would sap the councils of whatever legitimacy they might have acquired. To Ebert, the councils were not the embryonic form of a fully democratic society, one in which popular participation ran through all the institutions of society, including the workplace. He saw the councils, rather, as a dangerous radical experiment that smacked of Bolshevism. They had to be eliminated, but in the chaotic conditions of 1918–19, a direct assault threatened to backfire. With luck, elections and a constitutional convention would do the trick.

SOURCE

9   In this speech, given by Karl Liebknecht at a SPD/USPD meeting in Berlin on 10 November 1918, Liebknecht argues that the revolution is being betrayed and accuses Ebert of being against the revolution and the soldiers' councils.

I am afraid that I must try to pour cold water on your enthusiasm. The counter-revolution is already on the march; it is already in action! (Shouts: Where is that?). It is already among us. Those who have spoken to you, were they friends of the revolution? (Shouts: No! Loud retorts: Yes!). Read what Reich Chancellor Ebert (Shout: without him you would not even be here!) had printed in *Vorwarts* (SPD newspaper). It is a slander of the revolution carried out yesterday. Dangers to the revolution threaten us from many sides (Shouts: From you!) Danger threatens not only from those circles that up to now have held the reins – the demagogues, big landowners, Junkers, capitalists, imperialists, monarchists, princes and generals – but also from those who today support the revolution, but were still opposing it the day before yesterday. (Stormy interruptions: Unity, unity. Retorts: No! Shouts: Sit down!) Be careful whom you choose for the government and whom you trustingly elect to the soldiers' councils. The soldiers' councils must be in the vanguard of the defence of the councils' power. No significant portion of the councils' power can be placed in the hands of officers. The reins must be primarily in the hands of the simple soldiers. (Loud shouts: They are!) In the provinces several higher officers have been elected chairman of soldiers' councils. (Protests) I tell you: Enemies surround us! (Shouts: You're twisting the facts!) The revolution's enemies are insidiously using the soldiers' organisations to their own ends. (Persistent commotion) I know how unpleasant this disturbance is, but even if you shoot me, I will say what I believe to be necessary. The triumph of the revolution will be possible only if it becomes a social revolution. Only then will it have the strength to ensure the socialisation of the economy, happiness and peace for all eternity (Applause from some, persistent uproar, renewed shouts: Unity!).

ACTIVITY
KNOWLEDGE CHECK

1 Using Extract 3 and Source 9, assess the key ways in which Liebknecht and Ebert disagreed on the future of Germany after the fall of the Kaiser.

2 How far do Liebknecht and Ebert disagree? Are there any areas of agreement between them?

3 What do the interruptions of those listening to Liebknecht's speech (Source 9) reveal about the left-wing of German politics at this stage?

TO WHAT EXTENT DID THE FOUNDATION OF THE WEIMAR REPUBLIC IN 1919 ACHIEVE A NEW UNITY FOR THE GERMAN NATION BASED ON DEMOCRATIC VALUES?

The Weimar Republic

The election of January 1919

At the same time as Ebert was moving against the left-wing forces of the councils and the KPD, he had also made arrangements to hold constituent assembly elections so that Germans could elect the parties that would decide on the new constitution. The election took place on 19 January 1919 in the midst of the crackdown on the attempted Communist revolution in Berlin. It was also significant in allowing women to vote for the first time. The election was a success for the parties to the centre of German politics, supporters of parliamentary democracy who were opposed to further revolution. The SPD, Centre Party and the new German Democratic Party (DDP) won around 76 percent of the votes. The DDP was a centre party that promoted democracy and was against any form of extremism either to the left or to the right of politics. It was well supported by educated middle-class Germans, as well as the small but quite wealthy Jewish population of Germany. The DDP promised to promote democratic values and minorities such as Jews and Poles. The SPD had hoped to achieve a majority of the vote in its own right, but failed to achieve this, winning only 37.9 percent of the vote. This may have been due to many Germans turning against socialism due to the violence of the Spartacus uprising. Women voters in particular tended to favour the centre right parties as opposed to the SPD. However, the SPD, DDP and Centre Party shared a generally similar view on the type of political system Germany should become, and therefore formed what became known as the Weimar Coalition.

The first assembly met in Weimar, as it was too dangerous to meet in Berlin. Weimar was chosen as it was a place of political calm and was easily accessible for all the delegates, being located in the centre of Germany. Weimar also had historical resonance as a key city in German culture, particularly as it was where arguably Germany's greatest ever writer, Johann Goethe, had decided to live. It therefore represented a culturally educated Germany that the politicians hoped would resonate with the German people.

Divisions within the new republic

There were still critical divisions within German society that would hamper the new republic, even at this early stage. A large number of Germans still felt loyalty to the old Kaiserreich system and were opposed to the upheaval in society that had led to the proclamation of the new republic. They viewed the new government as illegitimate and were angered by the creation of the Weimar Republic from its very beginnings. In the Reichstag, the German National People's Party (DNVP) and the German People's Party (DVP) represented those opposed to the new democratic system. The DVP represented the industrialists and upper middle class; its members believed the rebirth of Germany had to be based on a strong economic basis that was free of trade union interference. They also campaigned for a return of the German monarchy. The DNVP was the strongest anti-Weimar political party. Its members viewed the Weimar as an aberration, believing that the republican democratic system was not suited to the country. They asserted that the socialists and Jews had been responsible for Germany's defeat during the First World War, due to the 'stab in the back'. In the election of January 1919, they won 10.3 percent of the vote. The divisions between the parties were clear during Ebert's opening speech at the assembly on 10 February, when he was constantly interrupted by right-wing parties, but cheered by the SPD and the other members of the Weimar Coalition. Two days after his speech, the first framework of the new republic was put in place, with the assembly granted the powers to decide on the new constitution and new laws. Ebert was elected Reich President by the National Assembly and tasked with appointing a cabinet to govern the country. The liberal lawyer Hugo Preuss was given the job of designing the new German constitution that would be put to the vote in the assembly in August.

SOURCE

10 President Ebert's address to the Opening Session of the German Assembly, 6 February 1919. In this section he challenges industry leaders and workers to compromise and work with each other, and then sets out what he hopes will be the future of the German political and social system.

Many employers, accustomed to the **high secured** profits which the war economy in the old monarchical and protectionist State created for them, have neglected to display the necessary initiative. Therefore, we address to the employers the urgent appeal to help with all their strength the restoration of production. (Applause.) On the other side we call to the workers to employ all their strength in work, which alone can save us. ('Hear, hear.') We understand the psychology of those who, after an undue expenditure of strength in time of war, now seek relaxation. We know how difficult it must be for those who have lived for years on the battlefield to settle down to peaceful work; but it must be. We must work and create values, otherwise we collapse. ('Hear, hear.') Socialism means organization, order, and solidarity, not high-handedness, perversity, and destruction. There must no longer be room for private monopolies and capitalist profit without effort in time of national emergency. Therefore, profit is to be methodically **obviated** where economic development has made a trade ripe for socialization. The future looms before us full of anxiety. In spite of all that, we trust in the indestructible creative power of the German nation. ('Hear, hear.') The old foundations of the German position based on force are forever destroyed. The Prussian hegemony, the Hohenzollern army, the policy of the shining armour have been made impossible among us for all future. As November 9, 1918, follows on March 18, 1848, so must we here in Weimar complete the change from Imperialism to Idealism, from world power to spiritual greatness. ('Hear, hear.') Now must the spirit of Weimar, the spirit of the great philosophers and poets, again fill our life, fill it with the spirit described in Faust and in Wilhelm Meister's *Wanderjahre* (famous German novels). Not roaming in the interminable and losing one's self in the theoretical, not hesitating and wavering, but with clear vision and firm hand taking a firm hold on practical life. So will we set to work with our great goal clear before our eyes: to maintain the right of the German people, to anchor firmly in Germany a strong democracy and to fill it with true social spirit and Socialist character. ('Hear, hear.') So shall we create an Empire of right and of righteousness, founded on the equality of everything that wears the form of mankind.

KEY TERMS

High secured
This refers to the fact that the war economy guaranteed wealth to many German employers.

Obviated
Removed or prevented.

A Level Exam-Style Question Section A

Study Source 10 before you answer this question.

Assess the value of Source 10 for revealing the political goals of Friedrich Ebert and the problems facing the new Weimar Republic.

Explain your answer, using the source, the information given about its origin and your own knowledge about the historical context. (20 marks)

Tip

This question requires you to question the evidence of the source and consider how a historian could best use it. With this source, think about how helpful it is for understanding the problems Ebert faced and what he hoped would be the future for the Weimar Republic. How far is Ebert's speech backed up by historical evidence? Are there any particularly problematic areas that are not discussed or are misrepresented by Ebert?

KEY TERMS

War bond
Used to fund governments' wars, by allowing groups and individuals within society to invest in the war effort. During the First World War, Germany would sell war bonds and use the money raised to buy German war equipment. German citizens were encouraged to buy war bonds to show their patriotism, and were promised that they could cash in their war bonds after ten years and be paid back by the government with interest. The war bond drive raised 10 billion marks. However, after the war, the amount of money the government owed to the public was quite high, due to the interest payable on the bonds. This would have been affordable if Germany had won the war, but the situation Germany faced at the end of the war meant the interest owed on the war bonds was a considerable economic strain.

November criminals
A term popularised by Adolf Hitler; he used it to refer derogatively to the leaders in Germany who had ended the war in November 1918. Hitler used this term to assert that those who established democracy in Germany were traitors and criminals, and thus the Weimar Republic was illegitimate. The notions of 'November criminals' and the 'stab in the back' were made official parts of German history, to be studied by school students after the Nazis came to power in 1933.

Parallel to the difficult political situation, the new republic faced severe economic and social problems beyond the attempted Communist uprisings. Germany had financed the war through **war bonds** and by printing more money, believing that it would be payable in the future through reparations imposed on the countries it had defeated. Germany now faced considerable economic problems, such as high inflation combined with continuing shortages of food caused by the ongoing British naval blockade. Socially, it faced the impact of millions of returning German soldiers, who needed to be integrated back into German society.

The Treaty of Versailles, 1919
Politically, the ongoing armistice negotiations with the Allies undermined the Weimar Republic from its creation. The treaty that was finally put to Germany imposed territorial losses, limited the German army considerably and humiliated the country by forcing it to accept Article 231, which declared Germany as solely responsible for starting the First World War. Ebert's successor as Chancellor, Phillip Scheidemann, resigned rather than sign the treaty. However, there was little choice for the Weimar Republic, as the British held the blockade in place and the Allies threatened to invade Germany unless the treaty was signed.

On 28 June 1919, two members of the SPD-led government signed the peace treaty. It was a critical event that would undermine the new republic, as it allowed the military and right-wing forces to blame the democratic republic parties for the surrender and now the humiliation of the Versailles Treaty, just as Ludendorff had hoped to achieve when he stepped down in 1918. The idea that the **November criminals**, Jews and socialists had caused Germany's defeat through 'the stab in the back' was a prominent message that the right used to great effect to undermine the Weimar Republic throughout its existence.

Summary: the strength of the new Weimar Republic
By the end of 1919, the prominent left-wing politicians, Rosa Luxemburg, Karl Liebknecht, Kurt Eisner and the former leader of the SPD and founder of the USPD Hugo Haase, had all been murdered by groups or individuals of the extreme right. The Weimar Republic had been founded, free and fair elections involving both men and women had been held, the peace treaty had been signed and the naval blockade had been lifted. The government had also maintained the territorial unity of Germany by ending the civil war in Bavaria and re-establishing calm in German streets. However, the new republic faced a considerable threat from extreme right-wing groups such as the Freikorps, as well as the old order of the Kaiserreich, which viewed the new republic as illegitimate and longed for a return to authoritarian government. Although the majority of the German people did not share these right-wing views, the humiliation of the Versailles Treaty undermined the new government's popularity as it tried to establish a new form of political order. These issues were to be compounded by the issues arising from the new constitution that was finally implemented in August 1919.

EXTEND YOUR KNOWLEDGE

The historical debate concerning Friedrich Ebert

Friedrich Ebert, the first SPD Chancellor of Germany after the First World War, remains one of most controversial individuals in 20th-century German history. For some, he was the founder of German democracy, who brought order and democracy to the country during the chaos at the end of the First World War and the German revolution. For others, he was a man who betrayed his own ideology, using the right-wing forces of the Freikorps to stop revolution in Berlin and Bavaria, thus allowing the Freikorps considerable power and legitimacy that would eventually contribute to the rise of the Nazis. In Ebert's defence, the events in Russia in 1917 had shown the dangers of left-wing revolution, and he firmly believed that such an eventuality had to be stopped from taking place in Germany, even if this meant the oppression and murder of his former political colleagues. He was a strong believer that only an ordered democratic system could bring about social reforms, not revolution and upheaval. It can be argued, however, that Ebert wrongly overestimated the power and support for the Communists in Germany, while ignoring the much more threatening right-wing forces who would constitute the greatest threat to democracy in Germany. His deals with the army and his unwillingness to reform the judiciary and civil service in the early stages of the Weimar Republic have also been criticised. It should be remembered, though, that Ebert was desperate to keep order and believed that massive reform of the German system would only cause further chaos and make the foundation of democracy impossible. Given the huge problems facing Germany, it is difficult to understand exactly what any leader should have done, thus ensuring that Ebert's choices continue to fuel historical debate some 90 years after his death.

 THINKING HISTORICALLY | Interpretations (6a)

Ever-changing history

Our interpretations of the past change as we change. This may be because our social attitudes have changed over time, or perhaps a historian has constructed a new theory, or perhaps technology has allowed archaeologists to discover something new. This can clearly be seen in respect to the changing attitudes towards Friedrich Ebert and his actions in 1918–19.

Work in pairs.

Make a timeline that starts with the death of Ebert in 1925 and ends around 50 years into the future from now. Construct reactions to Ebert that illustrate the point that time changes history. In the future box you can speculate how people might react to the event in another 50 years' time. Below is an example. (Hint: Consider the numerous changes in government and political systems in Germany between 1918 and 1991. How might they have shaped the historical interpretation of Friedrich Ebert?)

1914	1917	1932	1968	2066
Event: The outbreak of the First World War.	German patriot: 'The start of Germany's greatest war.' Farmer from northern France: 'A disaster.'	British diplomat: 'The start of Britain's greatest colonial era.' Unemployed German: 'A disaster.'	Farmer in northern France: 'The start of the war. I keep finding bullets.' British diplomat: 'The beginning of the end of the British Empire.' An Indian historian: 'A major step on the road to Indian independence.'	?

Answer the following questions.

1 Identify three factors that have affected how Friedrich Ebert's actions have been interpreted over time, or might affect these interpretations in the future.

2 If a historian were to write a book proposing a radically new interpretation of Friedrich Ebert, how might other historians react? What would affect their reaction?

3 How will the future change the past?

The importance of the Weimar Constitution, including its salient features and their strengths and potential weaknesses for achieving freedom and stability

The strengths of the new constitution

The Weimar Constitution was officially proclaimed on 11 August 1919. In many ways, it provided considerable democratic freedoms for the German people. Freedom of speech, protest and the press were all instituted formally in the constitution, and all Germans, men and women, over the age of 21 were able to vote in elections. Critically, the constitution established in law that men and women were to be considered equal citizens. In terms of social reforms, the constitution was a considerable change from the Kaiserreich. Union rights for collective bargaining were enshrined, as was the German state's responsibility in respect to welfare, pledging the state to protect the country's women and children and provide for the unemployed. The federal system was maintained, although the number of German states was reduced to 18, and the central government was given greater powers than in the Kaiserreich. One of the most substantial changes was that the army would now be a united German body, as opposed to the grouping of four different *Länder* armies under Prussian control, as it had been previously. For the first time since 1871, Germany had an officially national army. In terms of parliament, the head of government was to be the chancellor, who would be selected and held accountable by the Reichstag. The Reichstag itself was to be elected through proportional representation (see Chapter 1). An elected president, who had considerable powers, including the ability to make the final decision on the make-up of the government and the appointment of the chancellor, replaced the Kaiser as head of state. He could also dismiss the chancellor, dissolve the Reichstag and call for new elections. The German people elected the president every seven years.

Weaknesses of the new constitution

In many ways, the Weimar Constitution was one of the most democratic political systems of the time, and proposed a fairly radical break from the laws and values of the Kaiserreich. There were, however, some major issues with the constitution that hampered the Weimar Republic's ability to achieve a stable political system. There were some vague aspects in the constitution, due to disagreements between the SPD, the Centre Party and the DDP. The constitution, for instance, enshrined the right of Germans to private property; however, at the same time it allowed for the possibility of nationalising private industry. The constitution proclaimed that there would be no 'state Church', but still allowed religious education in German schools and retained important privileges for the Church in Germany.

The bigger issues, however, related to the political system it put in place. Firstly, the use of proportional representation meant that parties got one seat for every 60,000 votes they achieved. The system ensured that no one party was able to achieve a majority, but instead, a large number of parties were elected. This in itself was not a problem, and it could be argued that proportional representation was the fairest, most democratic electoral system. However, every Weimar government had to be made up of a coalition. The splits between the political parties and their unwillingness to compromise in order to maintain a stable political system ensured that coalition governments rarely lasted very long. More critically, Reichstag members did not run directly, but were selected by their parties after it was apparent how many seats they had achieved in the election. This caused a considerable distance between the voting public and the politicians, given that any Reichstag member had greater dependence on their party than they did on the German people. This factor, combined with the considerable changes in governments that took place without elections, meant that over time the distance grew between the German people and the democratic system that was meant to represent them.

Perhaps the biggest issue with the constitution was the powers of the president. The makers of the constitution had wanted to provide the president with substantial powers, so that if the Communists ever won power in the Reichstag, their attempts to destroy democracy could be stopped. Thus, in times of emergency, the president could enact Article 48, thereby suspending the Reichstag and ruling by decree. The president also had supreme command of the army. If used responsibly, the president's considerable powers would not be a concern. However, there was vast potential for any president to dominate the Weimar political system and undermine the democratic process of the Reichstag. It is perhaps not surprising that the Weimar president was nicknamed the *Ersatz Kaiser*, or replacement Kaiser, given how his power reflected much of that held by the monarchy in the Kaiserreich.

It would be unfair to argue that it was the constitution that undermined Weimar political stability. The use of proportional representation does not guarantee unstable coalitions and the presidential powers were meant to be used with extreme caution and only in emergency situations. However, the flaws in the constitution meant that irresponsible individuals and political parties had considerable potential to undermine democracy in Germany, something political parties such as the Nazis were all too happy to use to their advantage.

The Weimar Republic was also considerably weakened by three factors that the parties and constitution failed to reform: the army, the judiciary and the civil service. Although under the responsibility of the Reichstag, the army was still dominated by the Prussian Junker elite, who despised democracy and the new republic, and worked throughout this period to undermine and ultimately overthrow the political system. This was also the case for the civil service, which was never particularly loyal to the government it was meant to help function. The rule of law and the separation of the state and the judiciary were enshrined in the constitution, but the judges from the Kaiserreich still held their important positions. They despised the Weimar Republic and frequently interpreted the law in a manner that allowed violent, right-wing fanatics, who assassinated politicians or mounted attempted coups, to either go free or face little punishment. Ebert, and the politicians who came after him, had relied on the military and the experienced civil service and judiciary from the Kaiserreich to lay the foundations of stable government.

However, their unwillingness to challenge this old order left the entire system of the Weimar Republic in a dangerous position, undermined by the very institutions that were meant to uphold its laws and protect its values against those who would violently oppose it.

SOURCE

Gerhard Anschutz speaking on the guiding principles of the Weimar Constitution at the annual gathering of the University of Heidelberg, 22 November 1922. Anschutz was a leading academic on constitutional law. In this section of the speech, he asserts that the Weimar Constitution reflects the democratic will of the German people.

The Weimar Constitution is a *democratic* constitution, both in origin and content. Unlike its predecessor of 1871, its *origin* was not an agreement among the German states, but—like the Frankfurt Constitution of 1849—an act of the German *people*. Thus its introduction states: 'The German people has given itself this constitution'; this of course should not be understood literally, as if the entire people itself accepted the Constitution through plebiscite, but rather to mean that the people acted through a parliament that it elected and empowered: the National Assembly of Weimar. We should recall that the elections to this constitutional assembly took place on the basis of an extremely free right to take part in the full electoral process and with the participation of all political parties—*all*, including those that rejected the new state that was being created. Even these opponents consented to democracy in one main point; in their opinion, too, the new Germany could not be created otherwise than through the self-organization of the people, through the will of constitutive popular representation. If in addition one considers the fact that the Constitution was accepted in the National Assembly by a majority of more than three-quarters of those voting, it is clear how foolish the contention is... Like its origin, the *content* of the Constitution reflects the democratic idea in all its purity. The very first article states the guiding principle: 'State power emanates from the people.' The state power spoken of here, *Reich* power, is located and has its source not outside of and above the people, but in it; it is synonymous with the common will of the entire people. Two of the major organs that are to create, explain, and execute this common will, the Reichstag and the president, are filled by popular election, so that not only the *legislature,* but also the highest bearer of the *executive* are direct agents of the national will... If one adds to all this the fact that the Constitution also prescribes to the *Länder* a democratic, republican form and thus forbids them not only a return to monarchy but also the introduction of undemocratic forms of government, such as, in particular, the dictatorship of the working class or proletariat—it becomes apparent with what energy and consequence a democratic view of the state is expressed and implemented in the Weimar Constitution.

ACTIVITY
KNOWLEDGE CHECK

1 According to Anschutz (Source 11), in what key way does the Weimar Constitution differ from the 1871 constitution?

2 What is Anschutz's main evidence that the Weimar Constitution is truly democratic?

3 Imagine you were debating with Anschutz on the strength of the Weimar Constitution. What would your main arguments against his interpretation be? Consider, for instance, his arguments that the president's role is truly democratic and that the main concern for the Weimar is a left-wing dictatorship.

4 During this speech, the university students listening scraped their feet on the ground, a traditional German sign of student disapproval. This was unprecedented during an academic speech such as this. What does the students' action demonstrate about the problems facing the Weimar Republic at this stage, three years after it had been founded?

A Level Exam-Style Question Section B

How accurate is it to say that the Weimar Constitution of 1919 failed to make a significant change from the previous political system of the Kaiserreich? (20 marks)

Tip

This question is asking you to assess the extent to which the Weimar Constitution helped to bring about democratic change in Germany. This is a difficult question that is asking you to assess a range of factors. You may feel that in some ways it made a radical break from the authoritarian political system of the Kaiserreich. However, there are also key institutions that were left completely unchanged. You will need to assess the exact extent to which you feel that the Weimar system differed from the political system it had replaced.

ACTIVITY
SUMMARY

1 Construct an annotated graph showing the patterns of German support for the First World War from 1914 to 1918. What are the key events shaping the changing patterns of civilian support for the war throughout this period?

2 Using your work on Question 1, answer the following question: 'To what extent did the social and political tensions that existed within the Second Reich increase during the First World War?'

3 To what extent would you agree that, despite the upheaval following the First World War between 1917 and 1919, the German political system underwent surprisingly little change?

4 You have been asked to write the biography of Friedrich Ebert. How would you conclude your book? What is your overall historical assessment of his actions, and why?

5 What do you believe was the biggest issue facing the Weimar Republic in 1919, and why?

 WIDER READING

Bessel, R. *Germany after the First World War*, Clarendon Press (1993)

Bessel, R. 'Germany from war to dictatorship', in Fulbrook, M. (ed.) *German History since 1800*, Bloomsbury Academic (1997)

McElligott, A. *Rethinking the Weimar Republic: Authority and Authoritarianism, 1916–1936*, Bloomsbury (2013)

Weitz, E.D. *Weimar Germany: Promise and Tragedy*, Princeton University Press (2007)

3.5

A new Reich, 1933–35

KEY QUESTIONS

- How effectively did Hitler establish the Nazi dictatorship between 1933 and 1935?
- To what extent was Hitler a dictator by 1935?
- How successful was the Nazis' attempt to create a Volksgemeinschaft between 1933 and 1935?

INTRODUCTION

In January 1933, Adolf Hitler was appointed Chancellor of Germany. It was a dramatic rise for a party that only five years previously had achieved just two percent of the vote in national elections. Hitler had been largely helped into power by conservative elites, who believed they could use his popular support to achieve their own political goals before removing him. He was seen as a weak figure, with the Nazis making up the minority of the governing cabinet. However, within a short period, he had removed almost all opposition and imposed himself as Führer, leader of the Nazi dictatorship. Not only had he overcome political parties opposed to the Nazis, he had also undermined the conservative forces within Germany and wiped out potential opposition from within his own party in a dramatic fashion. Even the powerful German army found itself in an increasingly subservient position to him. By 1935, Hitler had also begun to pursue his ideological goals on Germany's Jewish population, enacting the first of his discriminatory laws that would lay a path to the horrific events of the Second World War and the 'Final Solution'.

However, despite this power, Hitler achieved his goals in a unique fashion, running a government that had little direction and which rested on a large degree of infighting and chaos that the Nazi leader was responsible for, and to some degree encouraged. How Hitler achieved his aims, and the means by which the Nazi dictatorship was imposed, despite his attitude and approach to government, is thus a historical puzzle that can only be solved through a fuller understanding of his position within the Nazi Party, and the way in which those under the Führer worked fanatically to make his 'world view' into a terrifying reality.

HOW EFFECTIVELY DID HITLER ESTABLISH THE NAZI DICTATORSHIP BETWEEN 1933 AND 1935?

Creating a totalitarian state

Hitler's appointment as Chancellor of Germany in January 1933 did not immediately signal that Germany had become a dictatorship. It must be remembered that between 1919 and 1933 there had been frequent changes in the chancellorship, with Hitler being the fifteenth appointment in only 14 years. Despite the rhetoric of the Nazis, which preached that the Weimar democratic system was weak, anti-German and should be destroyed, it was not apparent to many politicians in 1933 that Hitler's appointment as

1933 –

January: Adolf Hitler appointed German Chancellor. 50,000 SA, SS and Stahlhelm members deputised as auxiliary police in the Prussian police force

5 March: Nazis win 44 percent of the vote in German elections

20 March: First concentration camp for political opponents opens at Dachau

2 May: Trade union offices raided and leaders arrested; all trade unions apart from Nazi German Labour Front made illegal

14 July: Nazis declared the only legal party in Germany

| 1933 January | February | March | April | May | June | July |

27 February: Marinus van der Lubbe arrested for setting fire to the Reichstag

28 February: Order of the Reich President for the Protection of People and State (Reichstag Fire Decrees)

23 March: Enabling Act gives Hitler power to rule by decree and ignore parliament

31 March: Law for the Co-ordination of the *Länder*

21–26 June: 500 SPD members tortured and around 23 murdered by Nazi SA in Kopenick, Berlin

22 June: SPD dissolved as a party and key members flee Germany

20 July: Signing of Concordat between Catholic Church and Nazi Germany

chancellor marked a distinct turning point. There was still a functioning Reichstag that encompassed a range of political parties which opposed the Nazis. There were only three Nazis out of 12 members in Hitler's first cabinet, and Hindenburg was still president, a role that was meant to ensure that it was not possible to impose a dictatorship on the German system. Importantly, Hitler had been helped to power by the vice chancellor, Franz von Papen, of the Centre Party, as well as other powerful conservative forces who believed they could control the Nazi leader and use him to achieve their own political goals. Crucially, within Germany, although the Nazis were popular, it must be noted that in the elections of November 1932, the Nazi vote had declined from 37.27 percent to 33.09 percent, and although they remained the most popular party in Germany, this meant that two-thirds of the German voting public had cast their votes for parties other than the Nazis. The imposition of the Nazi dictatorship was therefore not a straightforward process.

Yet despite these obstacles, by July 1933, Hitler had largely achieved his aims, cementing power for himself and the Nazi Party in a totalitarian dictatorship that would dominate Germany until its ultimate demise in 1945. The key aspects of this rapid imposition of a dictatorship related to four interlinking factors: violence; propaganda; *Gleichschaltung*; and pseudo-legal methods. Hitler was also helped by the miscalculations of others. The right-wing political elite of Germany who had helped Hitler become chancellor had hoped to use Hitler's popularity with the German people to impose a dictatorship, but then remove him and replace the Nazis with a conservative, military-style government. Hitler, they believed, could easily be controlled due to the fact that only three Nazis were in the cabinet. However, this was somewhat deceptive, as these Nazis held key positions from which they could exercise significant power. Beyond Hitler as chancellor, the Nazi Herman Goering had control over the large and powerful Prussian

police, while the other Nazi, Wilhelm Frick, held the important position of Reich Minister of the Interior.

The role of violence in establishing control

Violence was another key aspect in allowing the Nazis to establish their dictatorship. In this sense, Goering's position was critical. He was able to utilise his control over the Prussian police force by deputising 50,000 **SA**, **SS** and **Stahlhelm** members as auxiliary police, with the official goal of assisting the regular police to keep law and order in Germany following the Reichstag fire (see page 110). This essentially legalised these violent organisations and their attacks on Communist and socialist members. It was a key combination of violence and legality; the Nazi paramilitary organisations were essentially the police as well, making it extremely difficult for persecuted groups to mount any kind of opposition against the Nazis. New laws were also passed in February 1933, banning any newspaper from speaking out against the new government. This pseudo-legality, backed up by violence, was a key part of the Nazi establishment of its dictatorship in a manner that made it difficult to resist.

KEY TERM

Gleichschaltung
The term essentially translates in English as 'switching on', as in a light switch. The term was used by the Nazis, however, in terms of 'co-ordination' or 'bringing into line', and describes the policies that brought German society under the overall control of the Nazi Party. In this way, it could be said that German society was 'switching on to the Nazis'.

KEY TERMS

SA
The *Sturmabteilung* (Stormtroopers), became the official paramilitary wing of the Nazi Party in 1921. They were also referred to as the Brown Shirts, due to their uniform. Their main role was to protect Nazi rallies and meetings and violently disrupt the activities of the Nazis' political enemies.

SS
Schutzstaffel were the special protection squad that acted as Hitler's personal bodyguard. They swore direct loyalty to Adolf Hitler. The SS had stricter joining requirements than the SA and were considered a more elite body of men.

Stahlhelm
(Steel Helmets) This was a separate paramilitary organisation that pre-dated the Nazi Party, having been formed in 1918. It consisted of war veterans and young men opposed to democracy and the Weimar Republic. The Stahlhelm aimed to establish a fascist (though not necessarily Nazi) dictatorship in Germany. By 1930, it was the largest paramilitary organisation in Germany, with around half a million members. After 1933, considerable pressure was placed on the Stahlhelm to align with the Nazis, and in 1934 they were renamed the League of National Socialist Frontline-Fighters.

1934 –
30 January: Law for Reconstruction of the Reich ends all state parliaments in Germany

1 August: President von Hindenburg dies. Hitler combines role of chancellor and president into one office known as the 'Führer'

1935 –
March: Military conscription introduced for German men

1934	1935

17 June: Papen delivers Marburg Address criticising some aspects of Nazi rule
30 June: Night of the Long Knives – Hitler has SA leadership and key political opponents executed

19 August: Hitler's role as Führer passed by German plebiscite with 90 percent approval
20 August: Army implements new oath of loyalty for Adolf Hitler to be taken by all soldiers in the German military

15 September: Nuremberg Laws severely restrict legal rights of German Jews

Hitler was then aided considerably by the events of 27 February 1933, when a young, disturbed Dutch Communist, Marinus van der Lubbe, was arrested while burning down the Reichstag. Inciting the fear of a Communist revolution, Hitler was able to convince President Hindenburg to utilise Article 48 and proclaim a state of emergency. The emergency decrees that followed, officially titled Decree of the Reich President for the Protection of People and State, but commonly known as the Reichstag Fire Decrees, essentially destroyed all democratic liberty in Germany. All the personal rights granted to the German people through the Weimar Constitution were suspended, including freedom of speech and protest. Unlimited periods of detention for political prisoners were introduced; in Prussia, for example, 25,000 members of the political opposition were held in custody by April. Violent action against the opposition accelerated from this point onwards, and on 20 March the first concentration camp was opened at Dachau for political prisoners. This provided a significant insight into the means by which the Nazis aimed to rule the country.

Following the Reichstag fire, Hitler had called elections for the 5 March 1933. The election campaign was tainted by repression and violence against the Nazis' political opponents. The Nazis were able to use their control of the German press to perpetuate the idea that only the Nazis could save Germany from a Communist revolution. Despite this, the Nazis were unable to win a majority of the vote, taking 44 percent. It is thus interesting to note that at this point, the majority of the population was still not voting for the Nazi Party. However, the Nationalist allies of the Nazis won around eight percent of the vote, allowing the Nazis a small majority in the Reichstag, albeit in a coalition government.

EXTEND YOUR KNOWLEDGE

The Reichstag fire (27 February 1933)

The controversy over the real culprit of the Reichstag fire has raged since the fire took place in February 1933. Was it really the responsibility of deranged Dutch former Communist member Marinus van der Lubbe? Given that the Reichstag fire was a convenient means for the Nazis to move against the Communist Party and weaken German political freedoms, is it more likely that they had something to do with the fire? The Nazis themselves claimed that van der Lubbe could not have started the fire alone. Four other Communists were arrested and tried alongside van der Lubbe, but much to Hitler's anger, the courts found these other defendants not guilty due to lack of evidence. This led to the Nazis establishing special courts so they could control future trials of political opponents. Van der Lubbe was found guilty and executed on 10 January 1934.

The speed of the fire, plus the convenience for the Nazis, has led to many claims that the Nazis themselves were responsible. A bestselling book was released in the United Kingdom as early as 1934 asserting that the Reichstag fire was a Nazi plot. However, prominent historians such as Kershaw and Mommsen have argued that van der Lubbe probably did start the fire on his own. They point to the fact that close sources to Hitler at the time report that he and the Nazi leadership were in a state of panic and believed that the fire really was the start of a Communist revolution, hardly the actions of a party that had set up the fire themselves. It was the Dutch Communist Party itself that spread the rumour that van der Lubbe was mentally unstable, as they wanted to distance themselves from his actions. These historians also point out that, given the political goals of Hitler, the Nazis would have come up with another method of restricting the Communists if the fire had not happened. The skill of Hitler was in his understanding of how he could use the fire to achieve his political aims. Recently, however, there have been new studies coming from German historians that have argued that the Nazis were responsible for the fire, clearly showing that 82 years later, this remains an ongoing area of debate.

ACTIVITY
KNOWLEDGE CHECK

1 With reference to Source 1, what do the Nazis claim the Reichstag fire was meant to do and what evidence do they have to back up this assertion?

2 This official announcement came one day after the fire. What does this demonstrate about Hitler's ability to take political advantage of the Reichstag fire?

3 How does Source 1 contribute to an understanding of why Hindenburg passed the Reichstag Fire Decrees with little protest from the German people?

SOURCE 1

The official Prussian Press Bureau Release on the Reichstag fire, 28 February 1933. Here, the Nazi Party sets out its official statement on the fire.

On Monday evening a fire broke out in the German Reichstag. The Reich Commissar for the Prussian Ministry of the Interior Reich Minister Goering, on arriving at the scene of the fire immediately took charge of operations and issued the necessary orders. On receiving the news of the fire Chancellor Adolf Hitler and Vice Chancellor Papen at once betook themselves to the scene. This is unquestionably the worst fire that has hitherto been experienced in Germany. The police inquiry has revealed that inflammable material had been laid throughout the entire building from the ground floor to the dome... A policeman saw people carrying torches moving about in the dark building. He immediately opened fire upon them. One of the criminals was arrested. He was a twenty four year old mason named van der Lubbe from Leiden in Holland, and was found to be in possession of a properly visaed Dutch passport. He stated that he was a member of the Dutch Communist Party. The central portion of the Reichstag has been completely gutted and the chamber in which the Reichstag held its meetings has been destroyed. The damage runs into the millions. This act of incendiarism is the greatest terrorist achievement of German Bolshevism. In the hundreds of tons of pamphlets found by the police in the Karl Liebknecht House were instructions for carrying out a Communist terror after the Bolshevist patterns. According to these instructions government buildings, castles, museums and vitally important factories were to be set on fire. Instructions were also found ordering that women and children, and wherever possible the wives and children of policemen, were to be used as cover by the Communists, in cases of rioting and street fighting. The discovery of this material prevented the Communists from systematically carrying out their revolution. Nevertheless, the burning of the Reichstag was intended to serve as the signal for bloodshed and civil war. Raids on business houses and shops had been ordered for Tuesday at four in the afternoon. This terror was to signal the commencement of civil war.

Gleichschaltung

Parallel to this gradual erosion of civil rights and political freedom was the process of *Gleichschaltung*. This essentially meant the gradual assimilation of all aspects of the state into the Nazi Party. You have already seen the example with the Prussian police, whereby Nazi organisations became part of the official police force. In other important elements of German society, such as the judiciary, political opponents and Jews were removed from their positions, and professional Nazi organisations were set up which workers were encouraged to join. This 'co-ordination' or 'switching on' of society with the Nazis was a powerful means by which Hitler was able to establish his dictatorship.

German citizens co-operated with the Nazis and joined their professional organisations for a number of reasons. In such an atmosphere of repression, there could be a fear of seeming as though you were opposed to the Nazis by not joining their organisations. Also, for professional reasons, associating with the Nazi Party was then of great benefit in German society. There was also a large number of Germans who agreed with the Nazis' policies and believed that socialism and Communism were a danger to German society and needed to be destroyed. Whatever the case, *Gleichschaltung* had its own perpetual dynamic, as more and more Germans associated with Nazi organisations, thus accentuating the Nazis' control over daily life. Alongside this was the control that the Nazis, led by Joseph Goebbels, head of the Propaganda Ministry, had over the German media. Press, radio and films were a means by which the Nazis could disseminate their message to the German people, restricting all other dissenting voices. Using these critical factors of violence, pseudo-legality, propaganda and *Gleichschaltung*, the Nazis were therefore able to move towards a totalitarian state in the first few months of their government. Freedoms were eroded, political opposition arrested, anti-Nazi messages restricted and Nazi organisations imposed on society.

SOURCE 2

Hermann Goering was arrested at the end of the Second World War, and between 8 and 22 March 1946 he faced trial on war crime charges, for which he was eventually found guilty and sentenced to death. During the trial that took place in Nuremberg, he discussed several aspects of the Nazi dictatorship. Here, he explains what measures were taken to strengthen the power of the Nazi Party after Hitler's appointment as Chancellor in 1933.

In order to consolidate this power now, it was necessary to reorganise the political relationships of power. That was carried out in such a manner that, shortly after the seizure of governmental authority in the Reich and in Prussia, the other states followed automatically and more or less strong National Socialist Governments were formed everywhere. Secondly, the so-called political officials, who according to the Reich Constitution could be recalled at any time - that is, could be dismissed - would naturally have to be replaced now according to custom by people from the strongest Party - as is everywhere customary.

For the further seizure of power, main political offices were now likewise filled with new appointments, as is the case in other countries when there has been a shift of power among the political parties. Besides the Ministers there were mainly – I take Prussia as an example – the heads of provinces, the official heads of administrative districts, the police commissioners, county heads. In addition there were certain further grades – I believe ministerial directors were considered political officials, and so also were district attorneys. This on the whole described the group of offices which were filled anew when a shift in political power took place and had previously been bargained out among the parties having majority... In spite of that we did very little in this direction at first. First of all, I requested Herr von Papen to turn over to me the position of Prussian 'Minister President' since he, as he had no Party behind him, could not very well undertake this reshuffling, whereas I – that is one of us – could do so. We agreed at once. Thereupon I filled some, a relatively small part, of the offices of the highest administrative officials of Prussian provinces with National Socialists. At the same time I generously allowed Social Democrats to remain in these posts for many weeks... slowly, in the course of time, these offices, in so far as they were key presidential positions, were, of course, filled with National Socialists... In the case of police commissioners, I should like to emphasise for the information of the Tribunal that the police commissioners at first had nothing to do with the Gestapo... I filled these offices of police commissioners partly with National Socialists but partly with people who had nothing to do with the party.

ACTIVITY
KNOWLEDGE CHECK

1 According to Goering in Source 2, how did the Nazis go about consolidating their position shortly after coming to power?

2 How does Source 2 demonstrate the importance of the government control over Prussia?

3 How does Goering try to defend the Nazis' actions?

Abolition of political parties and trade unions

Despite the repression following the Reichstag fire and the restrictions and violence against political opposition during the election campaign, the Nazis were still unable to achieve a majority in the Reichstag. This was important, as they required a two-thirds majority vote in parliament in order to change the constitution and thus fully implement their dictatorship. Even with their coalition with the other right-wing nationalist parties, they still only constituted 52 percent of Reichstag seats. Despite these difficulties, the Nazis were able to achieve their political goals through a variety of means.

The necessity of Hindenburg's support

Firstly, they required the crucial support of President Hindenburg, without whom no change to the constitution could be implemented. Goebbels used the opening of a new Reichstag, at Potsdam on 21 March 1933, to ingratiate the Nazis with Hindenburg. The event was named 'The Day of the National Uprising' and was timed to coincide with the anniversary of the opening of the first Reichstag in 1871. The event was stage-managed by Goebbels, with Hitler appearing in formal black attire, as opposed to his military uniform, and using the opportunity to show his gratitude and subservience to the President. At the tomb of the Prussian King Frederick the Great, Hitler spoke of his respect for the President and his belief in the union of his young regime with the older order of Germany. The event was shown in cinemas and broadcast on the radio. It was critical in reassuring the powerful conservative forces that Hitler respected their position, and thus strengthened Hindenburg's support for the constitutional changes the Nazis proposed.

The Enabling Act

Only two days after the opening of the new Reichstag, the Reichstag met to debate the Enabling Act that would allow the Nazis the power to alter the Weimar Constitution and give the Chancellor, Adolf Hitler, the power to legislate and enact his own laws. Hitler was able to achieve this through a variety of means:

- The Communist Party of Germany (KPD) had won 81 seats, but members were by this stage either in concentration camps or had left the country, ensuring that they would offer no political opposition to the vote. The Reichstag Fire Decrees had come too late to stop the KPD running in the election, but the party had subsequently been repressed and its members were not able to take up the seats they had actually won.

- The SPD members who were able to make the debate (94 out of 120 members who had won Reichstag seats) faced an intimidating atmosphere. The Reichstag was decorated with swastikas and filled with SA members. The SPD leader, Otto Wells, tried to speak against the Enabling Act, but was drowned out by SA members and faced verbal abuse by an enraged Hitler. As the SPD discussed the vote, the SA men present chanted 'We want the Enabling Act – or there'll be hell to pay'.

- In terms of the Centre Party, Papen, the vice chancellor, was a strong supporter of Hitler's dictatorship, believing it could later be overthrown and a military dictatorship of the upper-class elite implemented. As a key member of the Centre Party, his encouragement of the Enabling Act was one reason why the party voted in favour of the legislation. Additionally, the Centre Party feared the political consequences if they did not support the Enabling Act, and hoped that Hitler could be restrained by President von Hindenburg.

The Enabling Act was initially for only four years, and many members of the Centre Party naively trusted that Hitler would restore political and civil rights after this time. Thus the Enabling Act was overwhelmingly passed by 444 votes to 94. The Enabling Act did not abolish the Reichstag, nor did it immediately outlaw other political parties, but the Reichstag had now lost all political relevancy and acted simply as a body from which Hitler could make major speeches.

SOURCE 3

Hitler shows his respect for President von Hindenburg during the opening of the new Reichstag, 21 March 1933.

SOURCE 4

Hitler addresses the Reichstag during the Enabling Act debate, 23 March 1933.

Kopenick Blood Week

Within four months of the Enabling Act, all political opposition had been abolished. The SPD faced ongoing violence and repression, particularly during the so-called **Kopenick Blood Week** between 21 and 26 June, when 500 SPD members and known anti-Nazi political opponents were gruesomely tortured by the SA, SS and Gestapo, and at least 23 people subsequently died. On 22 June, the SPD was dissolved as a party after its key members fled to Prague. The DNVP was subsequently absorbed into the Nazis after its leader, Alfred Hugenberg, resigned from Hitler's cabinet as a protest against Nazi attempts to dissolve his party.

ACTIVITY
KNOWLEDGE CHECK

1 What does the photo of Hitler with Hindenburg (Source 3) demonstrate about Hitler's actions during the opening of the new Reichstag?

2 How does the photo of the Reichstag on the day of the Enabling Act debate (Source 4) help to demonstrate some of the ways in which the Nazis tried to intimidate their political opponents?

3 How do the two photos (Sources 3 and 4) support an understanding of the differing ways in which Hitler consolidated his dictatorship?

KEY TERM

Kopenick Blood Week
Events between 21 and 26 June 1933 that took place in the working-class Berlin area of Kopenick, after SPD member Anton Schmaus resisted arrest by shooting dead three SA members. The SA reacted in a horrific fashion, arresting and torturing some 500 SPD members. The events led to much of the SPD fleeing to Prague. It also demonstrates why political resistance against the Nazis was so difficult. Schmaus did resist, but the outcome demonstrated that any attack on the Nazis would simply be responded to with even greater violence and repression.

The Centre Party was weakened by the Concordat negotiations between Hitler and the pope, in which the Nazis promised to respect Catholic institutions in Germany if they refrained from political activities (officially signed on 20 July 1933). On 5 July, the Centre Party thus dissolved itself as a political party. On 14 July 1933, the Nazis were declared to be the only legal party in Germany, and a decree was passed making it illegal in Germany to form any new political group. It had essentially taken only seven months for the Nazis to destroy the Weimar political system and impose a totalitarian dictatorship on Germany.

SOURCE

5

Nora Waln was a bestselling author and journalist who lived in Germany in the late 1930s. In her book *Reaching for the Stars* (1940), she describes the spread of the Nazi movement and her belief that the German people would rebel against what she saw as an evil ideology. Here she describes a conversation with a German friend about Nazi violence against political opponents in the period after they came to power.

I now asked about this brother in law, and learned that during the Republic he had been an outspoken Social Democrat. When President von Hindenburg appointed Herr Hitler Chancellor on 30th January 1933, this man issued a pamphlet warning citizens against the encroaching dangers of dictatorship. After the Reichstag fire on February 27th he stated, without reserve, his opinion that the National Socialists had done this themselves to unloose a wave of terror and ride to power on it. He had worked hard to oppose them in the March elections, and issued a pamphlet against the proclamation of the anti-Jewish boycott of April 1933. He had tried to form a league of men and women organised to fight the 'Law of April 7th' when publicised because he felt that its 'reform of the organisation of the Reich' simply meant the handing of government over to complete Nazi control. He had issued a pamphlet telling Catholics that the Concordat signed between Hitler and the Vatican on July 8th would be betrayed by Hitler as soon as he made what use he could of the Catholics. On July 16th, not quite six months after Hitler became Chancellor, a law was published forbidding all parties except the National Socialist Party. Shortly afterwards, this man went for a walk one evening and did not return. At Christmas the wife shot their five year old son and herself 'while of unsound mind'. She had that morning received a package – a cigar box – marked with a swastika and the word 'traitor' before her husband's name. It contained ashes.

ACTIVITY
KNOWLEDGE CHECK

1 What does Source 5 argue was a key means by which the Nazis imposed their dictatorship?

2 How useful is Source 5 to historians? Consider the strengths and weaknesses of the source, including the background of the book and the use of this dramatic example.

3 How far can individual stories, such as that in Source 5, advance historical understanding?

The destruction of the trade union movement

Parallel to the brutal suppression of political opponents was the destruction of the politically powerful trade union movement. The popular Christian trade union was dissolved due to the Concordat. The socialist trade unions, however, were destroyed through deceit and violence.

The socialist trade unions had over four million members. Hoping to preserve their institutions in the face of Nazi pressure, they promised to remove their association with the SPD and co-operate with the Nazis. At first the Nazis seemed agreeable to this idea; 1 May 1933 was designated the Day of National Labour and a holiday for workers was held. On the following day, however, as the trade union members slept off the effects of their holiday celebrations, the SA raided the trade union offices, destroyed their organisations and arrested trade union leaders. In an example of *Gleichschaltung*, the trade unions were replaced with the Nazi organisation the German Labour Front (DAF), which was then the only legal trade union represented by German industry.

Thus, those previously powerful institutions that had exerted political influence throughout the Weimar period, whether trade unions or political parties such as the SPD, were repressed, attacked, arrested and then outlawed between January and July 1933. Although there were still areas of concern for Hitler, he had essentially imposed the foundations of the Nazi dictatorship that would rule over Germany during the following tumultuous 12 years.

The establishment of DAF

The destruction of the trade unions took place in parallel to the establishment of the Nazi workers' organisation, the German Labour Front (DAF). This is a good example of *Gleichschaltung* in action, the implementation of a Nazi organisation as the only legal institution for workers in Germany. The DAF was established shortly after the Nazi raids of 2 May. In the same month, all independent labour unions in Germany were outlawed. The DAF, which replaced the trade unions, was not established to defend the rights of workers or push for greater pay or conditions, as the old trade unions had done. All previous contracts agreed during the Weimar Republic were dissolved and workers now had to accept new contracts set by employers. With the lack of worker representation, there was a clear advantage for industrial bosses and this was shown in the increased hours and wage freezes workers had to accept. Within the context of Nazi Germany there was also no way workers could voice their opposition, and this was obviously not the role the DAF was meant to play. Instead, its primary purpose was to control German workers and ensure that political agitation was silenced. In November 1933, its key goal was set out as 'educating all Germans engaged in the life of labour in Nationalist Socialist conviction'.

The leader of the DAF, Robert Ley, believed that it was crucial that the Nazis provided some form of workers' organisation after the destruction of the trade unions. He believed that given the distrust many workers in Germany had of the Nazis, without some form of representation for German labourers their opposition would simply grow further. The Nazis instead had to demonstrate that they could provide benefits for the German working class. In some ways, the DAF did aim to protect workers' rights. In the period after 1936, as German industry was focused predominately on rearmament and preparation for war, the DAF opposed attempts to restrict workers' wages and hours or impose stricter controls on their ability to move jobs. Ley argued that such attempts would increase worker opposition to the Nazis, forms of which would be manifested in lower productivity and potential sabotage of German industries. Goebbels and other important Nazis, who believed that keeping working-class support was essential to Nazi power, generally supported this argument.

The 'co-ordination' of regional and local government

One of the key issues Hitler faced in terms of the imposition of his dictatorship was Germany's federal system. Not only did he need to overcome the federal system represented by the Reichstag, but Germany's numerous local and state institutions as well. In this sense, he was helped by events that had taken place before he had been appointed chancellor. The previous chancellor, Papen, had deposed the Prussian Socialist/Centre Party coalition government in July 1932. He had justified this questionable action, known as the Prussia coup d'état, by the supposed inability of the Socialist/Centre Party coalition government to control street violence between the SA and the Communists in the state, therefore requiring a state of emergency to be declared and the central government, under the chancellor, to take direct control. The real reason had been that Papen hoped the destruction of the SPD's powerful base in Prussia would gain him favour with right-wing Germans and organisations in the lead-up to the 1932 July elections. Although this goal failed, a key significance of Papen's actions was the precedent it allowed Hitler to take advantage of.

Goering was appointed Reich Commissioner for the Prussian Ministry of the Interior when the Nazis came to power, and he had used this powerful position to control the Prussian police and civil service. It was also this position that allowed the Nazis to 'legally reinforce' the Prussian police with 50,000 SA, SS and Stahlhelm members. Further to this, Article 2 of the Reichstag Fire Decrees, using the precedent of the Prussian coup d'état, enabled the Nazis to take control of any state that could not control law and order. In March 1933, the SA and SS were put to use, causing disorder and violence in states where the Nazis had yet to take control. Utilising Article 2 and the fact that these states could not control law and order, despite the fact that it was the Nazis themselves accentuating the problem, the Nazi Party was able to replace the governments of Wurttemberg, Baden, Bremen, Hamburg, Saxony, Hessen, Bavaria and Lubeck with their own Reich commissioners.

Prussian coup d'état (July 1932)

Despite the fact that the Nazis had nothing to do with it, the Prussian coup d'état was a crucial event that would help Hitler cement his dictatorship when he came to power in 1933. When he became chancellor in 1932, Papen had hoped to implement a nationalistic dictatorship supported by the military. Prussia was Germany's largest and most important state and was ruled by a left-wing coalition of the SPD, Centre Party and German Democratic Party. It was the last major power base of German centre-left politics. Papen required Hindenburg to use Article 48 to remove the constitutional government of Prussia. He used the violence then taking place on the streets of Prussia, primarily caused by the SA from which Papen had just lifted a ban, to pressure Hindenburg into granting him emergency powers over Prussia. On 20 July 1932, Hindenburg granted Papen direct control over Prussia and dismissed the parliamentary government of the state. The move was contested in the German courts by the SPD, but in October, Papen's coup was deemed legal.

The coup severely weakened the SPD and removed the last democratic, centre-left government in Germany. It also provided the Nazis with significant powers when Hitler became chancellor in 1933. Goering's cabinet role meant he essentially ruled Prussia, and he was able to use its police force, in particular, to move against the Nazis' political opposition. Critically, the constitutional precedent set by the coup was replicated by Hitler, who used the SA to create violence on the streets of differing German states and then simply asserted that, as the states could not stop street violence taking place, he would have to impose centralised, governmental control over the states, just as Papen had done to Prussia in 1932.

Gauleiters

This was a unique Nazi organisation. Originally, they had been heads of electoral districts that assisted the Nazi Party with its campaigns in specific regions. On taking power in 1933, they became Nazi governors of the regions. They had enormous power and ruled their regions as 'regional Hitlers'. They were usually loyal Nazis who had been members of the party since the early 1920s. Whether they strengthened or weakened Hitler's power is a matter for continuing debate among historians.

By the end of March, all regional and local governments were under Nazi administration. On 31 March, the Law for the Co-ordination of the *Länder* was instituted, allowing the Nazi governors, known as **Gauleiters**, to implement laws and administer their states without having to consult the state parliaments. This essentially gave the Gauleiters considerable power, installing them as dictators over the areas they controlled.

The final destruction of the German state system that had existed since 1871 came on 30 January 1934, with the Law for Reconstruction of the Reich. This law officially ended all state parliaments, made all rights of administration of the *Länder* subservient to the central government and abolished the upper house created by the Weimar Constitution, the Reichsrat, which had represented the state assemblies. By January 1934 then, through a combination of violence and legislation, the Nazis had imposed their dictatorship firmly on Germany, becoming the only legal party in both federal and state government. The main concern of Hitler now focused on powerful institutions within his own party.

The impact of the Night of the Long Knives

As you have read previously, the SA was an important aspect in the implementation of the Nazi dictatorship. Their use of violence against the Nazis' opponents enabled the party to intimidate those who may have threatened their power. The SA was led by Ernst Rohm and had played a key part in Hitler's ascension to the chancellorship; in numerous violent confrontations they had imposed Nazi control in the streets of Germany and weakened political opponents, particularly the SPD and the KPD. The Brown Shirts, as they were known due to their uniform, were a violent and revolutionary group of men who now believed that Hitler's dictatorship would provide them with the reward they were due in response to the efforts they had made throughout the 1920s and early 1930s. They expected Hitler to go further with the Nazi revolution, allowing the SA a crucial role in the state, particularly in respect to the military, which the SA hoped to control. The SA was also more radically anti-capitalist in its ideology and expected a greater revolution in the German economic system, and a prioritising of unemployed SA men in terms of employment. Hitler, however, was concerned that such disruption would upset those in the economic system, particularly the wealthy industrialists, who he needed to implement his economic plans.

After the banning of other political parties in July 1933, SA violence, which had been so helpful in the past, now became counterproductive to Hitler's plans. With the Communists and SPD gone, SA violence seemingly had no purpose, and the continuation of the violent behaviour of the SA now grew in unpopularity, particularly with the middle classes who were supportive of Hitler. The military also despised the SA, seeing it as a group of undisciplined, violent thugs who were a threat to the army's privileged position in German society. The SA believed that it should take control of the military, implementing a so-called 'people's militia'. This was a serious threat to the military's position, particularly given the size of the SA, which at this stage numbered around two million. The army, on the other hand, was limited to only 100,000 men by the terms of the Versailles Treaty. Hitler had already clearly demonstrated that in respect of this argument the army was more important to his aims, having informed the SA in February 1933 that only the military was legally allowed to carry weapons. In terms of both his political goals and his foreign policy, Hitler understood that having support from the military was absolutely essential. Also concerning for Hitler was the growing opposition of the conservative right in Germany against the Nazis and calls for a 'second revolution'. Some of these powerful conservatives, including Papen, had even raised the possibility of the monarchy being restored on Hindenburg's death. While Hitler had some sympathy for Rohm's politics, he also understood the power that the elites of Germany held, and that compromise was required at this early stage of his dictatorship if he was to strengthen his power. He was particularly worried about Hindenburg. The President was elderly and nearing death. Hitler aimed to take over the role of president on Hindenburg's death. In this sense, he needed the President to grant Hitler these powers by not appointing a new president before he passed away. To achieve this goal, Hitler needed to assure the President and the military that he would respect the power of the Junkers. Rohm's calls for a 'second revolution' were therefore problematic to Hitler's political goals.

On 17 June 1934, Papen spoke at Marburg University, criticising calls for a 'second revolution', as well as Nazi intimidation of German churches and its refusal to listen to other political viewpoints. Hitler was now seriously concerned that the actions of the SA would fuel opposition from the military and the conservative right. The tension was accentuated further when the head of the military, Werner von Bloomberg, threatened to impose military control over Germany if the Nazis could not stop SA disorder still taking place in German towns. Other Nazis, such as the SS leader Heinrich Himmler and Goering, who despised Rohm, had been spreading false rumours that Rohm was about to launch a takeover of government against Hitler. With this building pressure, Hitler finally decided to act on 30 June 1934. The SS moved against any powerful opponents to the regime, arresting Rohm and other SA leaders and having them executed. Other conservative opponents were executed, including the previous chancellor Schleicher and the author of Papen's Marburg university speech, Edgar Jung. Papen himself was arrested and kept prisoner for four days, where he was continually threatened with execution. Two of his closest advisers in government were executed. When he was finally released, he was a severely weakened figure who posed no further threat to Hitler's dictatorship. In total, around 200 of the key SA leaders were executed, as well as around 100 other political opponents.

The impact of the Night of the Long Knives was overwhelmingly positive for Hitler's dictatorship. It completely destroyed any potential threat from the conservative right. It was popular with the military, who appreciated Hitler's destruction of the SA. This was clearly shown on 1 August, when Hindenburg passed away and Hitler was able to take the role of chancellor and president under a new title, Führer, without any opposition from the military. On 20 August, the army showed its appreciation further by implementing a new oath whereby all soldiers would swear absolute loyalty to Adolf Hitler.

For the German people, the Night of the Long Knives had shown Hitler as a decisive and daring leader, who would even be willing to move against his own party if he believed that it represented a threat to German society. The SA violence had become unpopular and many German people believed that the SA was planning to overthrow the German state; thus its destruction was greeted with widespread support. Alternatively, for those Germans opposed to the Nazis, the Night of the Long Knives showed the consequences of opposition and provided a stark example of the vicious tactics the Nazis were capable of to maintain their dictatorship.

Overall, then, the Night of the Long Knives was a critical moment, confirming the nature of Hitler's dictatorship. He was not in favour of any further revolution, but was instead determined to work with the traditional powers of German society to fulfil his goals. It destroyed any form of opposition and firmly entrenched the Nazi dictatorship. It had taken only 18 months, from January 1933 to August 1934, for Hitler to impose an unchallenged totalitarian system over Germany.

SOURCE 6

Hitler's speech to the Reichstag on 13 July 1934, in which he explains his motivations for the Night of the Long Knives and argues why he had to move against Rohm and the SA.

Without ever informing me and when at first I never dreamt of any such action, the Chief of Staff Rohm, through the agency of an utterly corrupt swindler – a certain Herr von A – entered into relations with General Schleicher. General Schleicher was the man who gave external expression to the secret with of the Chief of Staff, Rohm... He it was who defined the latter's views in concrete form and maintained that: 1. The present regime in Germany cannot be supported. 2. Above all the army and all national associations must be united in a single band. 3. The only man who could be considered for such a position was the Chief of Staff, Rohm. 4. Herr Von Papen must be removed and he himself would be ready to take the position of Vice Chancellor, and that in addition further important changes must be made in the Cabinet of the Reich... However in the course of the 29th June I received threatening intelligence... At 1 o'clock in the night I received from Berlin and Munich two urgent messages concerning alarm summonses. Firstly that for Berlin an alarm muster had been ordered... for 4 o'clock in the afternoon, that for the transport of the regular shock formations the requisition of lorries had been ordered, and that this requisition was now proceeding, and that promptly at 5 o'clock action was to begin with a surprise attack: the Government building was to be occupied. In these circumstances I could make but one decision. If disaster was to be prevented at all, action must be taken with lightning speed. Only a ruthless and bloody intervention might still perhaps stifle the spread of revolt. If anyone reproaches me and asks why I did not resort to the regular courts of justice for conviction of the offenders, then all that I can say to him is this: in this hour I was responsible for the fate of the German people, and thereby I became the supreme Justiciar of the German people!

SOURCE 7

A report by the German Social Democratic Party in Exile (Sopade) on the public reaction to the Night of the Long Knives. Here, the report considers the reaction in Germany in general and then reports on the reaction in some specific states.

The immediate result of the murders was great confusion, both as regards the way they were viewed and as regards their future political consequences. On the whole, Hitler's courage in taking decisive action was stressed the most. He was regarded practically as a hero... Our comrades report that Hitler has won strong approval and sympathy from that part of the population which still places its hopes in him. To these people his action is proof that he wants order and decency. Other sections of the population have been given cause for thought. East Saxony: A small businessman told me that he and his colleagues had known for a long time that Hitler was going to strike at Rohm and his associates. He still sees Hitler, even now, as an utterly honourable man who wants the best for the German people... When I tried to explain to him that Hitler alone bore the responsibility for all the murders, these and earlier ones, he said, 'Still, the main thing is, he's got rid of the Marxists... Bavaria: First report. By slaughtering his 'best friends,' Hitler has forfeited none of his mass support as yet; rather he has gained. Reports from different parts of Bavaria are unanimous that people are expressing satisfaction that Hitler acted so decisively. He has produced fresh proof that he will not settle for second best and that he wants decency in public life.

ACTIVITY
KNOWLEDGE CHECK

1 In Source 6, what does Hitler claim are the reasons he had to move against his opponents?

2 In what ways is Source 6 useful for historians? In what ways is it not useful?

3 Looking at Source 7, why had Hitler's actions been popular with the German people?

4 Why is the Sopade source (Source 7) particularly strong in showing Hitler's popularity? (Hint: Consider the provenance of the source and what the main goal of Sopade was.)

TO WHAT EXTENT WAS HITLER A DICTATOR BY 1935?

Hitler's approach to government

Given the power that Hitler was able to impose over German society, it would seem logical to imagine that he approached government in a centralised fashion, proclaiming numerous orders that had to be fulfilled by his subservient party. It can therefore be surprising to learn that Hitler's approach to government was in many ways the exact opposite of this. In fact, it was quite disordered and lacked a strong direction. However, this does not mean that it was inefficient or incapable of reaching its goals; rather, it was a unique system that centred on Hitler's role in the party.

By August 1933, the unique nature of Hitler's approach to government was becoming apparent. Hitler had no interest in the discussions or design of new legislation. Instead, it was up to the initiative of the ministers to draft new legislation and then discuss it with other relevant ministers. Once the legislation was redrafted and organised it was presented to Hitler, who would read through it (sometimes only briefly) and either sign it into law or reject it. Hitler played no role in co-ordinating the ministerial departments, so at any one time different ministers could be working on drafting legislation that contradicted or replicated other departments' proposed legislation.

SOURCE

8

Here, Albert Speer comments on Hitler's peculiar working habits and how he made political decisions. Speer met Hitler in 1933 and subsequently became his friend and personal architect, later becoming Minister of Armaments and War Production. He was sentenced to 20 years in prison after the war ended. His book, *Inside the Third Reich* (1970), gives an important and detailed account of his relationship with Adolf Hitler and the functioning of the Nazi dictatorship.

I myself threw all my strength into my work and was baffled at first by the way Hitler squandered his working time. I could understand that he might wish his day to trail off in boredom and pastimes; but to my notion this phase of the day, averaging some six hours, proved rather long, whereas the actual working session was by comparison relatively short. When, I would often ask myself, did he really work? Little was left of the day; he rose late in the morning and conducted one or two official conferences, but from the subsequent dinner on he more or less wasted time until the early hours of the evening. His rare appointments in the late afternoon were imperilled by his passion for looking at building plans. The adjutants often asked me: 'Please don't show any plans today.' Then the drawings I had brought with me would be left by the telephone switchboard at the entrance, and I would reply evasively to Hitler's inquiries. Sometimes he saw through this game and would himself go to look in the anteroom or the cloakroom for my roll of plans. In the eyes of the people Hitler was the Leader who watched over the nation day and night. This was hardly so. But Hitler's lax scheduling could be regarded as a lifestyle characteristic of the artistic temperament. According to my observations, he often allowed a problem to mature during the weeks when he seemed entirely taken up with trivial matters. Then, after the 'sudden insight' came, he would spend a few days of intensive work giving final shape to his solution. No doubt he also used his dinner and supper guests as sounding boards, trying out new ideas, approaching these ideas in a succession of different ways, tinkering with them before an uncritical audience, and thus perfecting them. Once he had come to a decision, he relapsed again into his idleness. I went to Hitler's evenings once or twice a week. Around midnight, after the last movie had been run, he sometimes asked to see my roll of drawings and studied every detail until two or three o'clock in the morning. The other guests withdrew for a glass of wine, or went home, aware that there would be little chance to have a word with Hitler once he was caught up in his ruling passion.

There were several reasons why Hitler allowed this chaotic system to develop. In a unique way, this system, whereby he played little role in day-to-day government, actually allowed Hitler to focus on his key goals: primarily, rearmament and the imposition of German power against the terms of the Versailles Treaty. He also had no real interest in the details of government. It should be noted that Hitler had no experience in political legislation; his career since the First World War had consisted of nothing except constant campaigning for the Nazi Party. His work habits were disorganised and he frequently worked throughout the night but slept in late during the day. He disliked Berlin and therefore spent most of his time away from the capital, at his home in the Bavarian Alps. Once he became Chancellor, Hitler made some efforts to work in a more regulated fashion. However, on becoming Führer following the death of Hindenburg, he made no further effort to order his working life and the Nazi state developed around his particular style of government. Hitler also believed in using the theories of evolution in his governing style, believing that if different government ministries were working on similar areas, the competition would ensure that the best departments would eventually emerge. Hitler would only meet with his favourite ministers and Nazi officials, while for others it was increasingly difficult to present legislation to the Führer. As the Nazis perpetuated the idea that the Führer was never wrong, it was impossible to admit that any legislation was unworkable or had failed in its goals. Instead, the legislative policies were never formally ended, but left unfulfilled. Rivalries between departments developed as differing departments battled for the Führer's attention. Furthering the chaotic nature of the Nazi government was the fact that Hitler declined to take a strong direction in relation to these rivalries, preferring not to take a firm stance on one department over another.

A Level Exam-Style Question Section A

Study Source 8 before you answer this question.

Assess the value of Source 8 for revealing Adolf Hitler's attitude and approach to government.

Explain your answer, using the source, the information given about its origin and your own knowledge about the historical context. (20 marks)

Tip

Consider how Speer's account (Source 8) helps to illuminate the unique nature of Hitler's governing style. Can Speer's assertions help develop understanding of Hitler's attitudes and approach, and in what way? Also look at Extract 1 and consider in what ways Speer's argument is backed up or debated by historians. Make sure you clearly evaluate the source using valid criteria backed up by historical evidence.

The 'Führer's Will'

Despite this chaotic approach to government, the Nazis still achieved their political goals. This was possible only due to the unique position of Hitler. The Nazi Party may have been somewhat fractured between competing agencies, but they were united by their overwhelming loyalty to Adolf Hitler. Even without clear direction, Nazi officials were encouraged to use *Mein Kampf* and Hitler's speeches to understand his ideology and form legislation that would fulfil his goals. There may have been competition between differing departments, but the legislation being produced was therefore committed to the ideas of Hitler. Hitler would sign off on initiatives that he favoured, therefore ensuring that his ideas were becoming reality. If Hitler did not favour legislation, it would be either rejected or, as discussed previously, would not be pursued further. Only a small number of ministers, primarily Goering, Goebbels and Himmler, favoured by Hitler, could gain personal meetings with the Führer to present legislation. The majority of ministers had to gain access to Hitler through the head of the Reich Chancellery, Hans-Heinrich Lammers. This gave Lammers significant power. He could present ministerial proposals to Hitler in a form that would favour agreement or disagreement from the Führer, or choose not to present the proposals at all. Thus ministers had to find favour with Lammers if their legislation was going to gain the final approval from Hitler. This style of government has been described by the historian Sir Ian Kershaw as fulfilling the 'Führer's Will'. It was up to the other Nazis to understand Hitler's will and create legislation that would make it reality. However, it is of key importance to remember that Hitler was in ultimate control; no legislation could be enacted without his final approval.

'Cumulative radicalisation'

This style of government, despite its chaos, had its own dynamic. As Hitler himself was ideologically extreme, he tended to favour legislation that was extreme in its nature. The competition between departments meant that government departments would enact legislation that was more and more extreme in its elements, in order to outdo other competing agencies and gain the favour of Hitler. Historians have described this as the process of 'cumulative radicalisation', whereby Nazi policy, towards the Jews for instance, got progressively more radical, despite Hitler never making any firm legislative decisions on how the Jews should be treated. Thus Hitler's approach to government was not detrimental to his goals, but instead ensured that his ideas took on the most literal and terrifying reality, as Nazis desperately competed to 'fulfil the will of the Führer'.

KEY TERMS

Plebiscite
Electoral vote in which people vote on one particular issue.

Machiavellian
Niccolò Machiavelli was an Italian philosopher from the 16th century who is best remembered for his political work called *The Prince*. In this book he sets out the personal cunning, deceit and acceptance of immoral and hypocritical actions needed to obtain political power and ensure the defeat of one's political enemies. Machiavellian thus refers to political actions that lack morality and are simply aimed at achieving personal gain, no matter what the cost.

EXTRACT

1 Ian Kershaw, in *Hitler* (1991), describes Hitler's peculiar style of ruling and the chaos this caused in Nazi government.

Once he had been confirmed as head of state, with the sworn support of the army and civil service as well as the popular acclaim provided by the **plebiscite** of August 1934, Hitler's working style as head of government changed. Increasingly, now, he reverted to the irregular, non-bureaucratic style which had characterised his Party leadership prior to 1933. His temperament and personal indolence [laziness] inclined him more towards the 'genial' idea on the spur of the moment and a premium upon public display and maintaining appearances than to poring over lengthy memoranda and complex government papers. According to a former adjutant, 'he took the view that many things sorted themselves out on their own if one did not interfere.' Access to Hitler was increasingly difficult for all but the most favoured ministers, impossible for some. Pinning him down to a clear reasoned decision in disputes, especially on sensitive issues, was far from easy. Important matters could be shelved for months before a decision could be extracted from him. When they came, his 'decisions' were often arbitrary, even casual utterances in an informal setting. They were, however, regarded by those who took them away to use in defence of some policy initiative as anything other than loose recommendations. Where, on occasion, such an initiative, apparently backed by Hitler, met with such hostility that it proved unworkable, it was not revoked – which would have been incompatible with the Führer's prestige – but simply left as a dead letter, or remained 'pending' indefinitely. Hitler's non-bureaucratic style was a recipe for general structural governmental disorder. That it was the product of a well conceived **Machiavellian** strategy to 'divide and rule' is scarcely likely, even though Hitler had extremely sharp antennae towards any move to impair his authority. Rather, it was the practical application of the principle of letting the stronger in a dispute arise through a process of struggle.

ACTIVITY
KNOWLEDGE CHECK

1 To what extent does the primary account in Source 8 back up the historian's argument in Extract 1?

2 Using Source 8 and Extract 1, summarise Hitler's style of government.

3 In what ways was Hitler's style of government damaging to the Nazi dictatorship?

4 In what ways was Hitler's style of government a strength?

Decline of cabinet meetings

In parallel to Hitler's unique approach to government was the decline of direct discussion between Nazi ministers at cabinet meetings. As previously set out, Hitler's first cabinet was a coalition and included only three Nazi ministers. At this early stage of his chancellorship, Hitler had to maintain the support of these other politicians to ensure that the Nazi Party could impose its dictatorship. Thus, despite his aversion to meetings, cabinet meetings continued as they had done previous to January 1933. Yet even from this early stage, Hitler ensured that the cabinet would be progressively weakened in its power. Despite allowing discussion and debate, Hitler would not allow the cabinet to vote on legislation, instead ensuring that he would solely make the final decision on any proposals. The Enabling Act confirmed the weakening of the cabinet further, by allowing the chancellor the power to enact legislation agreed on by the cabinet without the president's signature. Thus a key part of the Weimar Constitution that asserted all legislation had to be confirmed by the president was destroyed.

There was now little point in cabinet meetings, as Hitler's supreme legislative powers meant that debate over legislative proposals was pointless, as all decision making was subservient to Hitler's position. As the Nazis imposed their dictatorship and the role of other politicians weakened in the cabinet (the cabinet still contained non-Nazi members), the need for cabinet meetings became increasingly unnecessary. Some cabinet members complained that they only found out about crucial decisions made by Hitler from listening to the radio or reading the newspaper. While the cabinet had met 72 times in 1933, in 1935 it met only 12 times. Even at these meetings it was rare that Hitler was even present, preferring instead to stay in his Bavarian home rather than travel into Berlin. Discussions between ministers concerning government initiatives declined until they were non-existent, thus contributing to the style of government discussed previously.

Relations with the army

As mentioned earlier, Hitler's relationship with the army between 1933 and 1935 was shaped intrinsically by the events concerning the Night of the Long Knives. From the very beginning of the Nazi regime, Hitler was focused on overcoming the restrictions of the Versailles Treaty and regaining areas of Germany that had been lost after the First World War. He also aimed to go beyond this, claiming living space, *Lebensraum*, for the German people through an expansion of their territory. To achieve these goals he required the support of the military and a disciplined, well-equipped, well-trained army. Arguments by Rohm calling for the establishment of a people's militia were thus detrimental to Hitler's goals. Hitler demonstrated that he favoured the military over the SA when he asserted in February 1933 that only the military could carry guns. In January 1934, he followed this up by ordering the SA to limit its activities to political agitation, a move that pleased the military, but drove Rohm to further anger at the direction of Hitler's dictatorship. The military was still concerned with the SA, and one of the key motivations for the Night of the Long Knives was the threat by the military not to support Hitler's ascension to the presidency if he did not move against the SA.

As previously set out, following the events of 30 June 1934, the army chose to implement the 'Hitler oath' for all servicemen in the army, promising 'I swear by God this holy oath, that I will render unconditional obedience to the Leader of the German Reich, Adolf Hitler, supreme commander of the armed forces, and that, as a brave soldier, I will be ready at any time to stake my life for this oath'. This was a significant move, tying all German soldiers intrinsically to the goals of Adolf Hitler, a move that would not be fully understood in its ultimate consequence until the Second World War. Rearmament and the focus on redeveloping the German army gained further approval from the military for Hitler's policies, particularly in March 1935, when conscription was reintroduced.

However, Hitler was also concerned about the military's traditional political influence and worked on slowly weakening it.

It could be argued that the focus on National Socialist ideological education for new recruits conscripted in the army from 1935 had the effect of diluting the traditional Prussian values that had shaped the military ideal in Germany since 1871. Hitler also paid less attention to challenges from the military. Although supportive of his decision to reintroduce conscription, the military chiefs were concerned by the fact that they had not been consulted in any way about this significant move. Additionally, despite promising to respect the army as the only military force in Germany, he allowed the head of the SS, Heinrich Himmler, to create SS regiments to control the growing concentration camp system. Under the command of Sepp Dietrich, the Order of the Death's Head reached 2,000 men by the end of 1934. Despite concerns voiced by the army, who felt that these new regiments impinged on roles that should be carried out by the military, the regiments under Dietrich continued to grow. Thus, while the policies of Hitler mostly pleased the military and Hitler was careful to nurture their support, as the Nazi dictatorship grew in power, the army leaders found that they were undoubtedly becoming more and more subservient to Adolf Hitler's leadership and ideology.

SOURCE

Military recruits take the oath of allegiance to Adolf Hitler, 2 August 1934, Potsdam. After Hindenburg died, the traditional oath to the supreme commander was changed so that it swore allegiance to Hitler by name, as opposed to the political office of supreme commander. This picture shows some of the first soldiers to swear allegiance to Hitler directly.

ACTIVITY
KNOWLEDGE CHECK

1 What can you learn about the military oath to Adolf Hitler from the photo (Source 9) alone?

2 Photos such as Source 9 were widely published by the Nazi Party. Why do you think the Nazis would have wanted Germans to see military recruits taking the oath to Hitler?

The extent of Hitler's power by 1935

When one considers the progress of Hitler's dictatorship from 1933 to 1935, it is clear that he had amassed significant power within this two-year period. He had destroyed all opposition, undermined the traditional institutions of government (such as the cabinet) and imposed Nazi ideology across society. The Nazis had oppressed all state institutions and were able to use their control of the German media to ensure that their world view was largely disseminated across Germany. Hitler even felt confident enough in his position to no longer believe it necessary to consult with the leaders of the military before making critical decisions relating to the German army. He had merged the two most powerful roles in the German political system into the new position of the Führer, and he alone had the power to decide on legislation. No German leader had held such unlimited power since 1871, not even the Kaiser, who had still been restricted somewhat by the Reichstag. Hitler had no belief in a system of law or constitutional government and boasted that he was answerable to nothing except history.

There were areas in which the extent of Hitler's power was somewhat restricted. The Gauleiters had considerable autonomy and opposed legislation emanating from central government if they thought it impinged on their power. Hitler never made it clear who had supreme authority in terms of these disputes, but he was reticent to challenge the power of the Gauleiters. As Hitler refused to take a pro-active role in legislating, this allowed other Nazis, such as Goering, Himmler and Goebbels, to develop their own power bases within the party. Both the Gauleiters and the role of favoured ministers allowed areas of autonomy with the Nazi system; however, this was based centrally on complete loyalty to Hitler. Although Nazi institutions frequently competed with each other, there was no attempt to challenge the overall power at the head of the system. As previously set out, the chaotic system actually enabled Hitler's ideology to become reality in spite of his distance from the decisions that led to the drafting of political legislation. Despite not having completely imposed his leadership over the military, Hitler's position by 1935 was extensive. He dominated the political system in a manner that was unique in its structures of power, and despite its chaotic nature and Hitler's peculiar governing habits, the loyalty of all within the Nazi system ensured that his extreme goals in both foreign and domestic policy were fulfilled within a short period.

A Level Exam-Style Question Section B

'The consolidation of Hitler's dictatorship between 1933 and 1935 was primarily achieved through the use of violence.' To what extent do you agree with this statement? (20 marks)

Tip
This question requires you to assess the use of violence as the primary means of establishing Hitler's dictatorship. You need to weigh up this key factor with other factors that helped him to consolidate his power. What other factors did he use and are these as important as, or more important than, violence?

HOW SUCCESSFUL WAS THE NAZIS' ATTEMPT TO CREATE A VOLKSGEMEINSCHAFT BETWEEN 1933 AND 1935?

The relationship of state and party

One of the key aspects contributing to the chaos in the Nazi political system discussed previously was the complex relationship between the party and state. Nazi institutions such as the SS came to play a significant role in the German system, but Hitler never fully allowed the Nazi Party to take total control over the state. Instead, state institutions such as the ministries (labour, education, transport, etc.), the police, army, judiciary and civil service remained in place. The Nazi Party reformed and controlled these state institutions, with both the judiciary and civil service purged of Jews and political opponents, for instance. However, it was never entirely clear whether the institutions of the state or the institutions of the party were the dominant aspect in German politics. In terms of the military situation, it was very clear that Hitler favoured the traditional state institution of the army over the party group of the SA, but in other areas the boundaries between state and party were complex and ever-changing. Robert Ley, for instance, attempted to use the DAF to try to influence economic affairs, but was mostly unsuccessful. Instead, from 1934 to 1937, the Minister of Economics, Hjalmar Schacht, was the main figure in charge of the economy, thus showing the dominance of the state institution on the economy during this period. The Gauleiters, on the other hand, were largely independent Nazi institutions and frequently clashed with the Minister of the Interior, Frick, who found it difficult to centrally control these regional Nazi leaders.

EXTEND YOUR KNOWLEDGE

The role of state and party – dualism in Nazi Germany

To understand Hitler's unique form of government, it is crucial to understand the difference between state and party structures. In the United Kingdom it is clear that the state plays the dominant role in government. The state institutions such as the chancellor and the ministers run the country through the cabinet, and the civil service, which helps to run the differing state institutions, supports them. If the party changes through an election, the prime minister appoints new ministers, but the actual state structures do not change. The civil service remains largely unchanged and carries on working for the same government organisation, albeit for a different minister. There are party organisations in the United Kingdom, but these seek to influence decisions made by the party leaders; they do not play any specific governing role. In countries such as the USSR up to 1991, or Communist China today, the party is the main body. These are one-party Communist states, where it is clear that party organisations play the primary role in governing the country. In Nazi Germany, however, the question of whether the old state structures of German politics or the Nazi Party organisations were more important was never clear. Instead, Hitler supported a system that has been described as 'dualism', whereby two parallel organisations – government and party – operated in competition with each other; neither being clear which exactly was in charge. This undoubtedly led to a chaotic system of overlapping bureaucracies. However, as the historian Richard Kershaw has argued, this confusion and 'dualism' actually helped to strengthen Hitler's own power in a unique fashion.

To add to the confusion, Hitler frequently created party institutions that paralleled state institutions and set out overlapping tasks. For example, in 1933, instead of using the Ministry of Transport to manage the construction of the Autobahn, he created a totally new party institution to oversee the Autobahn, Organisation Todt, led by Fritz Todt, who he appointed General Inspector for German Roads. In terms of the police, as early as 1933 the lines were blurred between state and party when the SS, Stahlhelm and SA were inducted into the Prussian police force. From 1933 to 1936, the Minister of Interior and Himmler clashed over whether the party or state had control of the police, but in 1936 the SS was officially placed in charge of the German police force. This enabled the police to become a key instrument in the imposition of Nazi policies, as opposed to an independent organisation upholding the rule of law. As you have previously read, there was even the creation of separate SS divisions, a move that challenged the dominance of the army as the sole military institution in Germany. The military was also angered by the fact that the building of the new German air force, the Luftwaffe, was placed under the newly created Reich Aviation Ministry, controlled by Herman Goering, as opposed to the state institution of the Ministry of Defence. The overlapping responsibilities of the state Ministry of Education and the party institution of the Hitler Youth, run by Baldur von Schirach, also confused policies concerning young Germans.

It may seem confusing to understand exactly why Hitler implemented this difficult relationship between state and party. Why did he not simply implement total party control over all aspects of German politics? If he wanted Todt to be in control of the building of the Autobahn, why did he not sack the Minister for Transport and appoint Todt? However, what needs to be comprehended is that this confusion enhanced Hitler's power. He was happy to use state institutions when they benefited his aims at that point in time. A perfect example is Schacht. In the early stages of his dictatorship, Hitler needed to assure influential industrialists that the Nazis would not make radical changes to the running of the economy. Thus, it was to Hitler's advantage at that stage for the Ministry of Economics, under a conservative economics expert, to be in control of the economy. This was to change after 1936, as the party institution of the Plenipotentiary of the Four-Year Plan came to control the economy. However, in key areas of Hitler's interests, namely the police, the Autobahn and German youth, appointing new organisations that were directly answerable to him alone allowed Hitler to subvert the potential controls of the state and his own party. Instead, the leaders of these institutions were loyal to Hitler and committed to enacting his 'will'. Both the party and the state therefore eroded in power during the Nazi period, in turn enhancing the personal power of the Führer.

EXTRACT

2 Ian Kershaw, in *Hitler* (1991), here describes how the confusing dualism between state and party accentuated Hitler's power.

More important than the unresolved Party-state dualism was the creation of new institutions, usually straddling Party and state though belonging to neither, and owing their very existence and their power to their position as direct executive agencies of the 'Führer will.' They were an expression of the fact that from the very outset the 'Führer will' formed a separable – theoretically all encompassing and in practice dominant – category of power to that of the apparatus of state government and administration itself. The 'state' which in German political thought since Hegel had enjoyed such an elevated status, was, as a structured apparatus of 'rational' government and administration, for Hitler no more than a means to an end – to be exploited where possible, but to be discarded where the end could be better achieved without it. Hence in policy areas which Hitler regarded as of especial importance, new instruments of executive implementation were established... Through the erosion of central government, the accompanying proliferation of agencies of policy making and administration and the creation of new hybrid executive organisations, the autonomy of the 'Führer's will' could expand dramatically, freed of any constitutional or institutional restraints. Even Hitler's official title suggested the change which was taking place: in 1933 he was officially 'Reich Chancellor,' after Hindenburg's death this was altered to 'Führer and Reich Chancellor.'

ACTIVITY
KNOWLEDGE CHECK

1 According to Extract 2, why did Hitler maintain state organisations?

2 Using Extract 2 and your own studies, explain how the confusing relationship between state and party in Nazi Germany actually strengthened Hitler's power.

Attempts to create a *Volksgemeinschaft*

One of the key goals for the Nazi dictatorship was the implementation of a people's community, a *Volksgemeinschaft* that would unite the fractured aspects of German society into one united communal body. The *Volksgemeinschaft* was a rather vague idea that was older than the Nazi Party itself and related to the spiritual connection that all Germans should feel in respect to their nation. In Nazi propaganda, this connection between Germans was brought about by shared loyalty to the nation and to Hitler. The two aspects were inseparable, as belief in Germany was belief in Hitler; it was therefore not possible to be part of the *Volksgemeinschaft* and not support the Führer.

The exploitation of propaganda was the key means by which the Nazis attempted to create the *Volksgemeinschaft*. The Weimar Republic was portrayed as the worst point in German history, its politicians having betrayed the German people after the First World War and then implemented a fractured and weak political system that accentuated the divisions within society. In comparison, the Nazis had brought about strong, central government that was regaining the pride of the German people. The key figure was Adolf Hitler, who embodied the hopes and dreams of the German nation and was committed to overcoming the humiliation of the First World War. Class divisions that had been so prevalent during the Weimar were to be overcome; the most important aspect of any German's identity was not their earning power or their occupation, it was the very fact that they were German and that they supported Adolf Hitler. The national community was also shaped by a clearly articulated concept of exclusion. Some people could never be part of the *Volksgemeinschaft* due to their race or political outlook. Only true Germans could be part of the *Volksgemeinschaft*, with Nazi propaganda depicting Communists and Jews as disease-like, poisonous and harmful to the strength of the national community. The *Volksgemeinschaft* was thus shaped by a clear identification of who it did not include, as well as who it did.

The vagueness of its concept was one of the *Volksgemeinschaft*'s key strengths. Germans across society could relate to differing aspects of the Nazis that they supported. Big business, farm owners and the military, for example, shared support for the end of democracy and the imposition of a centralised dictatorship. Both the Protestant and Catholic Churches supported the strong movement against Communism and the imposition of a more structured, less liberal German society that shared many of the Churches, own values. Many Germans supported the end of a political system they had become disenchanted with and supported Hitler's opposition to the hated Versailles settlement.

The key aspect of the *Volksgemeinschaft* was consent: it was a powerful uniting force that encouraged Germans to support the Nazis for many differing reasons. It did not mean that all Germans agreed with every single aspect of the Nazi state, but instead that they shared support for key parts of the regime they believed were positive. Oppositional voices were excluded and instead, German people were repeatedly told that fanatic support for the Nazis, and willingness to commit one's life to the Führer, were the key principles that united the national community. The old, more selfish divisions based on personal motivations were to be given up and, instead, the new values of self-sacrifice and belief in Germany, as represented by Hitler, were to be embraced. In the period between 1933 and 1935, the concept of the *Volksgemeinschaft* was thus a powerful idea that wedded German people to the new dictatorship and encouraged a united support from across society. Additionally, the parallel belief that there were people within Germany who could not be part of this national community, that instead were a danger to the unity and strength of the German people, was an intrinsic aspect of the *Volksgemeinschaft* that would have significant and tragic consequences, particularly for the country's Jewish population.

SOURCE 10

In *The Political Testament of Hermann Goering* (1938), Goering here discusses the success of the Nazi *Volksgemeinschaft*.

The national socialism of our Weltanschauung [world view] came therefore at the right time. Our movement seized hold of the cowardly Marxism and took from it the meaning of socialism. It also deprived the cowardly middle class parties of their nationalism, and throwing both into the cauldron of our Weltanschauung, there emerged crystal clear the synthesis: German National Socialism! That was the foundation of the rebuilding of our nation. That is why the revolution was a national socialistic one. The idea grew out of the nation itself – and, because it grew out of the nation, led by the unknown corporal of the Great War, therefore this idea was also chosen to put an end to the dissension among the people and once more to unite them into one unit. The outer frame of the Reich was weak – it was only in existence on paper; inside there was the people, torn apart and bleeding from a thousand wounds; inside there was opposition – of all parties, professions, classes, confessions and occupations. Our leader, Adolf Hitler, realised that the Third Reich could only be saved and rebuilt if one could put inside this outer frame a united people. And that was the work of our movement during the past fourteen years – to make out of a people of divergent interests, religions, classes and occupations – a new and united German people... I do not ask you all where you come from! I have on my staff, officers specially selected from among the common soldiers, and have learned to respect them as real men. One may come from the poorest of conditions; from the most insignificant family, yet in truth he carries in his rucksack the marshal's baton. How much he may make out of himself in life depends entirely on him alone. Today, nothing is a drawback. Conceited appearances of accident may have been wiped away, the individual man is tested and stands, as a result of his own value. Therefore, I desire and command of you, that you take the people's community, created by the Leader, as an example, and that you become part of it – and that you count more valuable the poorest companion, than perhaps the richest and most prominent foreigner. Only when all of us think and feel like that will we become an unconquerable people's community.

SOURCE 11

In *Inside the Third Reich* (1970), Albert Speer discusses the contradictions and hypocrisy of Nazi claims concerning the *Volksgemeinschaft*.

The ordinary party member was being taught that grand policy was much too complex for him to judge it. Consequently, one felt one was being represented, never called upon to take personal responsibility. The whole structure of the system was aimed at preventing conflicts of conscience from even arising. The result was the total sterility of all conversations and discussions among these like minded persons. It was boring for people to confirm one another in their uniform opinions. Worse still was the restrictions of responsibility to one's own field. That was explicitly demanded. Everyone kept to his own group – of architects, physicians, jurists, technicians, soldiers or farmers. The professional organisations to which everyone had to belong were called chambers (Physicians Chamber, Art Chamber), and this term aptly described the way people were **immured** in the isolated, closed off areas of life. The longer Hitler's system lasted, the more people's minds moved within such isolated chambers. If this arrangement had gone on for a number of generations, it alone would have arrived at a kind of **caste society**. The disparity between this and the *Volksgemeinschaft*, proclaimed in 1933, always astonished me. For this had the effect of stamping out the promised integration, or at any rate greatly hindering it. What eventually developed was a society of totally isolated individuals. For although it may sound strange today, for us it was no empty slogan that 'the Führer proposes and disposes' for all.

KEY TERMS

Immured
Imprisoned.

Caste society
A way of dividing a community based on, for example, inherited characteristics or the type of job someone is employed in.

1 According to Goering in Source 10, what was the problem with German society that the Nazis wanted to overcome?

2 According to Goering in Source 10, how did the Nazis achieve their goals and what has this success meant for the German nation?

3 What evidence does Speer in Source 11 offer to show that Goering's claims are exaggerated?

4 Which source (10 or 11) do you find more convincing in its argument, and why?

THINKING HISTORICALLY   Cause and consequence (6c)

Connections

Read this view of the Roman Empire written by Diodorus of Tarsus, who was writing in the 4th century AD.

'The Roman Empire acquired its stewardship of the world from God. For, as the Saviour was about to appear among men, God, in anticipation of his arrival, sent forth the Roman Empire in his service, so that through it, He might establish a calm and more peaceful life for men. Thus he delivered men from warring upon each other, and gave them the leisure to make His acquaintance.'

Work in groups or individually.

1 Read the quote from Diodorus above and then answer the following questions.

   a) What did Hitler believe about the Nazis and the establishment of the *Volksgemeinschaft*?

   b) How is this similar to Diodorus's ideas about the Romans?

2 Are there any other similarities between the Nazis and the Romans that you can find through your own research?

3 Why it is important for historians to see these links across time and be able to explain how causal factors can influence situations much later in time?

Racial policy, including the significance of the Nuremberg Laws

The racial policy of the Nazis was a core element of their ideology. Although they had toned down the focus on anti-Semitism during the election campaigns of the early 1930s, it came back to the fore after Hitler came to power in 1933. Hitler's extreme anti-Semitism formed the basis of his world view, his *Weltanschauung*; in *Mein Kampf* he had written that 'the personification of the devil as the symbol of all evil assumes the living shape of the Jew'. Nazi propaganda depicted Jews as parasites, intent on feeding off German society and destroying it from within. They were outsiders, not only unable to be part of the *Volksgemeinschaft*, but actually a danger to it, their very presence having the potential to weaken the German race. Ideas of purity of blood and race were key aspects of the Nazi ideology; the belief that races could become tainted by interbreeding with so-called 'inferior races' and that this would inevitably lead to the fall of the nation as a world power.

While these policies underlined Nazi thinking, the development of racial policy was not simplistic. Despite his extreme anti-Semitism, Hitler's style of government meant that racial policy lacked clear direction, just as it did for other aspects of policymaking. Hitler was also concerned about uncontrolled violence against Jews, with chaotic violence unpopular with the majority of the German public. This was clearly demonstrated in early 1933, when the SA used the Nazi electoral victory in March to begin a rampage of violence against the Jewish population in Germany. Under pressure to maintain law and order and to rein in the actions of the SA, Hitler instead agreed to a systematic one-day boycott of Jewish shops. On 1 April 1933, SA members were placed outside of Jewish businesses and encouraged Germans to shop elsewhere. Revealingly, at this stage, the boycott was overwhelmingly unsuccessful and was never extended beyond one day.

Thus, it is clear that Hitler's need to maintain order over the SA, and concerns about political stability, took priority over racial policy at this early stage in Hitler's regime. Other anti-Jewish policies were also watered down due to economic and political concerns. The reduction in unemployment meant that the government agreed that Jewish firms could still bid for public contracts, and pressure from President Hindenburg meant that the April Civil Service Law, which purged Jewish civil servants, did not include Jews who either fought in the First World War or had family that had died in the war.

As Hitler's position was strengthened, however, particularly after Hindenburg's death, racial policy became a greater focus. This is clearly demonstrated by the Nuremberg Laws in 1935, although again, their implementation was not a simple process. By 1935, anger at the lack of progress in anti-Jewish legislation was becoming a prominent aspect in Nazi journals and there was a resurgence of unco-ordinated violence against Jews, most prominently in Munich and Berlin during July and August. More conservative forces within the Nazis, led by Schacht, were concerned that these anti-Jewish riots needed to be controlled, with the best recourse being legislation. Hitler had ordered the end of random attacks in August, but by the time of the Nuremberg rally of September 1935 there was still no clear direction on government policy. He had originally planned to give a speech concerning foreign policy. However, prompted by a speech by the Reich Doctors' leader Gerhard Wagner, on 12 September, which hinted that a new racial policy was imminent, Hitler decided to act. He demanded that legislation be drawn up to restrict the Jews in Germany. Four drafts were presented, with Hitler selecting the one that would form the basis for the Nuremberg laws alongside the hastily drawn up Reich Citizenship Law. Thus, what became the basis of Nazi racial policy was created and announced in haste as Hitler reacted to the direction of his own party.

Hitler summoned the Reichstag to Nuremberg and the parliament met on 15 September to pass the laws. The Nuremberg Laws made it illegal for Germans and Jews to be married or have sexual relationships, and barred Jews from employing German women as domestic servants. Jews could not display the German flag. Critically, Jews were no longer German citizens, instead being designated 'subjects'. Hitler did not set out who was to be classed as Jewish and who was not until November, when it was decided that any German would be classed as Jewish if they had either three Jewish grandparents, or two Jewish grandparents and were a practising Jew, or had a Jewish husband or wife. It meant that a German who did not believe in God and never went to the synagogue would still be deemed Jewish if they had three Jewish grandparents, but would not be classed as Jewish if they only had two Jewish grandparents. The restrictions relating to the First World War on removing Jews from the civil service were also now lifted, and Jewish First World War veterans were removed from all state employment. Jews were legally second-class citizens living under legal repression. This pleased all elements within the Nazi Party: those who wanted strong action against the Jews and those who wanted to use legislation instead of random violence to control the Jewish population. For the Jewish population, it was the first step in a process of increasing legal constraints and discrimination that would progressively grow in its radicalisation over the next seven years, culminating in the horrors of the 'Final Solution'.

ACTIVITY
SUMMARY

1 Construct a timeline of Hitler's consolidation of power between 1933 and 1935 and use this to answer the following questions.

   a) Why do you believe Hitler was able to impose his dictatorship so rapidly?

   b) How far were Hindenburg and Papen's mistakes to blame in enabling Hitler to establish his dictatorship?

   c) How far was the weakness of the SPD, Centre Party and the Trade Unions to blame for enabling Hitler to establish his dictatorship?

   d) What does Hitler's unique style of government demonstrate about his power within the Nazi movement? Use evidence to back up your argument.

   e) What do the Nuremburg Laws and the way they were developed reveal both about Hitler's style of government and his ideology?

WIDER READING

Bullock, A. *Hitler and Stalin: Parallel Lives*, HarperCollins (1991)

Evans, R.J. *The Coming of the Third Reich*, Penguin Allen Lane (2003)

Evans, R.J. *The Third Reich in Power*, Penguin Allen Lane (2005)

Fulbrook, M. *Dissonant Lives: Generations and Violence through the German Dictatorships*, Oxford University Press (2011)

Gellately, R. *Lenin, Stalin and Hitler: The Age of Social Catastrophe*, Vintage (2007)

Kershaw, I. *Hitler*, Longman (1991)

Kershaw, I. 'Hitler and Nazi dictatorship', in Fulbrook, M. (ed.) *Twentieth-Century Germany: Politics, Culture and Society 1918–1990*, Bloomsbury (2001)

Noakes, J. 'Hitler and the Nazi State', in Caplan, J. (ed.) *Nazi Germany*, Short Oxford History of Germany series, Oxford University Press (2008), pp. 73–98

Stephenson, J. 'Inclusion: building the national community in propaganda and practice', in Caplan, J. (ed.) *Nazi Germany*, Short Oxford History of Germany series, Oxford University Press (2008), pp. 99–121

Thacker, T. *Joseph Goebbels: Life and Death*, Palgrave Macmillan (2009)

3.6 Establishing and ruling the new Federal Republic, 1949–60

KEY QUESTIONS

- How successful was the constitution of the new West German Federal Republic in establishing a stable and long-term democracy?
- How effective was the new Christian Democratic Union of Konrad Adenauer and the reconstituted SPD in shaping the new Federal Republic from 1949 to 1960?
- To what extent did the FRG undergo a process of de-Nazification in the 1950s?

INTRODUCTION

Following the devastation of the Second World War, the Allied forces of the United Kingdom, the United States, the USSR and France occupied Germany. Germany was divided into four occupied zones to be governed by the respective occupying powers. What was to take the place of Nazi Germany, however, remained a difficult question. There was considerable debate and tension between the four Allied powers, as well as with the new German political parties, established in 1945, which also differed in their visions for the future of Germany. The growing tension between the USA and the USSR that would develop into the Cold War ensured that the division of Germany into two separate political entities was much more solidified by the late 1940s.

In 1948, German politicians within the Western occupied zones were instructed to draw up a constitution for a new nation, the Federal Republic of Germany (FRG), which would become a democratic, capitalist nation focused against the Communist system in the USSR-controlled East. Established in 1949, the FRG sought its basis in the values of the Weimar Republic, but attempted to improve its constitution in order to overcome the political issues and divisions that had led to the failure of Germany's first democratic experiment. Led by the powerful and dominating figure of the Christian Democratic Union (CDU) leader Konrad Adenauer, the FRG would establish itself as a leading member of an integrated Western Europe in the 1950s, become a member of the North Atlantic Treaty Organization (NATO) and develop a new economic, democratic and social system that would prove much more durable than the Weimar Republic. This was a West Germany that now worked with France, its traditional enemy, to develop a secure and prosperous Western Europe that provided a mutual defence against the Communist system to the East. However, for Adenauer, this stability would come at a controversial cost. In 1945, the Allies were determined to rid Germany of its Nazi past, prosecuting tens of thousands of Germans for being Nazi criminals. Adenauer, however, would pursue a policy in opposition to this, believing instead that social peace and the need to use the expertise of those who worked for the Nazis was more important to the foundations of the new Federal Republic than a full process of de-Nazification and an attempt to come to terms with a

1945 – 8 May: Germany officially surrenders to Allied forces, ending the Second World War in Europe

June: Christian Democratic Union Party (CDU) founded

July: Allied forces meet at Potsdam to discuss future of Europe

1949 – 23 May: Federal Republic of Germany proclaimed with capital in Bonn

14 August: CDU wins first election of FRG

15 September: Konrad Adenauer becomes first Chancellor of FRG

1945	1946	1947	1948	1949	1950	1951	1952

1948 – 20 April to 2 June: London Conference confirms permanent division of Germany

1951 – First amnesty law for Germans accused of being Nazi sympathisers passed by CDU government

controversial past. His decisions are still providing a source of critical debate among historians today.

Overall, the period from 1949 to 1960 was a critical time in German history, when a new state arose from the ashes of Nazi Germany. This new state set in place the basis of Germany's first successful democratic system, which would survive the test of time and prove that the problems that plagued the Weimar Republic could be overcome.

HOW SUCCESSFUL WAS THE CONSTITUTION OF THE NEW WEST GERMAN FEDERAL REPUBLIC IN ESTABLISHING A STABLE AND LONG-TERM DEMOCRACY?

The creation of the FRG and the impact of the new Constitution: the attempt to reconcile difference and liberty

The end of the Second World War brought about a period of significant upheaval in German society and politics. Hitler committed suicide on 30 April 1945 and Germany officially surrendered to the Allied forces on 8 May. Since 1943, when it became apparent that the Allies were going to be victorious, there had been a series of discussions on what shape Germany should take after the conclusion of the war. The United States, Britain and the USSR set up the European Advisory Commission and it engaged in complex planning for the future of Germany. However, the exact political structure of whatever was to take the place of Nazi Germany was unclear.

Deciding Germany's future at the Yalta and Potsdam conferences

Between 4 and 11 February 1945, US President Roosevelt, USSR leader Joseph Stalin and British Prime Minister Winston Churchill met at Yalta to discuss the future of post-war Europe. While they were in agreement with Stalin and Roosevelt's declaration at the Yalta Conference on the purpose 'to destroy German militarism and Nazism and ensure that Germany will never again be able

to disturb the peace of the world', how exactly Germany would be reconstructed remained uncertain. It was finally agreed that at the conclusion of the war Germany would be divided into four separate zones, with the United States, France, the USSR and the United Kingdom governing one zone each. Berlin, the capital, would be separately divided into four occupation zones. Importantly, this division of Germany was meant to be temporary, and it was not firmly envisioned that this arrangement would become a permanent solution. The question of reparations was a critical argument. The USSR and France wanted to punish Germany for its actions, but the USA and Britain, while agreeing that Germany had to be made to account for its aggression, were wary of imposing another Versailles Treaty, which had played such a role in undermining democracy during the Weimar period.

The critical meeting would take place at Potsdam in July 1945. Already the fractures that would lead to the Cold War were becoming apparent. Roosevelt died on 12 April 1945 and was replaced by his Vice President Harry Truman. Truman was much more suspicious of Stalin and the motivations of Communist Russia, which at this stage occupied much of Eastern Europe. At Yalta, all three countries had agreed that democratic elections would be held in all of liberated Europe, thereby allowing citizens to decide the type of government they wanted to live under. However, it was becoming clear that Stalin had no intention of allowing free elections in the areas under his control, instead wanting to ensure that Communist governments under USSR direction were imposed, regardless of the desires of the people living within these countries. There was some agreement made at Yalta that Germany would be de-Nazified and demilitarised, and would undergo economic restructuring. How this was to be achieved was not clearly answered.

Key disagreements concerning the future of Germany, reparations and political structure led to the permanent division of Germany (see Chapter 4: The birth of democratic Germany, 1917–19, pages 86–107). Even before the French, American and British zones were united into one entity in April 1948, significant political restructuring in West Germany had taken place. The American zone had moved the fastest in establishing democracy and the involvement of German politicians in administration. In January 1946, Germans within the American zone had been able to vote for local councils, and this was followed in March by elections for town and county areas.

1953 – 20 August: Post-Second World War leader of the SPD Kurt Schumacher passes away

Konrad Adenauer and CDU win second FRG elections

1955 – German Treaty between FRG and Allied forces

Hallstein Doctrine published by FRG

1959 – SPD publishes the Godesberg Programme

| 1953 | 1954 | 1955 | 1956 | 1957 | 1958 | 1959 | 1963 |

1954 – Second Amnesty Law passed

1957 – CDU wins majority in FRG Bundestag elections for the first time

1963 – Konrad Adenauer resigns as Chancellor of the FRG

The Americans constructed new *Länder* for their zone and held elections in June, followed by *Länder* elections in the French and British zones in May 1947. Thus, democracy was beginning to develop in the Western zones, with elected German representatives responsible for the administration of the *Länder* under Western occupation.

EXTEND YOUR KNOWLEDGE

The Cold War and the division of Germany

The Cold War was a conflict waged between the USSR and its Communist aligned allies, and the capitalist, democratic United States, Western Europe and their allies between the late 1940s and 1991. Europe was essentially divided into democratic West and Communist East, with Winston Churchill famously defining the dividing line between the two blocks as 'an iron curtain', behind which were the Communist-controlled Eastern European nations. It was known as the 'Cold War', as the United States and the USSR were technically never in direct conflict with each other, instead supporting differing sides in numerous wars across the globe during this time, such as the Korean War and the Vietnam War. During the Cuban Missile Crisis in 1962, the United States and the USSR stood on the brink of nuclear war, and although this particular event did not lead to global destruction, the fear of all-out nuclear war was a recurrent theme over the years in which the Cold War took place. The conflict was largely ideologically based, with the USSR supporting the extension of Communism throughout the world, and the United States alternatively trying to stop Communism's expansion, instead promoting capitalist democracy.

The Cold War ended with the collapse and end of the USSR in 1991. During this period, Germany was the front line of the Cold War. The growing antagonism between the United States and the USSR from the end of the Second World War meant that the two sides were unable to come to any agreement on how to reunify Germany, thus leading to the division of the country into the capitalist, democratic Federal Republic of Germany and the Communist Democratic Republic of Germany (GDR). In Berlin, the United States and the USSR military literally faced each other across the border, the division of the city the strongest representation of the division of Europe into two separate ideological camps. The reunification of Germany in 1989 was thus one of clearest signals that the long conflict between the United States and the USSR was finally coming to an end.

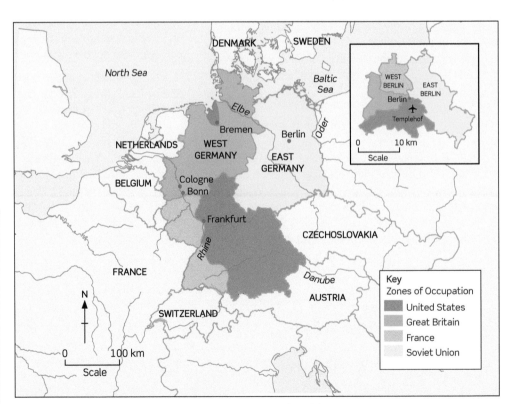

Figure 6.1 Division of Germany at the end of the Second World War.

Two main parties dominated the elections of 1946 and 1947: the reconstructed SPD, now led by Karl Schumacher, and the newly created Christian Democratic Union (**CDU**), led by Konrad Adenauer. The CDU was a conglomeration of supporters of the old Centre Party, German Nationalists and Populists. It differed from the Centre Party (which still existed) by representing both Catholic and Protestant middle-class voters in the north and south of Germany through the values of Christian Socialism. Importantly, the 'Union' aspect of its name asserted the idea that they were a confederation of differing political groups and ideas that were determined to work together for a common vision, unlike a more unified, centrally directed 'party' such as the SPD.

At the London Conference in February and March 1948 (covered in Chapter 2, page 59), countries in democratic Western Europe accepted the likelihood of a permanent division of Germany. This would consequently mean the creation of permanent democratic institutions in West Germany. Therefore, in July 1948, the *Länder* ministers were instructed to begin discussions on a new constitution.

SOURCE

Appeal to the German People by the Christian Democratic Union, of 26 June 1945. Here, the CDU sets out the problems it believes Germany faces after the Second World War and outlines how the country should be rebuilt.

German People! Amidst the most terrible catastrophe to ever befall a country, the party of the Christian Democratic Union of Germany, out of ardent love for the German people, calls upon Christian, democratic, and social forces to come together, work together, and build a new homeland. The deification of a criminal daredevil has left us in a turmoil of guilt and shame, and a free democratic order can only emerge if we reflect on the culturally formative moral and spiritual forces of Christianity and increasingly draw upon this as a source of strength for our people.

It is an unspeakably difficult task. After 1918, our political leadership saved state, cultural, and economic institutions from military collapse. The towns, villages, factories, workshops, fields and forests that had been spared went on to provide a foundation for the nation's gradual recovery... In the light of the terrible magnitude of the injustice perpetrated over Hitler's rule, we must be unrelenting in our quest to hold the culprits and their accomplices to account, ensuring that strict justice is served while relinquishing any thoughts of revenge. Hitler's rule presented a distorted version of a nation; this must now be replaced by a truly democratic state built upon on its people's commitment to loyalty, sacrifice and service to the common good, as well as respect for individual rights, honour, freedom, and human dignity. The rule of law must once again become the foundation of all public life. The lie 'that which benefits the nation is right' must be replaced with the eternal truth: 'the nation only benefits from what is right'. We must restore an independent and orderly course of justice. The call for just judges rings out across every corner of the German nation like a single cry. The law is never to be used in an arbitrary way. A Gestapo and the terror it brings must never again exist. With strict frugality, public life must largely be built on self-government and voluntary work. Parliament must ensure that all parties in favour of democracy and all forces prepared to rebuild the country can work together in brotherly, trusting partnership.

We demand a public life that is free of lies, mass hysteria, and mass sedition as well as a responsible press whose guiding principle is a commitment to truth. We call for spiritual and religious freedom of conscience, independence of all church communities, and a clear separation of church and state.

SOURCE

'Political Principles of the Social Democratic Party', published May 1946. Here, the SPD sets out what it sees as the main problems for Germany following the Second World War and how it believes the country should be rebuilt.

In the period between the two world wars, the forces of high capitalism and reaction sought to avoid the socialist consequences of democracy everywhere. In Germany, they were granted success as a result of the country's economic, historical, and intellectual-historical circumstances.

In the Third Reich, democracy was thrown off course by the suppression of the working classes' political power, and the key factor for the European catastrophe consisted of a lack of a democratic decision-making process and control. The failure of the German middle classes and the section of the workers' movement that did not recognise the value of democracy in terms of class politics is a burden that the German people must bear.

The Third Reich employed the very same methods it had used to forcibly suppress class conflicts within its own borders to foster antagonism among nations. The inevitable consequence of the dictatorship was war, which brought total military and political collapse and destroyed the existing foundations for economic, political and cultural life. These foundations are therefore no longer fit for the construction of a new Germany. In economic terms, a vast concentration of once immense productive force has given way to paralysis; it has closed its doors. As things stand, no class, no people, no form of economy is able to exist...

However, the Social Democratic Party has tasked itself with uniting all of Germany's democratic forces under the banner of socialism. The political balance of power must be transformed, along with its economic basis. A complete transformation is required if the German people are to be granted economic and social opportunities and if freedom and peace are to be secured. Present-day Germany is no longer in a position to sustain a private-capitalistic profit-based economy, nor can it pay profits based on exploitation, capital dividends or ground rents.

ACTIVITY
KNOWLEDGE CHECK

1 With reference to Sources 1 and 2, summarise the key aspects of the political programmes of the CDU and SPD.

2 To what extent do the political programmes of the two parties differ?

3 To what extent are their political programmes similar?

The new German constitution

Subsequently, 65 members of the *Länder* parliaments met in Bonn to draw up a constitution. This was known as the Parliamentary Council. At this stage they believed the constitution would only be a temporary legislation until the full reunification of Germany. Interestingly, the *Länder* ministers rejected calls from the United States that the constitution should be voted on by the German people, fearing that the Communists in the East would encourage voters to reject the constitution by claiming it would stop reunification from ever taking place. The constitutional convention was made up of 27 CDU members, 27 SPD members and 11 other smaller parties. Adenauer directed proceedings after being nominated as President for the Parliamentary Council. In respect to the SPD, Schumacher was too ill to attend, and the talented constitutional lawyer Carlo Schmid primarily led the Party.

From August to September 1948, legal experts designed the basis of the new constitution known as the 'Fundamental' or 'Basic' Law. The constitution eventually presented to the Parliamentary Council in September was in many ways very similar to the Weimar Constitution. West Germany was to be a federalised state and the proportional representative vote was reintroduced for federal elections to the Bundestag, which replaced the Reichstag. Just as in the Weimar Republic, the Bundesrat was implemented as the upper house that represented the *Länder*. There was also a fair degree of continuity between the West German constitution and the Weimar Constitution in terms of the roles of the judiciary and civil service in the state structure.

However, there were some fundamental differences that were established to ensure that the West German political system was more stable than the Weimar Republic's. Prussia was permanently erased as a state and the new *Länder* was reconstructed in a manner that was more balanced. A new voting system replaced the old Weimar list system, whereby Germans now voted twice: once for a direct representative for their electoral district and another for a party list. This aimed to connect politicians and the public much more in terms of local issues than during the Weimar period. Federal elections would take place every four years. There would be no more elected presidents (the president, or **Bundespräsident**, would be appointed by parliament instead), thus removing the constitutional ambiguity of the Weimar Constitution. Critically, Schmid ensured that there would be no continuation of Article 48 and the ability to either suspend parliament or change the constitution. The chancellor could be removed by a vote of no confidence by the Bundestag only if a new chancellor had already been elected by parliament. This was known as the 'constructive vote of no confidence'; it effectively stopped political parties from using continuous votes of no confidence to cripple the successful functioning of the Bundestag, as the Nazis and KPD (the Communist Party of Germany) had done in the Reichstag during the early 1930s. The president did not appoint the chancellor; instead the leader of the main party or coalition within the Bundestag was appointed chancellor, making their role both more representative and removing the possibility of the backroom intrigue that had led to Hindenburg appointing Hitler in 1933. Yet, given that Hitler had been leader of the most popular party in 1933, this constitutional aspect alone would not guarantee that such an event could not happen again, so a constitutional court was established with the power to outlaw parties it decided were undemocratic in their political ideology. Additionally, parties had to gain five percent of the vote or above to take their place in the Bundestag, thus guaranteeing that minor extremist parties could not gain federal seats.

KEY TERM

Bundespräsident
(FRG President) The FRG retained a president, but this was a very different role from the President of the Weimar Republic. They were not elected by popular vote but through an election by state representatives. Although they had an important constitutional role, their influence on the political system was not as great as it was during the Weimar period. In the Basic Law (see Source 3 on page 136) it was clear that the chancellor and the party system were the more powerful legislative bodies, a distinction that was not clear in the Weimar period and thus led to considerable political disruption, particularly when Hindenburg became president in 1925.

At this stage, the new constitution had no role for a reconstituted military; this would take place some years later due to growing concern regarding the USSR. The new constitution guaranteed a social welfare state, thereby establishing an area of continuity going back to the 1871 constitution. There was a critical argument between the political parties concerning how powerful the *Länder* should be. The key disagreements rested on whether the Bundesrat should be fully elected or made up of delegates from the *Länder* parliaments, and how much power the Bundesrat would have to block Bundestag legislation. Eventually, a compromise agreement was reached whereby the Bundesrat would not be directly elected and each state would be represented proportionally to its population. Economically, the central government would set taxes, but if the taxes affected the *Länder* they would have to be passed by the Bundesrat. Government revenue from taxes would be split between the *Länder* and the federal government equally. The *Länder* parliaments would have control over education and administration in their states.

The question of Berlin

The most complex question of the constitution was what to do with Berlin, as West Germany only controlled the western half. Berlin was geographically not in West Germany, and the political and military situation with the USSR that controlled East Berlin was tense. It was seen as being politically provocative to claim Berlin as part of the new West German Federation. Instead, it was decided that as Berlin's military occupation could only be ended through agreement with the USSR (at this stage unlikely), it would remain officially under the control of the Western Allies. It was a complicated situation. West Berlin citizens were considered citizens of West Germany, but could not vote in federal elections, nor was West Berlin considered a *Länder* and therefore it did not have state elections. Twenty-two members from the Berlin Assembly (elected by West Berlin citizens) could sit in the Bundestag and four members in the Bundesrat, but they had observer status only and no voting rights. Citizens in Berlin also enjoyed civil liberties and rights agreed by the West German constitution. A local authority led by a popularly elected mayor governed West Berlin, but this had to be ultimately approved by the Western occupying powers. West Berlin could reject federal laws, famously doing so with regard to military conscription in the 1950s, but the vast majority of laws passed by the West German government were implemented in West Berlin. Although its citizens could not vote in federal or *Länder* elections, they could join political parties and run in elections, albeit not as representatives of West Berlin. West Berlin was thus in a strange, complex and ambiguous position due to the complicated division of the city made at the end of the Second World War and its prominent position as the point of ongoing confrontation in the Cold War. The agreement on West Berlin ensured that it was engaged with the new federal republic, while officially being under continuous military occupation.

Proclamation of Germany's Federal Republic

With the complexities of the new system agreed upon, the Fundamental Law was put to the Parliamentary Council on 8 May 1949 and passed by the vast majority of members. It was agreed that the constitution would remain in place only until Germany was reunified, whereby it would need a new constitution.

On 23 May, the new FRG, with its capital at Bonn, was proclaimed. Federal elections were set for 14 August. The eventual constitutional make-up of the Federal Republic of Germany was a complicated arrangement. It had significant continuity with the Weimar, but differed in key areas. The Federal Republic of Germany was a functioning republic with its own constitution, but did not officially govern the western part of Berlin, nor did it control its own main industrial region, the Ruhr, which was at that time under the power of the International Ruhr Commission. Crucially, it was not even allowed to have its own foreign minister, with all foreign affairs of the FRG run by the Allied High Commission. There were still major concerns from other Western powers, primarily France, that the FRG should be strictly controlled in economic and foreign matters to ensure that it did not threaten Europe again.

The Allied powers officially recognised the FRG as a sovereign nation on 20 September 1949, but all laws passed by the FRG had to be signed off by the United States, France and the United Kingdom before they could become law. It has thus been described by some historians as a 'semi-sovereign' state.

EXTEND YOUR KNOWLEDGE

The choice of Bonn as capital of the FRG

The decision to make Bonn capital in 1949 can tell us a lot about the thinking of the politicians who founded the FRG. Bonn was not an obvious choice. It was a small city and most of the facilities required for a capital city were already located in Frankfurt. It was therefore much more expensive to locate the capital in Bonn than it was to make the capital in Frankfurt. Adenauer was from the Bonn area and preferred Bonn to Frankfurt, but this was not the main reason the city was chosen. The key factor was that the politicians in West Germany did not believe the division of Germany would be permanent. They still planned for the unification of Germany with the capital in Berlin. However, if the West German capital was in a large, important city like Frankfurt, it would make division seem more permanent. Thus, the choice of Bonn, a small, somewhat provincial city, as capital of the FRG was designed to show that the division of Germany was not an unending solution.

THINKING HISTORICALLY — Cause and consequence (7c)

The value of historical explanations

Historical explanations derive from the historian who is investigating the past. Differences in explanations are usually about what the historian thinks is significant. Historians bring their own attitudes and perspectives to historical questions and see history in the light of these. It is therefore perfectly acceptable to have very different explanations of the same historical phenomenon. The way we judge historical accounts is by looking at how well argued they are and how well evidence has been deployed to support the argument.

Here are three different approaches to the creation of the FRG.

Approach A	Approach B	Approach C
The creation of the FRG was the natural development from the Weimar Republic that had been temporarily halted by the Nazi dictatorship that ruled for only 12 years. Once it disappeared the politicians were able to reinstate German democracy.	The creation of the FRG was an anomaly of the Cold War. It came about because neither politicians in Germany nor the occupying powers could agree on the political system of a unified Germany. The FRG was thus a temporary solution to this problem.	The creation of the FRG was driven by the United States, which needed a strong democratic German nation to block the spread of Communism. The FRG was thus created to aid US foreign policy.

Work in groups of between three and five (you will need an even number of groups in the class).

1 In your groups, devise a brief explanation of between 200 and 300 words of the creation of the FRG that matches one of the approaches above.

2 Present your explanation to another group, who will decide on the following.

   a) Which of the approaches is each explanation trying to demonstrate?

   b) Considering the structure and the quality of the argument and use of evidence, which is the best of the three explanations?

   c) If you choose a 'best' explanation, should you discount the other two? Explain your answer.

SOURCE 3

The Basic Law of the Federal Republic of Germany, 23 May 1949. Here, the key points are set out.

The German people in the *Länder* of Baden, Bavaria, Bremen, Hamburg, Hesse, Lower Saxony, North Rhine-Westfalia, Rhineland-Palatinate, Schleswig-Holstein, Wurttemberg-Baden, and Wurttemberg-Hohenzollern, conscious of its responsibility before God and man, animated by the resolve to preserve its national and political unity, and to serve the peace of the world as an equal partner in a united Europe, desiring to give a new order to political life for a transitional period, has enacted, by virtue of its constituent power, this Basic Law of the FRG. It has also acted on behalf of those Germans to whom participation was denied. The entire German people is called on to achieve by free self determination the unity and freedom of

Germany... Article 20: (1) The FRG is a democratic and social federal state. (2) All state authority emanates from the people. It is exercised by the people by means of elections and votes and by separate legislative, executive, and judicial organs. (3) Legislation shall be subject to constitutional order; the executive and the judiciary shall be bound by law... Article 21: (1) The parties participate in the shaping of political will of the people. Their foundation is free, their inner structure must correspond to democratic principles, they have to account for the source of their funds in public. (2) Parties which are inclined to harm or to overthrow the free democratic order or to endanger the existence of the FRG according to their goals or to the behaviour of their supporters are unconstitutional. The Federal Constitutional Court decides on the question of constitutionality. Article 23: For the time being, this basic law applies in the territory of the *Länder* of Baden, Bavaria, Bremen, Hamburg, Hesse, Lower Saxony, North Rhine-Westfalia, Rhineland-Palatinate, Schleswig-Holstein, Wurttemberg-Baden, and Wurttemberg-Hohenzollern. In other parts of Germany, it shall be put into force on their accession... Article 116: (1) This Basic Law understands as German, except for legal stipulations, whoever lived as a refugee or expellee of German ethnic origin or as his spouse or descendant on the territory of the German Empire on 31 December 1937.

ACTIVITY
KNOWLEDGE CHECK

1 Read through Source 3 and then answer the following questions.

   a) Which aspects of the Basic Law are focused on the democratic freedom of the German people?

   b) Which aspects of the Basic Law are focused on ensuring that political extremism does not become a problem again in the new republic?

   c) Which part of the Basic Law opens up the possibility for the reunification of Germany to take place in the future?

2 Look back at your work on the Weimar Republic (Chapter 4). In what ways does the constitution try to ensure that the FRG is a more stable democracy than the Weimar Republic?

Problems with the new constitution

There were other issues with the constitution. Although more stable than the Weimar Constitution, the use of proportional representation ensured that the Bundestag would be made up of a large number of differing parties and that the ruling government would still be mainly constituted by coalitions. Thus, the political situation remained rather fragmented, although the ability of the parties to work with each other, plus the provisions made in the constitution, ensured that this would never become the issue it had been in the Weimar Republic.

There were criticisms, particularly from groups on the left, that the constitution simply re-established a capitalist system that did little for the German working classes. However, the members of the Parliamentary Council were not trying to impose a radical, new system that would alter the economic and political system of Germany. Instead, they were guided by the Weimar Constitution and determined to implement its broader, democratic ideals in a more sustainable and firm fashion. In this way they were successful. They faced the same problems as the Weimar: military occupation; a difficult economic situation; destruction and social upheavals caused by defeat in war, yet the democratic leaders of the FRG were able to overcome these issues in a manner that had been unattainable by the Weimar Republic's politicians. The FRG was obviously helped considerably by the occupying Allied powers, which were also eager not to repeat the mistakes of the Versailles Treaty, but the constitution also played a critical part. It implemented democratic rights for all citizens within a federalised system, yet ensured through a variety of measures that extremist parties would not be able to play a role in the FRG's political system. It ensured greater stability through the changing functions of the president, and, importantly, provided the German people with greater democratic connection to the Bundestag members who they were being asked to vote for. This is not to say that the FRG Constitution was perfect or never underwent political challenges; nor was it assured in 1949 that, once the shock of the war dissipated, the FRG would not undergo the same problems as the Weimar Republic. However, the fact that the FRG Constitution and its democratic system remained up to German unification in 1990, and that the FRG enjoyed a large degree of political stability during this time, appears to demonstrate the success of the 1949 constitution.

HOW EFFECTIVE WAS THE NEW CHRISTIAN DEMOCRATIC UNION OF KONRAD ADENAUER AND THE RECONSTITUTED SPD IN SHAPING THE NEW FEDERAL REPUBLIC FROM 1949 TO 1960?

The importance of Adenauer and the CDU in shaping the new Federal Republic

Konrad Adenauer was the most important political figure in the FRG during its first decade of existence. His political decisions would have a profound influence in shaping the social, economic and political structure of this new state. His dominance of the political scene has led to some historians classing the period between 1945 and 1963 as 'the Adenauer Era'.

Adenauer's politics

Adenauer had a long history in German politics before 1945. In 1918, he had been Mayor of Cologne, during the German Revolution. He had been removed from his position as mayor by the Nazis and was later imprisoned due to suspicions that he was involved in the 1944 plot to assassinate Hitler. On 3 May 1945, after United States' forces had liberated Cologne, he resumed his position as mayor. Adenauer had a significantly new vision of a future Germany, one that was based on a strong relationship with France. This was quite a radical step, considering that Germany had been unified in 1871 through war against France and had waged two major wars against the French, occupying the country during the Second World War. Adenauer believed that Prussia and its values of aggression and militarism were to blame for Germany's aggressive actions between 1871 and 1945, and he was determined to rid the new Germany of what he considered Prussia's dangerous ideals. Although it could be argued that the Nazis shared little with the Junkers (having essentially eroded their power and then largely wiped them out as a class in 1944), Adenauer still argued that Prussian militarism was the reason for the Nazis and their aggressive foreign policy. In 1947, Adenauer played a key part in the Allied Control Council, issuing Law No. 46: 'The Prussian State which from early days has been a bearer of militarism and reaction in Germany has de facto ceased to exist.'

Adenauer's political career, however, had been challenged in October 1945, when he was sacked as Mayor of Cologne due to a disagreement with the British military government in North Rhine. However, the British allowed Adenauer to continue to engage in politics, and it was actually his sacking that gave Adenauer the time to focus on national politics. His main focus now centred on leading a new national political party, the Christian Democratic Union (CDU), which had been established in June 1945. As discussed above, the party aimed to unite Catholics and Protestants through the values of liberal conservatism, an ideology the party considered 'Christian Socialism'. Adenauer believed that the Weimar had shown the danger of disunity between political parties, and therefore aimed for the CDU to unite a variety of class, religious and ideological groups from across all of Germany. The CDU was predominately centre right and had originally existed in both the British and Soviet zones of occupation. However, in August 1947, the Soviets moved against the CDU, arresting 600 members, and while continuing to exist, it was essentially transformed into a pliant puppet of the ruling Communists. Thus the independent CDU under Adenauer came to focus solely on politics in the Western-occupied part of Germany.

The rising influence of the CDU in West Germany

As tension between the USSR and the West grew in the late 1940s, the CDU began to find greater favour with the Western occupying powers of the United States and the United Kingdom. This was due to both its economic policies, as pursued by Ludwig Erhard (see Chapter 2, page 47), and Adenauer's strong anti-Communist policies. The latter saw Adenauer vehemently opposed to East Germany and any form of German unification that would require compromise with the German Communist Party in East Germany, known as the Socialist Unity Party (SED). It was for this reason that the CDU also enjoyed the support of the Catholic Church, which viewed the party as a strong power against Communism. This was crucial to the CDU, as the regions that made up West Germany meant the population was now 45 percent Catholic, as opposed to only 30 percent in the old post-1945 unified Germany. Thus, the fact that Catholics largely voted for the CDU was a key element in its popularity.

In the first election for the FRG on 14 August 1949, the CDU was victorious, winning 31 percent of the vote, with the SPD an extremely close second with 29.2 percent of the vote. The election had largely been fought on the issue of the nature of the FRG's economy, with the SPD proposing a more socialist, government-controlled economic system, against the CDU's proposed 'social market economy'. This idea centred on an economy run on a largely free market basis, but with a strong social insurance scheme built into it. You have already read in Chapter 2 (page 47) how Erhard's economic policies would drive the so-called 'post-war economic miracle'; thus the CDU's victory ultimately shaped the FRG's economic system for the next 40 years.

The CDU formed a coalition with the Free Democratic Party and the German Party to make up 208 of the 402 seats in the Reichstag. On 15 September 1949, the Reichstag elected Adenauer as Chancellor by only one vote (his own casting vote being decisive). Adenauer would remain Chancellor until 1963, and the CDU remained the party in power until 1969. Thus its values and the leadership of Adenauer had a large impact on shaping the structure of this new nation following its foundation in 1949.

EXTEND YOUR KNOWLEDGE

The Socialist Unionist Party (SED) and the political situation in the GDR

The political parties that formed after the Second World War in Germany were originally united parties with no East/West division. The USSR had actually encouraged and assisted the establishment of German political parties, hoping that this would enhance Soviet power across Germany. However, once it was clear that that KPD (the Communist Party of Germany) was not going to win elections in East Germany, the Soviets forced the SPD within their zone to amalgamate with the KPD to form a new party, the Socialist Unity Party (SED). As relations between East and West deteriorated during the Cold War, the CDU also began to split between a Western faction, under Adenauer, and an Eastern faction, under Jakob Kaiser.

Although the GDR was technically a democracy and the CDU continued to run in elections, it was essentially a dictatorship under the SED. The SED controlled the functions of government as well as those of the Supreme Court, the Department of Public Prosecutions and the secret police (known as the Stasi). Through pressure and intimidation they forced the other parties to agree that in elections the citizens of the GDR were presented with one united list of parties, all setting out exactly the same policies. The SED was essentially guaranteed over 60 percent of the vote and the elections were never free and fair. The other political parties accepted this situation, as they were desperate to remain independent, although they had no chance of taking power. The SED was thus able to claim that the GDR was a pluralist democracy, although until 1989 the citizens of the GDR had no ability to overthrow the SED from its position.

Adenauer's policies

Adenauer's belief that the future survival and prosperity of both the FRG and Western Europe required greater economic and political co-operation was intrinsic to the European Coal and Steel Community (ECSC) in 1951 and the European Economic Community (EEC) in 1957 (see Chapter 2, page 61). His ideals would forge a stronger relationship with France and set the basis for what would later become the European Union. As set out in Chapter 1 (page 27), the economic system and insurance policies pursued by Adenauer and the CDU in the 1950s led to greater social mobility, but in turn meant the FRG was a quite gender-structured society, whereby men would be the main workers and women would largely remain at home to bring up the family's children.

Another critical aspect of Adenauer's policies was in regard to the military situation of the FRG. This was an extremely controversial and difficult area given Germany's actions in the Second World War, and the fear, particularly in France and the USSR, of a remilitarised German nation. Indeed, the Petersberg Agreement, 22 November 1949, between the Allied High Commissioners and the Chancellor of the German Federal Republic asserted that the FRG would stick to 'maintaining the demilitarization of the federal territory and endeavour by all means in its power to prevent the recreation of armed forces of any kind'. However, events in the Cold War, primarily the Korean War, which Adenauer believed might encourage East Germany to replicate the actions of North Korea, led him to controversially propose the formation of an FRG army of 150,000 men in 1950. He faced considerable opposition from the SPD, Germany's churches (usually a major supporter of the CDU) and trade unions. However, Adenauer enjoyed the support of the West German people, who feared Communist aggression. This was clearly shown in the second FRG election in 1953, where the CDU won with 45.2 percent of the vote, a 14 percent increase from 1949. Adenauer thus had the mandate to push ahead with his plans for an FRG army. Through a series of discussions and compromises, particularly with France, on 5 May 1955 the new 'General Treaty' (also known as the German Treaty) came into force. This gave complete foreign policy sovereignty to the FRG within its membership of the **North Atlantic Treaty Organization (NATO)**. The FRG would be able to have its own military force, as proposed by Adenauer. Allied troops would still be in the FRG and the status of Berlin was unchanged, but this was a crucial agreement shaping the nature of the FRG all the way up to 1989. It established the FRG as a key member of the Western European community, both in a military and in an economic sense, and confirmed this newly sovereign nation as a firm part of the Western Bloc, opposed to the USSR and Communist Eastern Europe.

SOURCE 4

The General Treaty on Germany, signed 23 October 1954 (came into force on 5 May 1955), set out a new relationship between the FRG and the Western occupying forces. Here are the key elements of the treaty.

Article 1. (1) When this treaty goes into effect, the United States of America, the United Kingdom of Great Britain and Northern Ireland, and the French Republic (in this treaty and supplementary treaties thereafter also referred to as the 'Three Powers') will end the occupation regime in the Federal Republic, repeal the occupation statute and dissolve the Allied High Commission and the offices of the State Commissioners in the Federal Republic. (2) The Federal Republic will thereby have the full powers of a sovereign state over its internal and external affairs. Article 2. In view of the international situation, which until now prevented German reunification and the conclusion of a peace treaty, the Three Powers retain the rights and duties exercised or held by them with regard to Berlin and Germany as a whole, including German reunification and a peace settlement. The rights and duties retained by the Three Powers in regard to stationing armed forces in Germany and protecting the security of these forces are determined by Article 4 and 5 of this treaty... Article 7. (1) The signatory states agree that a significant goal of their joint policies is a settlement for all of Germany through a peace treaty freely agreed to by Germany and its former opponents, which will form the basis for a lasting peace. They further agree that a final determination of Germany's borders must be postponed until such a settlement is reached. (2) Until conclusion of a peace treaty settlement, the signatory states will co-operate by peaceful means to implement their common goal: a reunited Germany possessing a free, democratic constitution similar to the Federal Republic and integrated into the European Community... (4) The Three powers will consult the Federal Republic in all matters affecting the exercise of their rights with regard to Germany as a whole.

ACTIVITY
KNOWLEDGE CHECK

Read through Source 4 and summarise the significance of the General Treaty of 1954.

The Hallstein Doctrine

Parallel to the setting-up of NATO was the establishment of the Hallstein Doctrine, which was set out in 1955 (Professor Hallstein was State Secretary of the FRG Foreign Office). This followed on from the USSR's recognition of the GDR as a sovereign nation. It challenged Adenauer's assertion that only the FRG represented the legitimate continuation of the Germany founded in 1871. The Hallstein Doctrine asserted that the diplomatic recognition of the GDR by any nation apart from the USSR would be regarded as a hostile act against the FRG. No country could gain financial assistance from the FRG if it recognised the GDR. The integration of the FRG with NATO, along with the Hallstein Doctrine, confirmed the division of Germany over the next 44 years.

EXTEND YOUR KNOWLEDGE

The Hallstein Doctrine
A key part of the FRG's constitution was the strong assertion that it was the only legitimate representative of Germany and a continuation of the nation that was founded in 1871. When the USSR recognised the GDR officially in 1954, this challenged the FRG's assertion, as there were now technically two Germanys. The Hallstein Doctrine attempted to enforce the FRG's political role by threatening sanctions against any country that had diplomatic relations with the GDR. Thus, using its economic power, the FRG hoped to retain its position as the only official representative of Germany and to isolate the GDR. However, the Doctrine was difficult to enforce and constricted the FRG's political relations. In 1972, the FRG's Chancellor, Willy Brandt, heralded a new relationship between the two countries, when the FRG and GDR agreed to recognise each other as sovereign states, thus ending the Hallstein Doctrine.

Adenauer's policies essentially guaranteed that the reunification of Germany was now highly unlikely. The Hallstein Doctrine ensured that the GDR would become further integrated with the Soviet Bloc, just as the FRG was with the Western Bloc. This was most prominently confirmed by the building of the Berlin Wall by the GDR in 1961.

The CDU's continued successes under Adenauer

In 1957, Germany went to the polls again, with the CDU achieving a massive electoral victory, gaining 50.2 percent of the vote and the first majority government of the FRG era. The CDU had campaigned with the slogan 'No Experiments!', thereby calling on West Germans to stick with the party that had positively led the country through the 1950s and not to risk the unknown political direction the SPD represented. The 1957 landslide victory was a clear endorsement of Adenauer's policies throughout the 1950s. He would fight one more election, in 1961, winning again, but losing the CDU's Bundestag majority. He finally stepped down in 1963, at the age of 87, after 14 years as Chancellor of the FRG.

Adenauer's impact on the FRG is difficult to overstate. The economic and social policies of the CDU would set the basis for the FRG's development all the way up to 1989. His foreign policy led to the formation of the EEC, integrated the FRG into NATO, forged a new, peaceful relationship with France, and ensured the long-term division of Germany between the Communist GDR and the democratic FRG. Crucially, from the wreckage of the Second World War, Adenauer and the CDU built a stable and prosperous democracy that would exist up to 1989 and beyond, clearly achieving their goal of creating a Germany based on the values of the Weimar Republic, but with a more solid basis that would ensure its lasting success.

SOURCE

Konrad Adenauer presents the Hallstein Doctrine to the German Bundestag, 22 September 1955. The Hallstein Doctrine was critical in defining the relationship between the FRG and the GDR.

On the occasion of establishing diplomatic relations between the government of the FRG and the government of the USSR, I declare:

1. The establishment of diplomatic relations between the government of the FRG and the government of the USSR does not represent any recognition of present territorial possessions on both sides. Final determination of the German boundaries remains reserved for a peace treaty.

2. The establishment of diplomatic relations with the government of the Soviet Union does not signify any change in the legal standing of the FRG regarding its authority to represent the German people in international affairs and the political relationship in those German areas which presently lie outside its effective jurisdiction... All states having diplomatic relations with us can clearly see that the standpoint of the FRG toward the so-called 'GDR' and to boundary issues has not changed in the least... A settlement of Germany's territorial situation that is binding under international law does not yet exist. Such a settlement can be made only within the scope of a peace treaty to be concluded with a freely elected all-German government. The position of the government of the Federal Republic towards the government of the Soviet Zone – as follows from the first reservation – will not be affected by the establishment of diplomatic relations between the Soviet Union and the FRG. The government of the so-called 'GDR' was not formed on the basis of truly free elections and therefore has not received any real authorisation by the people. In fact, it is rejected by the overwhelming majority of the population; there is neither legal protection nor freedom in the Soviet-occupied zone, and the constitution exists only on paper. The FRG therefore remains the only free and legal German government, with sole authorisation to speak for all of Germany... We have notified the Soviet government of our viewpoint in order to remove any doubts whatsoever as to the firmness of our position. If the Soviet government nevertheless established diplomatic relations with us, it is doing so, though without granting approval, with full knowledge of our stand toward the so-called 'GDR'. I [Adenauer] must clearly and in no uncertain terms declare that the government of the FRG will interpret as an unfriendly act the establishment of diplomatic relations with the 'GDR' by third nations with which it has official relations, as this act would serve to deepen the division of Germany.

SOURCE
6
Political poster from the 1957 election showing Adenauer, along with the slogan 'No Experiments!'

Keine Experimente!
Konrad Adenauer   CDU

ACTIVITY
KNOWLEDGE CHECK

1 In what ways does the Hallstein Doctrine (Source 5) attempt to undermine the GDR's claim to be a sovereign nation?

2 Reading through Source 5, what would you consider the main purpose of the Hallstein Doctrine?

3 With reference to Source 6, what was the key message of the 1957 CDU electoral campaign?

4 Using your historical knowledge, explain why this message was successful in winning votes.

Changes in the nature of the SPD and their significance for the shaping of the Federal Republic

Alongside the CDU, the SPD was the other main party in Germany, and its political activities would also play a large part in shaping the Federal Republic. The SPD had been reconstituted in June 1945. In the USSR-controlled section of Germany, the SPD was forced to amalgamate with the KPD, to form the Socialist Unionist Party (SED) in 1946. In the Western-controlled sections, the SPD was led by the other dominant politician of the post-War period, Kurt Schumacher.

The politics of Kurt Schumacher and his rivalry with Adenauer

Schumacher was a charismatic leader who had spent ten years in the Nazi concentration camp at Dachau due to his political activities in the SPD. At the end of the Second World War he was the only SPD politician alive who had neither fled Germany nor collaborated with the Nazis, a position that gave him enormous prestige. He was convinced that he, not Adenauer, was the rightful leader of the new Germany. Despite some calls for the SPD to co-operate with the KPD in the Western-controlled area, he was determined to push the SPD in a socialist but anti-Communist direction. He was a strong nationalist who believed in the struggle for German reunification, and that only by appealing to middle-class voters, as opposed to just the working class, could the SPD win power in the new Germany.

Schumacher and Adenauer engaged in an intense political rivalry. Adenauer accused the SPD of being essentially Communist and unpatriotic to the new, democratic Germany. Schumacher argued that the CDU was a puppet to the Catholic Church, which simply wanted to exploit the German working class for capitalist economic profit. The differing background of the two men shaped their political disagreement. Adenauer was a Catholic, from the Rhineland, who – as you have already read – had a deep dislike of Prussian culture. Schumacher, on the other hand, was a Protestant from Prussia, who was determined to see Germany unified again.

In the election of 1949, in which Schumacher was confident of victory, the two parties presented very differing models for the future of the FRG's economy. The SPD proposed a 'planned economy', whereby the economy would be much more controlled by central government. Schumacher's policy, however, was somewhat undermined by the fact that Erhard's proposed 'social market economy' was already in place in Bizonia and was starting to produce positive results. Additionally, Schumacher's strong claims that the Catholic Church was the 'fifth occupying power' in Germany only alienated Catholic voters, who now formed 45 percent of the population. Importantly, the growing fear of the USSR and its actions in the east of Germany meant there was a stronger pull towards the conservative right of the CDU among West German voters. The CDU was also backed by the United States, which viewed it as a more reliable force against Communism than the SPD. Personality also played a role: Schumacher was in ill health, due to his mistreatment in Dachau, and had missed the Parliamentary Council due to medical complications that eventually led to him having his leg amputated (he had already lost his right arm during the First World War). There were therefore questions over whether he could handle the pressures of being Chancellor. It was these factors combined that led to the SPD's narrow loss in the 1949 election.

Electoral poster of the SPD for the 1949 election. The caption says, 'Who blocks the borders? The Communists! The way of the SPD leads to Unity in freedom'.

CDU electoral poster from 1949. It reads, 'With Adenauer for peace, freedom and unity of Germany, therefore CDU'.

Lothar Kettenacker, in *Germany since 1945* (1997), discusses the reasons for the SPD electoral defeat in 1949.

While the Economic Council in Frankfurt handled everyday business up to the last minute, West Germany experienced its first, shortest, and most critical election campaign. The political landscape was so diverse that there were no clear pointers to the future. Altogether sixteen parties campaigned for seats, and seventy independent candidates, but only four were represented in all *Länder*, apart from the big two, the Liberals and Communists. The CDU/CSU, on the advice of Adenauer, simply dropped its legendary 'Ahlener Programme,' which had rejected capitalism in favour of Christian Socialism, and now opted for Erhard's social market economy. Round faced Erhard, not yet a member of the CDU, exuded confidence and optimism. However, the economic miracle had not yet materialised and unemployment was still at 10 per cent, a level quite staggering at the time. Nevertheless, the Social Democrats lost the battle for nationalisation and for the soul of the country because they misjudged the public mood. Adenauer could afford to sit back and simply watch them ruin their chances. Schumacher reintroduced the language of class struggle and appealed to the national sentiments by attacking the victorious powers and their grip on German industry in the Ruhr. He also made a grave mistake by referring to the churches as the 'fifth occupation power.' Nor did his venomous attacks on Adenauer endear him to the German public, who were no longer used to the occasionally outrageous rhetoric of a democratic election campaign. Adenauer, through more restrained and statesmanlike, not only exploited the blunders of his opponent but also claimed the Social Democrats had joined forces with the Communists in the East and that a Socialist Germany would be 'no dam against Communism.' This was blatantly unfair, but probably quite effective.

The SPD as the party of opposition under Schumacher and Ollenhauer

In the three years following the 1949 election, Schumacher and the SPD vehemently opposed many of Adenauer's key policies. Schumacher opposed the FRG's integration with Western Europe and NATO, as it meant the unification of Germany was much more unlikely. He rejected the idea of Western European economic integration, arguing that it would enforce a free market capitalist economy across its member states. He argued instead that Germany could only integrate once it was fully unified and even then, only if Western Europe was based on socialist values. He argued that Adenauer was too eager to work with the Allied occupying powers and denounced the CDU leader as a puppet of the United States. For Schumacher, co-operation with France, Western Europe and the United States should be secondary to working towards German reunification; an alliance with the West should not be pursued to the degree that it would hamper this goal. Schumacher therefore fought against Adenauer's plans to create an FRG military.

Before he could fight another election, however, Schumacher passed away after suffering a stroke, on 20 August 1952. By this time, it was evident that Schumacher's policies were increasingly out of step with the German public. The success of the CDU's economic model combined with the fear of Eastern Germany and the backing for Adenauer's foreign policy had meant Schumacher's political direction had not helped the SPD, but had actually reduced its political support in the FRG. His replacement, Erich Ollenhauer, was not as strong a political opponent to Adenauer as Schumacher had been, and consequently, in the 1953 election, the CDU's vote increased considerably, while the SPD's vote remained the same as it had been in 1949. Under Ollenhauer, the SPD's political position weakened due to an inability to mount a clear and coherent opposition to the CDU, particularly in relation to foreign affairs. This was clearly shown in the results of the 1957 election.

SOURCE

9 From Kurt Schumacher's speech on the fight for Germany and Europe, 22 May 1950. The speech was made to party delegates at the first SPD conference since the foundation of the FRG. Here, in his general report, Schumacher strongly sets out his opposition to German membership of a more integrated Europe.

If, for instance, we now discuss problems of European organisation out of sincere and whole-hearted attachment to the international idea, which we have upheld for more than eight decades, we must realise that when people refer to Europe they do not always have in mind those things that make Europe worthwhile and capable of surviving... Foreigners who play at devising international schemes in an amateur fashion often misunderstand the German position... Meanwhile these matters are presented in a hysterical way, accompanied by dire threats. What happens if we join the Council of Europe, and what happens if we do not? I do not think that frontier barriers will cease to exist and the problem of Germany's military security will be solved if we go in, and no one abroad seriously believes that either. The creating of illusions is part of German internal politics, and the practice of the Council of Europe up to now also has a lesson for us. What then if we do not go in – will it weaken Europe? Does the Council of Europe in Strasburg represent the highest possible expression of democratic internationalism? If anyone disagrees with our attitude, let them prove it in this debate with genuine arguments and concrete proposals. Joining the Council of Europe will not bring about the opening up of frontiers, an international order or military service. And Germany will not be thrown out of Europe just because she refuses to join this particular institution on these particular conditions. The Germans, so far as we here can speak for them, are not willing to be excluded from Europe. Nor do I believe that those Allies who count in this matter wish to exclude Germany from it. An examination of the situation in Europe in relation to the dispute with the Soviets gives, it seems to me, a conclusive answer on both points. But what is missing – though I recognise that two Federal ministers have attempted to prove it – is a statement by the Federal government on the dangers that the present situation may involve for Eastern Germany. As I have said, we Social Democrats regard German unity as a European matter. But we reject the policy of certain Allies who, as I would put it, think that a better solution of the European problem can be obtained by keeping Germany partitioned.

The SPD under Willy Brandt and the Godesberg Programme

Ollenhauer's defeat in 1953 led to a revitalisation of the SPD, primarily led by the young, charismatic mayor of West Berlin, Willy Brandt. Brandt pushed the SPD in a new, more modern direction that accepted the realities of the FRG. In 1959, the party adopted the **Godesberg Programme**, which took the SPD away from its Marxist roots and fully endorsed the capitalist market economy. The party now supported the FRG's integration with Western Europe and membership of NATO, and moved away from its anti-Catholic rhetoric. The Godesberg Programme committed the party to becoming 'the party of the whole people'. In one of the most dramatic aspects of this new political direction, the SPD also asserted that it would now be willing to work with the CDU in a coalition, if requested. The Godesberg Programme therefore marked a change in direction for the SPD, one that would lead to its re-emergence as a political force. Under Willy Brandt's dynamic leadership, the SPD now gained the backing of the United States under President Kennedy. In 1966, the SPD and CDU entered into a coalition government, and in 1969, for the first time since the foundation of the FRG, Willy Brandt became the first SPD Chancellor of the FRG and the first SPD Chancellor in Germany since 1928.

It could be argued that the SPD under Schumacher failed to influence the FRG and only really came to prominence once it accepted a new political direction in the 1960s. It is also true that Schumacher was defeated on many of the key political arguments, and the SPD subsequently lacked direction in the 1950s, as West Germans enjoyed the fruits of the CDU's success. However, Schumacher and Adenauer's political rivalry helped to confirm that Germany could enjoy a constructive and vehement political debate without resorting to the fractious and destabilising politics of the Weimar period. Despite the differing visions between the CDU and SPD, they were united under a mutual respect for democratic policies and the rejection of extremist parties, and a firm belief that German nationalism could not be utilised by the extreme right to promote its political agenda (as had happened between 1918 and 1945). Together, the CDU and SPD thus forged a new, democratic and stable West Germany that moved the country decisively away from its authoritarian past.

EXTRACT

2 William Carr, in *A History of Germany 1815–1985* (1987), discusses why the SPD changed its political direction in the late 1950s and how this was significant to politics in the FRG.

During the Adenauer era, the FRG established itself as a major European power. As we have already seen, the 1950s was a period of unparalleled economic growth during which the GNP trebled, 'full' employment was achieved (by 1961) and the basis laid for what is today the third most powerful industrial nation in the world... During these years the SPD, for long a bitter opponent of all Adenauer stood for, changed course. Under Schumacher, party leader up to 1953 and then under Erich Ollenhauer the SPD strenuously opposed German membership of the Coal and Steel Community, the European Economic Community and NATO on the grounds that such commitments diminished the chances of re-unification. Although the Socialist vote rose steadily from 29.2 per cent in 1949 to 31.8 per cent in 1957, the CDU/CSU stayed well ahead, securing 50.2 per cent of the vote in 1957. At the Bad Godesberg Party Congress in 1959 the SPD took a decisive step away from its Marxist past. The new programme declared that democratic socialism was rooted in 'Christian ethics, humanism and classical philosophy.' In economics it was a pragmatic creed combining a belief in essential planning with a belief in the social market economy – 'as much competition as possible, as much planning as necessary' summed up the new position. The SPD no longer wanted to be a class party but aspired to be 'the party of the whole people.' Old fashioned anti-clericalism went out of favour and the party accepted the principle of national defence. In 1960 Herbert Wehner, the SPD defence spokesman, came out in support of NATO and a bipartisan foreign policy became a reality at long last. The Bad Godesberg volte-face was the end product of a reappraisal going on throughout the late 1950s. Electoral considerations were only one factor. Many Socialists now believed that excessive centralisation as exemplified by the GDR was inimical to human freedom. Willy Brandt, party leader since 1964 and a man who had spent his years in exile after 1933 in Scandinavia, brought a broader perspective and a new energy to an ageing party.

A Level Exam-Style Question Section B

How accurate is it to say that the SPD lost the 1949 election due to the leadership of Kurt Schumacher? (20 marks)

Tip
This question is asking you to weigh up the reasons for the SPD's loss in the 1949 FRG election. Consider Schumacher's leadership, his policies and the context of post-Second World War Germany. You could also consider other factors, such as the policies of the CDU. What do you consider the main factor in the SPD's defeat?

TO WHAT EXTENT DID THE FRG UNDERGO A PROCESS OF DE-NAZIFICATION IN THE 1950S?

The process and significance of de-Nazification and 'coming to terms with the past' in the 1950s

One of the key issues for FRG politicians after the Second World War was how to deal with the events of the previous 12 years. Many Germans had cheered Hitler's rise to the chancellorship and his subsequent actions, and millions of Germans had associated with the Nazi Party, whether as party members, members of the Hitler Youth or participants in the Nazi worker holiday programmes. This could not just be ignored and forgotten as though it had never occurred. For politicians such as Schumacher, there was a sense of bitterness that shaped his political outlook. He was seeking to represent the German people, but these were essentially the same people who had accepted, ignored or actually supported the destruction of his party and the brutal imprisonment of its key members, such as himself. Overcoming these issues would not be straightforward. At the Potsdam Conference in 1945, the United States, the United Kingdom and the USSR had agreed on the complete destruction of the Nazi Party and the trial of Nazi war criminals. Importantly, they also agreed that all members of the Nazi Party were to be removed from key positions in the public and private administration. These included positions such as teachers, civil servants and government officials.

The United States and the *Fragebogen*

In the part of Germany that the United States occupied, German citizens were judged through the *Fragebogen* or questionnaire, to decide who could be classed as a Nazi. These were extensive documents requiring Germans to answer 133 different questions concerning issues such as whether they had belonged to the German army, whether they had relatives or friends in a high position in the Nazi Party, who they voted for in the 1933 election, and whether they were a member of the Junkers. All Germans were required to fill out the *Fragebogen*, even those who had spent time in Nazi concentration camps or had faced persecution under the Nazis. Schumacher called this an outrage against those Germans who had tried to resist the Nazis, but this did little to deter US policy. Any German wanting to return to work had to be vetted through the *Fragebogen*; until then, they could not qualify for important state relief such as rations, let alone find a new job. The Americans ignored calls from prominent Germans that membership of the Nazi Party or affiliation with its organisations, such as the Hitler Youth, was almost compulsory under the dictatorship and that such association did not mean that one was necessarily a diehard Nazi.

The problem with the policy of the United States was that it depleted Germany of the key workers required to rebuild the state. Due to the growing lack of experienced German management in important areas of the economy, all four occupying powers slowly began to relax their previously strict de-Nazification policies by the end of 1946. There were also too many cases to get through: in one *Länder* alone, 2.5 million Germans were being investigated for possible Nazi sympathies. To deal with the problem, the Allies introduced a new means of judging the extent to which Germans had been associated with the Nazi Party. In October 1946, five categories were decided upon, with lesser offenders, such as those who had been members of the Nazi Party but were not seen as being involved in any serious political or military activity, placed on a probation period of two to three years in which they were allowed to return to work. Special tribunals run by Germans were established to deal with questionable cases, deciding in which category certain individuals would be placed. Although it was a more efficient process, it was still overwhelming: by 1947, 90,000 Germans found to be of the more serious Nazi offender category were being kept in prison camps. The process was also subject to corruption, with certificates of de-Nazification available on the black market. As the tensions between the USSR and the United States increased, de-Nazification also became less of a priority. The official United States programme of de-Nazification ended in 1951.

ACTIVITY
KNOWLEDGE CHECK

Study (Source 10) and its provenance. How does it help to explain why many Germans found the American de-Nazification tribunals demeaning and unnecessary?

The United States, de-Nazification and the *Fragebogen*

Of the occupying powers, the United States was the most vehement in its attempt to pursue de-Nazification. Its main method was the *Fragebogen*, a thorough questionnaire consisting of 133 questions over 12 pages. The questions covered a range of issues, such as who the respondent had voted for in 1932, how many bank accounts they had, how the bombing in Germany had affected them, what religion they were, what they did during the war, whether they were of Prussian royalty, what scars they had, and so on. The Americans printed 13 million *Fragebogens* and distributed them widely to Germans in their occupied zones, including those who had been arrested by the Nazis. The language in the *Fragebogen* was also difficult due to the inadequacy of the American–German translators. The vast majority of Germans who had to fill them out hated the questionnaires. They were long, intrusive and relied on Germans having a good memory of events that happened some time ago. They also asked Germans if they had hoped Germany would win the war, a difficult question, the answer to which could have changed several times in the 1940s. To answer any question in a way that appeared to show militarism or political sympathy with the Nazis would automatically mean that the German in question would not be able to return to work or claim much-needed social benefits, such as food coupons. It was also a bureaucratic nightmare, with the Americans having to assess millions of *Fragebogens* and try around 170,000 de-Nazification cases. As the Cold War made relations with Adenauer and the FRG more important, the Americans began to ease back on their de-Nazification processes, releasing thousands of those they had found guilty. It can also be argued that the *Fragebogen* process focused on Germans who had minor connections with the Nazis at the expense of trying those who played more vital roles in the Nazi state.

SOURCE

10

General Ludendorff's widow, Mathilde, at a de-Nazification hearing court in Munich, on 23 November 1949. She was a teacher and physician who had written anti-Catholic and anti-Semitic essays, although she was not a supporter of Adolf Hitler. The court found the 72-year-old guilty of Nazi sympathies, but she had her punishment reduced in 1951.

De-Nazification policies under Adenauer in the 1950s: the amnesty laws

After 1951, the FRG under Adenauer and his government was to pursue a very different direction. For them, the Allied policies had been too harsh and affected too many Germans. Instead, the 'politics for the past', or *Vergangenheitspolitik*, aimed at annulling many of the Allied punishments for millions of Germans deemed to be Nazi criminals. For Adenauer, the construction of the FRG as a stable society, as well as ensuring experience and proficiency in the government positions, were much more important than prosecuting Germans for their Nazi past. His government introduced amnesty legislation that by 1951 had benefited nearly 800,000 Germans who had previously been classed as Nazi criminals. He justified his actions by asserting that 'so long after the collapse of the National Socialist regime, the distinction between politically exonerated and non-incriminated persons should be ended'. He also asserted that 'the chapter of collective guilt for militarists alongside activists and beneficiaries of the National Socialist regime must be ended, once and for all'.

In May 1951, Adenauer's government passed the first amnesty law. It allowed 150,000 German officials who had been removed from their positions due to the Allied de-Nazification programme to return to government administration. Even more controversially, in 1954, his government passed the second amnesty law that annulled the British process of de-Nazification. The law led to some 400,000 Germans being granted amnesty after previously being declared Nazi criminals. While it is true that many within this 400,000 were probably not Nazi criminals, the law had important implications in weakening the legal focus on the investigation and prosecution of Nazi criminals in the FRG. From the early 1950s, high numbers of government civil servants in the foreign office and new government departments had previously worked for the Nazi Party. Adenauer's own chancellery head was Hans Globke, who had been involved in the legal process of the Prussian coup d'état, Hitler's Enabling Act and the Nuremburg Laws. Most controversially, former members of the Reich Main Security Office, an SS department aimed at fighting 'all enemies of the Reich', were able to take up positions again in the police and security forces. There was also political gain for Adenauer, as these policies allowed him to gain the support of more right-wing Germans. This point is significant, as Adenauer was reliant in the Bundestag on coalitions with right-wing parties which, controversially, justified right-wing politics in the 1920s and 1930s as a reaction against Communism and the possible breakup of the German nation.

This is not to say that Adenauer's government was completely ignorant of the threat of extreme right-wing politics rising again in Germany, or that he made no attempt to deal with the historical legacy of the Nazis. For example, in August 1952, the neo-Nazi **Socialist Reich Party** was banned. Furthermore, on 10 September 1952, his government signed an important agreement to pay the new state of Israel three billion German marks in compensation for the treatment of Jews during the Holocaust. Adenauer argued that such compensation was only the first step in dealing with the unspeakable crimes committed in the name of the German people. The issue with Adenauer instead focuses on the rehabilitation of Nazi Party members in government administration and FRG society. The British High Commissioner from 1951 to 1953, Sir Ivone Kirkpatrick, wrote that 'whenever I travelled, I ran into ghosts of Hitler's Reich, men who had occupied positions in the administration, in industry, or the society of the day. They were either living in retirement or were taking jobs in banks, commerce or industry.'

What was key for Adenauer was the fact that, despite their Nazi past, these Germans within government administration were prepared to work for West German democracy; this co-operation was built upon a shared foundation of anti-Communist ideology. The survival of the FRG as a democratic state was crucial in the battle against the Communist East. This set the FRG apart from the Weimar Republic, where civil servants, government officials and the judiciary still retained loyalty to the previous Kaiserreich, and actively worked against the Weimar democratic system they were supposed to protect. In 1952, for example, Adenauer told the Bundestag that although it was true that 66 percent of foreign office diplomats in high positions were former Nazis, this was necessary to ensure the proficient functioning of the foreign office, as former Nazis were the most experienced civil servants in the FRG. For Adenauer, it was unfeasible to bar hundreds of thousands of experienced Germans from working in professions from which they could make a significant contribution to the FRG. The Nazis had exercised significant influence across society, pursued through their policies of *Gleichschaltung* (see Chapter 5, page 109). Sympathy for some of Hitler's policies had also not simply evaporated since 1945. The relentless pursuit of Nazi criminals in the FRG could therefore affect a large number of Germans across the whole spectrum of FRG society and would possibly challenge the government's popularity. For Adenauer, the stability and survival of his government and the FRG took precedence over widespread de-Nazification. He believed that attacks against all aspects of the Nazi regime could open up mass societal divisions that had been so dangerous in the Weimar period.

The response to Adenauer's policies on de-Nazification
There were some public movements against the government's willingness to work with Nazi sympathisers. In 1955, the CDU/FDP coalition government in Lower Saxony had to withdraw its

appointment of Leonard Schluter (a Nazi sympathiser who described Hitler's party as the best political movement Germany had had in the 20th century) as Minister of Education, after protests from both professors and students at Gottingen University. Some SPD members, for example Carlo Schmid, argued against the FRG's willingness to forget the Nazi past. Most prominently, in 1955, the SPD parliamentarian Walter Menzel spoke out against the numerous amnesties passed by the government, saying 'through this amnesty, all those who had so murderously and bestially assaulted helpless and defenceless people before 1945 were pardoned, so long as no more than three years in prison were to be expected. This is what most deeply wounds our sense of justice: that individuals were treated so differently and unequally before the courts.' However, Adenauer's policies were largely supported. The SPD largely supported Adenauer's amnesty policies, believing that it was the only means of achieving social cohesiveness in the FRG. The older generation of Germans wanted to simply move on with their lives; the economic boom of the FRG in the 1950s and the resurgence in living standards following the destruction of the war were much more important than the pursuit of Nazi criminals and shining a spotlight on the past.

SOURCE

Norman Lindhurst, an American freelance journalist based in West Germany from the end of the war, reports on the FRG government's view on de-Nazification in an article titled 'Why Adenauer is opposed to more de-Nazification' (25 February 1960). Lindhurst was writing for the *Toledo Blade*, an American newspaper.

Gerhard Schroeder, West Germany's interior minister, was asked recently if the Adenauer government intended to attack anti-Semitism with a 'de-Nazification' campaign on a large scale. 'No' responded Mr Schroeder firmly, 'that would be like using a sledgehammer to kill a fly.' He reflected briefly and added, 'I am against this whole wretched business of de-Nazification. Most of these people (nominal Nazis) are leading decent lives.' The interior minister is himself a symbol of West Germany's Nazi travail. Mr Schroeder, a part of whose job is the suppression of neo-Nazism, is himself a former Nazi. From 1933 until 1943 he was a Nazi party member... The chancellor knew of Mr Schroeder's background, of course, before he picked him for his sensitive post... In practice de-Nazification degenerated into the worst fiasco of the occupation. It bogged down in backbiting, gossip mongering and corruption... As Mr Adenauer early discerned, Allied de-Nazification threatened to sunder German society into two perpetually warring groups: former Nazis and 'good Germans.' It threatened to create a pariah caste of erstwhile Hitlerites who would be permanent prey of extremist political movements, thus providing the 'new Germany' with built-in political strife. Proof of his fear was the early postwar mushrooming of extremist political movements, which despite the Allied occupation, openly rallied ex-Hitlerites under their banners. These movements became potent, if small, political forces with representatives in Bonn parliament and various state legislatures. Now they have all but vanished, but this is no accident. Mr Adenauer, with unanimous agreement of the German political parties, deliberately rang down the curtain on de-Nazification. Ex-Nazis were given to understand that their past, provided it was not too black, would not be held against them. To prove he meant it, the chancellor took former Nazis and bureaucrats who had served the Nazis, into his government wholesale. By so doing, he achieved two objectives. He ended class strife and paved the way for the recruitment of ex-Nazis into his government wholesale. By so doing, he achieved two objectives. He ended class strife and paved the way for the recruitment of ex-Nazis into his Christian Democratic Union. He thereby gained access to the old German government bureaucracy for staffing his new government. Thus, when Mr Schroeder states he opposes 'reviving this whole wretched de-Nazification affair,' he is speaking for Mr Adenauer as well. The problem is not a simple one.

A Level Exam-Style Question Section A

Study Source 11 before you answer this question.

Assess the value of Source 11 for revealing the attitudes and approaches to de-Nazification of the FRG government in 1960.

Explain your answer, using the source, the information given about its origin and your own knowledge about the historical context. (20 marks)

Tip

This source is from an American newspaper and uses quotes from Gerhard Schroeder to explain why the CDU government was no longer pursuing de-Nazification. Think about the argument being given and how well it is supported by your own knowledge. The source comes from the American press, so you might also like to consider the historical context at the time and how attitudes had changed to de-Nazification since the 1940s.

By the mid-1950s, the focus on de-Nazification had effectively come to an end. It was only in the 1960s that a cultural revolution led by young West German citizens challenged the policies of 'forgetting' and the high position of many former Nazis in government positions, and brought about a new democratic movement that openly faced, discussed and debated the legacy of Germany's Nazi past. Adenauer's actions in the 1950s have thus been a key area of debate ever since. On one side it can be argued that, despite its moral question, Adenauer's policies ensured stability in government, thus allowing FRG democracy to grow from a strong basis. He also avoided opening up substantial fractures within German society, particularly between left- and right-wing politics, which had so badly weakened the Weimar Republic in the 1920s. Members of his government were in no way Nazi sympathisers, and thousands of the most high-ranking Nazi war criminals faced imprisonment for their actions. Adenauer's amnesty policies were arguably justifiable as the most appropriate and effective direction for the immediate period after the Second World War. However, other historians have argued that such an assertion does not hold weight. The FRG could have functioned more effectively as a democracy if it had been willing to confront Germany's past in the 1950s, and a stronger pursuit of Nazis in the 1950s would have meant more war criminals being prosecuted, given the greater number of available witnesses at that particular time so soon after the Second World War. Adenauer's approach meant that the FRG was built on a morally questionable basis that undermined its supposed democratic values. These historians challenge Adenauer's belief (also shared by the majority within the SPD) that de-Nazification was not compatible with the maintenance of social peace and the building of democracy in the early years of the FRG. It thus remains a very difficult question, which you will have to weigh up carefully and decide on for yourselves.

EXTRACT
3

V.R. Berghahn, in *Modern Germany: Society, Economy and Politics in the Twentieth Century* (1987), here explains the unwillingness of many Germans in the early 1950s to properly face up to issues relating to the Nazi dictatorship that still remained, and the consequences this had on the social, political and cultural aspects of life in West Germany.

It was only now after 1949 that it became clear how much resentment had been generated by de-Nazification, **deconcentration** and a host of other measures, and not merely among those directly affected. By this time, the unwillingness and inability of Germans to face the past as well as the post war world squarely had become so strong that they voted for parties which promoted quite unreconstructed arguments about Nazism and the occupation period. The most successful among the extreme right-wing movements was the German Reich Party (DRP), which polled 1.8 per cent of the vote at the first elections to the Bundestag and dispatched five deputies to Bonn, the new capital of the Federal Republic. It was not a large number, but it must be seen in conjunction with the nationalism of some of the other smaller parties and of the FDP. As both the 'collective guilt' argument of the Western Allies and the Social Democrat interpretation of National Socialism had failed to gain wider acceptance, apologetic views of German history abounded. One of the more moderate interpretations, which probably shaped German perceptions of their history most powerfully after 1949, was the *Betriebsunfall* (accident in the works) theory. According to this theory, Hitler had not been brought to power by specific political forces, but had arrived on the scene virtually out of the blue. He and his band of criminals had then terrorised the country for twelve years before disappearing again like a bad dream. What this interpretation did was to cut the Third Reich out of the mainstream of German history. The Nazi period was an aberration without deeper roots. The beauty of this theory was that it did not require any agonising self-questioning, whether at a personal or institutional level. It seemed only logical that pre-1933 habits, traditions and institutions should be revived. If the Nazis had tried to destroy them, this merely seemed to prove their undiminished value. Consequently there were whole areas of social, political and cultural life in West Germany which experienced no institutional or attitudinal changes.

ACTIVITY
KNOWLEDGE CHECK

1 According to Extract 3 and your own knowledge, what were the key issues with Adenauer's de-Nazification policies?

2 Construct a two-column table setting out the overall positives of Adenauer's de-Nazification policy on one side and the negative aspects on the other. Using this, how far do you consider Adenauer's de-Nazification policies a success?

ACTIVITY
SUMMARY

1 To what extent had Adenauer's government built a successful and stable democracy in West Germany by 1960?

2 5-3-1 activity:

a) Summarise the history of the FRG from 1949 to 1960 in five sentences.

b) Choose three key words that you think best define this period.

c) Choose the one key word from the three above that you think best sums up the FRG in the period – be prepared to explain your answer.

 WIDER READING

Fulbrook, M. *Interpretations of the Two Germanies 1945–1990*, Studies in European History series, Palgrave Macmillan, second edition (2000)

Gehler, M. *Three Germanies: West Germany, East Germany and the Berlin Republic*, Reaktion Books (2011)

Judt, T. *Postwar: A History of Europe Since 1945*, Vintage (2005)

MacDonogh, G. *After Reich: From Liberation of Vienna to the Berlin Airlift*, John Murray (2008)

O'Dochartaigh, P. *Germany since 1945*, Studies in Contemporary History series, Palgrave Macmillan (2004)

Roseman, M. 'Division and stability: The Federal Republic of Germany 1949–1989' in Fulbrook M. (ed.) *Twentieth-Century Germany: Politics, Culture and Society 1918–1990*, Bloomsbury, second edition (2001)

Stone, D. *Goodbye to All That? The Story of Europe since 1945*, Oxford University Press (2014)

Thomaneck, J.K.A. and Niven, B. *Dividing and Uniting Germany*, Routledge (2001)

Williamson, D.G. *Germany from Defeat to Partition 1945–1963*, Longman (2001)

3.7

Reunification: recreating a united Germany, 1989–90

KEY QUESTIONS

- What caused the flood of refugees from the GDR in 1989?
- What impact did the revolution in the GDR and Kohl's Ten Point Plan in 1989 have on German reunification?
- What were the key reasons for German reunification in October 1990?

INTRODUCTION

On 10 September 1987, during a visit to the FRG, the GDR's Communist leader Erich Honecker predicted that the 'day would come when borders no longer separate us but unite us'. Honecker meant that the day would come when the FRG completely accepted the GDR's right to exist as a sovereign state. However, within three years his words were to take on a very different meaning that no one at the time could have foreseen.

At the start of 1989, Honecker himself announced that the great symbol of Germany's division, the Berlin Wall, might still be standing in 50 to 100 years. There were few German politicians on either side of the divide who would have argued against him at the time. It can sometimes be difficult to understand how people perceived momentous historical events at the time they were happening. Turning points in history, such as German reunification, can seem almost inevitable, as we can look over the entire narrative and know the end of the story. However, it is important to understand that those main figures involved in German reunification in 1990 did not always have a clear idea of what the outcome of their actions would be. The end point to them at times seemed vague and difficult to perceive.

The events that began in 1989 were not immediately seen as starting the process of German reunification. It is crucial to remember that politicians in the FRG, the GDR, and in Europe and the United States, did not actively work towards or even want German reunification at the start of 1989. What caused this change was the peoples of East Germany themselves, who rose against an oppressive regime that, for a variety of reasons, the majority of GDR citizens no longer wanted to be a part of. It was their actions that forced the FRG Chancellor Helmut Kohl to dramatically propose a road map to reunification in November 1989, and forced the leaders of Europe, the United States and the USSR to accept that the survival of the GDR and the continuing division of Germany were no longer possible.

1987 – September: GDR Communist leader Erich Honecker makes historic visit to FRG

1989 – 2 May: Hungarian government announces removal of barbed-wire fencing and fortifications on its border with Austria

Tens of thousands of East Germans travel to Hungary hoping to escape into Austria

7 October: GDR holds celebrations for its 40-year anniversary

GDR youth cheer enthusiastically for visiting reformist USSR leader Mikhail Gorbachev

1987	1988	1989

1 September: FRG announces it will accept 20,000 East German refugees from Hungary

17 October: 100,000 East Germans protest against the GDR government in Leipzig

18 October: SED decides to remove Honecker as leader and replace him with Egon Krenz

The reunification of Germany in October 1990 was one of the major events of the 20th century, one that many within Germany and the wider world never thought possible. Importantly, the Germany that emerged was one that fulfilled the dreams of those who created the Weimar Republic, a democratic, free and stable country that could play a peaceful and supportive role in Europe.

The story of German history from unification in 1871 to division and then reunification in 1990 is a tumultuous one. Germans had to pass through many dark periods before the country was able to emerge as the nation it is today. Studying the many interconnected factors that saw this happen at a rapid pace from 1989 to 1990 is therefore key not only to understanding how this important event came about, but also in helping us to understand the nature of Germany today, a country that continues to play a critical role in Europe.

WHAT CAUSED THE FLOOD OF REFUGEES FROM THE GDR IN 1989?

SOURCE

'Only the Germans want reunification' by Gwynne Dyer, published in the *Canberra Times*, 29 September 1987. Gwynne Dyer is a freelance journalist and historian who writes on international relations.

Concluding his historic five-day visit to West Germany, the first by any East German leader since the country was formally divided in 1949, Erich Honecker addressed the citizens of his home town of Neunkirchen. 'The day will come,' he said, 'when our borders no longer divide us but unit us.' Even if Honecker's words carefully excluded political unification of the two Germanys, such talk is as alarming to other Europeans as it is encouraging to many Germans on both sides of the border. He was only talking about easing travel and cultural contacts between the two parts of the German nation, but anyone with a feel for the way history works is aware that one thing quite often leads to another. If there is one thing on which most Europeans of both blocs can agree, it is the horror with which they contemplate the possibility of a reunified Germany. The Russian obsession with the 'German threat' is quite open – the unvarying response even from the most free-thinking Soviet official is that 'there is no German question' – but the Western allies are really just as opposed to German reunification. 'I love Germany so much that I am glad there are two of them,' French writer and sometime cabinet minister Andre Malraux once remarked, echoing the sentiments of almost every Frenchman. And the Belgians, the British, the Dutch and even the Italians generally agree, though with rather less emotional fervour. Indeed, the devotion of Western Europeans to the present alliance structure has at least as much to do with the fact that it perpetuates the division of Germany as with dwindling fears of a Soviet invasion. The first secretary-general of the North Atlantic Treaty Organisation, Lord Ismay, once put it quite bluntly. 'The object of the alliance is to keep the Americans in, the Soviets out, and the Germans down.'

This general satisfaction with the division of Germany has something to do nowadays with apprehensions about the emergence of a unified Germany of 77 million; people as an even more formidable trade rival. It lies rather more to do with nervousness about tinkering with what seems, at least in the short term, to be a relatively stable security structure in Central Europe.

ACTIVITY
KNOWLEDGE CHECK

Read through Source 1 and summarise the impression it gives of the relationship between the GDR and the FRG in 1987.

9 November: Travel restrictions for GDR citizens lifted, essentially bringing down the Berlin Wall

13 November: Egon Krenz removed as leader of the SED and replaced with Gregor Gysi

11 December: 300,000 East Germans protest against GDR government

1990 –

18 March: Elections held in GDR

SED no longer controls political system in East Germany

1990

28 November: FRG Chancellor Helmut Kohl announces Ten Point Plan for German reunification

19 December: 100,000 people arrive in Dresden for talk by visiting FRG Chancellor Helmut Kohl.

1 July: Monetary, economic and social union of GDR and FRG

3 October: From midnight, full unification of GDR and FRG

GDR ceases to exist

KEY TERM

Ostpolitik
This policy was pursued by Willy Brandt after he became Chancellor in 1969. It aimed to bring about a lowering of tension between East and West Germany and usher in a new, more mutually co-operative relationship. The high point of Ostpolitik came in December 1972, when both the GDR and the FRG recognised the sovereign right of each country to exist.

Reasons for the flood of refugees from the GDR in 1989

In 1969, Willy Brandt had become Chancellor of the FRG; he pursued a new relationship with East Germany, a policy known as **Ostpolitik**. A series of negotiations and new treaty arrangements had culminated in the Basic Treaty, signed in December 1972. This was a key turning point in East–West German relations, as it confirmed the division of Germany into two states and set out the basis for better economic co-operation between the two independent countries. The Hallstein Doctrine (see Chapter 6, page 140) was firmly repudiated and a new, more amicable relationship pursued. By the early 1980s, through the relationship between Erich Honecker in the GDR and Helmut Kohl in the FRG, the two countries appeared to have reached a somewhat comfortable accommodation. The long-term existence of two separate Germanys was a fact that most within German politics had accepted would continue into the foreseeable future. In 1987, Honecker had made a historical first trip to the FRG to meet with Helmult Kohl. However, from the mid-1980s, the GDR found itself facing new challenges that would ultimately cause it to cease to exist by 1990. This dramatic development was predominately driven by the new leader of the USSR, Mikhail Gorbachev.

The role of Gorbachev

When Gorbachev became leader of the USSR in 1985, he was faced with a nation that was declining economically and confronting a variety of social problems. Gorbachev's entire concept of Communism and the root to survival differed from Erich Honecker's. Through his twin policies of perestroika (restructuring) and glasnost (openness), Gorbachev attempted to introduce significant economic reforms in the USSR, as well as paving the way to greater freedom of speech and political participation for the Russian people. A critical part in his policies was the winding back of USSR economic aid to the Eastern Bloc countries, as the USSR had propped up their weak economies for decades. The USSR's military budget was also overstretched, using up a large percentage of the country's budget that was instead required to develop a better standard of living for the Russian people. Gorbachev therefore began to reduce the military presence of USSR troops in Eastern Europe. Gorbachev believed that only through reforms leading to a more open society and a better standard of living could he save the Communist system in the USSR.

EXTEND YOUR KNOWLEDGE

Mikhail Gorbachev and the end of the Cold War
Mikhail Gorbachev became the leader of the USSR in 1985 at the age of 54, making him the youngest ever leader of the USSR. By 1985, the USSR was facing considerable economic decline, and the Communist system faced growing pressures for reform. Gorbachev believed that economic, social and political reforms could revitalise the USSR and ultimately save the Communist government. Through his twin policies of peristroika (restructuring) and glasnost (openness), he introduced considerable reforms in the economic system, and greater political rights and freedom of speech for the USSR's citizens. Hoping to reduce the massive military budget that was bankrupting the USSR, Gorbachev pursued a reduction in tension between the United States and the USSR that would ultimately lead to the end of the Cold War. The fact that the USSR was no longer in a position to back up unpopular Communist governments in Eastern Europe, either economically or militarily, would set off a series of revolutions that would bring down the Communist system and change Europe forever. It was this pressure that would undermine Honecker's government in the GDR. For East Germans, Gorbachev was seen as a hero hungry for change, and his visit in 1989 was a crucial event that led to the overthrow of Honecker and the fall of the Berlin Wall. However, Gorbachev's hopes that greater freedom would actually strengthen Communism were politically naive; the change he brought about would not save the system he believed in, but instead prompted its complete downfall and ultimately the end of the USSR itself in 1991.

Changes in the GDR as a result of changes in the USSR

Gorbachev's policies had severe repercussions for the GDR. Honecker had no interest in pursuing a more open society or undergoing economic restructuring. Problematically, however, the economic situation in the GDR was declining, with money owed to Western financial lending institutions rising at an alarming rate. In the early 1980s, for instance, the GDR borrowed 1.95 billion German marks from the FRG. With the GDR's debt increasing, the country found it more and more difficult to maintain the policy of massive subsidies it paid in order to maintain a good standard of living for its citizens. The GDR could not afford to invest in industrial plants or research and development, and its economy was therefore stagnating. Additionally, Honecker's social policies were becoming more and more problematic.

The rise in immigration to the GDR

To appease the growing pressure from both the GDR's population and some within his own party over the question of free travel to the West, Honecker allowed a greater number of East Germans to visit relatives in the FRG. Between 1986 and 1988 there was a massive increase in the number of East Germans taking advantage of this policy. By 1988, the GDR had received hundreds of thousands of applications from essential skilled workers asking for permission to emigrate to the West. In 1988, the number of East Germans allowed to migrate to the FRG increased by 18,500 to a total of 30,000. By the start of 1989, it had reached 48,000 in the first few months alone. The number of Germans allowed to travel from the GDR to the FRG increased by five million, to 6.2 million, from 1987 to 1988. The GDR believed that if it allowed more of its citizens to visit the FRG, they would in turn be less inclined to seek permanent settlement there, although the increasing numbers seeking emigration appeared to demonstrate the limitations of this reasoning.

The FRG, on the other side, made it clear that it did not support a policy of encouraging emigration from the GDR. The FRG believed that if it pursued a direction of depleting the GDR, this would only lead to government repression and the decline of FRG–GDR relations, including the more liberal travel policy on behalf of the GDR. This meant that GDR citizens seeking refuge in the FRG's embassies in Berlin and across Eastern Europe were encouraged to leave and instead pursue emigration through the official channels of the GDR. The FRG itself attempted to reduce the number of GDR citizens seeking refuge in the West by decreasing the benefits Eastern European refugees would be entitled to when they arrived. Unemployment pay for GDR refugees, for instance, was removed and replaced by a lower rate of monthly payments. However, as greater numbers of East Germans were given the right to visit the FRG, so the demand for permanent emigration from the GDR rose.

The policy towards greater travel freedom for its citizens did not equate, however, to greater political freedom in the GDR. Honecker made it clear that the Communist government was not going to allow increased freedom of speech in the GDR; also, the political reforms taking place at the end of the 1980s, not only in the USSR, but also in Poland and Hungary, were not going to be replicated in East Germany.

The flood of East German refugees becomes a crisis

The growing increase in GDR refugees became a critical issue after 2 May 1989, when the reforming Hungarian Communist government announced that it would remove the barbed-wire fencing and fortifications along its border with Austria. This was a dramatic move that substantially undermined the GDR and led to a refugee crisis in the FRG. Hungary, as a member of the Communist East and therefore a permitted destination, had long been a prime location for East Germans during the summer months. The opening of the border between Hungary and Austria opened up a new route to the West, and over the summer of 1989, tens of thousands of East Germans flooded into Hungary on the pretext of going on holiday. In reality, they were hoping to leave East Germany. Austria was not part of the Eastern Bloc countries and GDR citizens hoped to enter Austria from Hungary and, from there, make their way into West Germany. Under the terms of the Hungarian government's treaty with the GDR, any East Germans caught attempting to flee to Austria should have been arrested and returned to the GDR. However, as the numbers of East German 'tourists' increased, implementing this policy became increasingly difficult.

At first, following the changes made on 2 May, the Hungarian government tried to stop East Germans from entering Austria. Then, on 9 August, Hungarian officials declared they would no longer stamp the passports of GDR citizens they caught attempting to flee to Austria. In practice, this meant that Hungary would no longer attempt to forcibly return GDR citizens to East Germany if they were caught trying to cross from Hungary over to Austria. This weakening of Hungarian attempts to stop GDR citizens fleeing to Austria in turn led to an even greater increase in the number of East German refugees heading to the Hungarian/Austrian border. Through July and August, there was a build-up of thousands of East Germans living in temporary refugee camps in Hungary along the border area with Austria. The events in Hungary led to an increase in East German refugees elsewhere in Europe. West German embassies in Prague, Budapest, Warsaw and East Berlin were inundated with GDR citizens desperate to leave.

As the numbers reached a critical mass, West Germany began to close its embassies in an effort to dissuade any more East Germans from seeking refuge in their grounds. On 20 August, around 500 GDR refugees successfully crossed into Austria illegally.

SOURCE 2

East Germans waiting in Czechoslovakia before being given asylum in West Germany, 4 November 1989.

The FRG's response to the crisis

The FRG decided to deal with the situation. On 1 September it announced that, together with the Austrian government, it would accept 20,000 East German refugees. Two weeks later, the Hungarian government opened its borders, with some 35,000 East Germans crossing into Austria and Western Europe during September alone. Honecker's government banned Hungary as a travel destination for East Germans, but this simply saw more GDR citizens head to Poland and Czechoslovakia. On 16 September, the GDR government agreed with the Polish government that East German refugees in Poland would be allowed to leave for the West. This was followed by an agreement reached with the Czechoslovakian government that the 4,000 East Germans camped out in the West German embassy in Prague could leave for West Germany. These concessions encouraged more East Germans to leave, and another 15,000 East Germans fled to the West via Czechoslovakia. As one mass of East Germans left Hungary, Czechoslovakia or Poland, another would turn up. By 7 October, 40,000 East Germans had crossed into Austria via the Hungarian border. Another 3,000 refugees invaded the grounds of the West German embassy in Prague, and just over a thousand more arrived at the embassy in Warsaw. By the end of October, the numbers were growing at an alarming rate. Soon, thousands were leaving Hungary for Austria every day, as thousands more GDR citizens entered Hungary to follow them. The West Berlin embassies in Prague and Warsaw continued to fill up every time they reached an agreement with the GDR for the last wave of thousands of East German refugees in their grounds to leave for the West.

On 3 November, an incredible 45,000 East Germans were camped out in or around the embassy grounds in Prague. When the GDR agreed that they would allow these refugees to leave for West Germany, thousands more entered Czechoslovakia. By the end of November, it was difficult to see how the numbers leaving could be sustained by the GDR. It was estimated that some 9,000 citizens were leaving the GDR every day, and it was becoming increasingly difficult for the FRG to deal with the massive numbers of East Germans arriving. Refugee camps were becoming inundated with arrivals, as around 200,000 East Germans left the country between August and November. It was estimated that around 1.3 million more East Germans hoped to join them.

Honecker's response to the GDR refugee crisis

The GDR's leadership appeared to be at a loss as to how to deal with the crisis. Honecker's first solution was to carry on as usual, presenting an image that there were no problems within the GDR. In September, he decided instead to launch a verbal attack on West Germany for supposedly promoting the depletion of the GDR's population, but contrastingly declared that he was unmoved by those leaving the GDR as they were traitors to the Communist system. Despite these claims, the situation within the GDR was chaotic. Mass numbers were leaving every day, and the state's survival was at stake. In the FRG, politicians grappled with how to deal with the thousands of refugees arriving every day, and the fraught and volatile situation challenged the stability of the large West German middle classes. The desperate social and economic situation in the GDR, however, led to over a million East Germans seeking a new and better life in the West.

The actions of the Hungarian government on 2 May 1989, in opening its border with Austria, set off events that would ultimately lead to the downfall of the GDR. The combination of the GDR's lack of reform contrasted with the fresh ideology of Gorbachev, and reforms in Poland and Hungary also encouraged a greater number of East Germans to seek a better life. Honecker's belief that he could prevent social and political change in the GDR through allowing greater freedom of travel was naive, and showed his lack of understanding of the core issues within his own state.

By 1989, East Germans did not just want the freedom to travel to West Germany; they desperately wanted to leave the GDR for the FRG permanently. The decision by the Hungarian government to open its borders with Austria on 2 May allowed this to become a reality. In October 1989, the GDR's Communist Party would desperately attempt to wrestle back the political initiative, making political changes they hoped would stop the huge numbers of East Germans leaving and save the GDR. However, events taking place in parallel to the refugee crisis would ensure that these attempted reforms came much too late to rescue the country and its Communist system.

EXTEND YOUR KNOWLEDGE

Erich Honecker (1912-94)
Honecker was the leader of the GDR from 1971 to 1989. In that time, he pushed through some economic reforms, as well as negotiating a better relationship with the FRG and achieving for the GDR a full place in the United Nations. By the 1980s, however, he refused to make either economic or political changes, as the GDR came under greater pressure. He also disagreed with the policies of Gorbachev, believing that any reform of the Communist system would lead to its ultimate destruction. He tried to resist the changes taking place in other Eastern European countries, but increased protests in the GDR and the continuing depletion of the GDR population as its citizens fled to the West undermined his leadership. In October 1989, the Socialist Unionist Party (SED) removed him from power in the belief that political reforms might save the GDR; however, the SED's political rule only survived a couple of months after Honecker's fall from power. Honecker was later given political asylum in Chile, where he died in 1994.

SOURCE

3

'Crisis of direction for East Germany' by Timothy Garton Ash, published in the *Canberra Times*, 1 October 1989. Timothy Garton Ash is a British historian whose work focuses on the history of Central and Eastern Europe. Here he assesses the problems facing East Germany in October 1989.

'The situation is complicated' officials gravely remarked when I visited East Berlin in July. But just how complicated was not apparent even then. For Hungary's removal of the barbed wire on its border to Austria proved to be, as it were, the last straw. Hundreds of East Germans made the dash for freedom. Hundreds more clambered into the West German embassy compounds in Prague and Warsaw. Then the Hungarian government, seeking full acceptance in the international community, made the brave decision to let the East Germans depart legally. More than 20,000 East Germans have arrived in West Germany so far. This is, let it be noted, only some 10 percent of the estimated 200,000 East Germans who spent their summer holidays in Hungary. Although more may still come out, it appears that more than 80 percent have gone back to the GDR. But the haemorrhage is still immense. As usual, those who leave are generally, the young, the active, the skilled, the independent minded. The visual, symbolic and emotional impact has been enormous, not just on East Germany, but also on West Germany, many of whose people, journalists and politicians seemed almost to have forgotten that they have compatriots ready to risk their lives for something they call freedom. Incidentally, 'risk their lives' is no hyperbole. According to a responsible source, 10 East Germans have already died trying to swim the Danube between Czechoslovakia and Hungary. And this is not all. In just the last few weeks, the demands for change inside East Germany have sparked and spread in ways few people thought possible. They have come from church leaders. They have come from new opposition groups. They have come from young people on the streets: as many as 8000 in Leipzig earlier this week, singing 'We shall overcome.' They have come even from the veteran leader of the puppet 'Liberal Democratic' party – the late blooming of a paper flower. In short, when Mikhail Gorbachev comes to East Berlin next Saturday he will be visiting a country in crisis.

ACTIVITY
KNOWLEDGE CHECK

1 What impression do Sources 2 and 3 give of the East German refugee situation in 1989?

2 What evidence is there in Source 3 that Honecker's attempts to deal with the situation will not be sufficient?

3 How far could you use Source 3 to argue that the fall of the GDR was becoming inevitable during the summer of 1989?

WHAT IMPACT DID THE REVOLUTION IN THE GDR AND KOHL'S TEN POINT PLAN IN 1989 HAVE ON GERMAN REUNIFICATION?

The revolution in the GDR in 1989, and its impact on the FRG

The refugee problem from August 1989 onwards ran parallel to a growing political protest movement in the GDR. Critically for the ruling Communist party, Honecker was taken ill with a gall bladder infection that meant he could not fulfil his leadership duties from 21 August to late September. Without his dominating position, the Socialist Unionist Party (SED) found it difficult to deal with the rapidly accumulating situation. New opposition movements began to appear in East Germany that challenged the dominant power of the SED. Mass protests against the Communist system broke out in Leipzig in September, following Monday evening church services and, despite the actions of the police to break them up and the threat from the SED that they would be crushed through a violent response, the protests in Leipzig continued every Monday. Honecker returned to work on 25 September and essentially acted as though there was no real danger to the GDR. He argued that citizens who were leaving the GDR were traitors anyway, so there should be no concern if they did not want to live in the socialist East.

EXTEND YOUR KNOWLEDGE

Leipzig Monday protests (1982–90)

The Leipzig Monday protest movement was a critical development in the fall of the GDR. From 1982, the Lutheran pastor Christian Führer had organised Monday 'Peace Prayers' for young East Germans in Leipzig. Using prayers and religious discourse as a way of discussing their frustrations with East Germany, these prayer meetings were one of the only ways in which young Germans could protest against the government. The Monday 'Peace Prayers' grew in numbers in 1989, as more young Germans were encouraged to engage in peaceful, non-violent protests against the East German government. The church in Leipzig became a focal point for the protest movement, with 120,000 people turning up to attend Führer's church service on 16 October 1989. Informed by West German television of what was happening, more and more East Germans began to attend the Leipzig Monday protests, which now spilled out of the church and were replicated across the GDR. By the end of October 1989, some 320,000 people were participating in the Leipzig protest movement. The government's inability to shut the protests down, and their unwillingness to stop the protests with force, made it one of the key developments leading to the fall of Communism in East Germany.

Events escalate: October 1989

At the beginning of October, there was a three-hour riot involving 10,000 people in Dresden, as East Germans tried to board a sealed train carrying East German refugees from Czechoslovakia through East Germany to the FRG. The incident occurred because, after considerable pressure, Honecker had decided to allow the 14,000 East Germans camped out in the West German embassy in Prague to migrate to the FRG. However, to reclaim East German pride, he insisted that they be transported in sealed trains through East Germany, so that it appeared as though it was the GDR that was expelling these 'traitors'. The move caused chaos as the train passed through the GDR. The passengers threw their East German passports out of the windows along the way, and in Dresden, 10,000 GDR citizens attacked the train, trying to get on it. The whole affair was a propaganda disaster for the GDR.

Honecker declined to deal with the mass protests by promising political reforms. Instead, he had the border with Czechoslovakia closed and persisted with the 40-year anniversary celebrations of the creation of the GDR, on 7 October. The celebrations were marred, however, by scuffles between the police and protestors in Berlin. The GDR youth, who had been officially chosen for the celebrations, embarrassed Honecker through their enthusiastic response to the reformist Gorbachev, who had come to the GDR for the anniversary. While not directly criticising the SED, Gorbachev encouraged the values of political and economic reform he was putting in place in the USSR, and confirmed that the USSR could no longer provide military or economic assistance to artificially prop up the declining GDR. Two days later, a crowd of 70,000 gathered in Leipzig to protest against the Communist system, and by 17 October it had grown to 100,000. In response to the growth of the protest movement and the mass numbers of East Germans fleeing the country every day, the leadership within the SED decided it needed to take action. On the same day as the mass Leipzig protests,

Honecker was removed as leader of the GDR and replaced with Egon Krenz. Krenz immediately announced that he hoped it was not too late to introduce political reforms in East Germany in order to develop a country which East Germans would want to live in and contribute to.

The new GDR government under Krenz

However, in reality, Krenz's new government was just as inadequate as Honecker's in producing the type of deep reforms that East Germans now desired. The SED still refused to accept any changes that might challenge its leading role within the GDR or to accept legalisation of the new opposition groups that had formed since September. The government attempted to introduce a new travel law that would give GDR citizens greater freedom, but it was so confusing and complex that it was rejected by the GDR's parliament. By this stage, in November 1989, around 750,000 East Germans had taken to the streets in protest across the whole of the GDR. On 4 November, mass protests took place in Berlin, with East Germans demanding political freedom, the legalisation of opposition groups and the freedom to unrestricted travel wherever and whenever they wanted. Under pressure, the SED's response was undirected and confusing. On 9 November, they convened a hastily arranged press conference, where Gunter Schabowski of the SED announced a new policy whereby any citizen with a passport would be granted greater rights of travel. When the press asked a clearly unprepared Schabowski when the regulations would come into place, he abruptly answered that they were in effect immediately, despite having no authorisation to say that. As the word spread that the border with West Germany was now open, tens of thousands of Germans flooded to the border gates in East Berlin; the guards were overwhelmed and were unable to stop the crowds.

The fall of the Berlin Wall: the barrier between East and West Germany comes down

At 11.20 p.m. on the night of 9 November, the border guards at Bornholmer Bridge decided to lift the barrier between East and West Berlin. The **Berlin Wall** that had held the division between West and East Germany in place since 1961 had now essentially ceased to exist. When the East German government border controls collapsed on the 9 November, Germans in both East and West Germany began to physically attack the wall. This was a powerful symbol of the German people destroying the most vivid sign of Germany's division. It also dramatically showed the powerlessness of the SED to uphold its dictatorship any longer.

KEY TERM

Berlin Wall
A wall constructed in 1961 by the GDR and USSR governments to cut off West Berlin from East Berlin and East Germany as a whole. This stopped the mass exodus of East German citizens, who had been leaving permanently for the FRG. The wall was heavily guarded, and between 1961 and 1989, East German border guards killed 150 to 200 people when they tried to escape.

SOURCE

4 Massive crowds of East Germans gather at the Check Point Charlie border crossing in Berlin on 9 November 1989, demanding access to West Germany.

KEY TERM

Keep one's powder dry
Remain cautious and alert.

The overwhelming pressure from the people of East Germany had challenged the system, and over the next few weeks, Germans from both sides of Berlin would attack the wall itself, destroying the most graphic symbol of German division. Critically, the 1.5 million Soviet troops stationed in the GDR remained in their barracks, confirming Gorbachev's promise that he would not use the military to defend unpopular Communist states against the will of their own people.

Political turmoil continues

On 13 November, the political parties within the GDR, such as the CDU, which had continued to exist in East Germany but had previously been subservient to the SED, reasserted their independence, announcing that they would now play a more independent, oppositional role in government. Desperate to save the situation and the GDR, the SED underwent another round of leadership changes, although this time they were more drastic: the entire leadership of the SED was removed; key figures were placed under arrest on corruption charges; and the party changed its name from the SED to the Party of Democratic Socialism (PDS) under the new leadership of Gregor Gysi and Hans Modrow. So-called 'Round Table' discussions were announced that would bring all political parties together in consultation on the future of the GDR.

The situation in the GDR, however, continued to unravel chaotically. Within only the first week and a half following the fall of the Berlin Wall, 17,000 East Germans left for the West. On 28 November, the West German Chancellor Helmut Kohl took the initiative to try to stabilise the situation by announcing to the Bundestag his Ten Point Plan, which he believed would first lead to a confederate structure incorporating the two Germanys, and then to full reunification of Germany some five to ten years after that.

SOURCE
5

Michael Simmons, in an article titled 'Honecker's choice **keeps his powder dry**' (*Canberra Times*, 20 October 1989), discusses the situation in East Germany and argues why Krenz will not be able to stop the protests in the GDR. Michael Simmons was a journalist who, at the time of the fall of the GDR, was working in Eastern Europe as a correspondent for Western newspapers.

Egon Krenz, who on Wednesday became East Germany's third leader in its 40-year history, was in Beijing when China celebrated its 40th anniversary. He told his hard-line hosts, 'The GDR will stick to the principle of combining the continuity of policies with reform.' As he spoke, the flow of GDR citizens heading westwards was already turning into a torrent, Neues Forum and other opposition groups were coming into visible being and the first street demonstrations in Leipzig, Dresden and East Berlin were just a few days away. None of these groups will have been heartened by what he said in Beijing and few, if any, will be heartened by his appointment. The demonstrations, in other words, will go on. It is a logical consequence of the ousting of Erich Honecker and his own succession that Krenz may now make some sort of heavily qualified offer to talk with the opposition. He may even, in the first instance, pronounce more in favour of reform than of continuity — but he will keep both heaps of powder dry. The Chinese, after all, thanked him for supporting the way they crushed the Tiananmen Square uprising and said they backed him in his fight against any efforts to 'sabotage' socialism in the GDR. As the communist party's chief man for both security and youth affairs, he knows the political opposition is a growing force. In the last few days alone, calls for change have come from all quarters. Regional party secretaries, some belonging to the country's new and educated elite, wanted Honecker to go; Neues Forum and other groups have gained in coherence and support; and the street demonstrations have grown in strength. By and large, the opposition consists of young people, sometimes disarmingly young, who are intelligent and simultaneously Left and Green in their persuasion, who like what Mikhail Gorbachev stands for, and who want to stay in the GDR. They have been unsettled and deeply dispirited by the exodus of nearly 100,000 of their friends and relatives, but they have not joined them... The summer exodus of so many of the country's brightest and best qualified young people, even though more than 99 per cent of the population stayed behind, did nothing to boost an economy which, although it is probably the strongest economy in Eastern Europe, has been showing serious signs of faltering.

ACTIVITY
KNOWLEDGE CHECK

1 In what ways does Source 4 demonstrate the problems facing the East German border guards on the night of 9 November 1989?

2 How far does Source 4 explain the reasons for the fall of the Berlin Wall?

3 Why does the writer of Source 5 argue that the replacement of Honecker by Egon Krenz would not help solve the problems of the GDR?

4 In Source 5, how far do you agree with the journalist's assessment of the situation in East Germany in October 1989?

The significance of Kohl's Ten Point Plan

The role of Helmut Kohl and the CDU

Helmut Kohl had been Chancellor of the FRG since 1982. During this period he had persistently pursued a policy of reasoned accommodation with East Germany that avoided any particular emphasis on German reunification. While concerned at the deteriorating situation in the GDR during the 1980s, there was little call from within Kohl's CDU to press for a dramatic change in the FRG relationship with the Communist East. The key focus for the CDU was to present the FRG's role in Europe as one of maintaining stability, not challenging the existing balance of power by seeking reunification. Within the West German public, calls for peaceful stability, in respect of ensuring that West and East worked together to overcome political divisions, were much more politically successful than renewed emphasis on the reunification of Germany.

In July 1989, Kohl's chief foreign policy adviser, Horst Teltschik, stated that the FRG's main focus was working towards stability and peace in Europe, not seeking to alter existing borders. Through the late 1980s, the FRG had shown its willingness to work with reforming Communist countries such as Poland and Hungary, and Mikhail Gorbachev had made a successful visit to Bonn in June 1989. While this appeared to be ushering in a new era of co-operation between Western and Eastern Europe, there was no indication that these new relationships would lead to a change in the status quo concerning the relationship between the FRG and the GDR.

Calls for German reunification

The events of late 1989 and the breakdown of the border after Schabowski's announcement caught Helmut Kohl's government somewhat off guard. It was only in mid-November, as thousands continued to leave the GDR, that East German protests began to call for reunification.

The FRG's politicians were initially unsure how to deal with this new emphasis on reunification. Most politicians within the FRG believed that reunification was virtually impossible, and the fact that the most vociferous calls for a new Germany came from the East was a complete surprise. Given the restrictive nature of the GDR, it had seemed inconceivable to politicians in the West that the main push for German reunification should come from the Communist East. Their immediate reaction was to provide humanitarian aid to the hundreds of thousands of East Germans arriving in the FRG, and to try to preserve some form of structured relationship with the collapsing government in the GDR. Kohl also announced that economic aid from the FRG to the GDR could be a possibility if the Communist government pursued substantial reforms. There was no word from Kohl at this stage that the actual existence of the GDR was in question. Kohl instead asserted that he believed the opening of the Berlin Wall would prompt the GDR to make the necessary reforms to ensure that more of its population would stay in East Germany. Politicians from both East and West argued that the continuing existence of the GDR was essential to European stability. However, in the weeks following the collapse of the Berlin Wall, these announcements seemed irrelevant to the thousands of people who continued to leave East Germany.

Kohl's Ten Point Plan

Hoping to seize the initiative, Kohl announced a Ten Point Plan that would first stabilise the current situation by the move towards a confederate state linking the two Germanys, and then move towards implementation of full reunification within five to ten years. Political motivations played as large a part as the ongoing collapse of the GDR in Kohl's announcement. The CDU's political polls were extremely low, and Kohl believed that taking the leadership towards reunification could boost his chances of winning the next election.

On 28 November 1989, Kohl made a dramatic speech in the Bundestag, announcing his Ten Point Plan for 'the regaining of Germany's national unity'. It was a clear reversal from the CDU's position that the main goal was stability in Europe. Before making this announcement, Kohl had consulted few people within his party, and most within the Bundestag had no knowledge of Kohl's decision to now work towards reunification. With his proposal, Kohl became the first German Chancellor for nearly 30 years to publically declare that his stated goal was reunification. The Ten Point Plan proposed 'immediate assistance' for the GDR, and the creation of 'confederative structures' between the FRG and the GDR, with the 'aim of creating a federation – that is, a federal order in Germany'. At this stage Kohl admitted that the outcome of his plan was quite vague and that the eventual structure of a unified Germany was difficult to envision, but that 'reunification – that is, regaining Germany's state unity – [remained] the political aim of the federal government'.

The response to the Ten Point Plan – in Germany and beyond

Kohl's proposal was greeted enthusiastically within Germany. On 11 December 1989, mass demonstrations of nearly 300,000 people took place in Leipzig, with the protestors carrying West German flags and calling for unification. When Kohl visited Dresden in the GDR on 19 December, he received a massive welcome, with 100,000 people gathering to hear him talk. From January to February 1990, high-level discussions began on how to best pursue the complex financial union between the two countries. Kohl believed that the first stages of reunification would probably take up to two years. Instead, reunification happened at a pace even Kohl had not envisioned, with Germany unified on the stroke of midnight between 2 and 3 October 1990. Kohl's Ten Point Plan had been hugely significant in providing the direction and impetus for this momentous event. He had seized the initiative and dramatically changed his party's entrenched policy on German reunification. However, the key negotiations leading to German reunification would not take place between the GDR and the FRG. Instead, they would take place between Kohl and the four powers that still technically occupied Berlin: the USSR, the USA, the UK and France, each of which had not greeted Kohl's Ten Point Plan with the enthusiasm it had found within Germany.

EXTEND YOUR KNOWLEDGE

The reaction of the United States and the USSR to the Ten Point Plan

Kohl's Ten Point Plan had been partly constructed due to advice he was receiving from Nikolai Portugalov, a key link between the FRG and the Soviet government. Portugalov claimed the USSR leadership was already discussing the possibility of confederation between the GDR and the FRG. However, Kohl did not realise that Portugalov's messages did not have the approval of Gorbachev himself. When Kohl made his speech on 28 November, he neither consulted the President of the United States, George Bush, nor Mikhail Gorbachev. Both of these leaders reacted angrily to Kohl's speech, although Bush and Kohl were able to discuss the matter on 3 December 1989 and come to a better understanding. Gorbachev, on the other hand, refused to discuss the matter with Kohl until February 1990, and the Russian leader made several angry remarks asserting that German reunification could lead to the death of Europe. Economic pressures on the USSR would, eventually, play a crucial role in changing Gorbachev's attitude to German reunification.

SOURCE 6

FRG Chancellor Helmut Kohl speaks in front of 100,000 people in Dresden on 19 December 1989.

SOURCE 7

Helmut Kohl's speech to the Bundestag, 28 November 1989. Here Kohl describes the key aspects of the Ten Point Plan, which sets out the process for German reunification.

We are all deeply impressed by the living, unbroken will for freedom that moves the people in Leipzig and many other towns. They know what they want. They want to determine their future themselves in the original meaning of the words. In this we shall of course respect every decision that the people in the GDR take in free self-determination... We cannot plan the road to unity in smoke-filled rooms or with a timetable in our hands. Abstract models are of no assistance either. But we can now, today, prepare the stages that will lead to this goal. I should like to set them forth on the basis of a ten-point programme: First: Right away, immediate measures arising out of the events of the last few weeks, particularly the refugee movements and the new dimensions of travel, are necessary... Third: I have offered to extend our assistance and our cooperation comprehensively when a radical change in the political and economic system in the GDR is bindingly decided and irreversibly set in motion. 'Irreversibly' means for us that the GDR national leadership should come to agreement with opposition groups on constitutional change and on a new electoral law. We support the demand for free, equal and secret elections in the GDR with the involvement of independent parties, including non-socialist ones. The SED's power monopoly must be removed... Fifth: But we are also prepared to take one further decisive step, namely to develop confederative structures between the two States in Germany, with the objective of then creating a federation, that is, a national federal system in Germany. This necessarily presupposes a democratically legitimated government in the GDR... How a reunited Germany will finally look is something no one today knows. But that unification will come if the people in Germany want it, of that I am certain... Seventh: The European Community's power of attraction and influence is and remains a constant factor in overall European development. We wish to strengthen it further. The European Community is now being called on to approach the reform-oriented States of Central, Eastern and South-Eastern Europe with openness and flexibility. We see the process of regaining German unity as a European matter. It must therefore also be seen in combination with European integration.

ACTIVITY
KNOWLEDGE CHECK

1 Read through Source 7 and summarise the key aspects of Helmut Kohl's Ten Point Plan. What differing goals does he set out for both the FRG and the GDR?

2 What does Source 6 demonstrate about how Kohl's programme was received by the citizens of the GDR?

WHAT WERE THE KEY REASONS FOR GERMAN REUNIFICATION IN OCTOBER 1990?

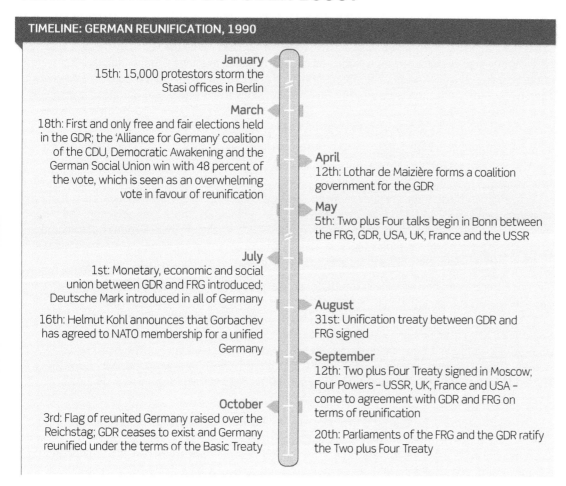

TIMELINE: GERMAN REUNIFICATION, 1990

January
15th: 15,000 protestors storm the Stasi offices in Berlin

March
18th: First and only free and fair elections held in the GDR; the 'Alliance for Germany' coalition of the CDU, Democratic Awakening and the German Social Union win with 48 percent of the vote, which is seen as an overwhelming vote in favour of reunification

April
12th: Lothar de Maizière forms a coalition government for the GDR

May
5th: Two plus Four talks begin in Bonn between the FRG, GDR, USA, UK, France and the USSR

July
1st: Monetary, economic and social union between GDR and FRG introduced; Deutsche Mark introduced in all of Germany

16th: Helmut Kohl announces that Gorbachev has agreed to NATO membership for a unified Germany

August
31st: Unification treaty between GDR and FRG signed

September
12th: Two plus Four Treaty signed in Moscow; Four Powers – USSR, UK, France and USA – come to agreement with GDR and FRG on terms of reunification

20th: Parliaments of the FRG and the GDR ratify the Two plus Four Treaty

October
3rd: Flag of reunited Germany raised over the Reichstag; GDR ceases to exist and Germany reunified under the terms of the Basic Treaty

Different levels of prosperity in the GDR and FRG

You have already read about the FRG's economic development in Chapter 2 (see page 59). By the 1980s, the FRG was a prosperous, developed member of the EEC, its citizens enjoying a high standard of living. The GDR's economy, on the other hand, had failed to develop in a sustainable fashion, and by the 1980s it was facing significant difficulties. From the very foundation of Germany's division, the FRG enjoyed significant advantages over the Communist East. The main industrial lands of Germany in the Ruhr and Saarland (from 1957) were part of the FRG and were crucial to fuelling its remarkable industrial growth. The GDR lacked any major areas of raw materials and was mainly agricultural. It had a much smaller population than the FRG and had suffered much more extensively from reparations demanded by the USSR. The GDR had attempted economic reforms in the 1960s, but these had failed to provide a basis for successful economic growth. The GDR's economic system also suffered from massive spending on defence and a huge bureaucracy. Additionally, it was committed to providing its citizens with a substantial social welfare system, which was increasingly difficult to sustain. By the 1970s, the combination of growing social welfare costs, a weak economic system and rising fuel costs were causing mounting problems for the GDR. To solve its economic problems, the GDR borrowed money through foreign loans and ignored the need for investment in its major industries. The GDR found itself more and more reliant on financial assistance from the FRG.

However, it should be noted that in terms of Eastern Europe, the GDR had the most successful economy, with the highest standard of living. Under Honecker, there had been a move to placate the consumer demands of the GDR's people, with fridges and televisions becoming more available. The GDR was the most advanced developer, within Eastern Europe, of microelectronics and computer technology, an area in which it concentrated much of its resources. By the 1980s, however, its economic system was in decline. In 1983 and 1984, it was forced to negotiate extensive loans from

West Germany in order to prop up its economic system. Honecker was determined to protect the East German people from the effects of this economic downturn by keeping up spending on the social welfare system, an action that simply pushed the GDR into more spiralling debts. Significantly, the GDR also suffered from some of the worst environmental conditions in Europe. Unable to afford investment in oil to run its factories, and unable to modernise equipment and reduce pollution, the GDR relied on highly polluting brown coal that could be sourced within the GDR. By the late 1980s, the GDR's level of harmful carbon dioxide and sulphur dioxide emissions was the highest in the world. Forests in the GDR were under threat from acid rain caused by the poor air quality. Respiratory illnesses caused by pollution were a particular problem, being twice that of the European average. By 1989, the average life span of a citizen of the GDR was two and a half years less for men and seven years less for women, in comparison to a citizen of the FRG.

By the mid-1980s, the GDR's economy was in a severe crisis: it could no longer afford the massive expense of its social welfare system, nor could it afford to invest in much-needed modernisation of its industrial technology. The economy was also hurt further by ill-thought-through prestige projects, such as the attempt to build 'the world's largest microchip' in the 1980s, which cost the GDR economy one billion marks and failed to achieve its goal. Economic growth was declining, and the ability of the government to supply the citizens of the GDR with the consumer goods they wanted was becoming more and more difficult. The quality of these goods, such as motor cars (particularly the **Trabant**) was low, and purchased goods took a long time to arrive.

The poor comparison between life in the GDR and life in the FRG was clearly seen through the West German television shows that East Germans were able to watch every day, and through contact with West German relatives and visitors, who had been given greater ability to travel to the GDR since the 1970s. These problems were accentuated by the policies of Mikhail Gorbachev in the USSR. The considerable economic reforms pursued by the Russian leader put Honecker under increasing pressure from within his own Communist party to develop similar reforms in the GDR. The leadership of the SED, however, refused to accept the need for any form of economic reform, believing this could weaken its control over the country.

As more East Germans travelled and then migrated to the West, there was growing awareness of the massive divergence between the GDR and the FRG. Additionally, the considerable loss of manpower weakened the economy even further. In October 1989, a report commissioned by the SED set out the grave economic situation, with GDR exports needing to rise by nine million German marks in order to stabilise the country's debt. However, to achieve such an increase, the GDR would need to restrict the import of consumer goods, reduce public spending and increase investments in national industries.

There is debate among historians as to how much economic uncertainties, as opposed to political freedoms, played a role in the growing protests from the GDR's citizens in the 1980s. Clearly, the growing discrepancies between the standard of living in the East and West added to the disenchantment felt in the GDR towards its government. There is no doubt, however, that the economic downturn played a critical role in reunification. Once the Berlin Wall came down, the mass exodus of GDR citizens accentuated the economic problems the country faced. Furthermore, now that the GDR was fully open to competition with West Germany, it found it impossible to compete. The GDR was the leading microelectronics producer in Eastern Europe, where it was seen as advanced in this field; however, in comparison to the West, its microelectronic goods were considerably outdated. As more East German citizens left the GDR, the ability of East Germany to sustain its existence was fundamentally challenged.

KEY TERM

Trabant
This was the GDR's car and it was an excellent symbol of the GDR's poor economic position in comparison with the FRG by the 1980s. While the FRG's car industry produced a range of high-selling vehicles with an excellent reputation (including Volkswagen, BMW and Mercedes-Benz), the GDR instead produced the Trabant. The Trabant was a small vehicle constructed with hard plastic made from recycled material. It ran on a combination of fuel and two-stroke oil and was highly polluting. The Trabant was produced for 30 years with little change to the design, and was the main car driven in the GDR. Nearly 3.7 million were produced from 1957 to 1991. When the Berlin Wall fell, GDR citizens had to get special dispensation to drive their Trabants into the FRG, where the cars did not meet the much more stringent anti-pollution laws. Trabant could not compete with the cars produced in the FRG and was a casualty of reunification, going out of business in 1991.

Continued migration from the GDR

As you have already read, the flood of refugees leaving the GDR after Hungary relaxed its border with Austria in 1989 was a crucial reason for the decline of East Germany. The desire of East German citizens to escape to the FDR had been a problem for the GDR since its creation. Up to the building of the Berlin Wall, hundreds of thousands of East Germans left the GDR for the FRG, thus leading to the decision to construct the wall in order to retain its depleting workforce. In the 1980s, the GDR relaxed its policy on emigration and travel for East German citizens. Hoping to enhance its relationship with the FRG, it allowed 40,000 East Germans to emigrate there in 1984.

SOURCE 8

East German inner-city Berlin covered in smog, February 1987.

ACTIVITY
KNOWLEDGE CHECK

1 What key problems facing the GDR in the late 1980s can be summarised from Source 8?

2 Why had the economic issues facing the GDR become so serious by the late 1980s?

3 To what extent did these economic issues lead to the collapse of the GDR?

In 1986, the GDR government relaxed its definition of what constituted 'urgent family matters', leading to 573,000 GDR citizens visiting the West, an increase of 400,000 on the previous year. In 1987, this rose again, to 1.2 million. The reasons for Honecker's decision to lower the restrictions for travel related to two factors:

• his attempt to build a stronger relationship with the FRG, particularly at a time when his government required further economic assistance

• his belief that if GDR citizens were given greater freedom, it would reduce political pressure and make them more likely to remain in the GDR.

Some historians have also pointed out that Honecker's inability to see how his policy would challenge his own regime came about because of the sheltered nature of his Communist party, which was unable to comprehend the growing agitation of its own people.

By 1988, Honecker was able to refer to figures that showed that only 1.5 percent of East Germans travelling to West Germany chose to stay there, as proof of the success of his policy. However, the truth was that a large majority of those returning from West Germany immediately sought permission to migrate permanently. The numbers leaving the GDR steadily grew through 1988 and 1989, depleting the country of much-needed workers. As you have previously read, this problem exploded from May 1989 onwards, when Hungary relaxed its border with Austria. With the fall of the Berlin Wall, the migration from East to West clearly accelerated the push for reunification; some 2,000 East Germans were leaving the GDR every day. In January 1990 alone, 60,000 GDR citizens left the country. These were mainly well-educated, young East Germans, and their absence impacted severely on the East German economy.

Productivity in East German factories declined by around 50 percent, and this, combined with the economic situation of the GDR, meant the state was nearing collapse. This pushed forward the drive for reunification. Kohl's Ten Point Plan took on greater emphasis within Germany, as it was increasingly clear that the GDR could not survive as a viable state for much longer. It was also important in Kohl's difficult negotiations with the four occupying powers. The fact that the GDR was on the brink of collapse, and the effects that the failure of this state might have for Europe as a whole, was used by Kohl to put pressure on the Four Powers to accept reunification.

SOURCE 9

Letter from Thorsten Muller to his cousin and her husband in West Germany, dated 13 November 1989. Thorsten Muller was a citizen of the GDR who had never been able to travel to the FRG before. Here he describes his experiences on entering the FRG for the first time.

Then on Thursday I watched the 'opening' of the wall and the whole confusion on TV until 2am. It was impossible to believe... Friday morning it was announced on the public address system that the Sperrgebiet had been lifted. The joy here knew no boundaries... But I didn't want to go right away. To be honest I was scared to see everything. And I was totally irritated at how everyone was after the 100 Western Marks... It's humiliating to get rich from your tax money. If we could at least have exchanged for it... Maybe the West Germans will destroy the GDR this way. It's like an investment. They buy the GDR citizens (their sympathy) and then they won't want to remain GDR citizens anymore. Anyway, I didn't want to go over to the West right away, but Katje talked me into it, especially when we heard that another border crossing had been opened near Heiligenstadt. We filled up the tank and left around 1pm. After four hours of stop and go traffic we came to the GDR control point, where they let us through without having to show our identity card, even without stopping. For us it was unbelievable. After a few hundred meters we came to the provisional Western control point. It was absolutely insane. It was already dark, and still there were people standing at the border shouting for joy. We honked and yelled. It was simply unbelievable. I was shaking so much I could hardly drive. People waved and greeted us more warmly than I've ever experienced. I had to fight back tears. It was great to drive on Western streets. We kept wondering what we should do... We decided to go to Göttingen... where we stopped at a rest area. How the parking lot was laid out, the neon signs, all the amazing cars. I walked around as if I were drunk. Katje absolutely wanted to go to a McDonald's restaurant [located at the rest area]. She stormed in, and I stood outside just opening my eyes as wide as I could. I was shaking so. It was all so modern, white and made of glass, the windows were so amazing, the roof was constructed in a way that's only familiar to us through Western newspapers... I felt like a convict who'd just spent 25 years in prison.

A Level Exam-Style Question Section A

Study Source 9 before you answer this question.

Assess the value of Source 9 for revealing the attitudes of East Germans to the fall of the Berlin Wall in 1989.

Explain your answer, using the source, the information given about its origin and your own knowledge about the historical context. (20 marks)

Tip

This question requires you to use this individual letter to assess the attitudes of East Germans as a whole to the fall of the Berlin Wall in 1989. Therefore, you will need to use your own knowledge of the historical context to judge to what extent this source is representative of the overall attitude of East Germans, and how it can help us to understand how the fall of the Berlin Wall affected the lives of the GDR's citizens.

The crumbling of the GDR state

You have already read about the mass exodus and deteriorating economic situation in the GDR at the start of 1990. In his maiden speech on taking leadership of the SED, Hans Modrow promised a new, more open era for the GDR, with economic and environmental problems being tackled directly and a new relationship with Western Europe. He asserted that the survival of the GDR was essential for the continuing stability of Europe as a whole. Despite his claims, the GDR appeared to be collapsing around him, as its citizens voted with their feet and left the country. West German goods and currency were flooding into East Germany, leading to further economic chaos. Modrow appeared to be unsure how to deal with the situation. He was prepared to make some concessions, but he still hoped that these would be sufficient to sustain the collapsing GDR. When he tried to replace the hated East German secret police (**Stasi**) with a watered-down security force, popular protests forced him to back down. It was indicative of Modrow's inability to understand that the GDR's citizens wanted a complete break from their oppressive system, not a weakened version of state control. This was shown further on 15 January 1990, when the Stasi headquarters in Berlin were overwhelmed by protestors. This was a dramatic event that saw East Germans rising up against the feared secret police service that had been a critical factor in the SED's maintenance of political power. With the Stasi itself no longer feared, the SED's own political survival was questionable.

Elections in East Germany, March 1990

In a desperate attempt to save the political system, Modrow announced elections for 18 March. West German politicians played a critical role in the campaign, openly supporting East German candidates who represented the same political party. The SPD leader, Oskar Lafontaine, encouraged East Germans to vote for the SPD in order to slow down the process leading to reunification, so that it could be approached in a more ordered and less chaotic manner. Helmut Kohl, on the other hand, in support of the CDU-led coalition known as the 'Alliance for Germany', asserted that East Germany's future lay in political and economic unification with West Germany. The result was a massive victory for the 'Alliance for Germany' coalition, winning 192 out of the 400 seats. The SED, now renamed the PDS, won only 66 seats, with the SPD winning 88. The Eastern CDU leader Lothar de Maizière formed a coalition government with the SPD and the League of Free Democrats. The success of de Maizière clearly showed the desire of East Germans to push ahead with rapid integration with West Germany. The survival of the GDR and the call to slow down the process of reunification had both been soundly rejected.

Setting a date for reunification

Working with the new government in the East, Kohl pushed forward with economic integration; within two weeks of de Maizière taking office, he and Kohl set 1 July as the date of the monetary, economic and social union of Germany. From 1 July, as the border evaporated, West German goods hastily replaced East German goods in the GDR. East Germans were offered a 1:1 currency exchange when changing their East German currency for FRG currency. The situation led to a complete meltdown in what still existed of the GDR economy. Unemployment and bankruptcy rose, and there was an even sharper decline in living standards. There was a considerable rush of GDR consumers for West German goods, and the market for GDR exports evaporated. From this point onwards, the drive for reunification was shaped by Kohl's negotiations with the Four Powers and paid little attention to the government in the GDR. The proposed date for reunification had to be brought forward, to avoid the complete collapse of the GDR before unification could take place. Economic disorder, the depletion of its population and the inability of SED to cope with a situation that had escaped its control, led to the crumbling of the GDR. On the stroke of midnight between 2 and 3 October 1990, the nation that had gained sovereignty from the Soviet Union in 1954 ceased to exist.

KEY TERM

Stasi
Founded in 1950, the Ministry for State Security (Stasi) was the GDR's secret security authority. It was one of the most effective and ruthless secret police agencies in history, running a massive surveillance operation that spied on GDR citizens and arrested and harassed suspected anti-government dissidents. Files were kept on millions of GDR citizens, and the Stasi ensured that any opposition to the SED was crushed. The Stasi's mass infiltration of the GDR caused fear and distrust within society. The storming of the Stasi building in January 1990 was therefore a key moment in the overthrow of the Communist government.

EXTEND YOUR KNOWLEDGE

The end of the East German mark and the adoption of the West German Deutsche Mark
One of the first issues arising in July 1990 concerning German economic reintegration was how to deal with the dual currencies of East and West Germany. It was agreed that the East German mark would be taken out of circulation and replaced with the West German Deutsche Mark. East Germans could convert up to 4,000 marks per person from their wages and basic savings at a rate of 1:1. For larger amounts, such as housing loans, the conversion was two East German marks to one Deutsche Mark. These were quite inflated exchange rates that were meant to help East German citizens and businesses to deal effectively with reunification. The real rate is judged to have been four East German marks for one Deutsche Mark. This amount was seen at the time as being too detrimental to the East German population. However, as wages were converted on a 1:1 basis, there was no incentive for profitable West German businesses to relocate to the East; nor were Eastern German goods cheaper than in the West, despite the fact that they were mostly of lesser quality. Thus, there have been many economists and historians who have argued that the process was flawed and accentuated the inability of East German businesses to compete with West German businesses, thus ensuring that the former GDR would remain poorer than the former areas of the FRG. The coins of East Germany were melted down, while the paper money was stored in a huge underground vault and eventually destroyed in 2002.

A Level Exam-Style Question Section B

How accurate is it to say that the GDR collapsed primarily due to economic factors? (20 marks)

Tip

This question is not about reunification, but focuses solely on the GDR's collapse. Weigh up the differing factors – political, social and economic – and consider which of these played the largest role in the GDR's collapse in 1990. Can you argue that economic factors played the major role, or was it something else?

 SOURCE 10 The left-of-centre West Berlin newspaper *Taz* reports on the GDR elections, the reaction of several politicians and what the results mean for the GDR and the FRG. From an article titled 'GDR Voters Hungry for All-You-Can-Eat Kohl-Slaw. Sensational Victory for the "Alliance"', 19 March 1990.

Federal Chancellor Helmut Kohl spoke of a 'joyous hour', because GDR citizens had voted against any form of extremism. He said that the result represented a clear rejection of the SED's successor party, the PDS, and that the people of the GDR had instead made it clear that they wanted to follow a path that led to a unified Germany together with the Federal Republic. At the same time, Kohl appealed to GDR citizens to 'stay home'. Together with the Federal Republic, they should help to 'build up this wonderful country'.

SPD chancellor candidate Oskar Lafontaine (SPD) predicted a rethinking process with regard to the promises made to the GDR. The CDU would 'depart from its designated course, just as it did with the issue of GDR resettlers'. The SPD would stay on its guard, he said, to ensure that election fraud did not continue to occur.

Following the initial predictions about the results of the first free elections in the GDR, Minister President Hans Modrow believed that his party, the PDS, would find itself in a 'position where it's possible to achieve something'. In his initial response, party leader Gregor Gysi said that the results show that the former SED has made 'considerable progress in the renewal process.' In future, he said, the party aims to practise 'modern, left-wing, and above all socialist politics against monopolies and autocracy'.

The revolutionaries of November 9 expressed bitter disappointment at the election results. Wolfgang Ullmann of 'Democracy Now' feared that 'a hurricane of national sentiment' is drawing in. Writer Stefan Heym was of the opinion that 'nothing will remain [of the GDR] but a footnote in world history' after the election results. Heym went on to say: 'The snake is swallowing the hedgehog; the snake will have digestive problems.' The elections, he claimed, were preceded by a revolution brought about by two groups. Whereas the first group took a significant risk in standing up for a better GDR, the second wanted to abolish it completely and ultimately prevailed... The results were seen as a 'victory for the Deutsche Mark' and a 'victory for Kohl' in East and West alike. According to reports, a swift unification of Germany is now to be expected.

ACTIVITY
KNOWLEDGE CHECK

1 With reference to Source 10, summarise the most important consequences of the GDR's elections in March 1990, according to the newspaper report. Would you agree with this assessment?

2 According to the newspaper article in Source 10, the revolutionary democratic groups, such as 'Democracy Now', were disappointed by the election results. Would you agree?

The process and problems of reunification and reasons for its acceptance by the Four Powers

Negotiating for reunification with the Four Powers

While the Ten Point Plan had been greeted enthusiastically within Germany, and the GDR elections in March 1990 demonstrated a willingness to push for reunification, the more critical aspect for Kohl related to his negotiations with the Four Powers that technically still occupied Berlin. There could be no German reunification without the support of France, the United Kingdom, the United States and the USSR. As you have already read, previous to the Ten Point Plan, Helmut Kohl had pushed forward a policy that proposed West Germany as a stable, prosperous and productive member of an integrated Western Europe that was not actively challenging the balance of power. His Ten Point Plan was therefore a shock for the Four Powers, who were not as enthusiastic for German reunification. Problematically for Kohl, the United States would not accept a unified Germany that was outside of NATO. However, he also needed the agreement of the Soviet Union for reunification, and he was sceptical whether they would accept a unified Germany that was also a NATO member.

The fact that Kohl had not consulted with France or the United Kingdom before announcing his Ten Point Plan also caused considerable anger. The French and leadership saw German reunification as a challenge to the European status quo, a dominant economic power that would seek to control Europe. The Prime Minister of the United Kingdom, Margaret Thatcher, was firmly against German reunification. France and the United Kingdom were also worried that Kohl's Ten Point Plan made no reference to Germany's eastern border, and were angered further when, at a meeting in December 1989, Kohl refused to make a commitment on the existing borders. Margaret Thatcher and the President of France, François Mitterrand, were also of the belief that it was still possible to save the GDR from economic collapse with Western assistance. Additionally, the spectre of a unified Germany haunted European thoughts, given the events of the 20th century. Leaders of countries affected by German occupation during the Second World War, such as the Netherlands, Poland and Italy, spoke out against German reunification, with the French President also asserting that Europe was not ready for the reunification of Germany.

SOURCE

11

Malcolm Booker, in an article for the *Canberra Times* titled 'Who will pull the handbrake on unification?', published 12 June 1990, discusses the problems facing the process of German reunification and the possible opposition of Gorbachev and the British Prime Minister Margaret Thatcher. Malcolm Booker was an Australian diplomat working in Eastern Europe. In 1990, he was writing as an expert on foreign affairs for the *Canberra Times*.

The drive for German unification looks more and more like a bus careering down a dark road with its lights out. Neither the driver nor its passengers are prepared to stop to see where it is going or what obstacles lie in its path. Helmut Kohl, the driver, sees early unification as ensuring his success in the next West German elections and his accession thereafter as Chancellor of a united Germany. Speed is essential if he is to realise his ambition. The elections are due next December or at the latest early January and his objective is to bring about unification in time for East Germany to participate. The passengers – France, Britain and the United States – would like to seize the wheel but dare not. They have deep misgivings about the re-emergence of a powerful re-united Germany but after decades of proclaiming support for re-unification they cannot now oppose it. Their main hope is to secure arrangements that would closely bind the new Germany to the western alliance... The attitude of the Soviet Union may offer one opportunity for applying the brakes. The Western leaders, including Mr Kohl, insist that East Germany should be embraced in NATO, but the Soviet President Mikhail Gorbachev refuses to agree. During the Bush–Gorbachev summit meeting in Washington an attempt was made to win his acquiescence by offering a 'nine point blueprint' of reassurances, but he remained unconvinced. The blueprint was endorsed at a meeting of NATO Foreign Ministers last week, and was again presented to Mr Gorbachev by the British Prime Minister, Margaret Thatcher, when she visited Moscow. Again he was not convinced... She nevertheless added, in terms more emphatic than used by other Western leaders, that a way must be found to satisfy Soviet concerns at having on its borders as a member of NATO a re-united Germany. She acknowledged that this prospect had revived memories of the devastation caused by the German armies during World War II, and said that no country was more entitled to reassurance about the future of Germany than the Soviet Union... Is she [Thatcher] getting ready to reach for the brake? Does she realise that implicit in Mr Gorbachev's attitude is the threat that the Soviet Union, which is one of the four Occupying Powers who still officially hold authority over Germany, might use his veto over any plan for re-unification? Would she mind if it did so?

ACTIVITY
KNOWLEDGE CHECK

1 According to Source 11, what were the biggest dangers facing German reunification in June 1990?

2 How would you summarise Margaret Thatcher's attitude to reunification, as set out by the writer of Source 11?

On 11 December 1989, the Four Powers met for the first time since the 1940s in the headquarters of the Allied Control Council. The West German leadership interpreted this as a sign that the Four Powers believed they could discuss the future of Germany without consulting with Kohl's government, leading to rising tension between West Germany and the Four Powers. In December 1989, the President of the United States, George H.W. Bush, made the critical assertion that the USA would only accept a unified Germany that was a member of NATO. This made reunification seem impossible; many believed it was inconceivable that the USSR would agree to a unified Germany as a member of NATO.

At this stage, Gorbachev believed that a reformed SED might even be able to save the GDR as an independent state, and he angrily rebuked the West German government for the Ten Point Plan. However, Kohl agreed to Bush's demands, fearing that a unified Germany outside of NATO would lead to its collapse and a Europe dominated by the United Kingdom and France.

As discussed previously, Kohl's strongest negotiating tool was the collapse of the GDR. It was becoming increasingly evident that, despite the hopes of the UK, France and the USSR, the GDR's whole political, economic and social system was rapidly crumbling. Kohl used this to predict chaos for Europe and beyond if a solution was not found to take control of the situation. By early 1990, the United States was becoming more supportive of reunification, believing that if it did not support Kohl, then West Germany might leave NATO. The SPD's leader, Oskar Lafontaine, had been critical of NATO, and the failure of Kohl's political programme might see Lafontaine elected. While Thatcher and Mitterrand still did not support a reunified Germany, they were aware that the collapse of the GDR was making reunification increasingly inevitable. For Gorbachev, it was clear that only a massive loan could prop up the GDR, and he was unwilling and economically unable to pursue this direction given the USSR's own economic problems. In mid-February, Gorbachev informed Helmut Kohl, during his visit to Moscow, that the Soviets now accepted that the question of reunification would have to be decided by the Germans themselves. It was a critical breakthrough. It was subsequently agreed that negotiations would take place between the Four Powers and the FRG and GDR. These were known as the Two plus Four negotiations.

The Two plus Four negotiations

Intense negotiations took place from March 1990, with the key question concerning Germany's proposed membership of NATO and the size of its military. The negotiations became bogged down, and there was a distinct feeling among German politicians that the USSR was aiming to slow down the process of reunification by dragging out the Two plus Four discussions. However, the elections in East Germany put renewed pressure on the USSR. The success of the 'Alliance for Germany' meant that the GDR's parliament was now in favour of reunification. By the terms of Article 23 of the FRG's constitution, the unification of Germany could take place if the GDR accepted unification under the laws and institutions of the FRG. Now that the 'Alliance for Germany' was in power, they requested membership of the FRG under Article 23. This, combined with economic unification in July, meant the USSR could no longer delay the process. Crucially, the USSR economy was in its own crisis and required foreign loans. When Gorbachev's request for financial help was rejected by the United States and the UK, he turned to West Germany. In May, Gorbachev informed US President George Bush that he would accept a unified Germany as a member of NATO. Further negotiations concerning the withdrawal of Soviet troops from East Germany, the eastern border of a new Germany and the size of the German army were concluded between Gorbachev and Kohl. With the agreements in place and the loan to the USSR agreed, German reunification was almost a reality. A final disagreement between the United Kingdom and the USSR concerning Western military activities in a unified Germany was overcome, and on the night of 12 September 1990, the foreign ministers of the Four Powers, the FRG Foreign Minister Hans-Dietrich Genscher, and the GDR's President de Maizière signed the 'Treaty on the Final Settlement with Respect to Germany'. The reunification of Germany, despite numerous difficulties, had been achieved with a speed that nobody had envisioned at the start of 1989.

A Level Exam-Style Question Section B

'It was Gorbachev's acceptance of German unification that made reunification between the GDR and the FRG inevitable in 1990.' How far do you agree with this statement? (20 marks)

Tip

This question is asking you to weigh up the key role of Gorbachev in respect to other factors that led to reunification in 1990. The key word is 'inevitable'. Other factors may have contributed, but was Gorbachev's final acceptance of a unified Germany in NATO the factor that made reunification inevitable, or was Gorbachev himself simply accepting the reality of a situation he could no longer stop?

EXTRACT

From Mark Allinson, 'The failed experiment: East German communism' in M. Fulbrook (ed.) *German History since 1800* (1997).

It is tempting to assume that the GDR was doomed to failure almost from the outset as a state founded and maintained against the will of its subjects. Certainly the GDR can be regarded as a dictatorship: the SED leadership and its many loyal and disciplined agents exerted fierce control over the rest of the population's lives, from frustrating careers to shooting would-be escapees at the border. However, historians who regard the June 1953 revolt as the root of eventual collapse neglect the fact that it was after 1953, not 1961, that the GDR properly stabilised, at least in terms of individuals' outward conformity, if not of their inner commitment. The later economic collapse resulted from external pressures as well as the SED's economic mismanagement, which sacrificed much to ideological demands and the USSR's interests, even when these clashed with the GDR's. Meanwhile, social and political stability essentially remained until Gorbachev's accession in the USSR, his policies wilfully refuted, despite popular aspirations to a freer society, by Honecker, who correctly perceived in them the seeds of the system's destruction. Ultimately it was this external impetus which disrupted and ended SED rule in 1989, just as it had established it 43 years earlier.

EXTRACT

2 From A. James McAdams, *Germany Divided: From the Wall to Reunification* (1993).

In spring 1988, for example, the Union leadership had come very close to endorsing in its annual platform language that would have played down the goal of German reunification in party policy in favour of broader **détente** initiatives in Europe. Over the following months, prominent CDU moderates, such as Horst Teltschik, went so far as to distance themselves from strictly 'territorial' solutions to the German question. And, in line with the party's desire to accent other issues and broaden its appeal to middle-of-the-road voters, even Helmut Kohl was known to soften his rhetoric. While frequently addressing the long-term goal of national 'unity in freedom' the chancellor almost studiously avoided the provocative term 'reunification' in his major speeches. Had any of these tendencies been formally adopted as Union policy, they could have had a major impact on the GDR's fall. Quite possibly, the confidence of those East German protestors who first called for German unity in November 1989 would have been dampened by the uncertainty of Bonn's commitment to reunification. It is more plausible that such a redefinition of the CDU's objectives would have had a decidedly negative impact on the party's electoral chances in 1990. The closer the Christian Democrats had come to endorsing the policy innovations of their rivals in the SPD, the harder it would have been for East German voters to distinguish among the competing parties in the FRG... For reasons that had much more to do with the party's changing electoral calculations and its need to appease its right-wing critics than with any unusual degree of political foresight, this shift was never formalised. Thanks to a continuing rhetorical commitment to the grand old goals of German national policy, the Union leadership, and Kohl in particular, were able to say that they had never wavered in their commitment to national unity. Thus, both party and chancellor were ideally positioned, first in the Volkskammer election of March 1990 and then in the national elections in December 1990, to capitalise upon the years of resentment and bitterness that had built up in eastern Germany.

EXTRACT

3 From Martin Kitchen, *A History of Modern Germany: 1800 to the Present* (2012).

The more familiar East Germans became with life in the West, the less enthusiastic they were about the idea of a reformed GDR. The slogan 'We are the People!' soon changed into 'We are One People!' All now depended upon Moscow's attitude. The Russians had refused to send in the tanks when the Berlin Wall was breached, and the 500,000 Red Army men in the GDR had remained in their barracks. Officially the Kremlin refused to accept any discussion of a change in the status quo, but unofficial talks began about a possible confederation between two sovereign states. Chancellor Kohl took this up, proposing a 'Ten Point Program' whereby after five to ten years of confederation the two states should reunite. The USA favoured Kohl's plan, but the Soviet Union, France and Britain were opposed. Opposition groups in the GDR argued that they should first set their own house in order along democratic socialist lines. They were supported by left-wingers in West Germany, while some argued that Germany should atone for its vast crimes by remaining divided. The ecstatic welcome accorded Helmut Kohl when he visited Dresden in December 1989 had indicated that the opponents of reunification in Germany formed a small minority. The mass flight to the West substantially worsened the economic crisis in the East to the point that by January 1990 the Soviets realised that there was no viable alternative to reunification.

KEY TERM

Détente
The easing of hostile or difficult relationships, particularly between countries.

THINKING HISTORICALLY   Change (8a, b & c) (II)

Judgements about change

Judgements about change depend on historians' assumptions, judgements and methodologies. If two professionals were asked to track a patient's health over time, one might approach this task by measuring heart rate, weight and cholesterol, while the other professional assessed the patient's mental well-being, relationships and ability to achieve their goals. Both are valid approaches, but result in different reports. What is true in this medical case is true in historical cases. Measuring change in something requires:

- a concept of what that something is (e.g. What is 'health'? What is an 'economy'?)

- judgements about how this thing should be measured

- judgements about what relevant 'markers of change' are (e.g. how we distinguish a change from a temporary and insignificant fluctuation).

Historians have differed in their accounts of why the GDR collapsed and Germany reunified in 1990.

Study Extracts 1, 2 and 3 about the collapse of the GDR and the unification of Germany, and then answer the following questions.

1 Do all three accounts agree on the main factors causing change in Germany in 1990?

2 Do all three accounts agree on the chronology of change concerning, for example, how events developed leading to reunification?

3 Do all three accounts agree in characterising change as (a) rapid, (b) dramatic and (c) impacting on both the GDR and the FRG?

4 Do the historians all think of the unification in the same way?

5 Generalising from these examples, to what extent do historians' judgements about change depend on what historians decide to look at and how they decide to measure change?

ACTIVITY
SUMMARY

1 Look over the key events leading to German reunification and organise them under these three factors:

   a) Problems with the GDR

   b) Political policies of Helmut Kohl

   c) Political decisions by the Four Powers.

   Once you have done this, decide: of these three factors, which would you consider the most important in German reunification, and why?

2 Which leader would you regard as the most important with regard to German reunification, Honecker, Gorbachev or Kohl? Why?

3 The arguments of historians are influenced by the way in which they view the underlying causes of change. Write a one-page argument on the reasons for German reunification that is based primarily on economic factors. Now write another one-page summary that is based primarily on social or political factors. How have your examples changed? What is the main difference in your explanations? How does this help to explain the differences between historical arguments writing about the same event?

WIDER READING

Haftendorn, H. 'The unification of Germany, 1985–1991', in Leffler, M.P. and Westad, O.A. (eds) *The Cambridge History of the Cold War Volume III: Endings*, Cambridge University Press (2010), pp. 333-55

Harrison, H.M. 'The Berlin Wall: looking back on the history of the Wall twenty years after its fall', in Kramer, M. and Smetana, V. (eds) *Imposing, Maintaining and Tearing Open the Iron Curtain: The Cold War and East-Central Europe, 1945–1989*, Lexington Books (2014), pp. 173–96

Osmond, J. 'The end of the GDR: revolution and voluntary annexation', in Fulbrook, M. (ed.) *Twentieth-Century Germany: Politics, Culture and Society 1918–1990*, Bloomsbury (2001), Chapter 12 – Aspects in depth 5

Roseman, M. 'Division and stability: the Federal Republic of Germany 1949–1989', in Fulbrook, M. (ed.) *Twentieth-Century Germany: Politics, Culture and Society 1918–1990*, Bloomsbury (2001), Chapter 8 – Aspects in depth 4

Smith, K. *Berlin: Coming in from the Cold*, Penguin Books (1990)

Preparing for your A Level Paper 3 exam

Advance planning

Draw up a timetable for your revision and try to keep to it. Spend longer on topics which you have found difficult, and revise them several times. Aim to be confident about all aspects of your Paper 3 work, because this will ensure that you have a choice of questions in Sections B and C.

Paper 3 overview

Paper 3	Time: 2 hours 15 minutes	
Section A	Answer 1 compulsory question for the option studied, assessing source analysis and evaluation skills.	20 marks
Section B	Answer 1 question from a choice of 2 on an aspect in depth for the option studied.	20 marks
Section C	Answer 1 question from a choice of 2 on an aspect in breadth for the option studied.	20 marks
	Total marks =	60 marks

Section A questions

There is no choice of question in Section A. You will be referred to a source of about 350 words long, printed in a Sources Booklet. The source will be a primary source or one that is contemporary to the period you have studied, and will relate to one of the key topics in the Aspect of Depth. You will be expected to analyse and evaluate the source in its historical context. The question will ask you to assess the value of the source for revealing something specific about the period, and will expect you to explain your answer, using the source, the information given about its origin and your own knowledge about the historical context.

Section B questions

You will have a choice of one from two questions in Section B. They will aim to assess your understanding of one or more of the key topics in the Aspect of Depth you have studied. Questions may relate to a single, momentous year, but will normally cover longer periods. You will be required to write an essay evaluating an aspect of the period. You may be asked about change and continuity, similarity and difference, consequences, significance or causation, or you may be given a quotation and asked to explain how far you agree with it. All questions will require you to reach a substantiated judgement.

Section C questions

You will have a choice of one from two questions in Section C. Questions will relate to the themes of the Aspects of Breadth you have studied, and will aim to assess your understanding of change over time. They will cover a period of not less than 100 years and will relate either to the factors that brought about change, or the extent of change over the period, or patterns of change as demonstrated by turning points.

Use of time

- Do not write solidly for 45 minutes on each question. For Section B and C answers you should spend a few minutes working out what the question is asking you to do, and drawing up a plan of your answer. This is especially important for Section C answers, which cover an extended period of time.
- For Section A it is essential that you have a clear understanding of the content of the source and its historical context. Pay particular attention to the provenance: was the author in a position to know what he or she was writing about? Read it carefully and underline important points. You might decide to spend up to ten minutes reading the source and drawing up your plan, and 35 minutes writing your answer.

Preparing for your A Level exams

Paper 3: A Level sample answer with comments

Section A

These questions require you to analyse and evaluate source material with respect to its historical context. For these questions, remember to:

- look at the evidence given in the source and consider how the source could be used in differing ways to provide historical understanding
- use your knowledge of the historical context to discuss any limitations the source may have
- use your historical understanding to evaluate the source, considering how much weight you would give to its argument
- come to a judgement on the overall value of the source in respect to the question.

Study Source 9 in Chapter 4 (page 101) before you answer this question.

Assess the value of the source for revealing the splits between left-wing German politicians and the difficulties facing the new German political system in 1918.

Explain your answer, using the source, the information given about its origins and your own knowledge about the historical context. (20 marks)

Average student answer

Following the First World War, Germany faced lots of problems. One of the key problems was what new political system was going to take the place of the previous Kaiser. Some German political leaders wanted a democratic, socialist system to take over that was not a massive change from the previous system. However, other leaders, like Karl Liebknecht, wanted a more extreme left-wing system, like Communism. There were therefore considerable arguments within German politics. The source clearly shows this.

In the source, Liebknecht is arguing with other members of the SPD and USPD parties about the type of government Germany should have. Liebknecht is arguing that the German system should include the soldiers' councils and needs to be defended. He says that the German revolution is threatened by 'big landowners, Junkers, capitalists, imperialists', but also by those within the SPD itself. Most controversially he accuses the SPD leader Chancellor Ebert of slandering the revolution. This clearly shows the splits within the SPD. At the end of 1918 there were lots of different ideas about what type of government Germany should have. The SPD took over in October, but the leader Ebert did not want to change very much from the previous reforms of Prince Max. Instead, he was very worried about the growing revolution in Germany and what might happen if it got out of control. He had seen what had happened in Russia. Therefore, he wanted to restrict the revolution, not encourage it. To achieve this he did a deal with the army. The soldiers' councils were organisations that were voted on by workers and soldiers and represented the views of these groups. They wanted to influence German politics. They were a challenge to the more conservative political system that was represented in the German parliament. Ebert feared that the soldiers' and workers' councils were a threat to German order and feared that they were creating a Communist revolution. Others, like Liebknecht, thought instead that the councils were a truly democratic system that represented the true beliefs of the German people. They were a big change from the previous system and therefore had to lead the revolution.

This is a fairly weak opening paragraph. It is too descriptive and only briefly mentions the source. It needs to set out a firmer argument on the source's value in relation to the question. It could be improved by using historical knowledge to briefly summarise the way in which the source is valuable and some of the potential problems with it.

This paragraph shows quite good own knowledge. It is clear that the student understands the historical context of the source, who Karl Liebknecht was and what his argument against Ebert and his supporters was based on. However, the answer would be helped by linking this to the source and using the historical context to answer the question. The paragraph is too descriptive. The historical context and source analysis should not be separate, but should be used together to evaluate the source in relation to what the question is asking.

The source is therefore very good in showing the splits within the SPD. Liebknecht argues against the leadership of the SPD and says that the councils are a good thing. While he speaks, other politicians yell out against him and call for unity in the party. He accuses Ebert of being an enemy to the revolution. It is a very controversial speech. The source is also good in showing the difficulties facing the German political system. Some politicians, like Liebknecht, obviously wanted a big revolution to change the German system. Others, like Ebert, feared revolution and the councils and wanted more ordered and conservative change. The arguments going on in this meeting show there were lots of arguments within the parties that would rule Germany after 1918. This is helpful in understanding why Germany would face so many problems after 1918. Liebknecht would eventually lead a Communist revolution to try to change the German political system and would instead be captured and executed on Ebert's orders. The source therefore helps us to understand the reasons for this split.

There is some good analysis here of the ways in which the source has value in reference to the question. There is some link to historical knowledge and how the source helps us to understand what problems the German system faced from 1918 onwards. However, it is a bit disjointed. The essay would be improved by a clearer explanation of exactly how the source helps us to understand the splits within the SPD and the problems facing German politics. The last sentence on the source's utility needed to be better supported by the student's historical knowledge.

The source is good at helping us to understand this point in German history. It is not so good in relation to understanding the exact problems with Ebert's leadership, as Liebknecht was much more radical than Ebert and did not like him. Therefore he would be against Ebert and his argument is biased. Therefore the source is good in showing the splits in German politics and the problems facing it, but is not so good in understanding who was responsible for these problems.

There is some attempt to show the weaknesses in the source, but it is not explained in enough detail. Additionally, the use of the word 'bias' is unsophisticated and lacks evidence to back up this assertion. The final conclusion does have a clear judgement, but it requires further development and a proper explanation relating back to the argument established throughout the essay.

Verdict

This is an average answer because:

- it demonstrates some understanding of the source material and the question but is not fully developed
- it shows understanding of the historical context but fails to fully use this to expand, confirm or challenge the source

- it ends with judgement but has limited justification to support its argument.

Use the feedback on this essay to rewrite it, making as many improvements as you can.

Paper 3: A Level sample answer with comments

Section A

These questions require you to analyse and evaluate source material with respect to its historical context. For these questions, remember to:

- look at the evidence given in the source and consider how the source could be used in differing ways to provide historical understanding
- use your knowledge of the historical context to discuss any limitations the source may have
- use your historical understanding to evaluate the source, considering how much weight you would give to its argument
- come to a judgement on the overall value of the source in respect to the question.

Study Source 9 in Chapter 4 (page 101) before you answer this question.

Assess the value of the source for revealing the splits between left-wing German politicians and the difficulties facing the new German political system in 1918.

Explain your answer, using the source, the information given about its origins and your own knowledge about the historical context. (20 marks)

Strong student answer

The source comes from a speech by the left-wing politician Karl Liebknecht, in which he accuses the leadership of the SPD of betraying the German revolution of 1918. The source is very valuable in demonstrating both the splits within the German left wing and the problems facing the new German political system in 1918. However, given Liebknecht's strong left-wing politics, it is not so useful in helping historians to evaluate the choices made by Friedrich Ebert, the SPD's leader, in 1918.

> This is a very strong introduction that directly relates to the question. It clearly sets out the answer to the question concerning the value of the source, but also points out potential weaknesses.

The source is very valuable in helping to understand critical differences between left-wing politicians during the 1918 revolution. Liebknecht accuses Ebert of threatening the revolution by opposing the councils. This is a very accurate depiction of Ebert's politics. Following the collapse of the Kaiserreich system, there were two main choices facing the left-wing political groups that now ruled the country. For the majority SPD and its leader Ebert, there was a clear belief in a stable, democratic system that was ruled by the elected Reichstag and directed by government. Other politicians, like Liebknecht, believed that instead the soldiers' and workers' councils that were forming in Germany at the time should be the basis of the new political system. These were grass-roots political organisations voted on by workers and soldiers and meant to represent their political views. Ebert and the SPD instead feared that the councils could take over from parliament and bring about a Communist revolution like in Russia. Ebert therefore opposed this form of government and moved against the councils. These arguments within the German left-wing political parties concerning the role of the workers' and soldiers' councils are clearly demonstrated by the source. The source is also a very accurate depiction of Liebknecht's strong backing for the councils and Ebert and the SPD's concerns and opposition. It is therefore a very strong source in revealing the clear splits between German left-wing politicians in 1918 on the future of the German political system.

> This is a very strong paragraph. The student uses the evidence in the source and links it to their historical knowledge to clearly show the way in which the source is valuable. The answer is clear and directly linked to the question. The historical knowledge used is not descriptive, but is used to explain how the source material can be utilised by historians.

The source is also very strong in showing the problems facing the new political system. As shown in Liebknecht's speech, there is a lot of argument between the different left-wing groups. Following the revolution, the left-wing parties of the SPD and the USPD formed a coalition, but this coalition fell apart over the question of Ebert's treatment of the councils. Liebknecht's speech shows quite clearly the importance of this issue. Liebknecht also argues that some of the old order within the Kaiserreich, such as high officers in the army, are taking up positions of power in the councils and therefore weakening the revolution. He says that the 'revolution's enemies are insidiously using the soldiers' organisations to their own ends'. This was definitely an issue for the new German political system. Ebert believed that the new SPD government had to work with the old order to bring about a stable political basis for the new Germany. Others, such as Liebknecht, instead asserted that this would only allow the old order to retain its power and challenge the new democracy. The source therefore has considerable weight in showing the divisions and problems facing the new political system. Eventually Ebert would violently move against the councils and shut them down, and Liebknecht was murdered when he attempted to create a Communist revolution in Germany.

However, the source has less weight in regard to whether what Liebknecht is arguing is accurate. Liebknecht was a strong left-wing politician who believed in Communism and wanted a Russian-type revolution in Germany. His accusations against Ebert, who he hated, and his belief that the councils were being weakened, are therefore very subjective. Ebert had seen what had happened in Russia and wanted a stable German system, not a violent revolution. Some of his choices are therefore understandable in this context. Liebknecht's claims about why Germany faces political problems therefore lack weight due to his political beliefs.

Overall the source is very valuable for revealing the splits between left-wing German politicians and the difficulties facing the new German political system in 1918. Liebknecht's speech and the reaction of other politicians to it helps us to understand what the issues were facing Germany's politicians in 1918 and why the left wing could not come to an agreement on how to create a new political system after the fall of the Kaiser.

> This paragraph clearly answers the second part of the question, using historical knowledge to explain how the source is valuable in understanding the political problems facing Germany. It is clear that the student has excellent historical knowledge and how this relates to the source's context and argument. The student then directly discusses the limitations of the source in respect to the historical context. This displays secure understanding of the source's strengths as well as its weaknesses.

> A short but strong conclusion that clearly summarises the student's overall argument in a way that is directly linked to the question.

Verdict

This is a strong answer because:

- it uses the evidence in the source with confidence, showing the differing ways in which the source is valuable through reasoned and supported argument
- it shows excellent historical knowledge and understanding, and uses this to discuss the strengths and weaknesses of the source in a sophisticated but clear manner
- it has a very strong judgement on the weight and value of the source that is clearly justified through valid points backed up by historical evidence.

Paper 3: A Level sample answer with comments

Section B

These questions require you to show your understanding of a period in depth. They will ask you about a quite specific period of time and require you to make a substantiated judgement about a specific aspect you have studied. For these questions, remember to:

- organise your essay and communicate it in a manner that is clear and comprehensible
- use historical knowledge to analyse and evaluate the key aspect of the question
- make a balanced argument that weighs up differing opinions
- make a substantiated overall judgement on the question.

'The reunification of Germany in 1990 was primarily due to the leadership of Helmut Kohl.' How far do you agree with this statement? (20 marks)

Average student answer

Helmut Kohl was Chancellor of West Germany when German unification took place with East Germany. He was very important and played a big role. There were many reasons why Germany unified, but Helmut Kohl was the most important.

Helmut Kohl became leader in 1982. He mostly tried to have a good relationship with East Germany and did not always think that unification would be possible. However, by 1989, East Germany was collapsing and its economy was in ruins. Thousands of East Germans were leaving the country and some East Germans were calling for unification. Kohl realised he had to do something to deal with that situation. He first offered economic aid to the East Germans, hoping that East Germany could continue to exist. Instead people just kept on leaving. Now Kohl announced the Ten Point Plan. This pointed the way forwards to unification. It was crucial as up to this point not many West German politicians were open about unification. Now Kohl had announced that unification was his policy and that he was prepared to make it happen. It was really important because it made unification a key policy and it was clear that this was now a possibility. There was a great willingness from both East and West Germans for unification. Kohl also used the collapse of East Germany to put pressure on Britain, the USSR, the United States and France to accept unification. This was very important during their talks. Overall, Kohl's leadership was really important in setting the direction for unification, and without him it would probably not have happened.

Other factors did play a role. A really important one was Gorbachev, who was leader of the USSR. Gorbachev became leader of the USSR in 1985. His country faced a lot of problems and he had to find a solution to their poor situation. He therefore decided that he could not use the USSR to help out countries like the GDR. He also introduced new open policies that had more freedom of speech for the people in the USSR. This meant other people in countries like the GDR wanted more openness too. The leader of the GDR, Honecker, did not want to make political changes for his country. However, Honecker was more and more unpopular and as the people wanted change and were inspired by Gorbachev this was a problem. Without the USSR it was difficult for East Germany to survive. When Gorbachev visited East Germany in 1989 he told the East German leader he would no longer support

This is a very short introduction. It does give an answer to the question that is clear, but it would be better if it briefly set out the other reasons for German unification that the essay will be examining.

The paragraph does set out an argument. However, the beginning of the paragraph needs to be less descriptive and establish its key point in the first line. It also lacks clear evidence to back up its argument. The paragraph establishes the importance of the Ten Point Plan, but it does not clearly set out why the plan was so crucial to reunification. The argument is very generalised and needs to be more specific on exactly why Kohl's leadership was so important to reunification.

Again, this paragraph has an argument that clearly relates to the question. However, it is over-generalised and lacks clear evaluation. Most importantly, it is never established exactly why Gorbachev's leadership is not as important as Kohl's leadership. The paragraph simply sets out Gorbachev's role but does not evaluate it directly in line with the actual question.

his government. This meant the system in East Germany started to collapse. This put lots of political and economic pressure on East Germany that it could not survive. Therefore, Gorbachev's leadership and his different ideas about Communism played a big part in German reunification.

Another important factor was how bad East Germany was. By 1989, it had big debts and lots of economic problems. Compared to West Germany it was very poor. As East Germans could watch West German TV they could see how bad East Germany was. Lots of people wanted to leave. When other countries in Eastern Europe like Hungary said they would change their border with Austria, thousands of East Germans went to Hungary hoping they could get out of East Germany. Soon millions of East Germans were trying to leave, as they hated the government and the system in their country. As the problem got worse the East German government tried to make changes, but it was too late. Huge protests were taking place and the East German people wanted to leave their country and some started to call for reunification with the West. When the Berlin Wall collapsed in November 1989, nobody wanted to stay in East Germany now. It was clear to everybody like Kohl and the United States and Britain that East Germany could not survive without money or people, so reunification became the only possibility. Therefore, the GDR's problems and the fact nobody wanted to live there anymore were also reasons for unification.

> This paragraph has the same problem. The argument is set out but it is generalised and not clearly linked to the question. It is clear that the GDR's problems contributed to reunification, but it is not clear why this is less important than Kohl's leadership. The student sets out an argument in the introduction, but it is not adequately supported by the arguments made in this paragraph.

It is clear that there were lots of reasons for unification. Helmut Kohl was very important with his policy on reunification called the Ten Point Plan. Gorbachev was also really important as he changed Communism and this made it difficult for the GDR. The problems in the GDR were also really important. They meant people wanted to leave the country. Overall, though, the most important factor for German reunification was Helmut Kohl's leadership.

> The conclusion fails to set out a direct, substantiated judgement on the question. It does agree with the question in a clear fashion but it is never clear exactly why. The student needs to summarise their argument in more depth and explain exactly what the reasons are for their judgement.

Verdict

This is an average answer because:

- it does analyse relevant key issues, but fails to give a sustained analysis of the relationship between these factors in relation to the question
- it demonstrates some good knowledge but lacks depth in some areas
- it attempts to make a judgement on the question, but the substantiation for this judgement is weak
- it shows clear organisation, but parts of it lack precise argument and judgement on the question.

Use the feedback on this essay to rewrite it, making as many improvements as you can.

Paper 3: A Level sample answer with comments

Section B

These questions require you to show your understanding of a period in depth. They will ask you about a quite specific period of time and will ask you to make a substantiated judgement about a specific aspect you have studied. For these questions, remember to:

- organise your essay and communicate it in a manner that is clear and comprehensible
- use historical knowledge to analyse and evaluate the key aspect of the question
- make a balanced argument that weighs up differing opinions
- make a substantiated overall judgement on the question.

'The reunification of Germany in 1990 was primarily due to the leadership of Helmut Kohl.' How far do you agree with this statement? (20 marks)

Strong student answer

German unification in 1990 was due to a range of interrelated factors. While it is true that Helmut Kohl played a crucial role in German unification, it is more difficult to argue that reunification was primarily due to his leadership. Instead, Helmut Kohl was reacting to events taking place that contributed to German reunification in a more important way. These aspects related both to the growing economic and social problems of East Germany and the leadership reforms of the USSR's leader Mikhail Gorbachev. While Helmut Kohl's role was important, it was not of primary importance to Germany's reunification.

> This is a good introduction that sets out a very clear argument to the question and gives a brief but well-defined justification for the student's answer.

The most important factor in Germany's reunification was the economic and social collapse of East Germany. By 1989, East Germany faced a range of economic problems. Its industrial base was outdated and it could not afford to invest to modernise its industry. Problematically, it was also in considerable debt due to its massive welfare system. The difference in the standard of living between East and West Germany was growing considerably. By 1989, 2,000 East Germans were leaving the country every day, weakening the workforce further. In total, 200,000 East Germans left the country to try to get to Austria via Hungary, hoping to then go on to West Germany. Mass protests broke out in East Germany, calling for political reform. When the East German government gave in to the pressure and opened the border with West Germany, the mass rush of East Germans for the West meant East Germany faced near collapse. The economic and social collapse of East Germany was the most important factor for reunification as it meant East Germany could no longer survive as an independent nation.

> This is an excellent paragraph. It starts with a very clear topic sentence that establishes the student's argument and then supports their answer with excellent historical knowledge. It also ranks the factor clearly, saying why this is the most important reason for German reunification.

Other factors did play a role. Critically, the role of the USSR's leader Mikhail Gorbachev put further pressure on the East German government and led to calls for political change. Gorbachev was a reforming Communist leader who implemented new policies of economic reform and freedom of speech in the USSR. This was a big change for the Communist country and led to calls in countries such as East Germany for more political rights. Gorbachev also informed the East German government that he would no longer use the USSR army to support them and would not help to crush any anti-government protests. Most importantly, he would not use the USSR to economically help the GDR. This enhanced the economic problems in East Germany. Gorbachev's new leadership encouraged East Germans to protest in larger numbers against the East German government. The economic and social problems were terrible and the people saw Gorbachev as an inspiration for change. The GDR's leader, Honecker, was removed from power by his own party, who believed that only political reform could save their system. Thus, Gorbachev's leadership played a large role in driving on the mass protests in East Germany that led to the collapse of the Communist system and the reunification of Germany.

> This paragraph sets out the student's argument clearly again, with well-supported evidence. Importantly, it links this factor with the factor considered in the previous paragraph and shows their relationship to each other. It then explains the importance of this factor in consideration of the question.

Helmut Kohl's leadership linked into Gorbachev's leadership and the collapse of East Germany. As the situation in East Germany deteriorated, Kohl realised he had to take charge of the situation. Before this, Kohl had hoped to keep stability by helping the East German government make economic reforms. However, by November 1989, Kohl believed that politically he needed to change direction. In his Ten Point Plan he set out his road map for the reunification of Germany. This was a big step, as he was the first German Chancellor for a long time to say that reunification was his goal. This set out a clear goal for reunification and pushed Germany towards this outcome. Thus Kohl's Ten Point Plan was very important for reunification. However, Kohl was reacting to events such as the East German economic collapse, not making them happen in the first place, so his leadership was therefore not as important as the other two factors.

Overall, Helmut Kohl definitely played an important role in reunification. His Ten Point Plan was very important in making reunification the political goal of West Germany and setting out a clear direction for Germany as a whole. However, more important were the events that led to the collapse of East Germany, its economic and social problems, and the decline of Soviet support for the GDR's government. This led to the fall of the GDR government and the migration of millions of its citizens. With this serious situation, Kohl chose to take control of the situation and define the way to reunification. He was therefore not the primary factor in reunification, as he was reacting to more important factors.

> This paragraph focuses on the key factor asked about in the question. It makes a clear argument as to why it was not the most important factor in reunification by showing its relationship to the other two factors focused on. This is a very sophisticated argument that links all the factors in a clear manner and uses this to support the student's answer.

> This is an excellent conclusion that gives a very clear judgement on the question. The links between the factors are explained, and a very clear and well-supported overall argument is set out. Importantly, the concluding judgement is the same as the argument being made by the student throughout the essay.

Verdict

This is a strong answer because:

- the key issues relevant to the question are explored through sustained analysis that also shows the links between the key factors examined
- it uses excellent historical knowledge to support the overall argument
- clear and relevant criteria are used to justify the overall judgement, and direct evaluation of the question is shown throughout the entire essay
- it is well organised, logical and coherent throughout.

Paper 3: A Level sample answer with comments

Section C

These questions require you to show your understanding of a subject over a considerable period of time. They will ask you to assess a long-term historical topic and its development over a period of at least 100 years, and they require you to make a substantiated judgement in relation to the question.

For these questions, remember to:

- organise your essay and communicate it in a manner that is clear and comprehensible
- use historical knowledge to analyse and evaluate the key aspect of the question covering the entire period
- make a balanced argument that weighs up differing opinions
- make a substantiated overall judgement on the question.

'Government economic policies had a mainly positive effect on the German economy in the period 1871–1990.' How far do you agree with this statement? (20 marks)

Average student answer

From 1871 to 1990, the German economy saw lots of developments. Some of this was because of government policies, although not all government policies were good. It can be argued that mostly government intervention had a positive effect on the German economy.

> The introduction sets out a clear argument, which is good, but fails to provide a clear, balanced analysis with some focus on evidence to back up the student's assertions.

One of the ways in which government policies were effective is during the Kaiserreich. In 1879, the government intervened in the economy to make imported goods more expensive through tariffs. This had a good effect on the economy as it made people want to buy German products, particularly in agricultural but also in heavy industry. Thus government intervention helped the German economy. Another way the government intervened in the economy was by pushing through policies to build a new navy. This again helped the economy by providing lots of jobs and work for German industry. Therefore it can be seen that government economic policies in the period from 1871 to 1914 had a good effect on the German economy.

> The structure and general ideas here are good. However, the argument lacks balance. It fails to provide a substantial assessment of tariff policy and provides an analysis that is too simplistic.

During the period from 1918 to 1931, however, government policies did not have an overall positive effect on the German economy. There were lots of problems that government policy made worse. For example, Germany had bad problems with inflation, but the government policy of printing more money instead of raising taxes made the situation really bad and there was hyperinflation in 1923. This meant money was pretty much worthless. There were agricultural problems, but the government policy of trying to introduce tariffs did not work and the crisis got much worse and many farmers went bankrupt. The worse problems came between 1929 and 1931 when the Great Depression happened. Germany was too reliant on American loans and when the American economy went badly so too did Germany's. The government was not sure what to do and its poor policies saw banks go bankrupt and millions of Germans become unemployed. This led to the collapse of the Weimar Republic. The Weimar Republic had some good policies, like introducing a new currency and getting loans from America, which meant the economy went well for a little while, but overall government policy did not help the economy.

> The Weimar period is assessed overall, but again the paragraph lacks balance. Government policy concerning the American loans is not well explained, nor is it set out exactly why Weimar government policy to try to help farmers failed. The paragraph is a bit unbalanced, with all the poor policies set out at the start and the positive policies of the government briefly mentioned at the end without any real explanation or assessment.

Nazi government policy mostly helped the economy. They used a clever idea called Mefo bills to pay industry and boost German employment. Because the Nazis wanted to start a war in Europe they invested massively in the arms industry. This provided lots of work for the German people. They signed lots of special deals with countries in southern Europe, which helped German trade and meant governments in these other countries bought German products. The Nazis also invested in public work schemes like building new roads, and unemployment fell considerably. By 1939, Germany had very little unemployment and people had work. However, there were problems as Germans did not have much to spend their money on and they were only focused on getting ready for war. Their economy had some problems that were difficult to solve. Overall, though, the German economy improved due to the policies of the Nazis.

Again, the paragraph is very unbalanced. Nazi policies are seen as overwhelmingly positive, with the issues caused by government economic intervention too quickly dismissed. There needs to be more depth to the analysis.

After the war, the West German economy boomed due to government policies. Despite the destruction caused by the war, the West German economy was soon one of the best in the world. Some of this was due to the help the Americans gave to West Germany through Marshall Aid. This helped the West German economy a lot. German industry was boosted by the strong global economy, which meant many countries wanted to buy West German products. However, government policies like co-determination and the guest worker scheme helped boost the economy. The German policy of creating a common European market was also really important. The EEC helped German trade, as more countries in Europe were able to buy German goods as tariffs were taken away. The Common Agricultural Policy also helped boost German exports of agriculture. Although there were some problems, the government policies helped with the change of the German economy from the 1950s to 1990, as it changed to a more service-based industry. Overall, government policies helped the German economy from 1950 to 1990.

Some good detail to this paragraph, but overall it focuses overwhelmingly on government policies that have been successful. It needs a bit more consideration of problems in the German economy. More depth and balance in the argument are required.

Overall, while in the 1920s and early 1930s there were lots of problems in Germany, most of the time the German economy went well. Thus, apart from the Weimar period, it can be seen that the German government introduced lots of policies that helped the German economy from 1871 to 1990, thus agreeing with the question.

The conclusion does set out a clear argument on the question. However, it lacks a clear overall analysis of the argument and is very short, giving a very simplistic and somewhat unbalanced assessment.

Verdict

This is an average answer because:

- key features of the question are analysed, although not all areas are explored with sustained analysis
- it demonstrates some good knowledge, but lacks range and depth in regard to some key aspects of the question
- it attempts to make a judgement on the question, but overall support for this judgement is weak and lacks depth

- it shows clear organisation, but parts of it lack a balanced, logical argument.

Use the feedback on this essay to rewrite it, making as many improvements as you can.

Paper 3: A Level sample answer with comments

Section C

These questions require you to show your understanding of a subject over a considerable period of time. They will ask you to assess a particular area for a period of over 100 years, and they require you to make a substantiated judgement in relation to the question.

For these questions, remember to:

- organise your essay and communicate it in a manner that is clear and comprehensible
- use historical knowledge to analyse and evaluate the key aspect of the question covering the entire period
- make a balanced argument that weighs up differing opinions
- make a substantiated overall judgement on the question.

'Government economic policies had a mainly positive effect on the German economy in the period 1871–1990.' How far do you agree with this statement? (20 marks)

Strong student answer

In the long period between 1871 and 1990, the German economy underwent substantial development, but remained overall one of the world's strongest and most important economic powers. Within this period, government economic policies mostly had a positive effect on the German economy. However, between 1918 and 1945, government policy was arguably less beneficial for the German economy. Therefore, it is only to some extent that the German governments' economic policies had a mainly positive effect on the German economy between 1871 and 1990.

Government economic policies during the Kaiserreich between 1871 and 1918 had a varied effect on the German economy, some of which was positive. Between 1871 and 1914, German industry grew massively, making it the biggest industrial power in Europe by 1900. Government policy aided this growth, providing large subsidies for German industry. The government encouraged the creation of cartels, providing a lack of competition that resulted in greater profits and economic stability for these companies. The heavy investment in creating a new German navy also provided employment and provided contracts for German industry. However, despite all these positive aspects there were problems, as the lack of industrial competition due to the power of the industrial giants meant products remained expensive for German consumers, a factor that was resented by the German working class. However, in terms of economic growth, it is clear that government policies had a positive effect on the German economy between 1871 and 1918.

The Weimar period from 1918 to 1931 was much more difficult in terms of the German economy and it is clear that government policies were not as positive as they had been previously. The Weimar Republic faced considerable problems after the First World War. The government refused to either raise taxes or cut workers' hours to try to rationalise the economy and instead printed more money, leading to hyperinflation in 1923, a considerable economic issue. Although they did develop the economy from 1924 to 1928 with the new currency (Rentenmark), this was done with a massive reliance on American loans that was never a safe basis for the economy. This was shown after 1929, as the economic issues facing the USA led to a collapse in the Weimar economy as American investment dried up. The government tried to make substantial cuts to deal with the crisis, but this only led to the further collapse of industry and banking, so contributing to mass unemployment. Overall, despite a period of growth between 1924 and 1925, government policy was not successful between 1918 and 1931.

Good overall argument set out in relation to the question. Importantly, the student has considered the idea of 'extent', clearly making a measured judgement and providing evidence for why they have come to this assessment.

The student has chosen to look at the question chronologically. This could lead to a narrative assessment that tells a story as opposed to making an argument. However, they have provided a strong analytical argument that weighs up government policies in this period and their strengths and weaknesses before ending with a clear assessment that relates directly to the question. The use of the words 'in terms of' shows the criteria on which the student is basing their judgement.

The first line relates to the idea of change, clearly showing that this period was not as successful as the one previously assessed. The student gives a very strong argument that understands how certain policies' successes can change over time. For example, the student argues that the Weimar government's policy concerning American loans

Nazi policy in the period from 1933 to 1945 is more difficult to assess, given its massive reliance on war armaments production. It is true that the Nazis lowered unemployment using policies such as deficit financing in German industry and massive investment in work schemes. Both these areas provided a huge boost in employment figures. However, this was done at the expense of the consumer sector of the economy. Wages were kept from rising and taxes increased to stop the rising demand of the German people for consumer products and the problems with inflation that this would cause. It is arguable that this policy was not sustainable, and the overall destruction of the Second World War, which the Nazi economic policy caused with its focus on war, makes it difficult to argue that its government policies were positive, despite the boost in employment they brought about.

Government policies in the period after 1945 through to 1990 were mostly positive, although some aspects concerning agriculture are debatable. The massive industrial growth of West Germany that saw them once again become Europe's largest economy was aided by the government's leading role in the creation of the European Economic Community, which helped to abolish tariffs between member states, and by 1981, 45 percent of all West German exports were with the EEC. Germany was the main economic power within the EEC, and co-operation between Western European economies definitely boosted Germany's economy. The agricultural policies were more questionable. Although Germany's small agricultural industry was helped by the Common Agricultural Policy, it meant the government had to pay a massive amount in subsidies to keep it viable and their policies restricted competition within West Germany's farming sector, thus encouraging inefficient farming practices. Thus, government policy between 1945 and 1990 was very successful in terms of industrial production, but less so in regard to agricultural production.

Overall then, government policies had some major positive effects on the German economy from 1871 to 1990, at times providing a strong boost to German industrial production. Between 1918 and 1945, it is more difficult to see the positives of the German governments' economic policies, with the Weimar period leading to the worst economic crisis in recent German history, and the Nazis focused overwhelmingly on the preparation for war. Therefore, overall government economic policies have, to some extent, had a positive effect on the German economy in the period 1871–1990.

was only positive in the short term, and overall was detrimental to the German economy. It is a balanced and knowledgeable argument that clearly answers the question.

This paragraph is strong in that it embraces the complexity of the issue. The judgement of the Nazi economy is difficult and the student clearly shows this. Instead, they argue that the Nazis were successful in terms of employment, but not so positive in relation to the consumer sector. It is this nuanced argument that makes the paragraph so strong, showing a clear comprehension that issues in historical analysis are not always clear, but at the same time providing criteria by which differing judgements can be made.

This is another balanced and strong paragraph that directly sets out the strengths and weaknesses of government policy within this historical period.

This is a strong conclusion that summarises the overall argument of the essay before setting out a clear answer to the question. Importantly, the overall argument is the same one established in the introduction, showing how the student has developed a balanced, coherent and well-explained argument throughout their essay.

Verdict

This is a strong answer because:

- the key issues relevant to the question are explored through sustained analysis that covers the entire time period and develops clear links between the paragraphs
- the student uses excellent historical knowledge to support their overall argument

- relevant criteria are used to make nuanced, complex judgements on the question, and a clear but sophisticated evaluation of the question is shown through the entire essay
- it employs a coherent approach that allows the student to cover the time period while also incorporating a clear and precise evaluation of the question.

Index

Acknowledgements

Acknowledgements
The authors and publisher would like to thank the following individuals and organisations for permission to reproduce photographs and text in this book.

Photographs
(Key: b-bottom; c-centre; l-left; r-right; t-top)

Alamy Images: akg-images 95, National Geographic Image Collection 6; **bpk:** Jürgen Bartsch 80; **Getty Images:** Culture Club 99B, Pascal George/AFP 156, Paul Popper/Popperfoto 122, Tom Stoddart 159, ullstein bild 26, 113R, Universal Images Group 15; **Mary Evans Picture Library:** picture-alliance/dpa 32; **Rex Shutterstock:** Courtesy Everett Collection 88, The Weiner Library 36, Universal History Archive/UIG/Rex Shutterstock 142, 143R; **TopFoto:** The Granger Collection 8, 74, 99T, The Print Collector/Heritage-Images 54, ullsteinbild 30, 45, 60, 67, 81, 147, 162, 165, 113L, 143L, World History Archive 42, 78

Cover image: Bridgeman Art Library Ltd: German Photographer (20th Century)/ © SZ Photo

All other images © Pearson Education

Tables
Source 2 on p.13 © Overy, R. and Ogilvie, S. (eds), 2003, *Germany: A New Social and Economic History Since 1800*, Vol. 3, Bloomsbury Academic, an imprint of Bloomsbury Publishing Plc. Table 2.3; Source 1 on p.39 © Overy, R. and Ogilvie, S. (eds), 2003, *Germany: A New Social and Economic History Since 1800*, Vol. 3, Bloomsbury Academic, an imprint of Bloomsbury Publishing Plc., chapter 'Government and the economy in the nineteenth century' by Tipton, F.B., p.133.

Text
Source 1 p.11 from J. Traynor, *Mastering Modern German History*, 2008, Palgrave Macmillan pp.32–3, reproduced with permission of Palgrave Macmillan (trans. from the German: *Der Junge Tobias, Eine Jungend und ihre Umwelt*, Insel Verlag (Scheffler, K. 1927) © Insel Verlag Leipzig 1927. All rights with and controlled through Insel Verlag Berlin.); Extract 1 p.14 republished with permission of Blackwell, from *The Origins of Modern Germany*, Barraclough, G. 1947, p.426 permission conveyed through Copyright Clearance Center, Inc.; Extract 2 p.17 © Overy, R. and Ogilvie, S. (eds), 2003, *Germany: A New Social and Economic History Since 1800*, Vol. 3, Bloomsbury Academic, an imprint of Bloomsbury Publishing Plc. Chapter 9: Social Structure in the Twentieth Century by Benninghaus, C., Heinz-Haupt, G. and Requate, J., pp.305–6; Source 5 p.19 from *Germany 1866–1945*, Oxford University Press (Craig, G.A., 1978) p.99; Extract 3 p.20 © Carr, W., 1987, *A History of Germany, 1815–1985*, Bloomsbury Academic, an imprint of Bloomsbury Publishing Plc., p.181; Source 6 p.25 from *The Weimar Republic Source Book*, University of California Press (Kaes, A., Jay, M. and Dimendberg, E. (eds) 1994) pp.182–3, Copyright © 1994 by The Regents of the University of California; Extract 4 p.28 from M. Fulbrook, *Interpretations of the Two Germanies, 1945–1990*, 2000, pp.58–9, Palgrave Macmillan reproduced with permission of Palgrave Macmillan; Source 9 p.31 from *The Weimar Republic Source Book*, University of California Press (Kaes, A., Jay, M. and Dimendberg, E. (eds) 1994) pp.206–7, Copyright © 1994 by The Regents of the University of California; Source 11 p.33 from *Nazism, 1919–1945, Vol. 2: State, Economy and Society 1933–1939*, University of Exeter Press (Noakes, J. and Pridham, G. (eds) 2000) pp.255–56; Source 12 p.34 from *Voices from the Third Reich: An oral history*, Da Capo Press (Steinhoff, J. Pechel, P. and Showalter, D. 1994) pp.465–6, reprinted with permission of Regnery Gateway Inc.; Source 6 p.46 from *A Life in Letters, 1914–1982*, Harvard University Press (Scholem, G. (Skinner, A.G. (ed. and trans.)) 2002) pp.193–4 (Letter written by Betty Scholem in 1931) Courtesy of the Leo Baeck Institute; Source 7 pp.47–8 translated from *Prosperity for All [Wohlstand für alle]*, Econ-Verlag (Erhard, L. 1957) pp.9–12, Reprinted by kind permission of Ludwig-Erhard-Stiftung e.V. Bonn – Germany; Extract 1 p49 from *Weimar: Promise and Tragedy*,

Princeton University Press (Weitz, Eric D. 2007) pp.159–60. Reproduced with permission of Princeton University Press in the format Book via Copyright Clearance Center; Extract 2 p.52 from *History of Germany, 1780–1918: The Long Nineteenth Century*, Blackwell (Blackbourn, David, 2003) p.239, Reproduced with permission of Blackwell Pub in the format Republish in a book via Copyright Clearance Center; Extract p56 'Guns or butter' speech, Goering, H., 17 January 1936 from *Encyclopaedia of the Third Reich*, Robert Hale (Louis L. Snyder, 1976) p.48; Source 10 p.57 from *Nazism, 1919–1945: State economy and society* University of Exeter (Noakes, J. and Pridham, G. (eds.) 1984) *Vol 2: State, Economy and Society, 1933–1939*, pp.293–4, Report of the Sopade; Source 11 p.58, Source 8 p.119, and Source 11 p.126 from *Inside the Third Reich* (Speer, A. 1995) Phoenix, a division of Orion Publishing London Copyright © 1970 The Macmillan Company, New York pp.67, 194–5, 300–301; Extract 3 p.61 from *Germany from Defeat to Partition, 1945–1963*, Williamson, D.G., Copyright © 2001 Longman. pp.70–71. Reproduced by permission of Taylor & Francis Books UK.; Extract 1 p.84 *Bismarck: The man and the statesman*, Hamish Hamilton (Taylor, A. J. P., 1955) p.155, reproduced with permission of David Higham Associates Limited.; Extract 2 p.84 © Carr, W., 1987, *A History of Germany, 1815–1985*, p.148, Bloomsbury Academic, an imprint of Bloomsbury Publishing Plc.; Quote p.87 'I know no parties anymore, only Germans', Kaiser Wilhelm II, August 1914, © Carr, W., 1987, *A History of Germany, 1815–1985*, p.213, Bloomsbury Academic, an imprint of Bloomsbury Publishing Plc.; Quote p.90, 'the fairly angel tied to the Christmas tree at Christmas for the children's benefit', SPD member, 1917 from © Carr, W., 1987, *A History of Germany, 1815-1985*, p.228, Bloomsbury Academic, an imprint of Bloomsbury Publishing Plc.; Extract 1 p.92 from *Germany 1866–1945*, Oxford University Press (Craig, G.A., 1978) p.384; Quote p.94, 'must now eat the soup which they have served us', General E. Ludendoff, 1 October 1918, from *Modern Germany: Society, economy and politics in the twentieth century*, Cambridge University Press (Berghahn, V.R., 1987) p.59; Source 5 p.96 from Diary entry of Colonel von Thaer, 1 October 1918, wwi.lib.byu.edu/index.php/From_the_Diary_Notes_of_Oberst_Thaer; Extract 2 p.98 © Fulbrook, M. (ed.) 1997, *German History since 1800*, 'Germany from war to dictatorship' by R. Bessel, pp.237–9, Bloomsbury Academic, an imprint of Bloomsbury Publishing Plc.; Quote p.98 'Long live the German republic!', Scheidemann, P., 1918, © Carr, W., 1987, *A History of Germany, 1815–1985*, p.241, Bloomsbury Academic, an imprint of Bloomsbury Publishing Plc.; Extract 3 p.100 from *Weimar: Promise and Tragedy*, Princeton University Press (Weitz, E., 2007) p.27 Reproduced with permission of Princeton University Press in the format Book via Copyright Clearance Center; Source 11 p.106 from *Weimar: A Jurisprudence of Crisis*, University of California Press (Jacobson, A.J. and Schlink, B., (eds) 2010) pp.144, 145, Gerhard Anschutz's speech at University of Heidelberg, 22 November 1922 Copyright © 2010 by the Regents of the University of California, (trans. from the German: *Drei Leitgedanken der Weimarer Reichsverfassung*, Rede, gehalten bei der Jahresfeier der Universität Heidelberg am 22. November 1922, Mohr (Anschutz, G., 1923) with permission of Mohr Siebeck Tübingen); Source 1 p.111 from *A History of National Socialism*, Methuen (Heiden, K., 1934) 28 February 1933 Prussian Press Bureau release, pp.220–1, Copyright © 1934 Methuen. Reproduced by permission of Taylor & Francis Books UK.; Source 2 on pages 111–2 from Trial of German Major War Criminals, HMS) (1946) Vol 7, pp.72–3, Contains public sector information licensed under the Open Government Licence (OGL) v3.0.http://www.nationalarchives.gov.uk/doc/open-government-licence; Source 5 p.114 from *Reaching for the Stars* The Cresset Press (Waln, N. 1940) pp.79–80 (Copyright © Nora Waln, 1940) Reprinted by permission of A.M. Heath & Co Ltd and The Random House Group (UK); Source 6 p.118 from *The Speeches of Adolf Hitler, 1922–1939*, Vol. 1, Oxford University Press (Baynes, N.H. (trans. and ed.) 1942) Hitler's Speech to the Reichstag, 13 July 1934, pp.311, 319–20, with permission of The Royal Institute of International Affairs, Chatham House; Extract 1 p.120 and Extract 2 p.125 from *Hitler*, Kershaw, R., p.114, pp.117–18 Copyright © 1991 Longman. Reproduced by permission of Taylor & Francis Books UK.; Extract p.121, 'Hitler oath', © Carr, W., 1987, *A History of Germany, 1815–1985*, p.319, Bloomsbury Academic, an imprint of Bloomsbury Publishing Plc.; Source 2 pp.111–2 from *Trial of German Major War Criminals*, HMSO (1946) Vol. 7, pp.72–3, Contains public sector information licensed under the Open Government Licence (OGL) v3.0. www.nationalarchives.gov.uk/doc/open-government-licence.; Quote p.135 'semi-sovereign' by Roseman, M. © Fulbrook, M. (ed.) 1997, *German History since 1800*, p.369, Bloomsbury Academic, an imprint of Bloomsbury Publishing Plc.; Source 3 pp.136-7, Source 4 p.140, and Source 5 p.141 from *Uniting Germany. Documents and Debates, 1944–1993*, Berghahn (Jarausch, K. and Grasnow, V. (eds) 1994) pp.6–7, 10–11, 12–13; Quote p.142 'fifth occupying power' Schumacher, K. from *Germany from Defeat to Partition, 1945–1963*, Williamson, D.G., Copyright © 2001 Longman, p.33. Reproduced by permission of Taylor & Francis Books UK.; Extract 1 p.143 from *Germany since 1945*, Oxford University Press (Kettenacker, L. 1997) p.44. By permission of Oxford

University Press; Source 9 p.144 from Lipgens, W. and Loth, W. (eds), *Documents on the History of European Integration, Volume 3: The struggle for European Union by Political Parties and Pressure Groups in Western European Countries 1945–1960*, Berlin: Walter de Gruyter, 1988 p.537; Quote p.145 'the party of the whole people' and Extract 2 p.145, © Carr, W., 1987, *A History of Germany, 1815–1985*, p.381 Bloomsbury Academic, an imprint of Bloomsbury Publishing Plc.; Quotes p.148 'so long after the collapse…', 'the chapter of collective guilt…', Adenauer, K., from *Adenauer's Germany and the Nazi Past: The Politics of Amnesty and Integration*, Columbia University Press (Frei, N., 2010) pp.48, 54; Quote p.148 'whenever I travelled…', Sir Ivone Kirkpatrick from *Modern Germany: Society, economy and politics in the twentieth century*, Cambridge University Press (Berghahn, V.R., 1987) p.215; Quote p.149 'through this amnesty…', Menzel, W., 1955, from *Adenauer's Germany and the Nazi Past: The Politics of Amnesty and Integration*, Columbia University Press (Frei, N., 2010) p.91; Source 11 p.149 from Why Adenauer is opposed to more de-Nazification, *Toledo Blade* 25/02/1960, p.12 (Lindhurst, N.); Extract 3 p.150 from *Modern Germany: Society, economy and politics in the twentieth century*, Cambridge University Press (Berghahn, V.R., 1987) p.200; Quote p.152, 'day would come when borders no longer separate us but unite us', Honecker, E., 10 September 1987, from *Germany Divided: From the Wall to Reunification*, Princeton University Press (McAdams, A.J., 1993) p.174; Source 1 p.153 from Only the Germans want reunification, *The Canberra Times*, 29/09/1987 (Dyer, G.); Source 3 p.157 from Crisis of direction for East Germany, *The Canberra Times*, 01/10/1989 (Garton Ash, T.); Source 5 p.160 from Honecker's choice keeps his powder dry, *The Canberra Times*, 20/10/1989, p.8 (Simmons, M.); Quotes p.161 and Source 7 p.162 from Helmut Kohl's speech to Bundestag: Ten Point Program for Overcoming the Divisions of Germany and Europe, November 28 1989, *Bulletin of the Press and Information Office of the Federal Government* (FGC Chancellor Helmut Kohl), www.tufts.edu/~bmartin/10pt.html; Source 9 p.166 from *Where the World Ended: Re-Unification and Identity in the German Borderland* University of California Press (Berdhal, D., 1999) Letter from Thorsten Muller to his cousin and her husband, p.157 Reproduced with permission of University of California Press in the format Republish in a book via Copyright Clearance Center; Source 10 p.168 translated from GDR Voters Hungry for All-You-Can-Eat Kohl-Slaw. Sensational Victory for the "Alliance" [DDR-Bürger haben den Kohl fett gemacht. Sensationeller Wahlsieg für die „Allianz], first published in *taz – die tageszeitung* on 19 March 1990; Source 11 p.169 from Who will pull the handbrake on unification?, *The Canberra Times*, 12/06/1990, p.9 (Booker, M.); Extract 1 p.171 © Fulbrook, M. (ed.) 1997, *German History since 1800*, 'The failed experiment: East German communism' by M. Allinson, Bloomsbury Academic, an imprint of Bloomsbury Publishing Plc.; Extract 2 p.171 from *Germany Divided: From the Wall to Reunification*, Princeton University Press (McAdams, A.J., 1993) p.234–5 Reproduced with permission of Princeton University Press, in the format Book via Copyright Clearance Center; Extract 3 p.171 from *A History of Modern Germany: 1800 to the Present*, 2nd ed., Wiley-Blackwell (Kitchen, M., 2012) p.356, Reproduced with permission of Wiley-Blackwell in the format Republish in a book via Copyright Clearance Center.